# Saving the Protestant Ethic

# Saving the Protestant Ethic

## *Creative Class Evangelicalism and the Crisis of Work*

ANDREW LYNN

OXFORD
UNIVERSITY PRESS

OXFORD
UNIVERSITY PRESS

Oxford University Press is a department of the University of Oxford. It furthers the University's objective of excellence in research, scholarship, and education by publishing worldwide. Oxford is a registered trade mark of Oxford University Press in the UK and certain other countries.

Published in the United States of America by Oxford University Press
198 Madison Avenue, New York, NY 10016, United States of America.



Library of Congress Cataloging-in-Publication Data
Names: Lynn, Andrew (Reverend) author.
Title: Saving the Protestant ethic : creative class Evangelicalism and the crisis of work / Andrew Lynn.
Description: New York, NY, United States of America : Oxford University Press, [2023] | Includes bibliographical references and index.
Identifiers: LCCN 2022029946 (print) | LCCN 2022029947 (ebook) | ISBN 9780190066680 (hardback) | ISBN 9780190066697 | ISBN 9780190066703 (epub) | ISBN 9780190066710
Subjects: LCSH: Capitalism—Religious aspects—Christianity. | Evangelicalism.
Classification: LCC BR115.C3 L96 2023 (print) | LCC BR115.C3 (ebook) | DDC 261.8/5—dc23/eng/20220907
LC record available at https://lccn.loc.gov/2022029946
LC ebook record available at https://lccn.loc.gov/2022029947

DOI: 10.1093/oso/9780190066680.001.0001

Printed by Sheridan Books, Inc., United States of America

# Contents

# Introduction

This book examines the intersection of religious beliefs and economic activity among a segment of conservative Protestants in the United States. At the center of this intersection are cultural frameworks related to "meaningful work." While economists typically examine labor participation in terms of supply, demand, and utility maximization, this book foregrounds the crucial interdependence between economic activity and the cultural frameworks that confer meaning on that activity. For many workers, their work "is about a search for daily meaning as well as daily bread," in the words of Studs Terkel.[1] This meaning can immerse our day-to-day routines with a sense of purpose, dignity, and even a sacred calling. This meaning can also serve to form the accounts we might give about ourselves, the sacrifices we have made in our lives, and our personal life trajectories. Work can of course also be "just a job," and for many workers today, work is precisely that. But even in cases of instrumental orientations to work, cultural frameworks are often still at play.

The religious movement studied in this book has set out to popularize very particular cultural frameworks for understanding one's work. A group of religious leaders—popular evangelical writers, pastors, theologians, artists, and organizational leaders—have united around these frameworks to form a movement commonly referred to as the "faith and work movement." This movement seeks to ennoble and sacralize work, imbuing it with the same religious significance as conventional religious activity. They want work to be a calling, a vocation, a channel for participation in a larger cosmic narrative of restoration. They see this vision as universal and inclusive: all work and all workers not only *can* view their work as service to God, but *must* view it in this way. Leaders of the movement adamantly protest anyone's work being "just a job" or work being compartmentalized from one's religious identity.

Following the lead of prior studies of work, this book is "at bottom a study not of work but of ideas about work."[2] The actors highlighted here has set out to transform such ideas. In recent decades a tremendous number of resources have been allocated to diffuse "theologies of work" through sermons, Bible studies, worship songs, seminary classes, gap-year vocation programs,

*Saving the Protestant Ethic*. Andrew Lynn, Oxford University Press. © Oxford University Press 2023.
DOI: 10.1093/oso/9780190066680.003.0001

and leadership courses. These cultural products have been injected into the central structures of the evangelical subculture, seeking to transform existing structures with institutional logics or frameworks originating from peripheral sites of culture production.[3] In terms of an infiltration effort, the movement has to date achieved remarkable success. The number of national "faith and work" parachurch ministry organizations—less than ten as recently as 1980—has doubled every decade since the 1960s.[4] National faith and work organizations have launched franchised-model "learning communities" in cities across the country, guiding clergy through discussions of faith-work integration. Local congregations have begun hosting "marketplace fellows" of young professionals being specifically trained in faith and work themes. Since 2002, evangelical leaders have begun seven different national annual conferences on the topic of work. Mini-conferences and special sessions have also been appended to existing conferences with established names and large attendance.Much of this drew on financial backing from private foundations, which began pouring money into the space around 2010.

Occuring at the same time was a notable uptick in the production of cultural resources. The number of books published on the "faith and work" topic surged around the end of the twentieth century: while all evangelical publishers together produced no more than five faith and work books per year up through 1978, a surge taking off in the 1980s would leave the market effectively saturated only a few decades later. One bibliography published by movement leaders found 350 "Christian faith and work" books in existence in 2000, which by 2005 had exploded to 2,000 books.

Channeling such energies and resources into the promotion of meaningful work holds significance on a number of levels. Scholars of work have long recognized how frameworks relating faith to work come to shape worker motivations and loyalties to assigned organizational roles. Critical theorists of various stripes have similarly been attuned to how such frameworks can serve the interests of those occupying positions of power, often consecrating submission to power structures as a divinely ordained duty. Prior studies operating in this vein have delivered insightful assessments that are worth considering here. We might consider two studies of related cases. One study of the evangelical-produced "Jobs for Life" curriculum found messaging about work that consecrated personal responsibility and disciplined work ethic as the needed virtue for those unemployed or underemployed.[5] Dubbed by researchers as a form of "religious neoliberalism," this curriculum primarily performed a conservative function of shoring up the stability of the social order by targeting those most likely to defect from their lower-status roles within it. Workers were effectively then sent out to "clean toilets for Jesus," as the title of the study labeled this effort.[6]

We might call this the "religion of the precariat" interpretation, updating the insights of earlier Marxist historians who saw in early British evangelicalism a new "religion of the proletariat."[7] A second study surveyed leaders of multinational corporations that targeted evangelical workers with frameworks that valorized lower paid retail work, deeming it "Christian service" work.[8] This "corporatized religion" then represented evangelicalism's entry into a growing set of "workplace spirituality" programs that frame faith commitments as a set of managerial techniques promising competitive advantage in business.[9] Evangelicalism's economic thinking in this case becomes a wing of corporate human resource (HR) strategies to optimize worker performance in religiously saturated regions like the Sunbelt and American South.

One thing we can say for sure: our era of capitalism has no shortage of leaders preaching religions of the precariat and corporatized forms of religion. But my observations and analysis of faith and work space uncovered compelling reasons to resist attributing the movement's emergence to either of these prior assessments. For one, in my research I met few bottom-line-driven HR gurus touting techniques for optimizing worker performance. But even more glaring was the absence of blue-collar or service-economy workers. Nearly every leader I interviewed lamented the universal absence of working-class populations at their events. The distinct demographic profile of faith and work leaders themselves likely plays some role in this. This group I interviewed represented a higher-educated stratum of American evangelicalism, with most leaders possessing advanced degrees (though, notably, not management degrees). The audiences that found their way to such leaders shared many of these characteristics: career-minded, creative-class professionals such as teachers, architects, software engineers, nurses, and small business owners. Few attendees to these events, then, would be trekking back to jobs in big-box retail or in places where they "clean toilets for Jesus."

We will return to these demographic factors as a crucial part of the larger story told here. But the real key to understanding the movement requires recognizing movement leaders as operating at a very particular place and time within a larger historical trajectory of American conservative Protestantism.[10] It was while observing two seminary professors teaching a week-long course on work—an experience described more in Chapter 4—that I began to recognize how the movement cannot easily be severed from this particular history. Faith and work leaders were not simply building a new Christian view of work: they were also aggressively trying to root out an oppositional view. These leaders were attempting to reconfigure precisely what is considered sacred, holy, or properly "Christian" activity in the lives of evangelical laity. In doing this, these leaders were waging war against ways of thinking they perceived to be both prevalent and harmful among American evangelical laity. What they were offering, in the words of one leader I interviewed, was a "remedial theology."

Theologians and religious scholars, in observing the development of this remedial theology, might reach for any number of evaluative descriptions: doctrinal development, theological resourcement, or even religious syncretism or accommodationism. My interest as a sociologist has been to interpret this phenomenon as primarily a case of cultural change and adaptation. American conservative Protestantism has long operated as a conglomerate of disparate theological threads that crystallized into a bricolage of a singular evangelical "tradition" at some point in the late nineteenth century.[11] The remedial efforts I observed were not so much introducing new frameworks, but reordering the frameworks already present within the earlier evangelical synthesis. Some theological ideas and orientations were made more salient; others were adamantly rebuked.

So why is this reconfiguration happening? Why does work suddenly "matter" to God? The guiding impetus of this book is to unpack not only the when, where, and what of the movement, but also the why and how. Certainly, playing some role in any sociological explanation would be social and economic factors related to the labor market, the political economy of advanced capitalism, the gendered nature of work, and the class and racial demographics of the relevant constituencies. But the explanations laid out here also incorporate the ineliminable role that changing *theological ideas* play in the movement. As Chapter 1 lays out in greater detail, the energies dedicated to making work meaningful seem to be *creating specific theological frameworks for a specific constituency confronting a very specific challenge*.Since its initial appearance in the mid-twentieth century, the faith and work movement has provided resources that empower laity to creatively examine and renegotiate their relationship the wider social and economic structures.

Clergy, writers, and laypersons leading such entities are typically serving a cohort of American evangelicals who have ridden a wave of social ascension into a social space for which they appear to be theologically ill-equipped. The world of "work" in these spaces—spaces I call "creative-class capitalism"—poses any number of threats to the spiritual health of the devout lay evangelical. The devout evangelical, after all, has historically been tasked to *evangelize*, or save souls, a task granted smaller and smaller space in the work and lifestyle cultures that characterize this creative-class space. Declaring "work" meaningful in such spaces then represents more than a recovery of the inner-worldly asceticism long associated with the Puritans. Movement leaders are also fundamentally renegotiating evangelicalism's "rules of engagement" with the wider social and cultural order.

I interpret such efforts as creative theological adaptation, as well as a reversion to earlier ideas. Leaders of the movement are effectively declaring war on many theological elements that American evangelicalism had inherited from an earlier era of conservative Protestantism. It was in this earlier era that Protestant forms of revivalism and fundamentalism began depicting the world through a dualistic lens that sharply separated religious activity from activity that happened outside the church. As a result, leaders of the era by and large said very little about economic activity. In places where work was engaged, it primarily fell on the "worldly" side of a sharp church-world dualism. Work was at best an activity to be instrumentalized for other ends, particularly for acquiring resources to fund missionary work. It was often viewed as an inconvenient diversion from more spiritually valuable activities and practices. Work, then, did not seem to matter to God.

Leaders of the faith and work movement today are doing everything they can to root out this way of thinking. Recognizing this reactionary dimension immediately illuminates how the claim "your work matters to God" is almost always taking aim at an otherwise-invisible theological sparring partner. The sentence "Your work matters to God . . ." is almost always completed with some sort of rejoinder aimed at fundamentalist ideas, whether the primacy of proselytization, the spiritual superiority of full-time proselytizers, the secondary status of money-making, or the "worldly" aspect of all activities not formally housed within the church. Regarding this latter idea, the movement often incorporates an underspecified conception of "work" in order to maximize the range of activities that are granted divine blessing. As we will see later, the central claim is really that your *Monday* matters to God.

Filling in this reactionary dimension also aided in locating the movement within the broader context of the American religious landscape today. Recent scholarship in American religious history has mined developments among conservative Protestants in the inter- and postwar years as key to deciphering the religious and political phenomena most visible in American public life today.[12] The faith and work movement, as a subcultural movement emerging from this same era, bears many commonalities with other forms of Christianity and often shares resources, constituencies, organizational backing, and leading figures. But the faith and work movement has by and large been eclipsed by both the more vocal Christian Right and the more ethnically and theologically diverse Prosperity Gospel movement. Part of the reason for exploring this particular case is the impressive institutional stronghold seized by faith and work leaders within the subcultural space of American evangelicalism in a relatively short time. And yet, for a variety of reasons, acquiring these institutional seats of power has not proven all that successful in exerting influence on the evangelical constituency as a whole. Throughout this book we will examine the various factors that appear to contribute to the faith and work movement's own provincialization within the wider evangelical subculture. As it turns out, an inner-worldly asceticism mobilizing zealous participation in secular institutions appears to be a tough sell in the current religious landscape.

## The Plan of the Book

Chapter 1 lays out the central arguments of the book in greater detail. Constructing a holistic interpretation of the present movement requires a great degree of context related to the sociological background of the faith and work movement. A key factor at play is the changing social location of white American evangelicals across the twentieth century. Chapter 2 backs up to the end of the nineteenth century to map out significant cultural and social shifts that began reshaping the "theologies of work" that prevailed among American Protestants of the era. A review of books and writings indexes the various historical and theological forces that went into constructing this earlier "fundamentalist work ethic"—a somewhat contradictory term—that located the central spiritual imperatives of the devoted layperson's life to non-work activities. The second half of Chapter 2 contends that this fundamentalist work ethic was not discarded by early neo-evangelicalism or even the evangelicalism that followed: in fact, Billy Graham's ministry and efforts served to preserve the core tenets of this "work ethic" among conservative Protestants. Chapters 3 and 4 survey the extensive resources devoted to replacing this fundamentalist work ethic with alternative orientations to economic activity. Chapter 3 tells the story primarily through the lens of social movement theory, surveying the various resources, organizations, and culture production that went into constructing a social-intellectual movement that sought to lay claim to the wider evangelical parachurch space. Chapter 4 then tells the story through the shifting theological frameworks that begin appearing in lay-targeted evangelical books in the mid-twentieth century. It was during the mid-century years that the secular realm of "Monday" came on the radar of popular writers, who urgently sought to envelop this world within an overarching framework for living as a devoted Christian. As the end of Chapter 4 makes clear, these efforts in many ways were circling back to recover something prevalent in earlier modes of Protestantism that had since been lost: an affirmation of the "ordinary" lay life. But the inner-worldly asceticism reconstructed by late twentieth- and early twenty-first-century Protestants also bears the marks of its more recent origins. Rather than cultivating a sober "deadness" to the world favored by the Puritans, the faith and work movement aestheticizes work as a creative arena where one can fulfill a greater cosmic and eternal purpose.

The second half of the book surveys internal tensions within this recovered or reconstructed Protestant ethic, probing the wider context in which the movement operates. Chapter 5 explores the varying exogenous and endogenous factors that shape the movement's offerings as primarily speaking to a particularly masculine and higher-status form of "breadwinner" work. While a handful of female religious leaders are active in the space, these leaders experience various challenges in working against the more commonly shared assumptions of the more male-dominant space. Women-centered discussions of work and career often instead get steered toward other spaces in the evangelical parachurch and conference universe, filtering away from the faith and work space all but a homogenous constituency of career-centered actors. Chapter 6 recounts the successes and failures of politicized voices and organizations in the faith and work space. Interviews with organizational leaders and review of disseminated materials reveal the challenges of appending to the movement a broader sacralization of economic participation and unregulated capitalism. Chapter 7 examines the manner in which higher-status evangelicals draw on particular theological streams of Calvinism to affirm the natural goodness or "common grace" present within work associated with high prestige and power in wider American culture. One form of Calvinist Protestant theology—Kuyperian humanism—proves instrumental in dissolving sharp antagonisms between sacred and secular or religious and "worldly" work, carving out space for the laity to faithfully serve the ends of existing institutions in government, commerce, the media, and the arts. Chapter 8 then zooms out the wider landscape of "Protestant ethics" today in order to locate the faith and work movement alongside and intersecting with other economic ethics active within a broader Protestant space. Briefly reviewed are the economic ideas and practices of sectarian religions, Prosperity Gospel, Dominionism, political evangelicalism, and Protestant traditions rooted in non-Anglo cultures.

Any work seeking to historically and culturally contextualize a contemporary religious phenomenon is of course constrained in a number of ways. It is worth flagging a few elements that are not prevalently featured in the pages that follow. First, there is notably no attempt to undertake an intensive survey of theological, doctrinal, or biblical sources on which contemporary evangelicals construct their understanding of work. Such projects have been more than adequately undertaken elsewhere.[13] Orientations toward work are examined in light of their "meaning-content of theologies, customs, worldviews, and rituals" through which actors make meaning of their worlds.[14] These orientations are framed as the cultural materials taken up, promoted, and legitimated by various actors working within a particular social context. The more in-depth overview of how theological ideas intersect, change, and evolve appears in Chapters 2, 4, and 7. Relatedly, this book also rarely draws on the sorts of formal pronouncements or systematic treatises that theologians and other scholars construct for those in their respective scholarly guilds. The methodology deployed here prioritizes the practices and ideas that make their way into the "lived religion" of those "in the pews," or in this case, those who regularly move from pews to workplaces.[15] The methodology that guided the selection of examined practices and ideas is described in greater detail in the Appendix. The individuals and organizations we will meet in the following pages have all exhibited "special competencies" to produce and transmit relevant cultural products to a wider population of religious laity.[16] They thus serve as "movement intellectuals" seeking to steer resources and efforts to "open a space in which creative interactions between individuals can take place."[17]

Another factor shaping what follows is closely tied to the particular subject matter. This study seeks to operate with a broader understanding of what the term "evangelical" signifies and who and what fits within this category. Central to this approach is attending to the complex cultural and social politics that have shaped on-the-ground usage of the term "evangelical," discussed in greater detail in the next section. Recognizing the diverse groups and actors that themselves identify with the term contributes to this complexity, as honoring their self-identity requires dispensing with narrower conceptualizations of evangelicalism that equate the phenomenon with white American Protestant identity.[18] But providing historical context for the emergence of the movement requires closely examining the particular subculture and institutions that have historically defined "American evangelicalism." In cases of looking at historical institutions, the modifier "white" is appropriately affixed to "evangelical" to reflect the manner in which these institutions have not only historically been composed of a white majority constituency, but have also practiced exclusionary practices that channeled non-white minorities away from leadership, sometimes appealing to explicit theological reasons, but other times more tacitly reproducing social structures related to the norms of whiteness. Such practices continue to shape inner-group hierarchies and leadership among the faith and work movement, as evidenced by the disproportionately white leaders occupying positions of power within the movement. These exclusivist structures—related to not only race but also gender—end up shaping the realm of culture-making studied here: individuals not admitted to leadership positions face limited access to the means of producing cultural products, whether authoring books, contributing to periodicals, leading organizations, or—perhaps most centrally—preaching or speaking on theological or doctrinal issues.

The larger methodology employed here seeks to describe this discursive space as it was and is actively constructed by culture-producing institutions and thus, to some degree, seeks to faithfully describes this realm as it exists. However, this book also examines voices operating at the margins or just outside the movement itself, particularly the voice of female leaders, in order to better contextualize precisely what or who counts as *the* faith and work movement. Careful attention was also given to not negating or diminishing the non-white participants, churches, church networks, authors, and speakers who are currently active in the faith and work movement: such actors weave their way through this movement and thus weave their way through the pages that follow.[19] The invisible sorting mechanisms that tend to keep these voices out of positions of power are also examined throughout this text. The evangelical "parachurch" space in which most of these actors operate often relies on white and upper-class resources in terms of both funding sources and organizational leadership, and this structure has historically reproduced the more homogenous and conservative interests of its donor class.[20] Thus, these organizational forms inherently favor the promotion of particular frameworks for seeing social issues and promoting accepted solutions that align with the conventionally white evangelical theology prominent in the mid-century.[21] The institutional approach to culture undertaken here attends to these cultural frameworks while also critically assessing the social conditions that directly shaped how they were produced and diffused.

Finally, it would be impossible to account for a religious group's changing position and orientations to social structures in American society without granting attention to the larger American political climate and the many political behaviors that appear to be mobilized by religious actors and resources. This study does not attempt to directly assess or predict the voting behaviors or political dispositions of the religious adherents examined: the "politics" explored in the following pages operates at a much deeper level, related to how economics and power are often mediated by particular cultural frameworks. However, the final two chapters of this book attempt to locate the phenomenon of interest amidst the more vocal and politicized forms of conservative religion.

## A Note on Terminology: What Makes This Movement "Evangelical?"

It is useful here to lay out the precise sense in which the term "evangelical" serves as a descriptor for the movement. Social scientists generally refrain from making such categorizations based on the perceived "genuineness" of faith or faithfulness to a particular theological creed. Categorization and labeling are instead undertaken for descriptive and classificatory purposes. The method employed here can best be understood as a hybrid form of the two most common classificatory approaches employed in studies of evangelicals, each outlined here.

The first approach is the most straightforward: in treating "evangelicalism" as a religious movement, its adherents are defined as those that explicitly draw on the term as their own self-identity. Uses of the term in this manner date back to eighteenth-century Anglo-Protestant writers and religious leaders who belonged to revivalist movements active among Calvinist, Methodist, and Church of England adherents. The term was steadily embraced by more Protestant groups across the nineteenth and twentieth centuries, and several immigrant churches and products of denominational mergers incorporated the term in their official titles around the turn of the nineteenth century. In the current religious landscape, with the notable exception of the Evangelical Lutheran Church of America (a Mainline Protestant denomination), nearly all groups, individuals, or organizations that self-identify as evangelicals bear some connection to ecumenical efforts of the early "neo-evangelicals" of the 1940s, who explicitly embraced the term and popularized it among conservative Protestants.

But this first approach always confronted certain limitations. For one, such measures were dependent on the evangelical label trickling down into the wider Protestant populace and coming to serve as a salient self-identifier alongside "Christian" or "Protestant." The evangelical identity would ideally operate somewhat analogously to national citizenship: there is a universally recognized means of acquiring the status, widespread self-knowledge of that status, some degree of shared in-group identity, and membership is dichotomous rather than fuzzy and open. Rarely have these conditions proven true. For one, denominational identity maintained an exclusionary hold on laity through most of the twentieth century, waning only in the latter decades. Particularly when combined with ethnic or regionally grounded cultural identities, the notion of being the "Church of Christ" was far more powerful than a self-identity of being an "evangelical."[22] A Southern Baptist leader speaking to a *Newsweek* reporter in 1976 made this clear: "Southern Baptists are not Evangelicals . . . we have our own traditions, our own hymns, and more students in our seminaries than they [other groups associated with evangelicalism] have in all theirs put together."[23] Denominations were able to preserve a greater stronghold on adherents' self-identity through their deep integration with family, kinship, ethnicity, and place. Denominations also kept a tight hold of their own educational institutions, missionary agencies, publishing companies, and clergy licensing. While a Baptist or a conservative Methodist might on occasion take part in an "evangelical" event or organization, these experiences failed to incite fundamental revisions to group boundaries related to doctrinal particularities, friendship networks, or even acceptable inter-religious marriage.[24]

In the 1970s, social scientists and pollsters began to realize some of these limitations. Much of this was brought to the attention of scholars and wider public discourse by President Jimmy Carter's publicized profession of being "born again," a term with which many scholars and the general public were unfamiliar. It was at this point that social scientists began employing an alternative approach: the "evangelical" was conferred not merely in cases of self-identity, but now as a post hoc categorization for either particular religious beliefs or affiliation with particular denominations. Some pollsters turned to the popular doctrinal definition of evangelicalism endorsed by historian David Bebbington and then created indexes that could score respondents against these beliefs.[25] Others imputed the label on all respondents who affirmed their status of being "born again." This approach revealed a much larger swath of the religious landscape that bore ties to evangelicalism, as the primacy of denominational self-identity was no longer competing with—and thereby obscuring—the less salient but shared adherence to evangelical beliefs. Many sociological studies today continue to use denominational affiliation or other measures as a means of determining who counts as an evangelical.

This study's particular interest in individuals and organizations producing cultural products related to American evangelicalism—rather than individual religious adherents—is able to employ a third approach that blends elements of these first two approaches. This approach could be shorthanded as the "guilty by (parachurch) association" approach. The first step is drawing on the strong consensus among historians of twentieth-century religious history regarding the organizations, groups, and denominations that are recognized as representing the theological, cultural, and institutional origins and lineage of American evangelicalism. This lineage, in brief, stretches from the era following the Civil War, through late-nineteenth-century revivalist efforts and the budding networks surrounding D. L Moody, and onward into a contemporary "neo-evangelicalism" or "evangelicalism" spearheaded by a more moderate and ecumenical-minded wing of fundamentalism.[26] The second step, then, identifies the "evangelical faith and work movement" as *those figures and organizations that have at least one substantive tie to institutions or organizations within this lineage.* Such ties could include partnering with parachurch campus ministry organization, taking part in a revivalist ministry organization, publishing with a religious publisher, or appearing in seminary classes or at conferences. Likewise, examination of fundamentalist orientations to work and economics of the earlier period draws out organizations and actors that have clear affiliation with fundamentalist denominations, organizations, or networks. This reliance on institutional affiliation overcomes some of the inherent challenge of studying an otherwise deinstitutionalized population of actors—itinerant ministers, freelance authors, self-employed popular speakers—by way of probing their intersection with institutions bearing more explicit affiliations.[27]

This approach has both strengths and weaknesses. Where it is at its strongest is in making the incontrovertible case that the leaders and organizations studied here presently occupy the institutional "seats of power" that descended from the evangelical parachurch and ecumenical efforts of the 1940s. They are editors of *Christianity Today*; they coordinate work-related efforts for Billy Graham's ministry organization; they head up vocation-related programming for evangelical student groups; they publish on evangelical presses; they preside over evangelical seminaries; and their work is promoted by the National Association of Evangelicals. But where this approach may confront challenges is its bult-in assumptions of a relatively static concept of evangelicalism that remains fixed through multiple eras of conservative Protestantism. This weakness is in many ways shared with the prior two approaches: existing measures of evangelicalism often struggle to take into account reinterpretations or changing significations of the term "evangelical" and how actors then actively negotiate and respond to this change.

On this front, all three approaches reviewed here must wrestle with the consequences of the politicization of many conservative religious groups beginning in the 1970s.[28] Several scholars contend that the politicization of religious identities sent lasting shockwaves through the wider American religious landscape, inciting many laity to permanently exit not just evangelical but all religious affiliation.[29] It was in the midst of the 1970s that a "political evangelicalism" gradually became more salient within broader conservative Protestant spaces, tightly weaving together conservative Protestant constituencies with political attitudes, political candidates, and governing agendas aligned with the "new right" ideology of the Republican Party. In the first decades of the twenty-first century, political evangelicalism's underlying dispositions shifted once again to more closely align with the paleoconservatism championed by Pat Buchanan. This conservatism more openly voiced support for anti-immigrant policies while embracing forms of nationalism and nativism that could protect ethnic homogeneity. Such views gained public prominence in the 2010s with evangelicals' unwavering support for the 2016 election and 2020 failed re-election of Donald Trump. It was in this era that self-identified white evangelicals have become the religious grouping most likely to support hardline immigration policies, hold dismissive views of racial justice efforts like Black Lives Matter, and report personal discomfort encountering non-English-speaking immigrants in the United States.

Studies of evangelicalism can ill afford to ignore how these events alter common conceptions and associations of what the term "evangelical" signifies. There is evidence that such reconceptualizations have effectively created a feedback loop that subsequently reconfigures what constituency identifies with Evangelicalism. Those self-labeling as "evangelical" today appear to be signaling that, relative to the wider populace, they hold outlier political views in how they evaluate particular progressive political movements, immigration, and overall threats to American identity in terms of ethnic and religious composition.[30] Political scientists have also charted *politically* motivated entrances into and exits from self-identity as evangelical.[31] It is important to remember that this phenomenon is relatively new. One poll from 1980 showed that over half of self-identified evangelicals—defined as those who claim to be "born again"—identified as Democrat, suggesting that many evangelicals would not see the term as signifying allegiance to any particular political party or ideology.[32] Evangelicals of the 1950s and 1960s also exhibited some of the lowest level of political activity of any group measured. Whereas even as recently as 1980, it was common to find Democrats or politically indifferent individuals identifying as evangelical, in the age of political evangelicalism such cases have become statistically rarer. And returning to the phenomenon of evolving interpretations of the term itself, a "Democrat evangelical" or a "politically indifferent evangelical" now seems to approach a contradiction in terms.

This book thus follows the lead of other scholars in recognizing that "evangelical" has today become more a term of political rather than religious identity.[33] Working in light of this recognition, I have deployed the term "political evangelicalism" to maintain an analytical precision that contrasts the evangelicalism crystallized around particular political views against more varied usages of the term "evangelical" among conservative Protestants, whether historically or globally.[34]

For readers more attuned to the illiberal and authoritarian voices that have come to represent political evangelicalism, there may be good reason to be skeptical that any form of predominantly white American evangelicalism can be all that different from "political evangelicalism." So here it may be helpful to directly ask: Precisely what is the evangelical faith and work movement's relationship to political evangelicalism? Is faith and work a subsidiary arm or more demographically targeted subset of political evangelicalism? One simplistic and categorical answer to this question is: not necessarily. This answer is derived from the classificatory method described above: the "guilty by (parachurch) association" approach, in the interest of consistent categorization over time, effectively imposes onto actors a more or less fixed meaning of the term "evangelical" without accounting for changing meanings of the term. This post hoc categorization then denies actors the ability to renegotiate or reject the resignification of the "evangelical" label as a political identity regardless of even an explicit and vocal rejection of what the term has come to signify.

But the real answer is likely more complicated. The movement does not a claim a formal set of members whose political views and behaviors might be surveyed, and no existing survey data have measured the behaviors of the evangelical constituency that gravitate toward faith and work resources. However, a few conjectural observations can be made. First, existing surveys suggest that evangelicals occupying creative-class spaces and careers—the population with the greatest proclivities to engage faith and work resources—have by and large remained loyal Republican voters and adhere to associated viewpoints on race, nationalism, and immigration that characterize political evangelicalism. There is no empirical evidence from national surveys, then, that faith and work resources are serving as "substitute goods" for political evangelicalism. My own observation of the faith and work space suggests that the two phenomena not only occupy the same universe but also prove capable of peacefully coexisting.[35] There is little question these leaders share organizational-institutional space with fervent political evangelicals, whether appearing on conference stages together, belonging to the same denominations, writing on the same religious presses, or working in organizations that draw on political evangelicals as donors. Some of this can likely be attributed to the shared origins of these movements: both the faith and work movement and political evangelicalism trace their historical developments back to similar cultural-institutional spaces within white conservative Protestantism. At a more cultural level, faith and work leaders largely preserve the individualistic notions of social change that have long characterized white American evangelicalism spaces.

But a caveat should be made: even if faith and work resources do not appear to be shuttling measurable portions of creative-class evangelicalism away from conservative American politics, faith and work leaders now represent a certain heterodox actor within political evangelicalism. This is because faith and work leaders fail to be "political" in the sense recognized by political evangelicalism. The leaders interviewed for this study, with only one exception, provided no public support for Donald Trump in the 2016 or 2020 elections. Some wrote widely distributed editorials denouncing his candidacy, while others signed statements and open letters that decried his policies. But the vast majority of leaders issued no writings or statements on the election.

There is an important implication to this heterdoxy: faith and work leaders' deficient or heretical views may be narrowing their potential to be heard within the evangelical constituency at large. One 2016 study provides a provocative take on *which* evangelical leaders' views seem to make their way into the evangelical populace at large. A survey of self-identified white evangelicals conducted by political scientists Paul A. Djupe and Brian R. Calfano revealed that the majority of those surveyed reported having little to no awareness of the political views of evangelical authors and church leaders like Rick Warren, Beth Moore, Jen Hatmaker, or Russell Moore, at least in terms of these figures' views on the presidential candidacy of Trump. But respondents *were* attuned to political leaders like Mike Huckabee, Pat Robertson, Jerry Falwell Jr.—figures who at that time all maintained a regular presence in popular media. While this study only looked at widespread awareness related to political views, this pattern of familiarity may very well hold for other sorts of views and positions. It follows that evangelical laity today may hold stronger awareness of—and loyalties to—the leaders of evangelicalism that hold court in highly visible media forms and deliver political pronouncements, but the figures who regularly appear in *Christianity Today*, dot the stages of evangelical conferences, or fill the catalogs of Intervarsity Press or other evangelical publishers do not share this recognition.[36] Such findings suggest the organizations and institutional positions once serving as powerful platforms within evangelicalism—many of which are now occupied by leaders active within the faith and work movement—have seen their influence drastically circumscribed by leaders more engaged in political rhetoric and regularly speaking on political platforms.

More research is needed on this front. But to return to this book's central interests, the faith and work movement is primarily engaged in an effort to alter the economic frameworks through which evangelicals view their workdays, not election days. The choice of prioritizing cultural elements of the movement—how it serves as a source of symbols, narratives, vocabularies, and frameworks that give meaning to actors' everyday lives—should not be dismissed as a turn to the apolitical or privatistic dimensions of religion. As will be clear in the pages that follow, these cultural elements speak to a broader conception of the political than what can be measured by political attitudes or voting patterns. Many aspects of the movement speak not only to the allocation of resources and power within dominant structures of American society, but also to the ethical criteria by which that allocation is properly evaluated. The faith and work movement can thus be aptly understood as a highly organized and well-resourced effort to renegotiate creative-class evangelicalism's place and relation to power within the institutions and social structures that make up American society today.

# PART I

# THE RISE OF THE EVANGELICAL FAITH AND WORK MOVEMENT

# 1
# More than Toil

Jakki Kerubo was exhausted. A writer and immigrant from Kenya living in New York, Kerubo found herself putting in sixteen-hour workdays as she pieced together enough projects to stay afloat. She was particularly on edge one Saturday morning after a delayed furniture delivery had thrown her morning schedule into disarray. A call from an unknown number set her off: she recounted later yelling, "What do you want from me?" as she answered what she assumed was a telemarketer's untimely intrusion. As it turned out, the caller was someone from her church—a bond trader employed by Goldman Sachs—who was inquiring whether she was going to make it to her church's "faith and work" event that day. Overriding her desire to brush off the event, Kerubo committed to attending.

The message Kerubo heard later that day, surrounded by other young professional Christians hailing from Manhattan, was not what she expected. Anticipating pastoral advice to slow down, do less, and "spend more time running on the beach," she instead heard the event's main speaker confer God's blessing on her time-intensive career. "God created the world to be a good place, for man to toil in it. It's dehumanizing not to work," the speaker assured the audience. Kerubo would later recount in a blog post that she found particular solace in this message: it was precisely what she needed to hear at that time. God was calling her not to work less, but to more effectively manage the stress produced by work. Kerubo found more opportunities to connect with the many professionals who also resonated with this message. She eventually became an "artist-in-residence" at her church—a program offered as part of the church's promotion of laity involved in the arts. At later events directed at workers, Kerubo herself came to serve as a featured speaker, sharing her own insights on integrating faith with her profession.[1]

Churches that bring together freelance writers, Wall Street traders, and other young professionals to discuss their day-to-day work lives may at first seem puzzling. Religion and economic life are not the most obvious pairing, particularly in our present cultural moment. The economic realm is thought to be governed by impersonal markets, material needs, and an amoral

*Saving the Protestant Ethic*. Andrew Lynn, Oxford University Press. © Oxford University Press 2023.
DOI: 10.1093/oso/9780190066680.003.0002

pursuit of self-interest. Religion—particularly in its more conservative forms—is thought to reside in the more intimate sphere of life, perhaps marshaled out into the public sphere only for particular political causes. So what was this "faith and work" programming about? Were these professionals commissioned to fight a new kind of "culture war" in their professions? Were they being coached in a "prosperity gospel" that valorizes personal wealth? Or perhaps, judging by Kerubo's self-reported transformation, were they exposed to more traditional Protestant ideas of a disciplined, methodical approach to work?

Over a period of four years, I investigated events, organizations, and individuals that shaped the world Kerubo entered. What I found was a complex set of moral and theological frameworks, weaving their way through a subset of actors within the American religious landscape. These frameworks sought to bridge the church-centered world of theologically conservative religion and the career-driven world of modern work. There could be no separation between "Monday" and "Sunday," these leaders proclaimed, nor should Christians distinguish between "working" for God and "working" in one's profession. This movement instead sought to extend a religious identity beyond Sundays, holy days, or election days into the realm of "Mondays." Monday was to be the arena in which one lived out his or her central calling, a place of worship and consecration that was thereby rescued from the clutches of insignificance.

The particular case of interest here—called by its own participants the "faith and work movement"—resides at the intersection of two dominant institutions in American culture: the institution of "modern work"—broadly defined as formal, paid labor taking place outside the home—and the evolving institutions that make up white evangelical Christianity. This is of course not a new pairing. Max Weber's classical study *The Protestant Ethic and the Spirit of Capitalism* has effectively cemented the Protestantism-capitalism intersection as a crucial part of the rise of capitalism itself. While many dimensions of his thesis have been challenged, Weber's explorations have been enriched by the later writings of social theorists like R. H. Tawney, Ernst Troeltsch, Thorstein Veblen, H. Richard Niebuhr, and E. P. Thompson. But probing the Protestant-capitalism intersection today proves more complicated than in prior eras: both components have mutated and have developed into far more forms than those observed by earlier theorists. Even if limiting one's scope to North America, studies of "Protestant ethics" today could probe a wide range of varieties: aspirations of social mobility among immigrant populations, pockets of Prosperity Gospel adherents stretching across racial and denominational lines, the unique sociopolitical experience of Black Protestant traditions, and the more establishment-oriented Mainline denominations. And capitalist settings also now serve up far more varied forms of labor participation. Protestant laity today experience work in settings of manufacturing, agricultural, service, and the knowledge economy, often combining these formal types of employment with unpaid labor of care work and various forms of volunteer work.

This book narrows in on one of the many possible intersections. The case of interest selected here captures an unusual phenomenon: a cohort of religious leaders and laity over the past century has become unusually reflexive regarding their faith system's ethical orientation toward economics. And then, judging that orientation to be entirely deficient, they have launched a movement to radically alter it. The pages that follow foreground how this set of actors, operating within the historical context of white American evangelicalism, have moved to confer new forms of meaning and significance upon the economic realm and the laity's role within it. Many of these efforts are spurred into action by any observation made again and again by evangelicals: the faith of the everyday Christian should never be compartmentalized into one's private life and sequestered from one's work life. Christianity is a whole-life faith. But how the religious world of "Sunday" and work world of "Monday" might be *integrated*—a favored word of the movement—required new vocabularies, symbols, frameworks, and other cultural elements that could be affirmed as theologically sound. And so, a movement was born.

Leaders of the movement largely focus on coordinating the production of new cultural products aimed at penetrating the evangelical subculture: new books, new lay-led organizations, new events, new Bible commentaries, new podcasts, new worship songs, and new teachings that can be incorporated within seminary classes, Bible studies, and local churches. The substantive alterations proposed by such products are best understood as altering what Max Weber labeled a religious system's *Wirtschaftsethik*, or economic ethic. In a 1913 essay called "The Economic Ethics of World Religions," Weber undertook a systematic exploration of how different religious systems orient themselves to economic activity and the class position of their adherents.[2] Weber's framework allows us to see the manner in which the faith and work movement responds to what it perceives as a moral crisis stemming from the existing evangelical economic ethic. Put simply, faith and work leaders see their religious tradition as completely devoid of *any theological frameworks that confer value on secular work.*

This perception is surprising on a few fronts. For one, it would suggest this mode of Protestantism does not see itself as an heir to the seventeenth- and eighteenth-century work-focused Puritans famously indexed by Weber and others. These leaders instead echo what surveys of American evangelicals had uncovered in the 1980s and 1990s: the majority of evangelical laity report seeing faith as having very little to do with their work lives.[3] Perhaps equally surprising is that this void was not resolved by the famous marriage of conservative politics and white evangelicalism in the latter decades of the twentieth century. Even the representatives of free-market organizations that I interviewed agreed with the common prognosis: evangelical laity struggle to see their economic participation as representing spiritually valuable activity. No invisible hand of the market seemed up to the task of consecrating "Mondays."

It then falls upon the faith and work movement to root out the deficiencies of this economic ethic and introduce something new. But altering their tradition's economic ethic entailed far more than promoting new moral imperatives. The movement also sets out to reconfigure the manner in which American evangelicalism locates itself within the dominant institutions of American society. Calls to withdraw and reject those institutions are replaced with calls to renew, transform, and ultimately work toward those institutions' own ends. The move to revise and ultimately discard prior economic ethics are closely tied to institutional factors related to class, family, and larger changes in the labor market that bore effects on the evangelical constituency at large. Accordingly, the next section surveys the sociological and historical conditions that gave rise to the movement, offering a fuller depiction of how this shift in an economic ethic emerges alongside the substantive socioeconomic changes of the twentieth and twenty-first centuries.

## Contextualizing Evangelicalism for Creative-Class Capitalism

The demographic profile I encountered in the faith and work space offered one of the key heuristics for making sense of its emergence, goals, successes, and failures. The faith and work movement in many ways represents an effort to recover and reconstruct a "Protestant ethic" that serves a particular class of workers who occupy a particular position in advanced capitalist societies. This explanation coheres with the observations of several classical theorists mentioned above—Weber, Troeltsch, Niebuhr, Tawney—who all indexed a visible affinity between Protestant Christianity and capitalist behavior in in prior historical eras. A similar phenomenon is almost certainly at play here. Evangelical laity on the whole have experienced substantial social class mobility as a religious group. In the 1920s and 1930s, white conservative Protestants were known for their cultural marginalization, lower social status, and militant rejection of the wider societal order. But most conservative Protestant groups quietly secured middle-class status through the mid-century decades, closing the education gap between themselves and the wider population by the 1980s.[4] Previous studies have narrated this embourgeoisement process of American evangelicalism as the postwar generation of laity riding the wave of middle-class affluence into the newly emerging knowledge economy.[5]

While this class shift captures one important part of the story, the faith and work movement also represents creative responses to *institutional* shifts taking place in the latter decades of the twentieth century. Substantive changes in gender and family have affected conservative religious adherents since the 1950s. In the postwar years, religious life and church membership were primarily structured around a "breadwinner-homemaker marriage" that thereby corresponded with religion, offering experiences tailored to reinforce the patriarchal structure of the home.[6] Higher percentages of conservative Protestants also resided in the South or Midwest and occupied lower or middle-class occupations that, at that time in history, made such an arrangement more achievable. But a variety of forces would come to undermine this religion-familism fusion: the next few decades saw a dramatic increase in female labor participation, overall gains in educational attainment, declining participation in civic associations, rising notions of gender egalitarianism, and a steady outflow of working-class populations from regular religious participation. The 1970s was also an era in which shifts in the labor market began exerting a significant toll on the breadwinner-homemaker family configuration, as workers in middle-class and working-class sectors began seeing flattened gains in wages, dwindling numbers of unionized jobs, and the first economic effects of global competition and outsourcing of manufacturing work. While white conservative Protestant denominations were often able to keep at bay the *cultural* challenges to their traditional familistic ideologies, they were not able to insulate their laity from the ways in which economic and institutional factors steadily chipped away at the predominant institutional arrangements of the 1950s.

While today few conservative Protestant denominations have explicitly broken ranks with the traditional familistic ideologies of the 1950s, they have long been navigating a world that has radically changed since the postwar years. Evangelical ministers and leaders have found themselves pastoring more and more congregants whose lifeworlds and life sequences are starkly different from patterns common to an earlier generation. For one, the evangelical constituency as a whole began to feel the effects of what demographers call the Second Demographic Transition, which shrank household sizes, delayed marriage and family milestones, and lowered fertility rates in evangelical families.[7] Other institutional shifts also altered the private lifeworld of religious laity: membership in labor unions or traditional forms of civic engagement all lessened their hold on occupants of the middle class. These shifts all served to weaken the demands of other institutions that had traditionally contended for time, energy, and identity. Those institutions that persisted—including religion—often moved toward "soft" forms of authority that were more affirming of individual life pursuits, rather than issuing hard demands on individuals.[8]

But while other institutional demands receded, the institutional demands of work remained strong. The faith and work movement represents an adaptive response to this phenomenon, specifically targeting the pastoral needs of a particular socioeconomic and institutional space born out of these changes. We might label this space "creative-class capitalism," building from Richard Florida's label for a stratum of workers in professional, knowledge-economy jobs.[9] But appending the word "capitalism" to the term highlights the underlying social formation, a formation that stretches beyond occupational groups or shared lifestyle affinities. Creative-class capitalism signifies a very particular subset of economic experiences born from the structures of advanced capitalism. Work is experienced in creative-class capitalism in a relatively distinct manner. Of course, many workers in the modern economy work demanding hours and are subjected to great physical toil through their work. But occupants of creative-class capitalism are subsumed into their work by forces other than economic necessity: they are more likely to feel the pulls of personal identitification with work, affective ties to workplaces, and larger personal narratives of achievement. The lifeworlds of those occupying creative-class capitalism become exceptionally shaped by the role of work and career: personal aspirations and lifegoals often correspond to "greedy" forms of work that assert demands related to emotional energy, geographic location, and the general ordering of one's life phase.[10]

Evangelical leaders took note of what emerged from these shifts: a species of a highly educated, career-driven, vocation-seeking professional class. What this population needed was a different sort of ministry strategy. "Home visits aren't common anymore, so we do work visits," a pastor recounted in a panel session I attended called "Shepherding Workers" at a faith and work event. Another faith and work leader used his platform of an evangelical college chapel service to promote the idea of a "take your pastor to work day," encouraging pastors to better familiarize themselves with the environments their laity occupied. What these religious leaders set out to do was essentially catch up with their own laity's social ascension and entry into higher-status jobs requiring a novel sort of personal devotion. What was needed was a remedial theology that aids the occupants of this newly entered social milieu, a milieu which initially posed substantive challenges to the existing frameworks for thinking about one's work. What evangelicalism suddenly found itself needing—and what the faith and work movement provided—was a theology of Monday.

## The Moral Crisis of Monday

Though religion and economics may at times seem to occupy different realms, social theorists have long been interested in their overlap and interplay. This particularly comes to head in the realm of work. Work has long been dependent on various cultural elements like religion to yield compelling "work ethics" or normative frameworks that temper and subordinate economic behavior.[11] And religious organizations have long occupied social positions that allow them to serve up such cultural elements. Here, it is helpful to make a distinction between "formal economics" and cultural frameworks related to economic activity, what Laurence Iannaccone has labeled "non-formal economics."[12] The former revolves around abstract sets of ideas surrounding economic phenomena and entities such as international trade and trade policy, government regulation, labor conditions, income distribution, and wider matters of political economy. Attitudes toward formal economics are generally measured with surveys and polls. But the sort of economic frameworks brought to the foreground by the faith and work movement are not so much formal but non-formal economics. Though certainly not void of political implications (as we will see later), the cultural frameworks promoted by this movement pertain to the vocabularies, narratives, symbols, and values through which actors make sense of their economic activities and the settings in which those activities take place. We might shorthand this non-formal economic content as part of a faith system's "economic imaginaries"—the underlying understanding of one's existence within, experiences of, and ethical responsibilities toward the part of society where goods are produced, circulated, and appropriated.[13]

While Max Weber at times depicts unavoidable clashes between many religious systems and the economic sphere, he also saw Protestant denominations and sects as helping to "deliver the 'spirit' of modern capitalism" and its "ethos of the modern bourgeois middle classes."[14] The interplay between religion and work, then, may take any number of forms, from inciting tensions, falling into a comfortable compartmentalization, or sparking transformation to either work or religion (or both).[15] This interplay can also take heterogenous forms even among adherents to the same religion, as religious traditions often provide an assortment of resources that might translate into contending orientations to work activity. But relevant to the particular inquiry here, we can narrow down the possible intersection between religion and work to three major forms. As a matter of terminological precision, these three orientations offer the categorical bins into which more specific "cultural frameworks" will be sorted later. At the most basic level, religious systems might be oriented toward the economic sphere in any of the following three ways.[16]

## Subordinating (and Shirking) Frameworks

Frameworks falling within this orientation promote a pragmatic acceptance of work when necessary, but overall lend little moral attention or valorization to work. Such frameworks include both withdrawal from the formal labor market, as well as cultural frameworks that merely divert moral and spiritual attentions away from work. Some frameworks may endorse "slacking off" as a result of this diverted energy, but more commonly, "shirking" frameworks are a product of workers embodying a more instrumental and selectively minimal commitment to their employment or labor. Subordinating and shirking frameworks provide minimal resources for a religiously grounded economic ethics and instead underwrite modes of compartmentalization that channel religious energies elsewhere.

## Sacralizing (and Stabilizing) Frameworks

These frameworks offer up a spiritually infused purposeful vision for secular work. That vision can be rooted in a divinely ordained vocation, a civic sense of responsibility, an eschatological or aesthetic appreciation for the fruits of one's labor, or the elevation of work as a site of proselytization. These frameworks typically do not incorporate an external criterion of normative evaluation for work, instead relying upon the norms of excellence and achievement that is endogenous to the work itself while overlaying it with spiritual significance

## Subverting (and Straining) Frameworks

These frameworks incorporate the external normative criteria absent in the prior category. They hold up the work sphere and its logics, practices, norms, and social relations to notions of justice, solidarity, and moral order, whether from a religious or secular perspective. Workers may successfully subvert the work sphere to the standards or criteria provided by their meaning system, they may engage in disruptive acts like strikes and sabotage, or they may find themselves locked in a perpetual struggle of being caught between two contradictory value spheres.

* * *

This classificatory tool serves to yield the most precise description of the faith and work movement: the movement at its most basic level represents an effort to mobilize material and organizational resources that steer more of the evangelical populace toward sacralizing and stabilizing frameworks. And in doing so, leaders are actively engaged in a two-front battle against forces that enforces subordinating and shirking frameworks by devaluing the activities of Monday life and compartmentalizing faith to one's Sunday life. On one front of this battle, leaders face off against the identity-fragmenting tendencies of advanced capitalism that led toward compartmentalization, generally simplified as the challenge of "Monday," discussed more below. On the other front, the adversarial force becomes the tenets of their own religious tradition that, only a generation earlier, had largely made peace with this compartmentalization. These tenets effectively shuffled religious energies away from the economic sphere and into a realm of inward introspection and church-related activities like proselytism and Bible study. Taking on both of these counter-forces at the same time, faith and work leaders declare the secular world of Monday to be just as sacred and spiritually infused as the world of Sunday. Their messaging declares an overarching harmony uniting work and worship, toil and transcendence, economics and eternal reward.

Driving this frenzied effort to make "work matter to God" are anxieties around "Monday." Again and again, faith and work leaders speak about the threat "Monday" poses to the Christian layperson. A 1961 evangelical book called *Monday Morning Religion* declares its central purpose is to "protest the heresy of compartmentalizing life" by showing "all days are God's days." A 1974 book on lay vocations identified a "great gulf" that has opened between Sunday morning and the activities in the workplace from Monday through Friday. A 1978 book describes Monday as a time of spiritual suffering for the Christian employee. A 1979 book worries of Monday's moral climate, suggesting there may be "little outer difference" between the Christian and the non-Christian once Sunday ends. These concerns all echo the charge famously delivered in a 1941 essay by British novelist Dorothy Sayers: "How can anyone remain interested in a religion which seems to have no concern with nine-tenths of his life?"[17]

Beginning in the 1980s, the evangelical publishing world began to seize upon the "problem of Monday" as a new genre of Christian books. A review of Christian publishers' catalogs reveal that twenty-six Christian books have incorporated the word "Monday" into their titles to express the challenges of the work since the 1980s.[18] Nine books chose an identical title—"Thank God It's Monday"—to signal triumph over Monday's woes and problems.[19] This genre does not take the challenges of Monday lightly: Mondays are seen to exert heavy demands on the laity's emotional lives, identities, and schedules. Inadequate response to these demands might even nullify one's status as a devoted Christian. One 2012 book warned against the compartmentalized life as a form of "Monday morning atheism."

"Monday" in many ways serves as a vehicle to address the larger spiritual implications of the economic realm. Some of these concerns mirror the well-established critiques of capitalism. Karl Marx saw the capitalism of his day as a social arrangement that permitted workers to be their full selves only in their leisure time, time spent outside the surveilling and dominating realm of the production process. Monday was no friend to visions of fuller human purpose, as it left no space for "a positive, creative activity" related to the human dimensions of life.[20] Later Marxists saw the need to address how a different problem of "Monday" emerged for those awaiting revolutionary change. Sociologist Paul Willis labeled this the "problem of Monday morning" that arose when political visions failed to wrestle with the "messy business of day to day problems" that dominated the average person's life, whether fulfilling one's economic role or raising children.[21] Such concerns were also voiced by the New Left of the 1960s, which often placed worries of spiritual alienation at the center of their critique of modern civilization and its impersonal economic structures.

This brings to the foreground one of the most unexpected dimensions of the faith and work movement: evangelical leaders are in many ways constructing their own account of alienation from their occupational positions within contemporary capitalism.

Few religious scholars—or even evangelicals themselves—would expect that some portion of American evangelicalism perceived itself to be estranged from the values, practices, or logics of capitalism. The scholarly consensus is in fact quite the opposite: many interpretations of white evangelicalism locate deep compatibilities between this faith system and wider capitalist values of individualism, therapeutic expressivism, and pragmatic openness to new techniques.[22] White evangelicals' steady social ascension amidst rising postwar affluence only deepened their comfortable position in the American middle class, presumably lessening any sense of alienation from capitalist materialism. Understanding the nature of this tension with Monday then becomes central to understanding the faith and work movement itself. The classificatory scheme outlined above provides an initial point of clarity: faith and work leaders certainly *do not* see their religious tradition as needing to be purified of subverting or straining orientations toward the economic sphere. They are not rushing in to stamp out anti-capitalist sentiments. They instead see their efforts as entirely reactive to the popularity of subordinating and shirking frameworks. To put this another way, tensions with Monday do not stem from judgment against capitalism being anti-Christian, but *judgment against Christians for failing to make capitalism "Christian" enough.*

This tension can be more fully unpacked when placed within the longer historical development of evangelicalism. The great sin of "Monday" is that it has somehow come to occupy a realm upon which the evangelical faith makes very little claims. This arrangement, when it comes into the view of religious leaders or the laity themselves, violates sensibilities lodged deep within the evangelical consciousness. Permitting one's work life to exist on a plane separate from one's faith life poses a great threat to being a "serious Christian." We find in the theological antecedents to American evangelicalism at least three streams that instilled a "whole-life" conception of religious identity: the Christian perfectionism teachings originating among German pietism and John Wesley that became popular through nineteenth-century revivalism; the fervent personal ascetism of Holiness and Pentecostal groups that cast off all activity judged to be frivolous or entangling; and Calvinism's "comprehensive vision of reality" that was mediated and injected into the American evangelical through several leaders and educational institutions. Though these theological streams differ in important ways, they together contribute to what Weber labels evangelicalism's "thoroughgoing Christianization of the whole life."[23] This totalizing dimension forbids any behavior or realm of activity that might possibly remain neutral in relation to the ends of the Christian life.

This helps us make sense of the perceived tensions with Monday. It was not white evangelicalism's embourgeoisement into middle-class and creative-class capitalism that drew leaders' concerns. Nor was it particular moral practices dominating those spaces. It was instead the shortage of *distinctly evangelical* frameworks through which evangelicals could interpret their relatively new social location and corresponding practices. Non-evangelical frameworks have always been readily available: a career-minded Christian has long had at their disposal cultural notions of hard work, personal ambition, or a drive to upward mobility that could all cast moral significance over a work-centric life. But for faith and work movement leaders, these frameworks were coming from wider American culture, not the relatively bounded world of evangelical theology. Even if these frameworks bore the lasting imprint of the more classical "Protestant" work ethic, in the eyes of faith and work leaders, they were not sufficiently evangelical. The needed intervention entailed recapturing the economic world of Monday and bringing it back beneath the umbrella of a whole-life faith. The overworking business executive or career-driven writer who, in the past, might have lurked on the edges of his or her church, could now be brought to the center of church, figuratively and also many times literally: today these workers are often prayed over by their fellow congregants and "commissioned" as part of faith and work programming. These workers are then sent out to do their work for God.

To translate this into Weber's language, the faith and work movement effectively constitutes a subcultural insurgency effort to restore some sort of inner-worldly ascetism, to "make work matter to God" in and of itself. Their desired outcome is consecrating the world of Monday as a realm permeated with the highest values of sacredness and worth and thereby on equal footing with the realm of "religious activity." As the next chapter outlines in detail, this effort represented a radical repudiation of some of the earlier orientations toward culture and economics that had come to be associated with white American evangelicalism.Work urgently needed to be reclaimed for God.

## Making Peace with the World of Work

One recurring theme of this book is that the central elements of the faith and work movement bear the mark of their sociological origins. This becomes most visible when questions of inclusiveness and scope conditions are posed: Whose work is actually acquiring spiritual status? In what institutions or sectors can one work to please God? And among what types of workers do these frameworks appear to take hold? As Chapter 5 will ask more directly, *whose work matters to God?*

In my interviews with faith and work leaders, the most common answer embraced an egalitarian inclusion: all work matters. The evangelical laity I met affirmed this point, speaking positively of their own acquired sense of a calling within their occupation or position. The movement in fact identifies itself as diametrically opposed to any hierarchy of vocations or rankings of work value. One anecdote provided by Hugh Whelchel, a popular speaker and writer in the movement, captured the movement's vision of a radical inclusiveness:

> I was asked to go to Missoula, Montana . . . [there are] four evangelical churches in the whole city. So they get together every six months and bring in a speaker, and one of them had read my book and asked me to come and do it so I did it. So I did a conference Friday night, Saturday morning, and then preached at one of the churches on Sunday morning and another one Sunday night. I think it was Sunday morning, this guy comes up to me after I preached and says, "I was at your conference, and I want you to know, I'm fifty-seven years old, I wash dishes for a living." And he said, "I

> heard everything you said . . . I became a Christian about ten years ago and I thought the best that I could do was occasionally witness to somebody about my faith at work, but I'm back in the back of the kitchen, it's hot, no one comes back there. But what you're telling me is that there's . . . there's an importance to everything I do to God. And every dish I wash for the glory of God, in ways I don't completely understand, fits with things other people are doing, and that brings flourishing to my community. . . ." I mean, tears were rolling down his cheeks. He said, "If that's true, that makes all the difference." I said, "Brother, that's true, that's why I'm here, to get that message out."

But the movement also entails aspects that counter this inclusiveness, even within the subcultural space of conservative Protestantism. For one, the repeated emphasis on the work of "Monday" creates a close association of "work" with formal, paid labor, the sort of work that one presumably leaves the home to do every Monday morning in a workplace outside the home. This subtly demotes care work, parenting, and volunteering, as well as any other activities that were not performed for pay. Those activities are not "Monday" work. Perhaps not surprisingly, then, the movement minimally engages many populations with only tenuous or highly obstructed access to Monday work.[24] Rarely are such populations discussed at events or mentioned in materials. This includes lower-educated workers, employed single parents, or those juggling unpredictable work schedules that interfere with any sort of regular church involvement. Absent as well from the movement are churches and denominations that have historically drawn marginalized populations navigating the challenges of discrimination and joblessness, two characteristics disproportionately found among African American neighborhoods and those institutions active within them.[25] While faith and work networks have made inroads into some non-white congregations, the movement remains largely sequestered from Protestant congregations that serve first-generation immigrants that often face credentialing or legal obstructions to maintaining or improving their occupational roles. Studies of such religious settings reveal an inverse dynamic often playing out: religious adherents—particularly men—often embrace a role and identity *through* their church body that may stand in place of the role and status that is no longer accessible to them within the wider social structure.[26] For these Christians—and many others—the "work" that matters to God is not primarily their participation in the paid labor force on Mondays.

Another self-limiting aspect of the movement relates to the affirming orientation toward dominant institutions of American society. Leaders are very cognizant of their battle against what Weber called "world-denying" modes of Christianity rooted in earlier modes of conservative Protestantism. This mode of Christianity commonly decried the insidious influence of the media, urban centers, the fashion industry, and "secular" arts. Yet faith and work leaders often find themselves ministering to laity working and even leading these "worldly" institutions. The call to affirm such institutions and the work within them runs against both historical and contemporary currents within conservative religious spaces. Much of the larger constituency of conservative Protestantism has come to view these same institutions through a lens of resentment, mistrust, and persecution. To invoke the "embattled and thriving" summation of American evangelicalism employed by sociologist Christian Smith, many white evangelicals have leaned deeply into the "embattled" aspect of their religious identity.[27] They sense adversarial threats lurking behind not only dominant institutions but also the larger demographic trends that have steadily chipped away their social status in the white Protestant majority in the United States. "Embattled evangelicals" have little interest in a movement promoting the "stewarding" of one's power *within* dominant institutions. Much of their religious identity is structured around a deep sense of betrayal by these institutions. Embattled evangelicals then flock toward leaders promising political action to counter or curb the power of such institutions.

The faith and work spaces I observed all appeared to the reside within the opposite pole of evangelicalism. None of the leaders I interviewed spoke in terms of embattlement. Compared to their embattled counterparts, these evangelicals appeared to be "thriving." The laity I observed all seemed largely at peace with the dominant institutions shaping the lifeworlds of creative-class capitalism—educational institutions, ethnically diverse urban centers, the media, and multinational corporations led by progressive leaders. At least some of this positive orientation toward institutions seems to be tied to socioeconomic position: faith and work adherents are almost exclusively white-collar workers who thereby possess access to jobs that more likely offer benefits, stability, and greater assurance of passing on financial security to their children.[28] They also tend to congregate in regions with more economic prosperity and that may have been spared the more enduring effects of the 2008 financial crisis. But while their socioeconomic position might be characterized as thriving, the thriving aspect is ultimately a cultural orientation not reducible to material resources. Whereas an earlier generation of conservative Protestants had moved toward a conspiratorial or Manichean orientation to the world, these conservative Protestants constructed a more harmonious view of the world.[29] They hold far less interest in charges to withdraw or war against the institutions they now occupy.

Pulling together these factors yields a supplementary if not alternative interpretation of the movement than what might be inferred from the story of the Montanan dish washer. The "work" most commonly targeted by the movement appears to bear strong affinities to a smaller subset of evangelical laity. Going further, faith and work resources appear optimized to speak to a particular orientation to work, one that for multiple reasons primarily dwells among creative-class evangelicals. These laity are more likely to find themselves deeply immersed in unusual levels of devotion to work and career. A highly shared 2019 article in *The Atlantic* identified the unusual orientations to work prevailing among the college-educated elite as a religion in and of itself."[30] Derek Thompson, the author of the piece, describes this religion of "workism" as the pursuit of identity, transcendence, and community by way of unyielding devotion to one's job. The prevalence of workism explains why American professionals work more hours than their professional counterparts in other countries, why their vacation days frequently go unused, and why even American teenagers identify having an enjoyable career as one of their highest life priorities. In places where creative-class work has come to possess its own endogenous "religion" of work, then, the faith and work movement appears to mount a particular sort of response. That response may very well be less an effort of enchanting otherwise meaningless toil and more an effort of assimilating otherwise contending religious devotion.

It is certainly worth indexing here how workism and evangelicalism bear similarities to one another and may set themselves up well for syncretization. Both religions imbue objects and activities with greater symbolic meanings that transcend daily life. This separates such objects and activities from a crude means-ends instrumentalism and moves them closer to the realm of the sacred.[31] The congruence becomes quite apparent in places: WeWork, a shared workspace company that came to represent the work-first "hustle" culture of millennial workers, often adorns its walls with "Thank God It's Monday" signage. Similarities also play out in terms of devotional practices. As an example from workism settings, a salaried consultant stringing together late-night work sessions is participating in practices that symbolically enshrine his or her place within and devotion to a larger community. The possibility that this worker would, at the end of this project, submit a carefully recorded time sheet demanding "overtime" compensation owed to him or her is judged highly inappropriate, a profane violation of the bonds to one's team, if not the larger profession. We could compare this to an evangelical layperson handing in a time sheet to a pastor for hours spent praying and reading Scripture: this represents a similar type of transgression. Both of these realms operate as "religions of the heart," a term religious historians use to describe the tradition of German pietism that bore significant influence on American evangelicalism. Pietists, in concerning themselves with subjective states and internal motivations, began to see external modes of control or authority as antithetical to true religion. So, too, workplaces among knowledge and professional work are characterized by internalized commitments and affectual loyalties. The stick-and-carrot bearing supervisor proves unnecessary. Workers' commitment instead stems from their own professional identities, which offer a fount of motivational energies to raise performance high above what they are formally rewarded to do.

But similarities can also incite conflict due to another shared characteristic of workism and evangelicalism: neither has a tendency to share space well. The American evangelicalism that gradually crystallized in the first half of the twentieth century drew from several sources that instilled the "thoroughgoing Christianization of the whole life" mentioned earlier. One of the lasting marks of this feature is the proliferation of evangelical "experts" and writers who speak on every imaginable topic and lifestyle activity, offering a distinctly "evangelical" insight on topics like dieting, marriage, parenting, grieving, financial planning, dating, and—as on display here—working. But today, we can just as easily speak of the "thoroughgoing *work-ization* of the whole life," as Thompson's workism concept highlights. The workism of creative-class capitalism extends a round-the-clock demand for observance, practices, and loyalties. Like evangelicalism, workism has a propensity to leave little of one's life unspoken for.

The faith and work leaders I spoke with were broadly cognizant of this tension. One faith and work leader recounted the biggest challenge of profession-centered ministry groups was getting anyone to show up: the high loyalty to work and career made the population difficult to court for regular evening or weekend programming. The workers I met certainly held their occupational roles in high esteem, seemingly incorporating the resources and events *into* their preexisting professional identities. This certainly presents the possibility that the key cultural resources of the movement might actually be subservient to the inexorable demands of workism.

Faith and work leaders routinely invoked a particular theological concept to ward off excessive work devotion: the threat of "idolatry." Idolatry is presented as a theological category for objects or activities judged to have accrued an inappropriate level of significance, diverting devotion and loyalty that should be directed to God. Idolatry of work, then, is a serious problem. But *identifying* idolatrous work proves tricky. The threat of work idolatry is generally spoken of in terms of an intersubjective orientation—once again, a matter of one's "heart"—that defies straightforward evaluation by an outside observer. Prohibitions against work idolatry can then easily be undermined by the absence of objective criteria that might be employed by a party external to the worker. Is an eighty-hour work week idolatry? There is no hard and fast rule. The effects of this ethical subjectivism are exacerbated by the supercharged spiritual value conferred upon work and work activities. What if work is a form of worshipping God? Or offers the highest form of participating in one's sacred calling? Seen from this view, the threat of excessive work becomes neutralized, seemingly comparable to excessive worship or service to God. Such an act becomes more difficult to condemn as sinful. "From a Biblical perspective, God is as present in your workplace—as present in Google—as he is your church," one leader of the movement likes to say. Another leader, in our interview, described his objective as helping laity see "that their primary place of worship is Monday and not Sunday."

Faith and work leaders seem remarkably lax about the potential impact of removing the "barrier" between Sunday and Monday, to use their own term. Weber, on the other hand, saw the potential for such transformations exerting a great psychic and spiritual toll on workers. His famous history of capitalism portrays the early Protestant reformers as ushering Christian laity out of the church and into the harsh light of the economic arena. This tore them away from any "magical" means of salvation conferred through the dispensing of grace and sacraments. They instead found themselves cast out into the theater (*Schauplatz*) of the world. In this performance venue, one's ability to secure ethical or moral merit is determined by the capacity to meet insatiable demands of achievement and self-perfection. This performativity quickly regresses into its own disciplining force, as the previous absolutions offered by the church and the "hope of grace" were no longer in a position to mitigate one's shortcomings and failures.[32] *The Protestant Ethic* quotes a sixteenth-century monk who saw this phenomenon play out in his time: "You think you have escaped from the monastery; but everyone must now be a monk throughout his life."[33]

Overworked high-status professionals are likely not what Weber himself had in mind, but we see much of this population today occupying its own secularized "monasticism." Workism in many ways represents the transposition of unforgiving frenetic pressure into the worlds of business, education, healthcare, artisan, and even nonprofit and religious work. These settings commonly present a high-achieving career as the exclusive means by which one attains a sense of personal worth, particularly in terms of constructing a coherent identity that enjoins the otherwise disparate components of one's life. We can again return to the famous observation by Weber at the end of *The Protestant Ethic*: "The Puritans wanted to work in a calling; we are forced to do so."[34]

One of the recurring arguments in the pages that follow is that faith and work efforts appear to be *optimized* for crafting a religious identity that can make peace with the workism-shaped worlds described by Thompson. But this interpretation has its limits. Not all creative class work has become workism. And not all laity who find their way to faith and work resources—even those occupying spaces within creative-class capitalism—exhibit exclusive devotion to workism. At the conferences I observed, I found myself regularly speaking with people from a range of professions, including nurses, teachers, architects, foundation managers, small-business owners, and artists. And all conference attendees, to their credit, had extracted themselves from their professional settings to attend at least *this* religious event, if not others.

This book ultimately sets out to explore how the faith and work movement aids a wide range of actors in constructing coherent religious identities that prove adaptive to their economic experiences and respective locations within broader societal structures. Seen again and again will be the recurring need for cultural-economic frameworks—whether grounded in traditional religion or a more-than-instrumental understanding of work itself—that transform Mondays into sacred sites for purposeful activity. This allows work to serve as sites for merging work with worship, toil with transcendence, and economics with eternal reward.

# 2
# The Fundamentalist Work Ethic

> *Wherever the sacred values and the redemptory means of a virtuoso religion bore a contemplative or orgiastic-ecstatic character, there has been no bridge between religion and the practical action of the workaday world. In such cases, the economy and all other action in the world has been considered religiously inferior, and no psychological motives for worldly action could be derived from the attitude cherished as the supreme value.*
>
> —Max Weber, "The Social Psychology of the World Religions"[1]

Lyman Stewart, a Civil War veteran-turned-oil-tycoon, had for years been pouring money into gospel missions and other Christian relief efforts. But his Christian faith took a sharp turn after attending a Bible conference in Ontario. There, he heard a pre-millennialist preacher speak of the dire conditions of modern American society. Only with the return of Christ could this depraved and dying social order be saved. Stewart returned from the conference with an urgent sense of impending eschatology: Christ would return soon. Setting aside his work in government reform, temperance, and poor relief, Stewart instead threw his energies into preaching "the gospel"—a call to personal repentance and conversion—in anticipation of the return of Christ. He drew on his vast wealth to support several efforts that were instrumental in creating a national movement of American fundamentalism, making significant contributions toward publishing the *Scofield Reference Bible*, the publication and distribution of *The Fundamentals*, and a massive distribution effort of the book *Jesus Is Coming*. He oversaw the publication and national distribution of several million copies of these resources, establishing one of the earliest networks of what would be a natural fundamentalist movement.

In 1908, Stewart teamed up with a minister to establish a Bible institute that could train other leaders and pastors in this pre-millennial faith. But

*Saving the Protestant Ethic.* Andrew Lynn, Oxford University Press. © Oxford University Press 2023.
DOI: 10.1093/oso/9780190066680.003.0003

after setting out the initial vision, the leaders confronted a haunting question: What if Jesus's return was truly imminent? How could they pursue a building project when the world might end in the coming years? Stewart initially opposed constructing new buildings due to "the imminence of the Lord's return": "I do not think it wise to use any portion of this fund in purchase of real estate or putting up buildings," he wrote in a letter to his brother. At that point in time, he felt it was a "serious mistake to put the Lord's money into brick and mortar." But by 1913, Stewart had come around: he recognized the next generation had to be educated one way or another. His institute, named the Bible Institute of Los Angeles (today, Biola University), constructed a thirteen-story building in downtown Los Angeles, making it the tallest building in the downtown area at the time. The building included a 3,500-square-foot theater and an impressive carillon of eleven bells that played hymns three times a day.[2]

Stewart's philanthropic activities happened at a time when close partnerships among economic elites and religious organizations were quite common. At the turn of the twentieth century, patron-like relationships permeated every major form of white Christianity, from fundamentalist Protestantism, Mainline Protestantism, more progressive forms of "Social Christianity," and even the steadily growing Catholic population, which often turned to wealthier Catholics to construct new parishes. Business owners were known to pay off churches' mortgages, support pastors' salaries, and encourage their employees to attend church regularly. Business leaders also used their societal influence to praise the virtues of religion as key to national prosperity. God was "the basis of successful commercial life," Howard Heinz of Heinz (Ketchup) Company told a group of two hundred sales workers at a gathering in the early 1920s. "There is no incompatibility between business and religion, and cannot be, seeing that the Lord has called us to both," declared a 1920 column in the *Watchman-Examiner*.[3] The column went on to identify the "foremost business men of our time" as those "whose Bibles were indispensable in their count houses, as daybook and ledger." Churches and religious leaders often reciprocated by also singing the praises of this happy marriage. Chicago Divinity School dean Shailer Mathews, writing in a leading business magazine of the era, praised the high calling and virtue of business owners: "Business cannot continue to be successful where human welfare is ignored," he declared. "When business men talk of rendering service they are not hypocrites, for they do serve their day. . . . Business does more than make money. It makes morals."

But against the backdrop of these collaborative relations, Stewart's frenzied apocalypticism captures the potential for fissures and consequential tensions. Even among conservative Protestants of the era, the logics of industrial capitalism and the logics of religious devotion did not always converge. For Stewart's case, fundamentalist theology conferred onto his enterprising efforts a very distinct understanding of history and time, with his business activity now interpreted against a backdrop of God's pending judgment of the world.[4] Conservative Protestantism also proved capable of creating bonds of solidarity among religious working-class populations that trumped loyalties to economic interests. Historian Liston Pope, in his classic study of a North Carolina mill workers' strike in the 1920s, found business elites facing off against the leaders of more sectarian faiths who, despite their emphasis upon "personal salvation," stood in solidarity with the strikers. Mill owners in the South would on occasion prohibit revivalist speakers from holding events in their communities, complaining their presence "just tear up a village and a community, keep folks at the meeting till all hours of the night so that they are not fit to work the next day, and they keep such meetings going for two months with shouting and carrying on." Historian Eric Hobsbawm records an account of a conservative preacher rousing up striking millworkers in a small town in North Carolina: "God's a poor man's God. Jesus Christ himself was born in an old ox-barn in Bethlehem. . . . It's sin that's causing this trouble. Sin of the rich man," the preacher told the strikers.[5]

These points of tension illuminate the heterogenous relationship between "conservative" religion and conservative economic interests. Some of this tension stems from imprecise usage of the term "conservative." As made clear in the preceding cases, adhering to theologically conservative ideas at the beginning of the twentieth century did not necessarily make one particularly committed to conserving the prevailing social order. This was particularly true for white Christian fundamentalism. Despite often being positioned as part of a lineage of "conservative Protestantism" (a convention I have reproduced here), fundamentalists were in many ways "savvy religious innovators," creating new things with little regard for the vitality of the old, as historian Matthew Avery Sutton points out.[6] This proves particularly relevant in how fundamentalists navigated questions of economics and economic life. Fundamentalist thought provided resources that could either challenge, resist, or—more commonly—demote the importance of prevailing economic mentalities, logics, and practices.

This chapter explores how fundamentalist orientations toward economics play a key role in setting the stage for later evangelical faith and work efforts. Here, we turn to writings dating from the era of conservative Protestant revivalism and fundamentalism (1890 to 1929). What we find in this era is the development and promotion of a "fundamentalist work ethic." This term is intended to capture some degree of contradiction, as many fundamentalist writers sharply deviated from what we conventionally think of as a "work ethic." The popular lay-targeted writings of the era contained little ethical instruction or spiritual content related to economic work and formal paid labor. In fact, activities related to economic life were granted little attention in these writings. Notably, this neglect was not rooted in any ascetic retreat from materialism itself, nor does it stem from rejection of the existing capitalist order. Rather, the fundamentalist work ethic channeled spiritual attention and energies toward activities other than economics. Returning to our categories from Chapter 1, these writers promoted subordinating and shirking orientations toward the economic sector that favored channeling energies toward the more important matters of faith.[7]

The emergence of the fundamentalist work ethic crystallized a number of ideas that shape the historical trajectory of conservative Protestant theologies of work. Many fundamentalists exclusively sacralized work that served ecclesial functions of ministry and proselytizing, the latter of which was perceived to be all the more urgent in the face of the imminent return of Christ. Work and wealth acquisition then become primarily framed as a means of acquiring financial resources to be given to the church in support of work of missionaries and clergy. The lack of worth conferred upon regular vocations and economic roles instills in fundamentalism what I call a "new clericalism," as those dedicated to full-time proselytization—ministers, missionaries, and evangelists—were granted a higher spiritual status than that of other vocations. Work, then, mattered to God provided that it was "Christian work," a term that fundamentalists used again and again to refer to evangelism and saving souls. This vocational hierarchy provides an important launching point for the twentieth-century faith and work efforts that will be explored in the next chapter.

## White Conservative Protestantism after the Civil War

For many Protestants, the question of "whose work matters to God" went back to Protestantism's beginnings. Martin Luther consciously broke with the Catholic doctrine on vocation by applying the term (*beruf* in German) to non-clerical positions for the first time, thereby flattening any vocational hierarchy regarding the value of work. Because all positions on earth can equally "participate in God's creating and sustaining activity on earth," Luther's proposal represented a radical equality in the "offices" in which Christians serve. Other Protestant reformers shared similar views: John Calvin commended Christians to enter into "worldly avocations" in the "right way when our hope depends exclusively on God."[8] Zwingli, too, pronounced labor "good and godlike" due to its ability to "make the body hale and strong and curse the sickness produced by idleness." "In the things of this life," Zwingli writes, "the laborer is most like to God."[9]

The white American Protestantism that prevailed after the Civil War exhibited similar views on labor, morality, and service to God. For one, most religious adherents preserved a close tie between the Bible, public morality, and the welfare of civilization. Many Protestant leaders also believed America was a Christian nation that continued to be guided providentially and covenantally.[10] Though the majority of the American populace was not affiliated with Protestant Christianity, white Protestant leaders governed key institutions of the era and ordered much of public and private life in accordance with Protestant values.[11] As George Marsden observes, the Protestantism of this era was dominated by a middle-class Victorianism that valued respectability, common morality, and order. Sensing little conflict with the wider institutional and cultural tenets of America, nineteenth-century white Protestants could still make plausible arguments for the public good based on a covenantal understanding of wider American civil society, serving as the nation's unofficial religious establishment. Even into the twentieth century, religiously led efforts like campaigns for Sabbatarianism and temperance would ground their moral claims in Christian values that they saw representing the "foundation of the Church and of our Christian civilization."[12]

Changes born out of the Second Great Awakening began reconfiguring religious converts' commitments to these older notions of Providentially ordered work. The individualistic, conversion-oriented mode of faith that prevailed in this era downplayed the degree to which many Christians were embedded within social relations and hierarchies that represented a covenantal or divinely established social order. Converts instead internalized an understanding of their faith that superseded external forms of authority, particularly those religious denominations that had previously been tightly intertwined with civic authorities.[13] This "revivalist protestantism," however, never completely severed the tie between religious life and the wider moral order: religious leaders still preached a unitive view of work, faith, and the moral order. "Faithfulness to secular engagements is a part of religion, and in observing this we render an acceptable service to God," a South Carolina minister pronounced in 1860, adding that "one may serve God in his field, his storehouse, or his workshop."[14] Charles Finney, one of the leaders of this era, leveled stern moral criticisms toward the growing credit systems and debt-taking made popular by the business class of his time.[15] Revivalist forms of pietism born from doctrines of "Christian perfection" also channeled energies toward reforming social systems, seeing such efforts as an outgrowth from the perfection achieved inwardly within the saved individual Christian.

Yet several developments originating in the 1870s would gradually widen the fissure between white conservative Protestantism and the economic order. It was in this decade that religious leaders began reacting to the rapid social transformations they witnessed around them, particularly due to the effects of industrialism and urbanization. These trends created a social order increasingly shaped by densely populated cities, many of them becoming homes to millions of European immigrants who were Catholics and Jews. Early advocates of "social Christianity" began to emerge in the North in the 1870s, with Washington Gladden, Richard Ely, and Jacob Riis making a mark on wider American society with bestselling books on a progressive and more political "social Christianity." Many of these leaders saw the changing features of American society as inciting a new imperative to "Christianize" the wider social order. Historian Christopher Evans traces the origins of such thinking to the older form of postmillennial evangelicalism—one that had shaped the prior era's abolitionist movement leading up to the Civil War—and growing currents of theological liberalism birthed out of Unitarianism. Social gospel advocates like Walter Rauschenbusch and Shailer Mathews came to embody the reform ethos of the emerging Progressive era, advocating for systematic, structural change in American institutions.[16]

But this same era also saw other white Protestant leaders move in a very different direction. Driving this turn was a reactionary opposition to perceived threats to traditional Christian belief. Darwin's writings had begun to disseminate in the wider public, challenging basic assumptions about the physical universe and the origin of human life. Scientific and "higher criticism" approaches to the Bible also began to disseminate from Europe, bringing scrutiny to orthodox beliefs in the historicity of the Bible and the accuracy of its accounts. Amidst these increasing intellectual challenges came rapid transformation in racial and religious demographics that made American society more difficult to reconcile with the prior notion of a "Christian nation." Feeling embattled by the combination of these threats, many conservative Protestant leaders began to lose confidence in American society's favored position in a providential order.[17] Two theological movements—both birthed from splinter groups of Anglicans in the United Kingdom—provided resources for these Protestants to locate themselves within a more reactionary mode of Protestantism, one operating from its own conception of history and an ongoing salvific drama.

The first movement, developed by John Nelson Darby, one of the founders of the Plymouth Brethren, was a frenzied concern for eschatology and a newfound commitment to pre-millennialism.[18] Darby's teachings stressed that the end of the current dispensation—the "church age"—was rapidly approaching and Scripture held clues of signs of a coming "rapture."[19] Darby initiated a series of American tours from 1862 to 1877 that diffused his teachings, quickly finding an audience among Northern Baptists and Presbyterians who found his high view of Scripture amiable to their own dispositions.

Darby's ideas enshrined themselves in the wider Protestant world with the publication of the prophecy-saturated *Scofield Reference Bible* in 1909. While the nineteenth century saw the formation of several groups pronouncing an impending judgment day (the Millerites, Jehovah's Witnesses, Seventh-Day Adventists, Christian Science), Darby's dispensationalist eschatology achieved a unique staying power by burrowing deeply into the forms of American Protestantism that would shape the next century. Revivalist D. L. Moody, who took in Brethren teachings during an 1867 trip to England, would come to incorporate Darby's eschatological urgency into his work and preaching. Moody's coordination of prophecy conferences and gatherings through the 1870s represented some of the earliest trans-denominational organizations that would give shape to a national fundamentalist movement. The 1870s also saw the establishment of several Bible institutes—in Chicago, Boston, Minneapolis, Los Angeles, Toronto, and Philadelphia—that sought to promote a defense of traditional biblical theology, pre-millennial prophetic teachings, and the urgency of evangelism.[20]

A second theological movement also made deep inroads into white Protestant Christianity at roughly the same time. A handful of Presbyterian, Quaker, and Methodist leaders began promoting what became known as the "Higher Life" or Keswick movement. Acquiring its name from an influential conference located in Keswick, England, this theology imprinted onto revivalist Protestantism a passion for fostering a robust inward spiritual life, fusing together Quaker and Wesleyan emphases on inward spirituality with a more optimistic view of the perfectibility of the human condition.[21] Keswick theology began channeling more energies toward seeking an indwelling of the Holy Spirit—a "second blessing" judged to warrant those energies that might previously be devoted to undertaking pious activities. Subjective experiences and laying claim to an inward "victorious life" began to consume greater focus and ministry resources. Those coming under the influence of Keswick theology did not abandon their occupations or economic roles, as Keswick teachings gave them little reason to do so. But shared experiences like baptism in the Holy Spirit and the felt urgency of eschatology led to cultivation of a more inward-looking religious faith that channeled energies away from "the world" and into the "harmless backwaters" of religious experience.[22]

These two movements together instilled within white conservative Protestantism what would become a potent combination of theological ideas: expectations of an imminent return of Christ, an inward-focused pietism focused on religious experience, and the primacy of proselytization as the laity's main spiritual directives. For many conservative Protestants, these ideas gave reason to abandon much hope for the "saving" of American society. An 1877 sermon by Moody articulated the revised understanding of society: Moody recounted a vision of a lifeboat at sail on a lake full of unsaved souls: "This world is a wrecked vessel. . . God has given me a lifeboat and said 'Moody, save all you can.' "[23] This turn toward saving of individuals would play out in different ways that were deeply related to race, region, and social status. Many white Northern Protestant groups that had only a generation earlier taken an active role in the abolitionist movement subsequently moved away from this earlier activism and relinquished any role in fighting for racial equality or racial justice. Similarly, many inner-city relief efforts led by middle-class churches began prioritizing evangelism and moral regeneration rather than working to resolve systemic issues. The heightened individualism of this theology proved easy to co-opt by both Northern and Southern currents of white supremacy that sought to maintain the social order by means of racial violence.[24] Methodist preacher Samuel Jones—who many saw as D. L. Moody's leading successor—openly professed racist views and defended the practice of lynching on the grounds of protecting "Christian morality."[25]

As examined below, these changes were accompanied with changes in the moral instruction directed toward the laity. The fundamentalist writers to emerge at the turn of the twentieth century began diverting far more of their attention to eschatology, missionary work, Bible interpretation, and personal piety, drawing sharp boundaries between these "spiritual" matters and those matters that were merely "worldly" diversions. The toils of present labor, now interpreted against the eschatological backdrop of dispensationalist theology, were downgraded in importance, a mere ephemeral state through which one must pass, en route to assured spiritual victories and relief. This orientation would prove remarkably enduring to the conservative Protestantism that characterized the American religious landscape for much of the twentieth century.

## Institutionalized Fundamentalism and Culture Production at the Turn of the Century

The particular institutional and cultural settings in which these work orientations were promoted prove to be a crucial part of this history. The institutions, organizations, and publishing enterprises piloted by conservative Protestant leaders from 1890 to 1930 would go on to place a formidable role in creating a theologically distinct movement within American Protestantism. The formation of new overlapping networks fueled by recurring prophecy conferences—combined with the culture production of periodicals and the acquisition of financial support from major industrial leaders of the time—all served to establish a crucial carrier for what became the fundamentalist movement of the early twentieth century. One of these biblical institutes founded in Chicago served as the epicenter for the movement. Its founder and namesake—the aforementioned Moody—made his most enduring impact on fundamentalism through building organizations and networks. Many of the pastors that worked closely with him until his death in 1899 had a significant impact on the next decades of fundamentalism, including Reuben A. Torrey, James M. Gray, Arthur T. Pierson, Charles A. Blanchard, William J. Eerdman, and Cyrus I. Scofield. Moody's

Bible institute became the preeminent Bible school of the era for training pastors, missionaries, and the laity, while also housing Torrey and Gray, both of whom served as public spokespersons for the movement.[26] The cultural materials produced by these institutions could for the first time connect rank-and-file laity with an extra-denominational, national religious network. Institutional leaders at places like Moody Bible Institute came to function as national spokespersons for a movement. Periodicals emerging in the era could boast subscription numbers (90,000 for *The Sunday School Times*, 60,000 for *The Defender*) that exceeded the reach of better-known twentieth-century periodicals like *Christian Century*. The generous support of financiers allowed for the distribution of over three million volumes of *The Fundamentals* to missionaries, ministers, and leaders of religious organizations across the country. The Moody Bible Institute alone could boast 14,000 students enrolled in its correspondence school by the 1930s and over 57 million pieces of literature produced by its publishing arm.[27]

Moody's influence also entailed the establishment of several early fundamentalist book publishers that flooded the market with mass-produced books carrying fundamentalist-grounded ideas about the Bible, theology, eschatology, and ethics. Fleming H. Revell was first established in 1869 by Moody's brother-in-law—the press's namesake—at Moody's encouragement. In 1871 the press went from producing Sunday School materials to books, first publishing Moody's transcribed sermons and several popular books on contemporary prophetic teachings. In 1894 Moody also founded the Bible Institute Colportage Association press (later Moody Press) to print inexpensive paperbacks, many drawn from Revell's own catalog. Soon after Revell moved from Chicago to New York in 1905, one of the press's vice presidents, George H. Doran, broke off to start his own publishing company. Doran's press and the two Moody-affiliated enterprises would together publish a significant portion of the books produced by fundamentalist leaders in the contentious decade of the 1920s.[28]

Despite depictions of fundamentalists as socially dislocated, backwoods populists, both fundamentalists and their theologically liberal or modernist foes drew from similar demographics that bridged the urban-rural and North-South divides of the era.[29] Both groups enlisted into their leadership positions a disproportionate number of college-educated clergy rooted in the Northeast.[30] Both groups were also tasked to pursue the support of wealthy donors whose ideas influenced their efforts.[31] And neither group was particularly successful in bridging outside of the white Protestant subculture to the concerns of Black Protestant or immigrant religious groups.[32]

Importantly, many religious groups did not map onto the "two-party" story of American Protestantism that pits revivalist, anti-modernist conservatives against more socially oriented theological liberals. Excluded from such a narrative are low-church Protestant sects, the early Holiness movement, and African American denominations that resisted the growing influence of pre-millennialist eschatology.[33] Various pockets of laity—particularly but not exclusively in the South—also preserved the classical link between the American social order and the demands of Christian faith, sensing little disruption to the Christian underpinnings of their public culture.[34] African American denominations within this era continued to confront a social and economic structure permeated by white supremacy, race demagogy, and threats of violence, which constrained any turns to an exclusively otherworldly or inward-facing religion. The modes of piety that persisted among such groups instead blended social and individual spiritual concerns while holding at bay the stronger currents of religious individualism.

But amidst this heterogenous landscape, key Protestant leaders established a lasting blueprint for trans-denominational networks or what would become "parachurch" organizations. This blueprint tapped wealthy donors to support not only publishing efforts but also recurring gatherings and conferences of religious leaders that provided a platform to disseminate theological ideas through wider culture. Analyzing lay-targeted resources produced and promoted within such institutions offers an avenue to excavate ideas, values, narratives, logics, and overarching orientations of cultural material being produced directly for (and, in some cases, by) the laity of the era.

This analysis should also be contextualized to the wider economic shifts that took place immediately prior to this era and that in many ways bore long effects into the twentieth century. The American economy underwent a significant "incorporation" between 1870 and 1890 as an early wave of mergers swept through industries, creating unprecedented corporate trusts. Whereas at the beginning of the nineteenth century the majority of American workers were self-employed entrepreneurs, by the end of the century approximately two-thirds had been absorbed into wage-labor positions.[35] This of course contributed to the diminishing number of those employed by small farms, family businesses, sole proprietorships, and artisanal trades.[36] This shift imposed a significant rupture on the "justificatory mystique" of work, in the words of Daniel Bell.[37] As Daniel Rodgers observes of the second half of the nineteenth century, "the factory system challenged each of the certainties upon which the work ethic had rested and unsettled the easy equation of work and morality in the minds of many perceptive Americans." At the center of this challenge was the jarring decoupling of a rugged individualist work ethic and assured economic success: the semi-skilled laborer may find himself "caught in the anonymity of a late-nineteenth-century textile factory or steel mill" in which "no amount of sheer hard work would open the way to self-employment or wealth."[38] This shrinking opportunity for upward mobility rooted in self-discipline took its toll on traditional work ethics that had previously couched such thinking within larger meaning systems.[39] All these factors also occurred within a period that saw a great amount of labor unrest, with labor organizing and protest movements seeking to resist the coercive factory discipline and control of production.

## The Fundamentalist Work Ethic in Popular Fundamentalist Writings

Books targeting Protestant laity in this era are uniquely able to capture the ways conservative Protestantism constructed and legitimated a particular economic imaginary for the fundamentalist laity of the time. Analyzing popular books written for lay audience attempts to get "below" better known top-down historical accounts that heavily rely on the writings and ideas of powerful institutional actors and economic elites. Within popular books one is much more likely to find the pastoral, the pragmatic, and the applied, as opposed to the systematic, the abstract, and the doctrinal.[40] Perhaps the most significant "finding" in analysis of these books is a non-finding. Surveying the fundamentalist era's popular periodicals and their frequent listing of books revealed just how little attention work and economics received in this era. With only a few exceptions, the books promoted by fundamentalist periodicals in this later era revolved largely around "spiritual" rather than material matters.[41] Topical studies of the Bible, studies of particular books of the Bible, or systematic theology grounded in the Bible dominated these publications. Other topics related to current cultural or social developments were explored, but far less frequently.[42]

The economic activity receiving attention within this space was personal finance. Titles like *Money: Thoughts for God's Stewards*, *Money Power*, *Money Mad*, and *About Money: Talks for Children* received praise for providing illuminating guidance for laypersons. Money stewardship, as discussed below, remained a concern of the fundamentalist author. A particular challenge of identifying relevant texts for this study also serves as an important finding: the popular lay books of this era almost universally used the word "work" to represent individual lay responsibilities of proselytization and ministry. As a result, the terms "Christian work" and "Christian workers," though commonly weaving through many texts and periodicals, were rarely connected with any sort of paid labor, occupation, or activity in the economic sector.[43] The majority of "work" prescribed to laypersons in these books and periodicals largely still looked like what the clergy were doing: preaching, winning souls, ministering to others, etc. While at times this religious meaning of "work" was merely the product of lexical imprecision, other cases clearly showed an intentional reappropriation of economic terms to describe church activity. Thus, the publication *The King's Business* in several articles compared proselytization to a business enterprise: "Our Lord was a business man. . . . He represented the great firm of 'The Trinity.' He exhibited the samples to the House—matchless grace, unfeigned love, limitless power, unending life, eternal joys."[44] A 1908 work declared the mark of a follower of Jesus is the "business to serve" and to make "living an investment for humanity."[45] Some of this framing was merely continuing an older strand of nineteenth-century revivalism: "Soul-Saving Our One Business," a sermon delivered by Baptist theologian Charles Spurgeon in 1868, was republished and widely distributed in the 1890s.

By and large, "faith and work" books or books devoted exclusively to theology of work were not a feature of fundamentalist book publishing for this era. One of the rare exceptions was Hugh Black's 1903 book simply entitled *Work*, published by Revell, which was indeed entirely about the laity's secular work and labor. Beyond this book, only a handful of books even saw the subject of work warranting its own dedicated chapter. Because of this lacuna, the books examined below were stitched together from several genres. A handful of books of this era explored faith's connection to business, such as *Their Call to Service: A Study in the Partnership Between Business and Religion* (1915, Revell) and *Making Good in Business* (1921, Revell). Other titles with relevant content appeared in listings designated as "Men's Library" or "Splendid Books for Young Men," with books blending pastoral guidance, career advice, and more general self-help themes. Other texts examined promoted missions support among the laity, personal evangelism among the laity, or financial stewardship. However, the dominant mode of writing speaking to work, lay vocations, or economic matters for this era came from more general applied devotional and pastoral books that spoke to "life" and contemporary questions. Two "practical theology" series of books described below wove in themes of work throughout their more spiritualized themes. Here, writers provide glimpses of the presumed role that work plays in the lives of the laity as they call them toward greater devotion to faith in everyday life. In total, fifty-two texts were compiled for analysis and coding. Three prominent themes emerged from this analysis.

## Instrumentalizing Work as Spiritual Discipline

Lay books appearing during the earlier portion of this era were more likely to promote a traditional or Victorian attitude toward work. Authors of such works differed from the later books' authors: in the earlier era, authors were more commonly ministers born in Scotland or England who only later came to the United States and subsequently published their works at an American press. Few of these authors played prominent roles in the later emerging fundamentalist-modernist battles. While Charles Spurgeon was active in the era prior to the 1880s, his work of satire, *John Ploughman's Talk; or Plain Advice for Plain People*, appeared on the Bible Institute Colportage Association press toward the beginning of the era of interest (1898). Spurgeon's work sounded many of the same themes that were harped on by earlier Puritan thinkers, including sobriety, discipline, and the dangers of recreation and idleness. "Nothing but rags and poverty can come of idleness," he warns his readers. Disorder and drunkenness are ever lurking threats. "He who plays when he should work, has an evil spirit to be his playmate, and he who never works to play, is a workshop for Satan. If the devil catch a man idle, he will set him to work, find him tools, and before long pay him wages. Is not this where the drunkenness comes from which fills our towns and villages with misery?" Hard work, Spurgeon recounted, is the secret to success; idleness is the root of all evil.

An 1894 text written by a Presbyterian pastor agreed: "Work is honorable. Jesus took his place in the ranks of the working classes. . . . Idleness is wrong. Idleness is the suicide of our noblest manhood."[46] A 1911 text called *A Christian's Habits* was equally concerned about a lack of discipline: "The habit of not dawdling is one of the most needed and most useful Christian habits. A dawdler can't really make a good Christian."[47] This text's praise of frugality and industry mirrored Weber's conception of work ethic down to even finer details: the author holds up Benjamin Franklin's discipline-themed autobiography as a compelling example of thrift for the Christian. The author, Robert Speer, went on to write two essays in *The Fundamentals* in the following years.[48] Dr. Hugh Black's book *Work*, published in 1903 by Revell, also reflects this work ethic. Black's book professes many classical Puritan themes surrounding work. Holding up trade and business against those who look down on labor, Black laments the societal values that evaluate individuals according to the amount of leisure enjoyed. This idea has permeated all social classes, observes Black, so that "to climb the social ladder means getting rid of work." Black praises work primarily as a vehicle through which character is instilled. The spiritual and moral threat of idleness still loomed large in his thought: idleness not only causes sickness to the body but is "also responsible for much sickness of the soul." "The most unhappy lives are idle ones," he writes.[49]

Clergy and the monastic life were not spared from this imperative to work, as Black revived the Reformers' criticisms of clerical and monastic life. Central to their shortcomings is their lack of economic self-sufficiency: "No amount of sanctity which might conceivably be attained by such abdication of the duty of work could make up for the selfishness of throwing the burden of their support on their fellows. . . . The holiness reached thus by casting an extra load on others is at the bottom selfishness, however religiously disguised. Christian independence is the other side of Christian charity." Black anticipated some of the compartmentalization concerns that will animate later writers of the century—particularly Dorothy Sayers—in lamenting the tendency of religion to "divide our life into a little snippet that we call sacred" while leaving the majority of our "secular" life unengaged by religion. Religion must "penetrate every detail, our whole manner of thinking, and acting, and living, our behavior to our fellows, our way of transacting business."[50] Black again and again portrayed the redemption of work as primarily a matter of correcting inner motives and subjective states, even in the face of work found meaningless, repetitive, or lacking any larger significance.

Black's wider work touched on many practical topics of lay concerns: from 1897 to 1911 he authored four works in his "Friendship Series" (largely reproduced transcripts of sermons) on Revell with the subjects of work friendship, comfort, and happiness each earning an individual book. Another writer of this era, also hailing from Europe but befriending D. L. Moody and making several trips to the United States, was also enlisted to write a similarly applied and practical series of works published by Revell beginning in 1892. Frederick Brotherton Meyer's series on "The Christian Life Series" was directly addressed to Protestant laity, with titles like *Cheer for Life's Pilgrimage*; *Christian Living*; *Saved and Kept: Counsels to Young Believers*; and *The Present Tenses of the Blessed Life*. Meyer failed to dedicate a book solely to work in the series, and indications that the "Christian life" featured any sort of work activity are sparse. However, the subject warranted its own chapter in Meyer's 1897 book *A Good Start*, which appeared outside "The Christian Life Series" by another publisher (Thomas Y. Crowell). Here, too, some of the core dimensions of the earlier Puritan orientation were present. Work must be done ". . . not for fee or reward, nor for wages which are, of course necessary and deserved, not for the applause and praise of one or many; but because work is honorable and noble, because a true man find his highest reward in putting his noblest self into all he does, because it is a scandal and shame to be content with anything less than the best, because God and his high angels are looking on, and because scamped work will return on us in other worlds to confront and shame us." Meyer warns of pending eternal judgment and shame for shirking or reserving one's best work "only for the best pay," echoing the earlier stern calls to obedient submission indexed in E. P. Thompson's historical survey of Methodism.[51]

But setting aside these work-focused passages, Meyer's larger corpus of applied teaching for laity captures the emerging ambivalence toward. While writers who come to dominate this era certainly preserve this paternalistic moralizing tone, the overriding concerns begin to shift toward specific moral and spiritual imperatives. Centrally, the moral grievance against sluggishness, shirking, or idleness begins diminishing as the threat of the idle worker does not seem to haunt these later Protestant moralists' imaginations the way it haunted earlier writers. Likewise, ideas about work inculcating character, channeling services toward God, or heading off the vices of idle hands also become less salient.

In many ways, this latter function of work—work's "virtue" of diverting busy-bodied workers from corruptive vice—perhaps shows the longest staying power of all early ideas. This is largely due to unwavering fears of encroaching amusements and recreational activities in the Christian life. Perry Wayland Sinks, in his 1896 work *Popular Amusements and the Christian Life*, praises work as a duty imposing natural limits on recreation in Christian life: "There will be preserved, in all reasonable and right amusements, a due relation between work and diversion—between the time devoted to pleasures and that taken up in duties. Christian ethics lay an abiding obligation to work upon every person capable of work. . . . We recognize the pleasure side of our nature; we must recognize the duty side as well." This obligation for Sinks serves as a welcome constraint on our nature, which might otherwise reach for the many popular amusements warranting his condemnation: dancing, card-playing, gambling, and theater. He concludes his argument by approving only of amusements sought after so that "we may be better fitted thereby for the work of life."[52]

But this means of valuing work captures the shift that is to come: work's primary good becomes its instrumentalization for purposes unrelated to work. This instrumentalization of work captures the beginning of its wider subordination in the Protestant moral universe. While for Black and many of the earlier Puritan writer coming before him, work had its own ends vested with inherent worth within a devout life, books emerging later in this era positioned work as a means—or commonly, merely a surmountable obstacle—to other spiritual ends. In addition to serving as a means to avoiding vice, work was also deployed as a means to two other ends or imperatives, each explored below. As laid out below, the major ethical imperatives for laity in this era revolved around a tranquil contemplation of inward piety and an active mobilization toward proselytization efforts.

## Subordinating Work to Contemplative Piety

Forms of pietism emerging from Keswick theology bore important consequences for moral instruction on work. This prioritization of inner spiritual states deals the first of two major blows to the traditional Protestant work ethic. Work largely takes a backseat as calls to "surrender," "yield," and inhabit a "victorious Christian life" come to shape more and more of the lay-targeted writing of the era.[53] Not only do the physical requirements of work hamper pursuit of these subjective states, but work also threatens to divert time and energy from the highest spiritual pursuits. There were certainly modes of interior-oriented piety prior to Keswick, but Keswick seems to have deepened a dualism that divided the spiritual and the material in a manner that would shape the theology of the next century.

Setting aside Meyer's chapter devoted to work in *A Good Start*, his wider body of writing was steeped in injunctions concerning this inward piety. The Christian life he envisioned predominantly centered on beliefs, assurances, states of being, and experiences. Chapter themes revolved around resting in wait, having assurance, abiding in Christ, living in victory. Little was said—or seemed needed to be said—of the readers' surrounding physical, social, or economic location: at times the intended audience seems largely disembodied and detached from any social or material reality. When the material world does make an appearance in these texts, it is generally portrayed as an undesirable encroachment—often cold, threatening, and perilous—juxtaposed against the warm, comforting life of the mind. "Let us bind his promise on our hearts as we descend each day into the arena of life, dreading the onset of men as wild beasts, and despairing of remaining steadfast or unmoved."[54] Or again: "And though outside there may be the strife of tongues, and the chafe of this restless world, like the troubled sea when it cannot rest, and the pressure of many engagements . . . whilst, within, the soul keeps an unbroken Sabbath, like the unruffled ocean depths, which are not stirred by the hurricanes that churn the surface into foam and fury."[55]

Rest occupies a central part of the Christian life: "It is just ceasing from your own works. The whole secret is in that word 'cease.' He that hath entered into God's rest *ceases* from his works as God did from His. Cease from self, from your own endeavors after rest, from going after this teacher and the other, sink down like a tired child on the pillow of God's loving care. Lean back on God."[56] From a later passage: "Christ's life was as free from care as that of the bees among the limes. Amid the strife of men and the fret of daily circumstances He leaned back on the bosom of God . . . always at rest, ever serene and tranquil."[57] "Dwelling" becomes a desirable state of rest: "How strong—how sweet—how happy—should we be, if only we could dwell in the unbroken enjoyment of the King!"[58] Here Meyer's work reflected a late nineteenth-century turn toward "quiet repose," a turn one historian sees yielding a number of Christian books that "advocated not effort or self-control but their psychological opposites."[59] Only a few decades earlier, Hannah Whitall Smith's bestselling 1883 book *The Christian's Secret of a Happy Life* called Christians to a similar rest: "Let your souls lie down upon the couch of His sweet will, as your bodies lie down in their beds at night. . . . Let yourself go in a perfect abandonment of ease and comfort, sure that, since He holds you up, you are perfectly safe. Your part is simply to rest."[60] There is likely no more apt representation of this shift away from the stern Puritan work ethic than this spiritualized imagery of pillows, couches, and beds.

Famed dispensationalist leader Cyrus I. Scofield built the case for inactivity—at least in disciplining the will exerting effort to build character—from a far different basis. Scofield's theology placed the modern Christian's life in a dispensation of the "church age," which must be sharply divided from other dispensations or ages. These divides must also be imposed on Scripture: Scofield's *Rightly Dividing the Word of Truth* asserted all studies of the word that ignored these divisions "must be in large measure profitless and confusing."[61] Scofield's divisions on Scripture diverted away from the modern lay Christian much of the ethical imperatives of Scripture: these directives, such as the Sermon on the Mount, were intended for another age. For this age, "walking in the Spirit" and its "increasing sense of peace, rest, and joy" were juxtaposed against "religionist" morality with its interminable self-discipline. Peace and rest were for this age; exerting effort was for another. Only Christians who understood their residence within the proper age of the church could avoid what Scofield identifies as "tragedy of the inner life": the "breakdown of the human will before the Christian ethic; the torment of an unattained ideal." Yet again, rest and tranquility—a "life of continual victory, peace and power"—mark the believer's life. Yielding one's powers to the "sway of the inliving Christ" was presented as an alternative ethical vision to strained efforts to self-discipline one's self.[62]

Books elevating inward states of being tended to neglect work as part of their larger neglect of the material world and social interdependencies, as outlined above. But where work does receive mention, it is subjected to two ethical admonishments. Commonly appearing in these texts was not praise of diligent industriousness but worries of shrewd materialism. A worker's ambition was recategorized from virtue to potential vice. Andrew Murray's 1896 work, *Money: Thoughts for God's Stewards*, took condemnation of "continuous money-making" to its extreme conclusion: the Protestant Reformers may have themselves mistakenly overlooked the value of a "holy poverty" in valorizing money-making, an activity Murray says drags the heart down and binds it to earth. "During the three years of His public career, Christ gave Himself and His whole time to direct work for God. He did not labor for His livelihood. He chose for Himself disciples who would follow Him in this, forsaking all for direct work in the service of the Kingdom."[63] Meyer offers a more tempered warning: "Don't drift into a mere money-making machine," he warns in *Light on Life's Duties*. Pursuit of money can disrupt the pursuit of God: "There is no harm in ambition when it is directed to doing the best you can to make the world better and those around you happier but it is a detestable passion to seek money for money's sake. Your aim must be to seek first the things that make for righteousness and peace for God's glory and man's good."[64] In another passage: "Suppose our one aim in life is to get money for our own enjoyment. Is it not clear that the meanness of the motive will react on the whole character behind it?" Pursuing profit is judged dangerous for the soul, which, "bathed in such atmosphere" of money making, will "become slovenly, careless, mercenary, and selfish."[65]

Other thinkers follow this line of thinking in tying the health of individual souls to wider cultural and social conditions, giving voice to an anti-materialist cultural critique. A 1906 book entitled *Money Mad* decries the modern age's "great modern peril" of "money-mad blindness and insanity," stating: "The ambition of young men and young women is almost entirely to have more of this world's possessions in their grasp when the ideal ought to be ahead of every man and woman to be right with God and have a character and have all life stamped with His impress."[66] A 1908 book takes similar aim at the wider culture: "Character does not develop freely, largely, beautifully in an atmosphere of commercialism."[67] Christians can possess a wealth that is different from that which the world pursues, according to a 1917 book by Robert Speer: "True wealth is inward resources, the love of God's world, of truth and holy thoughts, friendship with the living and the dead, the possession of the Son of God and His words which are spirit and life, and of His Spirit, 'whom the world cannot receive; for it beholdeth Him not.'" This "true wealth" is acquired independent of hard work: "We do not need to go anywhere for it. No man needs to bring it to us. It is here. It is Himself—the Bread of life." To be able to affirm our possession of this true wealth is, according to Speer, "our great American need."[68] The *Money Mad* text does not mince words on the perils of America's market society on this point, calling the stock exchanges of the day the "annexes of the insane asylum." Pursuit of wealth not only poses dangers to individual souls, but also can become substantiated in wider cultures of disorder.

Work was also subjected to a secondary ethical admonishment in cases where authors elevating the joyous and victorious inner lives paused to address how this experience can be reconciled with a mundane outer life. "The gospel is a call out of littleness, out of pettiness, out of insignificant things, to the breadth and sweep of great thoughts and forces, and to the wide horizon of limitless possibilities," Scofield wrote. But Scofield anticipated a resistant response: "You say, 'I live in obscurity; God has set me in narrow circumstances, in a routine of petty duties. I live in a farm house; I live in a village; I toil in a factory; I monotonously feed pieces of leather or wood into a machine and never see them again; I plow, I delve, I sell cloth by the yard, I wash pans and dishes. . . . I am no exultant young David, anointed of the Lord, free to go and come, to sing deathless songs, to rule over men.' " Scofield's response was summarized by a subheading: "What we are, not what we do, determines the largeness of life." Christians can "defy circumstances" that narrow their lives by being "lifted by the consciousness of divine sonship and divine fellowship."[69] There was little directive for fervent work and self-discipline; Christians already effortlessly possess what redeems their mundane activities. They must only come to terms with this reality "inwardly."

Likewise, Meyer also addresses a reader who "is tied by inexorable necessity to an office stool" and complains "his life afforded no outlet for the adequate exercise of his powers." Meyer admits the majority of Christians have monotonous lives that obstruct doing anything heroic or exceptional: "Each morning the bell calls to the same routine of common-place toil. Each hour brings the same programme of trifles." Meyer assures his readers they have been divinely placed in their work roles, which are "the likeliest and swiftest way for realizing His purpose." Meyer affirms the unimportant and obscure life in light of eternal considerations: "We need to look at our positions from the standpoint of eternity, and probably we shall be startled at the small difference between the lots of men."[70] At times Meyer turns to the more traditional directive of diligent and faithful work in whatever the role, in the interest of forming character and preparing for eternal reward. In other places the real redemption of work is rooted through the soul's imposition of beauty on all things: "Domestic servants, children at school, tradesmen, mechanics—let them not suppose that these spheres of duty are insusceptible of bearing treats of beauty. The heart can shed the light of its own ideals upon the commonest, meanest details until they wax lustrous. Many a beautiful life is being lived in top attics and cellar kitchens, because a beautiful soul is prompting every act irradiated by the gospel and irradiating it."[71]

## Subordinating Work to Proselytization

While the elevation of the inner life greatly tempered endorsement of the more classical work ethic, a more devastating blow to earlier work orientations was dealt by the era's obsession with evangelism. As described above, this prioritization not only drove out affirmations of meaningful "secular" work;

it also then lays claim to the term itself. For the devout Christian, "work" was disconnected from any sort of paid labor, occupation, or activity in the economic sector: it was instead the work of winning souls or undertaking the "King's business." A poem entitled "For Laborers" appearing in a 1921 issue of *Moody's Monthly* was clear on its referent: "For lab'rers on the mission field/To Thee, O Lord, we call;/To rave the blessing they so need—/Thy smile upon them all." Writers advocating this sort of work often exhibited the same sort of omission described above in failing to reference any economic or social interdependencies the reader might confront as they pursue the devout Christian life. Christian work was simply a universal calling imposed on all Christians, independent of one's position, occupation, or commitments in the economic sphere.

Samuel Dickey Gordon's 1906 *Quiet Talks on Service*, part of a very popular "Quiet Talks" series on Revell, was one of the earliest books to elevate missions to the highest calling for the laity. Gordon, a popular lay minister and lecturer who worked for the Young Men's Christian Association for much of his life, identified as "highly favored in privilege" three vocations that respond to the imperative to live an "active life of aggressive earnestness in winning men": those workers that can give "full strength and time" (professional missionaries), those workers that go to city slums, and those that dedicate themselves to evangelism in the places they are already located. Gordon then moved on to the "great majority" outside these groups who are "absorbed for most of the waking hours of the day in earning something to eat, and something to wear, and somewhere to sleep." Declaring this group does not warrant the "high favor" of privilege, Gordon was confident they too can locate "some bit of spare time, with planning, that can be used in direct service in church, or school, or mission." However, looking at this "great majority," Gordon decried "some new versions" of the last words of Jesus he saw being enacted by this group. Two "revisions" were articulated by Gordon, parodies of Jesus's "Great Commission" given to his disciples:

> All power hath been given unto Me, therefore go ye, and make—coins of gold—oh, belong to church of course—that is proper and has many advantages—and give too. There are advantages about that—give freely, or make it seem freely—give to missions at home and abroad. That is regarded as a sure sign of a liberal spirit. But be careful about the proportion of your giving. For the real thing that counts at the year's end is how much you have

added to the stock of dollars in your grasp. These other things are good, but—merely incidental. This thing of getting gold is the main drive.

Make a place for yourself, in your profession, in society. Make a comfortable living;—with a wide margin of meaning to that word "comfortable"—belong to the church, become a pillar, or at least move in the pillar's circle, give of course, even freely in appearance, but remember these are the dust in the scale, the other is the thing that weighs. All of one's energies must be centered on the main thing.[72]

Gordon's response to these revisions was a call back to the need for evangelism: "May I ask you to listen very quietly, while I repeat the Master's own words over very softly and clearly, so that they may get into the inner cockles of our hearts anew? 'All power hath been given unto Me; therefore go ye, and *make disciples of all nations.*' These other translations are wrong. They are misleading. *The one main thing is influencing men for Jesus*"[73] (italics in original).

Howard Pope's 1904 *What Every Christian Needs to Know: A Course Study in Personal Work* conscripted the laity into evangelistic efforts on account of the limitations of clergy to reach people. "The church must carry the Gospel to the world for the Gospel they must have. But who is to do it? The laymen and women. They know the people, they meet them in the shops, and stores, and on the street. They know their needs and dispositions as a minister cannot. . . . The church will never achieve any marked success until she trains and sets every available man, woman, and child at work." "Personal work" took priority over other work: ". . . every Christian ought to be a soul winner. Whatever a Christian's occupation may be his business is to win souls. Neglect to do it means failure in this life, and chagrin and remorse in the life to come."[74] R. A. Torrey's 1901 book, *Personal Work: How to Work for Christ*, made this imperative even clearer. Torrey indirectly expressed the low value afforded to a layperson's secular work by mentioning it only in relation to its capacity for providing a setting for evangelism. "At the Place of Business" was the sixth listed possible setting for evangelism (coming in right before "On [Train] Cars and Boats.") Torrey provided a rather tempered view of how much opportunity work really presents the aspiring lay missionary: "Of course we ought not to interrupt men and hinder their proper performance of their business duties. Many a work-man has rare opportunities to speak with his fellow workmen, sometimes during work hours, sometimes during the noon rest."[75] He was slightly more optimistic about nurses and physicians being able to carry out their "personal work" on the job. Overall Torrey's book resembled the contemplative spirituality books in imagining the great majority of the lay life distant from the encroachment of one's economic or social duties.

The prioritization of missions exerted a steady pull on not just teachings on work but also teachings on money. For practical reasons, the mission enthusiasts of the era also became the era's functioning moralists for questions concerning greed, mammonism, and financial stewardship. Books on missionary work at times included a special appendix for listings of books related to money and stewardship. A more moderately positioned Baptist periodical, *The Baptist*, laid out a special column for the "Stewardship Library," a listing of books presented as the latest "model missionary library prepared by the department of missionary education."[76] Some books of the era were not shy about preaching the duties of stewardship as responsibilities that could override private property. "There is an abundance of wealth in the possession of Christian people today which is absolutely unchristianed. Christians are holding God's money selfishly and the Church suffers and cause fails."[77] Andrew Murray's writing also delivers a sharp criticism of hoarding wealth: "Are there not many who say they have given their all to God, and yet prove false to it in the use of their money? Are there not many who say all their money is their Lord's, and that they hold it as His stewards, and yet who, in the amount they spend on God's work, as compared with that on themselves, and in accumulating for the future, prove that Stewardship is but another name for ownership?"[78]

This prioritization of evangelism subordinated the ends of work in a number of ways. The most common theme was the relegation of economic work beneath the responsibilities of "personal work." The layperson's central responsibility became conforming all of his or her life to the needs of the "king's business." John Horsch's 1921 polemic *Modern Religious Liberalism: The Destructiveness and Irrationality of Modernist Theology* lectures the reader on failing to distinguish between "Christian work" and work done only with a Christian motive: "It is quite true that the meanest manual labor is sanctified and becomes elevating when it is done from a Christian motive, 'as unto the Lord.' But this does not mean that such work is in itself of equal importance with the more direct Christian work which has to do principally with leading men to Christ and caring for their spiritual welfare." Horsch then remarked on the loss the world would have suffered had the apostle Paul dedicated all of his time to tent making.[79]

In addition, for some writers, work became the channel through which mission-supporting wealth could be acquired: the labor was not so much valorized in itself but rather its monetary rewards, as this wealth could be subsequently turned over to mission-coordinating agencies. This view failed to radically decouple and subsequently elevate the spiritual dimensions of work above the more material economic reward, a theological move made by Black, Meyer, and many others. A worker ultimately still worked to maximize his or her earnings. But injunctions to work for reasons other than wages—to build character, for eternal reward, to comply with biblical obligations to employers—became less applicable: the worker worked to earn money.

Finally, there were writers who elevated full-time missions to such a high level that all Christians not dedicating full-time efforts to missions owed restitution for their seemingly compromised vocation. Murray saw all labor as falling short of the full-time "work for the service of the Kingdom" that was commanded of Jesus's followers. In this case, all paid jobs were subject to severe scrutiny. This at times instilled ambiguity surrounding money-making activity, even if this money was reappropriated for missions.

Samuel Dickey Gordon and Howard Pope offered a more comprehensive ethic of money-making. For Gordon, all money accumulated in this life must be "exchanged" into the "current coin of heaven": redeemed souls. Gordon instructs those with wealth in this world to find their way to "foreign exchange desks" that specialize in this eternal currency: Bible Societies, international service and mission organizations, and local churches are all championed.[80] Prioritizing this exchange means forgoing certain luxuries: "Better turn your gown, and readjust your hat. . . . Wear your derby another season, and get your shoes half-soled, and some deft mending done. Let that extra horse go to other buyers, and the automobile be picked up by somebody who has not yet mined any of the fine gold of sacrifice."[81] Pope's proposed act of restitution is a more direct form of philanthropy: "I once wrote a leaflet entitled, 'Will You Go or Send?' It suggested that, as in war time when men could not go they often sent a substitute, so the Christian who could not go to the foreign field as a missionary, ought to try to send a substitute; that almost anyone by much prayer and some sacrifice could support one of those native preachers who can be maintained by thirty dollars a year."[82] In a later column published in the *American Messenger*, Pope proudly recounted an Illinois farmer whose entire life was reshaped by this pamphlet. On initially supporting a single missionary in Africa, the farmer enjoyed the assurance he now "worked" twenty-four hours a day, twelve on the farm and twelve in Africa. Six other missionaries were soon taken on by the farmer, who then became worried his "substitutes" were "doing better work for the Master than he himself was doing." After several years of reading the Bible in the poorhouse and smallpox ward, the farmer himself became a sought-after evangelist and eventually a missionary in China.[83]

For both Gordon and Pope, the real fruits of everyday economic work were what it yielded for ends exogenous to the activity itself. After all, the worker not on the mission field was the equivalent of the army draftee not at battle: restitution must somehow be made to offset his or her absence on the frontline. Financial support for missions became the redemptive act that can spiritualize and offset the less-redeemed day-to-day activities of the lay worker. And perhaps, in the case of the Illinois farmer, the absent soldier will eventually join the frontlines himself.

Orrin Phillip Gifford's 1922 work *Honest Debtors* provides a very practical explanation for this subordination of work to missions, in this case discussing the interaction between business and religion. Gifford has no doubts that religion and business share common tasks, but religion has the superior vision and ends: "In hunting whales the man in the topmast has the wider vision; if you will not launch out when he shouts 'There she blows,' then why send him aloft? . . . The man aloft, thinking only of [winning] men, has a clearer vision than the man on the deck thinking also of money."[84] What runs through all these visions is a deference to the vocation of missions and the "king's business" over non-mission vocations. "Money making" without this philanthropic end becomes deeply problematic within the emerging ethos of fundamentalist lay thinking.

## Fundamentalism's Other-Worldly Asceticism and New Clericalism

A character in Charles Dickens's *David Copperfield* at one point complains that his school's teachings on work seemed to radically vacillate in the course of even a single day: "From nine o'clock to eleven [they teach] that labour was a curse; and from eleven o'clock to one, that it was a blessing and a cheerfulness, and a dignity."[85] A similar observation could be made of the evolving moral instruction issued by American Protestant writers over the past two hundred years. The closing decades of the nineteenth century saw persisting vestiges of the stern inner-worldly asceticism that resonated with earlier

Protestant notions of work. The writings of Spurgeon, Vance, and Black preserved some of the moral consternation against idleness, shirking, or lack of discipline. Interestingly, conservative Protestant writers would also extend this endorsement of hard work to an endorsement of workers' interests. In 1908, the Moody Bible Institute periodical *Institute Ties* strongly affirmed the Federal Council of Church's "Social Creed of the Churches" as "a most righteous and reasonable appeal on behalf of laboring man which we should like to forward to the utmost of our ability."[86] Wealth inequality and consumerism also warranted spiritual concerns. In 1917, *The King's Business*, a periodical produced by Biola University, decried exuberant displays of the rich in a time of massive poverty with a surprisingly pointed reflection: ". . . is it any wonder that the poor laboring classes are increasing in discontent and that many are planning for a social war?"[87] Other fundamentalist writings also on occasion would voice support for economic populism, siding with the concerns of labor against the growing power of industrial capital.

But this same era saw the seeds planted for an ambivalence to economic matters in favor of those matters deemed more spiritually significant. A 1922 *Moody Monthly* column reprinted an editorial from an Indiana publication that is directly critical of the Federal Council of Church's establishment of a "Labor Sunday," judged to be a tactic for weighing in on industrial relations in an ecclesial setting. The editorial writer tentatively approved of a "Labor Sunday" to demonstrate the church's "interests in toil and the rewards of toil" but decries explicit support of the laboring classes on the grounds that it "smacks too much of the referee taking a hand in the fight."[88] Striving for a similar spirit of neutrality, Charles Erdman's 1915 essay "The Church and Socialism" that appears in *The Fundamentals* series calls on all parties to "live for Christ in every sphere and relationship of life, whether employer or employee, capitalist or laborer, stock-holder or wage-earner."[89] Black's 1903 *Work* also captures some neutrality on these contending forces, staking out his subject matter as "the more personal" problems of "our actual work and its claims on us and its lessons for us." "We are here not concerned with criticising the present state of industry or criticising the projects of reformers," Black assures his readers. ". . . Our subject is a primary one and simpler if narrower. . . . It is the personal duty incumbent on each in this or any other order of society."[90]

This era also saw the dominant interests in soul-saving and personal piety begin to eclipse the spiritual value or merit found within material work. This was found within the writings of Murray, Torrey, Scofield, Sinks, Gordon,

Meyer, Pope, Black, and others. The multivolume theological essays that make up *The Fundamentals*, produced between 1910 and 1915, had surprisingly little to say on the threat of idleness or the need for disciplined work. An essay on stewarding money makes clear that wealth can be ethically acquired and possessed by Christians, but then makes explicit a command to "subordinate" money to greater ends. By and large, questions of acquiring and possessing money appear to have been relocated to the less valued side of a spiritual-material dualism. John Horsch's 1921 *Modern Religious Liberalism* made clear what must take priority for fundamentalists: "It is more important to have the victory of the spirit through a personal relationship to God than to have one's social and political and economic desires satisfied." He lamented Unitarian sermons on "economics, sociology, labor parties, single tax, poetry, and the Bolsheviki" that have far less value than those that engage "innermost questions of the spirit."[91]

Horsch's contentious perspective captured one of the driving factors in this evacuation from concerns of work. "Social Christianity" and liberal Protestantism had already taken a firm hold of the economic realm, prompting fundamentalist writers to react by casting dispersion on religious leaders' meddling in such affairs. The moral or spiritual value of work likely fell victim to this reactionary disposition. As the 1920s progressed, economic issues began consistently falling on the wrong side of a spiritual-material ledger, seemingly having less to do with souls and more to do with liberal "sociology." A separate *Moody Monthly* editorial addressing Labor Sunday expressed a larger disapproval over the Federal Council of Churches' support for a pro-worker program slated for Labor Sunday. In this case, what was judged appropriate for the church was not neutrality but disengagement from the issue altogether. What industry really needed, the editors asserted, was "what the rest of mankind needs, the gospel of the grace of God proclaimed in Holy Ghost power."[92] Charles Erdman took a similar stance in his essay on socialism in *The Fundamentals*: "The hope of the world is not in a new social order instituted by unregenerate men; not a millennium made by man, not a commonwealth of humanity organized as a Socialistic state; but a kingdom established by Christ which will fill the earth with glory at the coming of the King."[93] Fundamentalist writers detected the dangerous "schemes of man" lurking in discussions of economics. Writers instead tied the economic imaginaries of the laity to ecclesial duties and eschatological urgencies. As historian Mark Noll assessed in his pointed reflection on Christian anti-intellectualism, fundamentalists of the twentieth century "fled from the problems of the wider world into fascination with inner-spirituality and the details of end-times prophecy."[94]

The fundamentalist writers surveyed above sought to usher conservative Protestantism toward an economic orientation that differed from its theological forebearers. Max Weber's classifications of religious systems proves helpful here. Fundamentalism, through its importation of pre-millennial apocalyptic anxieties and Keswick conceptions of inward piety, secured resources that weakened its ties with much of the "active" asceticism of seventeenth- and eighteenth-century Puritanism. What it came to resemble instead was other-worldly (or "world-flying") mysticism. In Weber's words, this mysticism "intends a state of 'possession,' not action, and the individual is not a tool but a 'vessel' of the divine." Laity were commanded to peaceably "lean back on the bosom of God," in Meyer's word, and take possession of their awarded state of grace. There was then no remaining action left to pursue. Action in the economic sphere came to appear as "endangering the absolutely irrational and the other-worldly religious state" venerated by this mysticism, to again draw on Weber's framework.[95] Particularly among adherents to the holiness movement, or even Keswick leaders who endorsed proto-Pentecostal forms of worship services, Protestantism had opened its doors to modes of religion Weber labeled "contemplative, orgiastic, or apathetic ecstasies."[96] But while these mystic forms of Protestantism favored religious experiences, they did not necessarily instill passivity or inaction. Energies for inner-worldly activity were now believed to be acquired through empowering experiences of baptism in the Holy Spirit, often described as an "enduement of power" that should be fervently pursued by the laity. These inward experiences were then believed to be the catalyst for taking one's place in the spiritual labor force of "personal work"" that would serve the cause of soul-saving.

Fundamentalists were at times surprisingly reflexive about their increasing detachment from "worldly" concerns. A 1921 column in the *Moody Monthly* proudly defended its other-worldly orientation against calls to improve social conditions: "Many claim that the premillennial doctrine makes of the people 'sky-gazers' instead of workers. Sky-gazers! That is just what the Lord Jesus wants us to be. Did He not command His disciplines, saying 'And when these things begin to come to pass, then look up and lift up your heads; for your redemption draweth nigh' (Luke 21:27)." The writer assured readers this proud sky-gazing does not lead to idleness but zealous mission work: ". . . the most zealous workers for the spread of the Gospel have been animated and spurred on to activity by their living hope of the early coming of their Lord."[97] But valorizing this sort of work had a consequential secondary effect: the flattened vocational hierarchy of Luther began to lose plausibility. With the dire state of unsaved souls looming large in the imaginaries of the laity, those who dedicated their full-time work to spreading the gospel seemed to exhibit a higher and holier Christian life than those constrained by full-time non-ecclesial work. Fundamentalist writers endorsed what was effectively a two-tiered understanding of Christian vocations, severing their own beliefs from Luther's spiritual egalitarianism. A 1921 book entitled *The Primacy of the Missionary* traced this spiritual hierarchy back to the early church: "Primacy belongs to the missionaries. They take the first rank because it was their duty to extend the boundaries of the church of Christ. . . . The early church so understood the teaching of her Lord."[98]

The result of such thinking was what might be called a "new clericalism" of fundamentalism, one that elevated evangelists, ministers, and particularly missionaries. Christian labor falling outside these occupations—and here, writers often explicitly included domestic and unpaid work—were only engaged in secondary callings. Meanwhile, the return for toil in higher callings—the saving of souls—was one of eternal value, whereas the return on labor from regular callings—money—was subject to moral scrutiny and often viewed with suspicion. Careful stewardship was commanded. Importantly, secondary callings possessed little hope of redemption in and of themselves: the pathway to redeeming such labor instead entailed "exchanging" the rewards of secondary callings into the rewards of the higher callings. But no redemptive act was necessary for the reward of higher callings, cementing a fundamental inequivalence between these two types of labor. Fundamentalist writers would occasionally invoke the metaphor of war to best flesh out this two-tiered hierarchy: the church was made up of those fighting on the frontlines—the missionaries and full-time ministers—whereas other laity, stationed in the rear, were tasked to acquire and transfer resources up to the frontlines.

In other historical reviews of religious orientations to economics, turn-of-the-century fundamentalism has at times been presented as deeply intertwined and at times a catalyst for the individualist ethos associated with modern capitalism. Alfred Griswold, writing in 1934, categorized the American Protestant preachers of the era as spokespeople for an emerging capitalist ethos: "From the pulpit you were told to get rich, and from the counting house to go to church."[99] Robert Wauzzinski pinpoints the origins of a marriage between conservative Protestantism and capitalism around the advent of the Second Great Awakening, inaugurating an era in which enterprise and public piety became sufficiently fused that one could "easily confuse enterprising inventors and pragmatically active revivalists."[100] Allan Lichtman argues the theology of fundamentalism had crystalized by the 1920s in a manner that "correlated, if not perfectly" with the conservative, pro-capitalist politics of the time.[101] Fundamentalist theology, in this portrayal, is judged far more compliant with the ideological needs of the industrial American economy. Fundamentalist leaders in this depiction conferred their blessings upon both individualistic wealth acquisition as well as the wider free market system.

Such assessments have some merit in identifying fundamentalism's propensity to accommodate and syncretize with the more dominant economic ethos of an era. Some of this accommodating likely dates back to the expanded individual autonomy promoted by the Second Great Awakening, a movement favorably disposed to the wider Republican ideology of the late nineteenth century that sowed the seeds for free enterprise.[102] But fundamentalism's complicity in perpetuating this accommodation may mainly be a product of neglect: many fundamentalist leaders and writers by the beginning of the twentieth century had turned their attention elsewhere.[103] The texts analyzed here also suggest that fundamentalist moral instruction may have undermined some of the key capitalist-affirming aspects of earlier modes of Protestant Christianity. Both money-making ambition and enterprising industriousness become subject to new suspicions of perhaps signaling a failure to "yield" to God. Fundamentalist spirituality recharged interest in an alternative, other-worldly temporality, which could at times bring into questions the pursuit of long-term economic endeavors. It is important to note that fundamentalism certainly bore affinities with a modern consumerist ethos in its adoption of modern technological and advertising methods, as several historians have pointed out.[104] But this relationship between evangelism and modern capitalist techniques seemed to heavily favor one direction of influence: modern business practices were instrumentalized to serve the gospel—often appeasing the demands of efficiency-minded donors—but the fundamentalist gospel was not so commonly instrumentalized for business and consumerist ends. Put differently, fundamentalists were quick to economize the sacred, but they did far less sacralizing of economics.[105]

Most importantly, the valorization of missionary work and its interminable dependence on voluntary philanthropy instituted a subcultural status system that stood outside the wider social order.[106] In this status system, feats of evangelistic effectiveness were rewarded with the highest spiritual status. The heavy production of stewardship books advanced the case that those occupying the lower positions on *this* status system owed portions of their income to support those at the top, who dedicated full-time efforts to proselytization. Popular writers depicted an interlocking system in which those who "those who preached" were dependent on "those who worked." As *The Fundamentals* commanded, wealth acquisition must then be "subordinated" in the interests of maintaining this system. A 1915 fundamentalist book called *Their Call to Service: A Study in Partnership Between Business and Religion* captured how this vision assigns social status. The "business leaders" selected to be featured in this study were honored for their giving to ministries, their founding of ministries, their service as chaplains, and in some cases their eventual conversion to full-time ministries. The lesson was clear: "good" business was that which was subordinated to church work. Fundamentalist literature could very well be fond of certain "businessmen," but that fondness did not necessarily extend to business itself.[107] Injunctions to subordinate money and money-making, to exchange wealth for "souls" through supporting missions work, and to forgo frivolous consumer spending all represented challenges to the popular economic mentalities of the twentieth century.

Fundamentalism also entailed a key deficiency that inhibited its ability to serve as the "priestly" religion of capitalism. By and large, when it came to responding to the woes of the modern world, fundamentalists simply did not "do" economics or, for that matter, any sort of abstract political thought.[108] Eschatology generally trumped all. The woes of the world would not be solved until Christ's return, and any positive improvements made prior to that would be a product of individual regeneration spurred by supernatural intervention.[109] A report on more than sixty creeds on social ethics issued by Protestant churches between 1908 and 1919 located only one creed from a conservative denomination of the time.[110] Conservative leaders instead advanced spiritual interpretations of economic phenomena. A Moody Bible Institute periodical linked the 1907 financial panic as an indication of a "cluelessness" haunting leaders' social unrest that was ultimately rooted in spiritual unrest. A *King's Business* diagnosed the cause of the Great Depression as the consequences of a "departure from God and ordained condition" that resulted from the churches of America "losing their grip on troubled millions of Americans."

This did not necessarily signal a surrender to quietistic fatalism. As Joel Carpenter observes, most fundamentalist leaders did not relinquish hopes for influencing society; they just saw culture and politics as unusual tools to achieve their goals. Carpenter identifies a "revivalist individualism" that placed regeneration of the individual as central to any mode of "redeeming" the worldly order.[111] Activism and reform efforts were channeled through this "salvational model" of influence.[112] A *Moody Bible Institute* column from 1922 heartily condemned "world *conversion*" which relied on a "steady, cumulative, evolutionary process" as government leaders slowly came to adopt Christian ideals. The biblical way forward, the writer argued, was "world *evangelism*."[113] A 1909 editorial in Moody's monthly periodical asserted that all "sociology" of radical change harmfully misdirected attention from what was actually "a question of soteriology."[114] Even the end of the First World War was interpreted in light of the larger salvational drama: a writer lectured against any declarations of "lasting peace" prior Christ's return.[115]

Fundamentalists would have certainly had good reason to consecrate the laissez-faire principles of free market capitalism in 1920s. At that time, they were fighting a two-front battle against not one but two movements associated with anti-capitalist sentiments. The "social Christianity" that became institutionalized in the Federal Council of Churches represented a dire threat emerging from the United States, while a godless "Bolshevism," coming from overseas, represented a foreign enemy. But the fundamentalist writers looked at here undertook a strategy that becomes a signature aspect of conservative Protestantism's social engagement: they refused to meet their opponents on the same theoretical plane. Instead of constructing robust apologetics against either industrial democracy or Leninist revolutionary tactics, fundamentalists sought to relocate their ideological foes into the languages and moral worlds where they had more resources to respond.[116] Both social Christianity and Bolsheivism were deemed mere symptoms of the greater disease: human sin. Bolshevism fundamentally represented a threat to moral order: its godlessness was judged a Satanic deception in both its intellectual atheism as well as its immorality. Bolshevism's sins are identified as anarchy, affinities with Darwinism, endorsement of free-love clinics, and the destruction of families. Reactions to such forces often indicted an assortment of parties judged complicit with such evils: teachers teaching godless science, baseball teams playing on the Sabbath, and preachers not committed to proper doctrines of the atonement.[117] Likewise, social Christianity's sins were primarily intellectual and doctrinal: Darwinism, Bolshevism, liberalism, and atheism were routinely stitched together as representing the same spiritual affront to the faith.[118] Even the Great Depression was still interpreted through this moral-theological lens: the root problem, as it appeared to leaders of the Christian Business Man organization, was hedonistic consumption, the liquor trade, and commodification of sexual activity.[119] This strategy repositioned appropriate response to such threats: rather than pronouncing the virtues of free enterprise, unfettered markets, or individual wealth acquisition, fundamentalists fell back on biblical injunctions revolving around personal renunciation of sin and affixing one's hope on the return of Christ. The salience and urgency of eschatology—combined with the primary concern for saving and regenerating souls—left only marginal space for the development of systematic positions on economic policy or—more importantly for our own historical inquiry—the economic life of the laity as a whole.

## Grahamism and the Long Afterlife of the Fundamentalist Work Ethic

How did the fundamentalist work ethic fare over the course of the twentieth century? Chapter 4 probes the content of white conservative Protestant books appearing after 1940 to find the emergence of some of the first faith and work thinking that would try to displace the fundamentalist work ethic. But setting aside these efforts to steer conservative Protestantism in a different direction, there is strong evidence that vestiges of the fundamentalist work ethic persisted well into the twentieth century and even remain salient today. One of the key carriers of the older economic ethic was the movement that purportedly usurped or splintered away from early twentieth century fundamentalist: the "neo-evangelicals" of the 1940s. This was an orthodoxy-defending but more culturally engaged mode of faith for which revivalist Billy Graham offers the most succinct representative archetype. While this form of Protestantism certainly predated Billy Graham—as Graham and many of his close associates had conversion experiences at town-wide revival services in the 1920s—we might simply label this theological stream "Grahamism" in recognition of the institutional and subcultural power exercised by Graham himself and those around him.[120]

Graham and other mid-century evangelical leaders such as Carl Henry and Harold Ockenga are often recognized for breaking with the earlier mode of fundamentalism and its sectarian infighting and anti-intellectualism. While their efforts certainly broke new ground in ecumenical cooperation among conservative Protestants, the neo-evangelical movement appeared to do far less for altering how conservative Protestantism engaged culture and economics. Much of what the leaders advanced in terms of a more "engaged orthodoxy" focused on establishing an assortment of new organizations that bridged denominational groups: Bible institutes, liberal arts colleges, missions organizations, media outlets, and summer camps.[121] The cornerstone organization within this space was the National Association of Evangelicals, founded in 1942, joined by Fuller Theological Seminary in 1947, and *Christianity Today* in 1956. But as sociologist John Schmalzbauer observes, "engaging" wider culture often meant merely creating parallel institutions in education, media, and other realms, rather than stepping into mainstream institutions.[122] This strategy effectively mirrored the earlier practice of churning out new religious organizations, media forms, and associations that came to characterize the fundamentalism of the 1920s and 1930s.

The "engaged orthodoxy" mindset charged those occupying or graduating from these institutions to be "ambassadors" in wider society, but the duties of this ambassadorship rarely diverged from the conversionist-centric impulse of Graham's own ministry, which in turn perpetuated that of D. L. Moody and other revivalists. This orientation doubled down on the "revivalist individualism" or the "salvational model" of influence discussed earlier.[123] Grahamism's orientation to culture and the world at large assigns the highest value to three things: eschatology, conversionism, and individual moral regeneration. To begin with the first, Christ's impending return overshadows nearly all of Graham's engagements with social, political, and cultural issues over his long career. Graham's writing in 1965 largely reproduces the same pre-millennial-focused approach to world issues that was common in the fundamentalist era:

> The salvation of society will come about by the powers and forces released by apocalyptic return of Jesus Christ. . . . There is nothing on today's horizon or in contemporary thought that offers an alternative hope that is better. Someone has said, "No arrangement of bad eggs can give you a good omelet." These successive civilizations of the past have been different

> arrangements of human institutions, but we have never had a lasting, satisfactory, peaceful social order. It is impossible to build a peaceful world on the cracked foundation of human nature.[124]

Likewise, in the face of difficult questions on civil rights, Graham turned not to ethics but eschatology: "Only when Christ comes again will the little white children of Alabama walk hand in hand with black children."[125] Such statements reveal little alteration from the earlier apocalyptic views of fundamentalism and the primacy of eschatology over social reform.[126] Such an orientation effectively dismisses efforts at social reform as poor imitations of the "lasting peace" to be established only on Christ's return. This pending apocalypticism drives energies toward the second priority, which is the primacy of conversionism. The priority of saving souls was often deferred to in place of any systematic engagement with ethical or political issues, a trait that runs through Graham's speaking on issues of civil rights, the Vietnam race, or labor issues. Closely following this conversionism, Graham elevated individual moral regeneration as the solution to particular social divides or conflicts. His hope for resolution within labor disputes relied on implementing regular acts of piety: "A good slogan might be: 'The plant that prays together profits together.' It is difficult to imagine labor trouble in such an atmosphere."[127]

Relevant to economic activity, all "Monday work" within Grahamism was still evaluated against its capacity to achieve the ends of "Sunday work." And with this standard of value established, it became clear that some occupations and jobs were better positioned than others to achieve spiritual ends like soul-winning, effectively preserving fundamentalism's "new clericalism." The result of such understandings is that successful evangelists, full-time ministers, and missionaries maintain the top spot on the vocational hierarchy. For the rest of the evangelical laity, the mundane pursuits of Monday should be subordinated to eternal matters. This view remained strong even into the twenty-first century. "The consequences of your mission will last forever," wrote evangelical leader Rick Warren in his bestselling 2002 book, *The Purpose Driven Life*. "The consequences of your job will not. Nothing else you do will ever matter as much as establishing an eternal relationship with God."[128]

Not all leaders, faith traditions, and organizations that operated within the evangelical space were equally committed to Grahamism. There were various pockets of evangelicals who held ambivalence toward conversion-inciting revivalism. Some of these outliers adhered to distinctly Reformed accounts of soteriology and culture that still provided resources for affirming a wider range of "secular" vocations among laity.[129] Authors and leaders operating from these theological views were often the first to write evangelical faith and work books in the age of Grahamism. As Chapter 4 reveals, some of these thinkers would even directly challenge Grahamism's conversion-centric ethic. Other religious groups adhered to amillennial or post-millennial accounts of eschatology that also tempered the primacy of soul-saving.[130] But setting aside this theological heterogeneity, Grahamism seems to have deeply instilled the dominant orientation for white evangelicals making sense of their work through most of the twentieth century.

The most salient challenges mounted against Grahamism appear to have come not from theological dissidents but from particular propagators of economic or political ideas. These challengers offered laity the ability to confer spiritual value on work in a manner not accounted for by Grahamism. Some of the most publicized efforts for baptizing economic prosperity in the name of Christianity appeared in the period between the 1920s to 1940s, with the Bruce Barton's bestselling 1925 book, *The Man Nobody Knew*, representing perhaps the high point of a celebrated Christian-business alliance. In 1935, Congregationalist minister James W. Fifield founded Spiritual Mobilization, a national organization that distributed periodicals and radio broadcasting aspiring to steer pastors away from the more progressive economic politics of the Federal Council of Churches.[131] But with only few exceptions, this "business Christianity" made limited inroads among the fundamentalism and neo-evangelical populations, largely due to the leaders' proud embrace of liberal theological beliefs.[132] And as the earlier account of Lyman Stewart revealed, the ticking clock of apocalypticism kept many conservative Protestant "businessmen" far more deeply invested in soul-saving rather than shoring up their own personal empires of wealth.

A different stream of leaders, often working from the opposite end of the theological spectrum from Barton and Fifield, valorized capitalist mentalities by way of a "Christian economics." Fundamentalist leaders like Carl McIntire and reconstructionist theological writers like Rousas Rushdoony both contended the tenets of capitalism were biblically ordained and "given to Moses on Mount Sinai."[133] While this veneration of capitalism was primarily intended to counter the progressive economics of the Federal Council of Churches, the enthusiasm for providentially guided invisible hands could very well have yielded a "Monday" ethic for conservative Protestant laity. American economists had long questioned the "unproductive labor" of missionaries that might be better channeled toward self-interested projects that yielded greater wealth for society.[134] Evangelical laity with an ear to such efforts could easily abdicate (or at least subordinate) their soul-saving responsibilities by appealing to the Providentially ordained outcomes achieved by "just doing their jobs." Sanctioning self-interested economics would then seemingly provide special blessing for entrepreneurs and those working directly in commerce, recreating a more conservative variant of "business Christianity."

But ultimately, these notions of a Christian economics failed to take hold among the wider evangelical laity. Much of this was likely due to these leaders repeatedly launching vitriolic attacks against many central evangelical leaders, which lent to their own marginality. Proponents of Christian economics also lacked reputable educational credentials, which seemed to limit the inroads made in evangelical scholarly circles.[135] A 1981 survey of faculty at schools affiliated with conservative Protestantism found no particularly strong consensus among faculty regarding economic views, suggesting the "Sinaitic" view of capitalism never secured a strong hold among educational institutions.[136] But more relevant to history outlined here, few conservative Protestant business leaders of this era seemed to indicate they had encountered these Christian interpretations of economic systems, which prompted them to construct the newer theological frameworks described below.

In the 1970s, Grahamism began facing off against its most reputable challenger: the political and religious alliances that formed the rise of the "Christian Right."[137] Leaders of the Christian Right were fully aware that their aspiration to transform a conservative religious constituency into reliable voters required confronting and overriding the other-worldly and privatistic elements of evangelical beliefs, which up to that point had yielded some of the lowest rates of political engagement of any religious group.[138] Some of this political apathy stemmed from the persistent rejection of religiously rooted political activism, which at that point was associated not only the Federal Council of Churches but also the Civil Rights movement. It was religious liberals who wanted to save society; Grahamism wanted to save souls. A fundamentalist Baptist preacher from the South delivered a 1965 sermon called "Ministers and Marches" that spurned all efforts to reform the "external" elements of society or "wage war against bootleggers, liquor stores, gamblers, murders, prostitutes . . . or any other existing evil as such." Drawing on the tenets of Grahamism as the appropriate response to activists like

Martin Luther King, Jr., this preacher went on to declare: "Preachers are not called to be politicians but to be soul winners . . . if as much effort could be put into winning people to Jesus Christ across the land as is being exerted in the present Civil Rights movement, America would be turned upside down for God."[139]

But this particular preacher, the well-known Jerry Falwell, would completely change his tune in the 1970s. Falwell's Moral Majority organization and other conservative political operatives began promoting more alarmist rhetoric surrounding encroaching threats to religious adherents, from forced school integration to liberalizing gender ideologies, increased visibility of lesbian and gay populations, the legalization of abortion, and the growing threat of "secular humanism." Grahamism's patient, prayerful response to these realities was judged much too tepid: Moral Majority board member and popular author Tim LaHaye framed political mobilization as a reluctant defensive move against politicians "intruding into areas of morality and the family and attempting to legislate outside their domain."[140] The Christian Right gained visibility and prominence through the 1980s and 1990s, celebrating Republican presidential victories in 1980, 1984, and 1988. Its power and influence within the Republican Party are generally thought to have peaked with the (ultimately unsuccessful) presidential bid of Pat Robertson in 1988. However, the infrastructure and network were very much part of President George W. Bush's electoral strategies in 2000 and 2004 and crystallized into new energies to support the election of Donald Trump in 2016.

But while the Christian Right conferred upon Christians sacred duties for election days, they appeared far less invested in conferring sacred duties on workdays. Certainly, rallying cries to oppose "godless communism"—an issue on which religious conservatives fell into perfect harmony with the New Right—instilled a deeply religious opposition to all things socialist or collectivist.[141] But Christian Right leaders, in their strategic promoting of social and cultural issues as central to the Republican cause, were far more tacit on Christianity's relationship to the mundane elements of day-to-day economic participation. Even LaHaye, who was never short on vitriolic charges against the threat of communism, framed the necessity of Christian activism as taking action in the *social* realm to challenge improper government overreach: he saw government oversight in realms of economics to be entirely appropriate.[142] But even more consequential than the Christian Right's underdeveloped economic policy was the minimal attention afforded to the day-to-day, "non-formal" economic orientations. Setting aside those

Christians working at flashpoints of culture war conflict, the laity drawn to the Christian Right did not seem to find resources for conferring religious significance on their Monday lives.

Measured by other standards, the efforts of Business Christianity, Christian economics, and the Christian Right achieved remarkable success in mobilizing resources and winning hearts and minds to their respective causes. But what they appear to have failed to do was dislodge Grahamism's hold on the economic imaginaries of conservative Protestant laity.[143] None of these efforts managed to claim the prize of overthrowing the vocational hierarchy that subordinated all non-proselytizing forms of work to those vocations that performed "work for eternity." Failures to displace Grahamism and its associated fundamentalist work ethic then kept alive the need for efforts like the faith and work movement, which would later assert, in a challenge to Grahamism, that *all* work matters to God.[144]

## Breaking Out of Grahamism: The "Problem" of Success among Conservative Protestants

We can learn quite a bit about Grahamism's persisting hold from the recurring pattern of protests mounted against it. There is a remarkable consistency in not only how individual evangelical laity protest its strictures, but also the identities and social locations of those leveling such protests. Going back to the early decades of the twentieth century, we see that Grahamism is generally challenged by a particular type of religious adherent: "worldly successful" Christians. A handful of successful business elites navigating their higher professional status were propelled into a social space where few fundamentalists or revivalist before them had tread. In each case, we see actors making sense of their new social location by confronting and creatively responding to the limiting strictures of Grahamism. What emerges from each of these cases is a theological interpretation that has far more to say to the world of "Monday," effectively forging a proto-theology of work. These individuals could be seen as conservative Protestantism's "social pioneers"—drawing on a concept developed by historian Eric Hobsbawm—in entering into spaces that few had tread before but many would come after. Later faith and work events held in the 2010s in fact recognized some of these individuals as the movement's "pioneers" who had blazed a trail many would subsequently follow.

The presence of committed Protestant "churchmen" among the upper stratum of economic elites had become a common feature of American capitalism at the end of the nineteenth century: Cornelius Vanderbilt, John D. Rockefeller, and Andrew Carnegie represented some of the most famous Christians occupying this space. But the cohort of interest here comes along a generation later and hails from revivalist and fundamentalist background. Henry Parsons Crowell, the founder of Quaker Oats Company, grew up Presbyterian but had a life-altering religious experience at a D. L. Moody revival service. Crowell's biography recounts a period where he initially felt an obligation to leave behind the world of business to become an evangelist like Moody. But Crowell came to discover his own calling soon after this:

> God didn't need his men educated, or brilliant, or anything else! All God needed was just a man! Well by the grace of God, I would be God's man! To be sure, I would never preach like Moody. But I could make money and help support the labors of men like Moody. Then I resolved, "Oh God, if you will allow me to make money to be used in Your service I will keep my name out of it so You will have the glory."[145]

His biographer frames Crowell's life as serving to resolve history's underappreciation for "factory builders" and those who "valorously rode the money tides and created great estates." Crowell's biographer identified him as a business "autocrat" on whom the "continuity of American life" depended: this providential purpose was of equal or greater value to what God might accomplish through successful evangelists.[146]

Another Christian business leader, Carl Gundersen, underwent a near identical experience. Gundersen, like Crowell, became involved in the Moody Bible Institute of Chicago, after graduating with a theology degree in the 1920s. He then briefly considered pivoting from managing his successful construction company to becoming a full-time pastor. According to Gundersen's biography, it was at this point that a pastor helped Gundersen recognize the merits of business: "Carl, God needs Christian businessmen just as much as he needs preachers. You have a talent for making money. If you will use that talent for God's glory He can take your service and multiply it many times, and you will know the blessing of God upon your life."[147] We find a very similar story in the same industry in the biography of R. G. LeTourneau. LeTourneau recounts being saved at sixteen in response to a week-long revival crusade in Portland.[148] But later in life, he had become involved in a Christian and Missionary Alliance church, which put a strong emphasis on evangelism. After joining a street corner "gospel singers" band and teaching a young men's Bible study, LeTourneau recounts feeling deeply unfulfilled with his calling in business and wanting to commit more to his faith: "To me service to the Lord, to which I had just dedicated my life, meant the ministry or missionary work." His biography records a pastor stepping in with the same message heard earlier: "You know, Brother LeTourneau, God needs businessmen as well as preachers and missionaries." LeTourneau credits that moment with showing him "a layman could serve the Lord as well as a preacher."[149] He would go on to become a significant booster and close friend of Billy Graham.

These individuals served as the test cases for a certain mode of revivalist Protestantism grappling with higher socioeconomic status. With that higher status came the enlarged role that work and professional identity came to play in the lives of the successful.[150] Yet because of Grahamism's stronghold on conservative Protestant laity, the achievement of success in one's profession initially posed conflict and tension for the devout layperson, who came to recognize that their professional status and worldly toil did not directly translate into the primary religious imperative of soul-saving. This brought them face to face with the question of whether they should in fact be channeling greater time and energy to evangelism efforts, as opposed to utilizing their professional gifts for God. The latter eventually won out.

The ministers who most frequently counseled these individuals toward this outcome were often far from neutral parties on this matter: Crowell, Gundersen, and LeTourneau all went on to be generous supporters of those working in full-time ministry. But the crucial element captured by these episodes are the particular means by which the imperative of soul-saving could be subordinated to a layperson's career ambitions. Returning to our three categories of religion's orientation to the economic realm, these actors all slipped through the cracks of Grahamism's subordinating and shirking orientations and entered what was then largely uncharted territory: an evangelical-grounded stabilizing and sacralizing orientation. As the next chapters explore, the evangelical theologies of work that emerged around the mid-century all tread similar paths in working to overcome the sharp Sunday-Monday or church-secular dualism. They did so by rehabilitating theological themes and imperatives that consecrated an even broader range of professions and trades as doing work that mattered to God.

# 3
# The Making of a Movement

*We are going to sell laymen the idea that they are going to work for Jesus Christ seven days of the week or not call themselves Christian.*
—R. G. LeTourneau, Christian Laymen's Crusade Meeting, 1941[1]

*You are most likely struggling with Monday Morning Atheism right now without even knowing it.*
—Promotional material for *Monday Morning Atheist: Why You Switch God Off at Work* by Doug Spada[2]

## "Are You Headed to the Work Event?"

I had just parked my car a few blocks from my destination, an older historic church located in a dense residential neighborhood. Before I could even close my car door, a woman driving by had spotted me and apparently judged me to be non-local. When I confirmed she had guessed correctly, she enthusiastically celebrated that we could walk together to our shared destination. As we walked, we worked through introductions and small talk as we made our way toward our shared Friday evening activity: an evangelical faith and work event called the Gospel at Work Conference. My companion on this stroll was an African American woman, probably in her late twenties, and professionally dressed, likely having come directly from work. She offered up a contagious enthusiasm for what the evening promised. On asking if she was familiar with any of the event's fairly well-known Christian speakers, I came to discover it was not the speakers but the topic itself that was behind her enthusiasm. She had heard the event advertised on a local Christian radio station and recounted that she knew immediately she "had to come." The event's advertised purpose had resonated with her: she felt personally called to "take the gospel" to her workplace, which was a small local company where she served as the branch's payroll manager.

*Saving the Protestant Ethic.* Andrew Lynn, Oxford University Press. 
DOI: 10.1093/oso/9780190066680.003.0004

Much of this interaction reset my expectations for the evening. At this point in my research I had attended a number of faith and work events, but they were in large cities, hosted in downtown hotel conference spaces, and frequently drew the "business class" professional crowd, the types of workers who could easily get away from work and family commitments for multiday gatherings. Local attendees were not a complete anomaly, but I generally found myself surrounded by jet-setting small business owners and an abundance of ministry leaders. Payroll administrators were far from the norm. But as it turned out, this event diverged in many ways from what I was expecting.

My companion and I entered the church at the basement level, greeted by about twenty volunteers, young adults wearing matching T-shirts branded with the event's logo. Modern-sounding rock music blared from somewhere in the building. The church itself was an early twentieth-century building with the smell and feel that only older churches can have: the green square tiled floor, the slight musty smell, and wooden paneling that marks a previous era's interior decor. This was not a state-of-the-art, amenities-loaded megachurch, as the long lines for tiny, outdated bathrooms immediately attested. A simple coffee station located along my path offered up the white Styrofoam cups one has come to associate with church basements. This was a no-frills Friday night church gathering. Amidst the frenzied enthusiasm of the assisting volunteers, I somehow lost my walking companion as I was herded from registration tables to the sanctuary. In a two-level room that easily held three hundred people, I could spot about five empty seats. A volunteer directed me up in the balcony. Here the remaining seats were on the far edges of a full U-shaped second level, placing me almost directly perpendicular to the front of the stage. The source of the modern rock music became clear: a band playing loud contemporary worship music had the room's full attention. I took a spot at the end of a long wooden pew. On stage below me, a bearded acoustic guitarist in stylish clothes led the band through several songs while the congregation sang along, aided by lyrics being projected on a large screen at the front of the room.

Setting down my pen and notepad, I stood with the crowd through several songs. This unexpected musical opener gave me time to survey the other attendees from my bird's eye view of the room. The crowd appeared to range from college students to middle-aged adults and was probably 95 percent white, a profile that also captured the entire band on stage and the front row of keynote speakers waiting for their moment. Just as the band wrapped up their final song, I spotted my newly made friend on the far side of the sanctuary. As the lead singer offered up a prayer to end his set, a late-arriving group of college students fanned out across the balcony and began filling in every open spot on the floor, filling the room far beyond capacity.

The number of volunteers, the local band leading the music, and the many local speakers sprinkled through the event program might suggest this to be the one-off program of a local church. The event program featured ads from local businesses, one of which sent a representative to raffle one of their products—appropriately, an office chair—in the closing moments of the program. But these local touches had been skillfully integrated by the coordinating hands of an international parachurch organization called Gospel at Work. This was in fact one of thirteen near-identical events sponsored by the organization. Incorporating some of the same strategies adopted by the famous traveling revivalists like Billy Sunday and Billy Graham, event coordinators from the international organization take time to form ties with local churches, recruit and train volunteers, and secure local advertising and sponsors. "Our end goal is that every church makes this part of what they do—thinking about the workplace and how the gospel intercepts it," Sebastian Traeger, founder of Gospel at Work, would tell me in our interview a few weeks after this gathering. It was safe to say that nothing about the efficiently coordinated, packed-to-the-rafters gathering I attended was merely a product of local circumstance.

One particular sequence of the event helped bring clarity to gatherings such as these: Who attends? As the band filed off the stage, the event coordinator requested that attendees stand as their respective profession was named from a list he then began reading. The first three professions named—healthcare, education, and finance—were each represented by about twenty-five people in the room. A slightly larger number stood for the technology industry. For industrial and manufacturing work, the number dropped to six for each. Ten attendees stood up for sales and marketing. Around thirty students stood up, college students and a handful of teenagers. When thirty people stood up for the "ministry or nonprofit" identifier, the rhythm of the exercise was disrupted when spontaneous applause broke out. This occurred again for the next category: military and civil services. Finally, the speaker got to hospitality and retail: roughly five people stood, one of them unabashedly letting out a proud cheer for their relatively small representation. Likely not wanting to break the pattern, the crowd chuckled while applauding politely. Finally, the speaker asked for those working in administrative work to stand.

As luck would have it, I had met the room's single payroll manager at my parking spot. She stood to another round of polite applause.

This breakdown of audience by occupational representation—which clearly favored middle-class to professional-class occupations—seemed to align with the event coordinator's expectations. "As you can see we have a very diverse group of people, and I am so thankful for that," the event coordinator said. "Our professions may make our 9-to-5 lives very different, but we're all brought here by the same question." That "question" was: How do Christians integrate faith with their work? The coordinator then handed the platform over to the first keynote speaker with a stately introduction: "He will come deliver the word of God to us." As nearly everyone around me pulled out their Bibles, I again realized how much this event took on the form of an evangelical church service. The relaxed stand-and-be-recognized exercise had served as the lighter interlude between the emotionally intense music and a more cognitively engaged sermon. As the first keynote speaker, a popular author and speaker named Greg Gilbert, took the stage clutching his black leather Bible, the attendees around me assumed the posture of attentive congregants, many joining me with pens and notepads out, poised to record the insights provided. It may have been a Friday night, but the audience had gone into Sunday morning mode.

Gilbert, a Southern Baptist early-career pastor from Louisville, Kentucky, began his talk by laying out the basic outline of the story of Joseph from the book of Genesis. Joseph, as the narrative revealed, was a favorite of his father and seemingly destined for greatness early in life. However, he hit rock-bottom early in the story when his brothers, seized with jealousy for his favored status, dumped him into a well and then sold him as a slave to Egypt. Yet Joseph persevered and rose in the ranks of servants in Egypt to eventually manage the household of Pharaoh's captain of the guard. After being falsely accused of sexual assault, Joseph finds himself back in prison, where he again rises in the ranks when his dream interpretation skills gain him an audience with Pharaoh. The tale of Joseph, we are told, is a rags-to-riches story, but the main character in this story is not actually Joseph but God, who divinely coordinated these events. "Whatever the circumstances of your job," Gilbert told us, "whether you like it or not, remember that God has a purpose for it all. And this has relevance to every single fact of your life."

The sermon transitioned from Scriptural exegesis to expressions of encouragement for resilience in the face of employment precariousness, with the assurance of God's sovereignty over all offered as a sharp juxtaposition.

"God is sovereign over every detail of your life, including your job." Even in cases where it appears our lives face trials, God is still working, just as he worked through Joseph in prison. We can have assurance in the face of evil and struggle that God is ultimately intending to bring about the outcomes that he wants: a statement Joseph made to his brothers after he had turned around his own life trajectory was applied to our own scenarios: "What you intended for evil God intended for good." After asserting this intentionality for our lives, the sermon delivered repeated calls for perseverance over struggles in one's workplace: "Whatever circumstances you find yourself in, remember that you are working ultimately for your God." "Just as God needed Joseph to be in prison, God needs you to be there [at your job] right now." "If you have a job or employment, it's because God has deployed you to it." "What matters is not your perfect job but faithful service to the king." Gilbert concluded his sermon with an assurance that Christians could weather even the worst employment conditions or instability: "God is sovereign over every detail of your life and you don't know how it will work out. It doesn't matter because it all ends up at the feet of Jesus anyway. At the end we will say to the Lord, 'To you belongs all the glory, honor, and praise.'"

This was not the rosy vision of the prosperity gospel that promises all blessings and no suffering for Christians. The constant returning to themes of God's sovereignty and a pessimistic view of ameliorating one's predicament revealed a low view of human agency, a central theme of the Protestant Reformation. Challenges faced in life were not downplayed. This was not "your best life now," to draw on a phrase of another popular evangelical figure. Work, it seemed, meant surviving undesirable and uncertain conditions by staying rooted in the unshakable character of God. You can depend on God; but work, not so much.

The second speaker of the evening, David Platt, was perhaps the event's "headliner," due to a fairly successful book-writing career and a rising career in the Southern Baptist world. Platt had entered the national landscape in 2010: he had released a *New York Times* bestselling Christian book called *Radical: Taking Back Your Faith from the American Dream*, which called on evangelical laity to dedicate themselves more fully to the Christian life by supporting missionary work and dedicating more resources to the poor. The book largely addresses an audience of comfortable megachurch-attending Christian laity, a demographic Platt had come to know well as a megachurch pastor in Alabama. While his book ruffled some feathers among more conservative evangelicals, it also garnered significant attention outside the

Southern Baptist Convention, earning a summary in a 2010 column by David Brooks in the *New York Times*. Likely due to Platt's ability to mobilize energy around mission work, the Southern Baptist Convention in 2014 elected him head of the denomination's International Mission Board. Platt and Gilbert both share similar physical characteristics: both are slender white men with tightly cropped haircuts and sharp jawlines that could easily allow them to pass as bright-eyed mid-twenties seminarians, despite their actual ages being closer to forty. At times I had trouble telling them apart from my vantage point in the second level. But Platt, like Gilbert, took the stage like a Sunday morning pastor, settling in behind the podium with Bible open in front of him.

"I want to show you how the gospel turns upside down our work and sees it as a component in God's gospel," Platt told us before laying out central doctrinal views of "faith in Christ" and the sufficiency of Christ as a means to secure our salvation. Practical takeaways concerning work were sprinkled through the teaching, also incorporating major theological themes of God's character, humankind's depravity, and God's redemption of the world. "God delights in work," Platt told us, "and he himself enjoys working." To make the point that God works through our work, Platt turned to a quote by Martin Luther: "God milks the cows through the milkmaid."

A high view of work landed on a far more direct imperative this time around: "Work is a mark of human dignity, and many people in the church work only as a necessary evil, in order to make money in order to get by. This type of thing is unbiblical." Here the sermon teetered on the edges of the "Protestant ethic" famously mapped out by Max Weber: work was being both sacralized and uplifted as a vehicle of living in the "urgency of eternity." Yet the conclusion took a sudden turn away from any Puritan veneration of toil to land in a more modern Protestant imperative: evangelism. We must work "from an eternal perspective" by "expressing the truth of the gospel" at work: "If you're the lazy one, unpleasant, the first to complain, then you aren't ordaining the gospel. Work hard to ordain the gospel. Work strategically to advance the gospel." Evidently it is not the Christian worker's salvation at stake here—what Weber saw at the center of an angst-ridden Puritan asceticism—but the soul of the ever-surveilling unsaved co-worker.

As I filed out of the church with the other attendees—many of them hopping into church vans with markings of local churches—I thought more about what attendees were taking from this event. Cultural sociologists studying religion have for some time made the case that a religion's meaning-content—"theologies, customs, worldviews, and rituals"—actually matter for its adherents, producing effects not reducible to structural factors.[3] But the precise meaning-content of the evangelical faith and work theology can be rather tricky to nail down. The frameworks promoted at this event seem to drift in divergent directions, at times generating enthusiasm for the experience of work, while other times cultivating a stoic resolve in the face of assured disappointment. And in the last moments of evening, work was noticeably subordinated to other ends altogether, the imperative of proselytization. In reviewing my field notes later, I realized the speakers I heard shuffled through a number of reasons for asserting that Christians owe something to God through their work. But precisely what they owed was less clear. What they were certain of was that, one way or another, God was not permitted to stay on the sidelines of modern work.

## Awakening the Laity

Conference gatherings have long been a staple of white American conservative Protestant subculture for nearly a century and a half. The annual "Bible conferences" initiated in in the 1870s by conservative Protestant leaders represented the first national organizational efforts of what would become American Protestant fundamentalism. Many of the same leaders continued to organize prophecy and mission conferences across the early decades of the twentieth century. Postwar neo-evangelicalism largely continued these practices. Since the 1990s, evangelical leaders have coordinated annual conferences around themes like worship music (Hillsong Conference), organizational leadership (Willow Creek's Global Leadership Conference), college students (Passion), and "biblical manhood" (Promise Keepers).

Conferences on work, however, have not been a prevalent feature of evangelical subculture prior to the first decade of the twenty-first century. But this is changing. Seven different nationally marketed annual events on work have now emerged within the evangelical subculture. These conferences served as part of a wide range of strategies to promote distinctly evangelical frameworks for understanding day-to-day secular work. As Chapters 1 and 2 have outlined, leaders of the faith and work movement understood these frameworks as key to overcome the shortcomings of the fundamentalist work ethic that proved inadequate for many portions of the evangelical constituency. Readers more interested in the cultural and theological content promoted to counter earlier moral instruction may want to skip ahead to Chapter 4. The present chapter explores the resources harnessed by the movement to diffuse these frameworks into a wider population.

Drawing on the insights of social movement theory, successful movements require both material and symbolic resources, including money, facilities, networks, and labor.[4] As we will see throughout this study, rarely have faith and work leaders articulated distinctly new ideas related to work and vocation: their real contribution is disseminating older but reconfigured ideas through books, networks, events, and organizations, eventually moving to contend with (and in some contexts, replace) existing frameworks. Movements diffuse cognitive content by drawing on organizational creation and transformation open up new spaces where types of "creative interactions" between individuals could occur, structured around certain ideas. Without the opening up of these spaces, such interactions—a pastor discussing vocational issues with a congregant or a theologian thinking through workplace ethics, for instance—would be infrequent, rare, and likely left up to chance.[5] Thus, the key driver of the movement was the construction of what sociologist Robert Wuthnow labels "special purpose" groups that could move ideas across churches and denominations, disseminating the cultural frameworks that might have otherwise remain marginalized.[6]

The present chapter maps several measurable dimensions of growth across the twentieth century and into the twenty-first, drawing on a range of data sources that are described in more detail in the Appendix. Where noted, responses from movement activists themselves supplemented the quantitative measures accessible from archived sources [7]

## Organizational Growth and Expansion

The phenomenon of parachurch organizations reflects an enduring attribute of American evangelical ecclesiology: American evangelicalism has since the very beginning been fueled by a democratic, entrepreneurial impulse toward innovative forms and practices. While circuit riders and tent revivals characterized the Second Great Awakening of the nineteenth century, the postwar twentieth century saw a surge of new laity-focused special-purpose groups. These groups and organizations might be understood as a unique twentieth-century form of the evangelical entrepreneurial impulse, as ministries, associations, and charities began to span local churches and denominations at the beginning of the century. Groups operating outside denominational identities and structures can easily escape empirical study: social scientists frequently adopt the unit of denominations to study and understand shifts, realignments, revivals, and contestation within American evangelicalism. Yet these parachurch organizations have in recent decades arguably absorbed from denominational leadership a greater share of moral energies, identity affiliation, and symbolic legitimation struggles occurring within American Evangelicalism. What is of central interest in the present analysis is the growth of parachurch efforts pertaining to theological doctrines and issues, concerning work.

Mid-century organizations like the Full Gospel Business Men's Fellowship International (1952), Laity Lodge (1961), and the Fellowship of Companies for Christ International (1977) were some of the earliest organizations providing conferences, networks, and resources for business leaders actively integrating faith and work. Organizations varied in theological emphasis—some focusing more on evangelism, others on ethics, and others on more transformational visions of culture change—but by and large they shared a commitment to overcoming the compartmentalization of one's faith and one's work.

The past three decades have seen an unprecedented explosion in these types of organizations. Table 3.1 demonstrates a surge in the founding of new evangelical faith and work organizations over the last decades of the twentieth century. Prior to 1980, there were a handful of organizations, primarily networks that built cells or local chapters for mid-to-late career male Christian business leaders. By the 1990s, new organizations were emerging with wider audiences than just business executives: organizations began producing vocational frameworks for a wider variety of economic actors and worker identities. In the two most recent decades, at least one new evangelical faith and work organization emerged every year.

This growth becomes even more pronounced if one includes "marketplace ministry" organizations in the post-1980s growth—an inclusion not pursued here for methodological reasons. These organizations are faith-affiliated professional associations focused on a specific industry, like Christian Coaches Network or Crown Financial Services. Previous research on organizational growth that *does* include such organizations confirms the same rapid expansion in recent decades: a 2000 "Faith & Work Directory" that spanned only North American and European groups charted around 750 faith and work and marketplace ministry organizations listed, while the same directory in

**Table 3.1** Growth of Evangelical Faith and Work Organizations, 1930–2020

| Time Period | Year Founded | Name | Mission (excerpted from websites or tax filings) |
|---|---|---|---|
| 1930–1949 (1 org) | 1930 | Christian Businessmen Connection | To evangelize and disciple business and professional men for Christ. |
| 1950–1969 (2 orgs) | 1951 | Full Gospel Business Men's Fellowship International | To witness to God's presence and power in the world today through the message of the total Gospel for the total man, and by this to reach men for Jesus Christ, especially those having the same social, cultural, or business interests as the person doing the witnessing. |
| | 1961 | Laity Lodge | To serve God by creating opportunities for people to encounter God for the transformation of daily life, work, and our world |
| 1970–1979 (3 orgs) | 1977 | Fellowship of Companies for Christ International | . . . united by a vision that the Lord can transform people, business, cultures, and nations through how we do business. |
| | 1977 | Needle's Eye Ministries | Connecting business and professional men and women to life-changing faith in Jesus—encouraging them to impact our community with His values, ethics, and love. |
| | 1978 | Pittsburgh Leadership Forum | To equip, connect, and mobilize leaders to serve that business in every sphere of influence in our city. |
| 1980–1989 (3 orgs) | 1983 | MBA Ministry (Intervarsity)* | . . . raising up Christian leaders who seek God in their professional and private lives. |

(*continued*)

Table 3.1 Continued

| Time Period | Year Founded | Name | Mission (excerpted from websites or tax filings) |
|---|---|---|---|
| | 1984 | Marketplace Ministries | . . . to share God's love through chaplains in the workplace providing a personalized and proactive Employee Care Service for client companies. |
| | 1985 | International Christian Chamber of Commerce | . . . to encourage and equip Christians to experience in a release into a new dimension of Faith, Hope, Love, and Freedom in their business and working lives and to better understand our time. |
| 1990–1999 (8 orgs) | 1991 | International Fellowship of Christian Businessmen* | . . . designed to bring Christians together to change the world and the workplace. |
| | 1992 | C12 Group* | . . . helping Christian leaders achieve excellence through best-practice professional development, peer sharpening, consistent accountability, and learning with the eternal perspective in mind. |
| | 1993 | Full Gospel Business Men's Fellowship in America | To reach men everywhere for Jesus Christ, taking particular note that in many instances men can reach others of their same social, cultural, or business interests more readily than anyone else. |
| | 1994 | Mockler Center for Faith and Ethics in the Workplace | To explore and promote biblical Christian ethics, values, and insights for today's workplaces—and to bring helpful insights and experiences from workplace laity to the church and its leadership. |

Table 3.1 Continued

| Time Period | Year Founded | Name | Mission (excerpted from websites or tax filings) |
|---|---|---|---|
| | 1995 | CEO Forum (Focus on the Family) | . . . to develop spiritual statesmen among senior executives of major corporations, and through them, advance the Kingdom of God and impact the business and social cultures of America. |
| | 1995 | Pinnacle Forum | To build a network of leaders committed to personal and cultural transformation centered on the values of Jesus. |
| | 1996 | Convene Now | To connect, equip, and inspire Christian CEOs and business owners to grow exceptional businesses, become higher-impact leaders, and honor God. |
| | 1996 | Marketplace Leaders | . . . to create tools that inspire, teach, and connect Christian believers to resources and relationships in order to manifest the life of Christ in their workplace call. |
| 2000–2009 (15 orgs) | 2001 | Kiros | . . . to connect, encourage, and equip Christian business people in the marketplace. |
| | 2001 | Life Chasers LLC | . . . equipped, inspired and encouraged Christians who were leaders in the marketplace to live out their faith with purpose, passion and commitment and to be a greater influence in our culture (disbanded in 2009). |
| | 2001 | Center for Integrity in Business | . . . to serve, inspire, and equip business leaders for positive impact, by being an accelerator of business and faith integration. |

(*continued*)

Table 3.1 Continued

| Time Period | Year Founded | Name | Mission (excerpted from websites or tax filings) |
| --- | --- | --- | --- |
| | 2002 | Kingdom Companies | To challenge, equip, and encourage followers of Christ to impact their personal and professional arenas of influence in business as together we "seek first His Kingdom." |
| | 2002 | Global Think Tank for Business as Mission | To champion the role of business in God's plan for the world |
| | 2002 | Center for Faith and Work (Redeemer Presbyterian, NYC) | . . . to foster, shepherd, and empower the church as it is scattered, not the church as it is gathered. That is to say, our focus is with the church body as it lives and works out in the world, beyond the walls of any one place of worship. |
| | 2003 | Marketplace Institute (Regent College) | . . . to provide and embody fresh, reliable, and well-informed expressions of the gospel that reveal its truth, necessity, and relevance to all spheres of public life. |
| | 2003 | At Work on Purpose | . . . to restore a full Christian commitment and contribution to the work world, one irresistibly transformed work life at a time. |
| | 2005 | Workplace Ministries | . . . made up of individuals who have a call to encourage, support, and train Christians in the workplace, so that they may enjoy God's grace while at work as well as in all other facets of their lives. |
| | 2005 | Transforming Business | . . . analyzes and catalyzes the contribution of Christianity and entrepreneurship to human and environmental well-being. |

Table 3.1 Continued

| Time Period | Year Founded | Name | Mission (excerpted from websites or tax filings) |
|---|---|---|---|
| | 2005 | Washington Institute for Vocation and Culture | . . . to advancing the idea that vocation is integral, not incidental, to the mission of God in the world. |
| | 2007 | Theology of Work Project | To help people explore what the Bible and the Christian faith can contribute to ordinary work. |
| | 2007 | WorkLife* | To collaborate with God to empower people to thrive at work. |
| | 2008 | Made to Matter* | . . . to introduce people to the great love of God by translating His truths and His Word into the language of the layperson. |
| | 2009 | Oikonomia Network | . . . to equip pastors to connect biblical wisdom, sound theology, and good stewardship to work and the economy. |
| 2010–2019 (16 Orgs) | 2010 | Praxis Academy | . . . equipping and resourcing a growing portfolio of faith-motivated entrepreneurs who have committed their lives to cultural and social impact, renewing the spirit of our age one organization at a time. |
| | 2010 | Work as Worship* | . . . helping people realize that there isn't a divide between the sacred and secular parts of our lives and that working with our God-given skills can be an act of worship. |
| | 2011 | 4Word | To connect, lead, and support women in the workplace to achieve their God-given potential. |

(*continued*)

Table 3.1 Continued

| Time Period | Year Founded | Name | Mission (excerpted from websites or tax filings) |
|---|---|---|---|
| | 2011 | Institute for Faith Work & Economics* | . . . promoting biblical and economic principles that help individuals find fulfillment in their work and contribute to a free and flourishing society. |
| | 2011 | Center for Faith and Work at LeTourneau University | . . . to help Christians understand how their work matters to God and His kingdom and experience Christ's transforming presence and power in every workplace in every nation. |
| | 2012 | Denver Institute for Faith and Works | to help men and women understand their work in light of the Christian faith and better serve others in their organizations, communities and professions. |
| | 2012 | Kingdom Driven Entrepreneur | . . . to inspire, teach, mentor, and advise entrepreneurs who desire to be led by God in their business. |
| | 2012 | Reintegrate | . . . equips God's people to reintegrate the Christian faith with vocation so that they can participate in God's mission on earth. |
| | 2013 | Kingdom Way Ministries | . . . to incite and outfit marketplace leaders and pastors to thrive in life, business, and ministry. |
| | 2014 | Nashville Institute for Faith & Work | . . . to equip, connect, and mobilize Christians to integrate their faith and their work for the flourishing of Nashville and beyond. |
| | 2014 | Talbot Center for Faith, Work, & Economics | . . . to equip churches to help Christians live integrated lives—at home, in their communities and in the workplace. |

Table 3.1 Continued

| Time Period | Year Founded | Name | Mission (excerpted from websites or tax filings) |
| --- | --- | --- | --- |
| | 2016 | Center for Faith, Work, and Innovation | . . . to help people discover and revive the God-given purpose to their everyday work and to help followers of Jesus Christ make for the new in all they say, in all they do, for the life of the world. |
| | 2016 | Kingdom at Work | . . . to inspire, equip, and ignite leaders to advance God's Kingdom through their influence in the marketplace. |
| | 2017 | Center for Faith and Work Los Angeles | . . . to equip, connect and mobilize the church, sent out to care for the world of work. |
| | 2017 | Chattanooga Institute for Faith & Work | . . . to engage women and men to live to live more fully with Christ through all of life, to bear witness to the gospel in all of culture, and to serve the needs of the world through their day-to-day work. |
| | 2019 | Center for Faith & Work St. Louis | . . . to transform the workplace for God's glory and our neighbors' good. |

*Indicates founding year was taken from first public tax filing.

2003 had over 1,200 listings. Theologian David Miller's history of the faith and work movement suggests that, at least up to 2007, the number of such groups has doubled every decade.[8]

## The Explosion of Evangelical Faith and Work Books

Growth in the number of books published pertaining to faith and work follows a similar trend to the organizational growth: there is a surge in production of books over the final two decades of the twentieth century and into

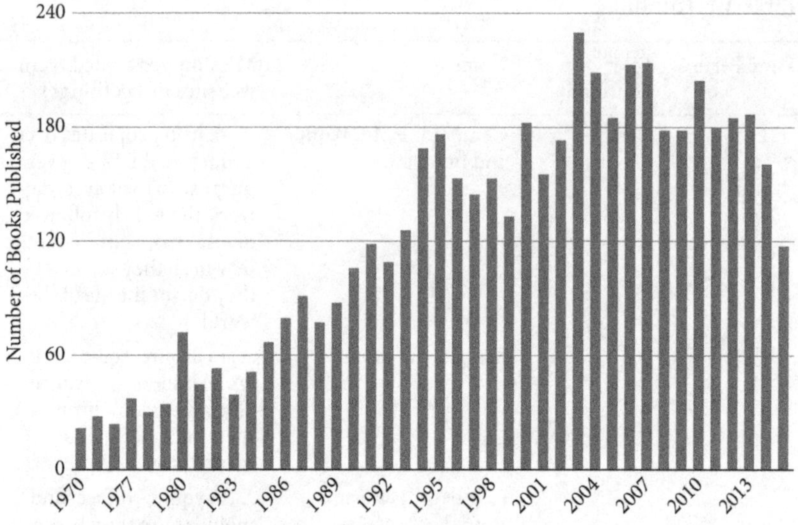


**Figure 3.1.** Publication Years for Christian Faith and Work Books, Global Database of Library Books
(listed subject matter: Work—Religious Aspects of—Christianity).

the first two decades of the twenty-first century. While neither the actors themselves nor the secondary literature employs a straightforward definition of a "faith and work book," the analysis here pieces together multiple methods of evaluating change in production over time to chart different dimensions.

A global database of published materials in libraries worldwide (worldcat.org) was consulted for the first measure. Figure 3.1 draws on the publication years of printed books (published in English) that were categorized in the database as pertaining to the subject "Work—Religious Aspects—Christianity." This subject shows steady growth from the 1970s to the 1990s, with a plateauing around the turn of the century.[9] Since 2000, on average 185 new books appear in this category every year. This gives some idea of the rise in faith and work books but, importantly, this measure is not limited to books written for or by evangelical authors. In general, then, this uptick reflects a wider uptick in the faith and work topic across the American religious landscape, an upsurge also observed by David Miller. But we must turn to other data sources to explore the specifically evangelical forms of growth.

Drawing on a different data source, Figure 3.2 shows publication dates from a curated database of 1,648 "faith and work books" collected and curated by Seattle Pacific University's University Library. This is a collection

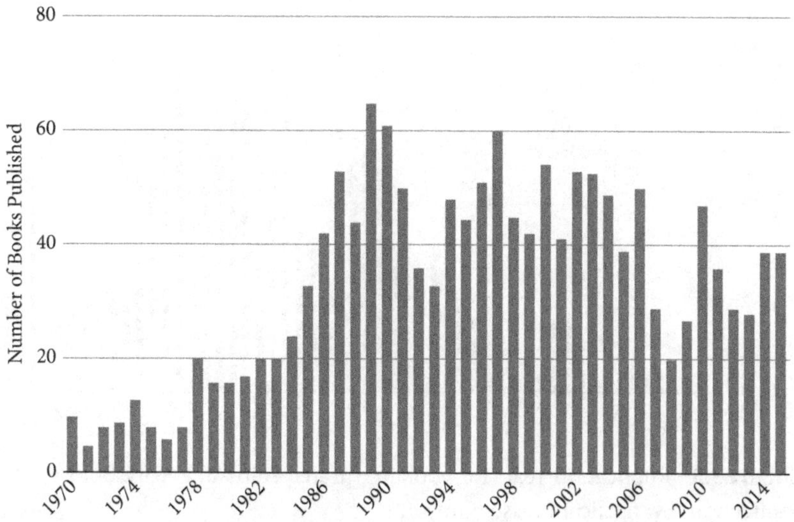


**Figure 3.2.** Publication Years for Books in Curated Faith and Work Book Collection

of faith and work books that is built, maintained, and shaped by the work of a committee of evangelical scholars and leaders. Each year these scholars meet to carefully select which new books will be added, guided by a written guide of principles, objectives, and priorities for the collection. This database, then, in many ways serves as a canonized bibliography for how evangelical leaders approach the topic of work. One observes a similar rise in production over period as the previous figure, with a similar climb in production from the 1970s to 1990s before this increase plateaus around 2000.

The curated collection of books also includes theoretical, sociological, and historical works on the intersection of religion and economics, which, while valuable for the purposes of those maintaining the list, limits one's ability to ascertain trends in books specifically directed toward laity. Figure 3.3 attempts to capture the growth of specifically lay-targeted books, here defined as books published by evangelical publishing companies. This definition of an evangelical faith and work book operates from the assumptions that books published by these publishers are responding to perceived interests of evangelical laity and are then marketed to and read by evangelical laity.[10] Once again, we see the same general trend as displayed in the earlier figure: a steady growth from the 1970s and 1980s to the turn of the century and then a plateau since the year 2000.

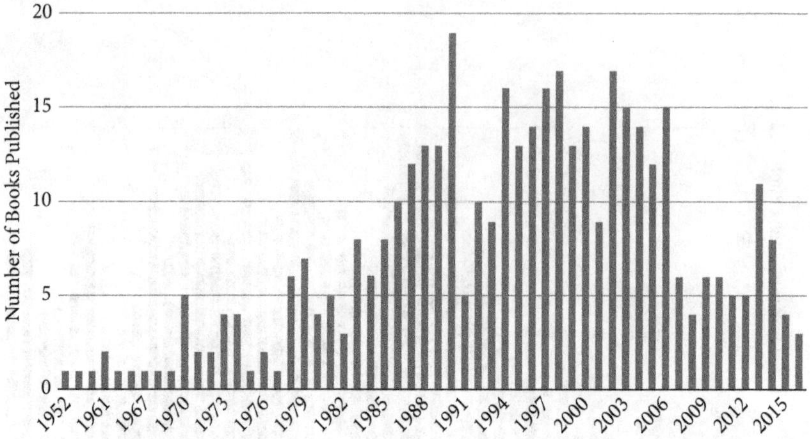


**Figure 3.3.** Publication Years for book in Curated Faith and Work Book Collection, Evangelical Presses Only

To assess whether this production surge was a product of wider publishing trends, the global database of books was also drawn upon to measure the total number of published books (on any topic) by year for evangelical publishers. This inquiry revealed the overall rate of evangelical book publishing rose several decades prior to the 1980s and 1990s surge in faith and work book production. This would suggest causes for the production surge in faith and work books are likely independent from overall trends in evangelical publishing.

One interviewed leader and author recounted Christian publishers in the 1980s giving a cold response to her proposal for a book on Christian business practices. Publishers at that time saw books that tread toward economics as having "no clear connection" to evangelical theology. This is somewhat surprising in view of the production levels depicted here, which appear to be ramping up by the 1980s. But this anecdote nevertheless captures that there was an era not long ago when publishers had little interest in an evangelical book on business or economic conduct. Several interviewees report this has drastically changed: one interviewee reported publishers now see the market of faith and work books as reaching a saturation point.

## Establishing the National Conference Circuit

From my time in the field I observed that national faith-based conferences serve as central, public-facing events for parachurch evangelical organizations. Because of the publicity efforts to draw attendees, conference logistics and planning can hold significant symbolic meaning that extends beyond the attendees and a one-time gathering. Conference speaker selection can incite national controversies, celebrity authors gain legitimation within these sites, and doctrinal controversies may spill out from conferences into the wider evangelical world through Twitter and blog posts. Al Hsu, lead editor of Intervarsity Press, observed that national "mega-conferences" have become a "big sort" mechanism of the larger evangelical world, offering branded identities, affiliation status, and a closed-off tribalism to their respective attendees.[11] While little sociological research has been conducted on this phenomenon, my own experience in this subculture supports Hsu's claim that conferences hold significant influence in relation to both individual and collective identity formation within American evangelicalism. Particularly as the prevalence of more locally autonomous "non-denominational" churches have grown, mega-conferences likely inherit from traditional denominational structures many important functions related to solidifying group identities, drawing group boundaries, shoring up doctrinal issues, sharing resources, and providing a means of legitimating new pastors and speakers. Building from this cursory understanding of legitimizing function of conferences, we can trace how the faith and work movement accumulated both valuable symbolic power and organizational resources through its entrance into the national circuit of mega-conferences.

To build a sociological-historical account of conference growth, existing histories of the faith and work movement were combined with interviewees' own accounts and archival research on specific conference histories. This mode of evaluation illuminated at least two major branches of faith and work gatherings, rather than a single lineage. The earliest gatherings—emerging in the 1980s--operated with a high degree of cultural legitimacy from evangelical leaders but can be demarcated by particular theological orientations, demographic reach, and logistical-organizational dimensions. A later developing movement of conferences—which only emerges in the first decade of the twenty-first century--absorbed a handful of earlier figures, but largely forged a different theological and institutional path. The following analysis traces the each of these waves and their distinctive techniques and cultural frameworks.

## First Wave: Marketplace Ministries and the Charismatic-Transformationalist Political Visions

For most of the twentieth century, the faith and work organizations that were founded by lay leaders did not coordinate national faith and work conferences. It was not until the 1980s that a particular type of gathering emerged: a gathering that sought (at least in its promotion) to appeal to all workers rather than a particular occupational field, that tried to downplay any specific denominational affiliation, and that was advertised widely to clergy, laity, and ministry organization leaders beyond those affiliated with the coordinating organization. Consequently, earlier twentieth-century gatherings coordinated by groups like the Christian Businessmen's Committee (founded in 1930), the Full Gospel Businessmen International (founded in 1952), and the Fellowship of Christian Companies International (1977), while chronologically preceding the first wave of national conferences, did not produce anything that looked like a national faith and work conference. Earlier organizations also focused on building local chapters to be networked together by an overarching organization rather than coordinating elaborate one-time events to draw in those with little previous engagement with the organization. The first wave of national gatherings, then, represents a moment of innovation for organizational leaders.

The first coordination of a national conference gathering was headed up by Os Hillman.[12] Hillman was a successful advertising executive until he hit several personal crises in 1994: his advertising agency's major client failed to pay its bills, he lost half a million dollars in investments, and he and his wife separated.[13] Seeking a new calling, Hillman found mentorship from several organizational leaders already active in the faith and work space and soon began his own magazine and daily-devotional newsletter on faith and work issues. In 1997 he partnered with Larry Burkett, president of a group called Christian Financial Concepts, to coordinate a gathering of "marketplace ministry" leaders, the first gathering of its type. To the surprise of the organizers, the gathering drew participants from over forty-five different workplace organizations. This gathering, combined with his magazine and daily devotional, put Hillman on the radar of the Billy Graham Evangelistic

Association, who contacted him in 2002 about coordinating a larger conference. Hillman and others worked with the Billy Graham Evangelistic Association to create four gatherings entitled "His Church in the Workplace," the most significant of which was hosted at the Billy Graham Training Center in North Carolina. According to the press release recounting the event, "nearly 300 pastors, marketplace business leaders, and workplace ministry leaders" attended the three-day gathering "designed to create an action plan to bring God's presence into the workplace." The participant list included major international organizations like the Fellowship of Companies for Christ and the International Fellowship of Workplace Ministries, then headed by Hillman. Other "His Church in the Workplace" gatherings, coordinated with the help of the Billy Graham Evangelistic Association, took place in San Antonio in 2004 and Silicon Valley in 2005. Hillman's wide network of contacts through his daily devotional newsletter—reaching 75,000 by 2004—and his success with the 2003 conference allowed him to organize an even larger gathering in 2007. Then heading the Atlanta-based group Marketplace Ministries, Hillman coordinated the first "Church in the Workplace" conference in downtown Atlanta in January 2007, targeting Christian pastors and workplace leaders. The conference featured well-known Fuller Seminary professor C. Peter Wagner and author Henry Blackaby, as well as Kent Humphreys, who was then leading the Fellowship of Companies for Christ International. One of the speakers, Linda Rios Brook, also coordinated a "Women in the Workplace" conference immediately preceding the event that aimed at bringing together working women to "foster spiritual and professional alliances to more effectively influence the transformation of culture." Both events keyed in on the transformational opportunity that workplaces held, as sites where believers could live out their callings and "impact their city through their authority."[14]

These events expanded their speaking lineup in the 2008 and 2009 versions of the Church in the Workplace gathering.[15] The attendees roster continued to represent a who's-who of the existing faith and work organizations of the time, and coordinators were able to legitimate their efforts by citing ties to central evangelical figures. A quotation attributed to Billy Graham frequently appeared on marketing materials at the time: "I believe one of the next great moves of God is going to be through the believers in the workplace." Another regular source of affirmation came from C. Peter Wagner, an academic advisor to bestselling author Rick Warren and often seen at the forefront of the "church growth" movement."[16]

Hillman's early events stand out among the wider evangelical faith and work space. The press release and schedule of sessions for the 2003 event frame the workplace as a crucial "mission field" to reach the unsaved. But the advertising and summaries for the later events (2007, 2008, and 2009) began speaking more directly about "transformation" of particular occupations, cities, and societies. The speaker pool began to shift toward a theological movement called "Dominionism," a branch of reconstructionist theology that propels Christians to seize control over major institutions and governments. Two particular themes of Dominionist theology gain prominence within these efforts: the New Apostolic Reformation and Seven Mountain Theology.[17] The websites advertising these events recounted aspirations to seize "dominion" over cultural spheres, with the business sphere occupying the central of these events.[18] Oddly, after these 2007–2009 events, the group of speakers assembled to promote these ideas appear to have exited the faith and work space. There is no obvious explanation for why this exit occurred: I explore some possible explanations and traces of lingering Dominionism in Chapter 8.

## Second Wave: Faith and Work Conferences Go Reformed

A second wave of faith and work conferences got off the ground around 2008–2009, drawing in a distinct lineup of theologians, pastors, and popular thinkers who had little role in the earlier wave. In 2008, the California-based Faith and Work Life organization offered their first annual Faith at Work Leadership Conference. Though never stretching beyond a single day of programming, this conference began identifying itself as an international gathering in only its second year and drew a lineup of speakers comparable to the later efforts of the Center for Faith and Work. This conference ran five consecutive years.[19] Another gathering founded in this era continues to exist: in 2007 David Miller (at that time a Yale faculty member, now a theologian at Princeton whose work is cited throughout this chapter) founded the Believers in Business Conference. The group held its first gathering at the Yale School of Business. This gathering explicitly targeted Christian MBA students and soon formed a network of Believers in Business that drew representatives from all major business schools in the United States. After its first few years, Believers in Business partnered with Intervarsity, an ecumenical parachurch organization focused on higher education. The group moved its annual event to Redeemer Presbyterian Church in Manhattan, a church that comes to play an important role in the movement.

These conferences set off a flurry of national events. In 2012, a Christian nonprofit in Texas called Right Now Ministries launched their first Work as Worship Conference, which became an annual gathering and by 2017 had expanded its gatherings to three different cities.[20] The same Redeemer Presbyterian Church mentioned earlier held their first faith and work conference in 2011, then called the Gospel and Culture Conference. This conference established itself as an annual gathering that generally sells out and has drawn well-known speakers like *New York Times* columnist David Brooks. In 2014, the evangelical magazine Christianity Today launched a conference initiative themed around "redeeming work," with conferences taking place in six different cities over the next two years. Capitol Hill Baptist Church out of Washington, D.C., also established a Gospel at Work ministry—based around a book written by Sebastian Traeger and Greg Gilbert—that launched eight "Gospel at Work" conferences across the country, pairing the book's authors with other authors, pastors, and local business leaders. This same era also saw the Kern Family Foundation provide support for conferences with nationally recognized speakers in Texas, Michigan, Illinois, and Minnesota, all since 2014. Three of the largest conferences in the movement—measured by both attendees and speakers—were "Faith and Work Summits" that took place in Boston in 2014, Dallas in 2016, and Chicago in 2018.

Perhaps just as significant as launching new conferences is the movement's ability to inject its theological wares into existing gatherings. Many established evangelical parachurch conferences have added workshops, themed tracks, and mini-conferences themed around faith and work. Generally pulling from the same pool of speakers that appeared at the national conferences listed above, these established conferences aid in granting legitimacy to both the speakers and their cultural frameworks. These prior established conferences include the Gospel Coalition's "Together for the Gospel" Conference, the Gospel Coalition Women's Conference, Urbana, the Christian Community Development Association, and Acton University, a free-market oriented summer school for pastors and laypersons sponsored by the Acton Institute. The emergence of these tracks, workshops, and sessions at lay-centered evangelical conferences represents a diffusion of faith and work frameworks, resources, and thinkers into the wider conference world.

It is difficult to overstate the rapid growth and legitimation of these actors by the core culture-producing institutions of evangelical culture. In the closing decades of the twentieth century, an evangelical layperson likely could not conceive what might constitute a "faith and work" event. By the late 2010s, evangelicals active in the parachurch space would have a hard time avoiding them. This sort of rapid penetration of evangelical subculture had no single origin—and certainly no single mastermind behind it—but did exhibit a sophisticated strategy of injecting a new subset of thought leaders and experts into already established networks and gatherings. If, following Hsu's observations, these national gatherings really are the subcultural "kingmakers" in terms of legitimacy and tribe formation, the faith and work movement acquired a significant amount of influence and power in a remarkably short time. Diffusing their ideas to the larger evangelical constituency, however, continues to prove challenging for the leaders.

## The Entrance of Foundations and Outside Funding

Indexing and assessing sources of material and financial resources provide important insights on how movement actors can sustain themselves and their organizations. While these outside sources are crucial to the growth of the movement, not all the organizational or conference growth has any observable ties to these sources. Many leaders and organizations generated support and resources from sources more internal to the evangelical subculture, such as speaking fees, book royalties, conference fees, or charitable giving from evangelicals themselves. But these sources certainly injected a new surge of resources and support into the space, particularly in the later part of the first decade of the twenty-first century and into the second. After providing an overview of the source, I will summarize the particular interests the organization appears to have in the space, drawing on interviews with leaders and materials produced by the organizations. The first funding source examined here, the Lilly Endowment, possesses the deepest pockets of all sources analyzed, but also embodies an unusual ambivalence regarding how faith and work leaders use their funds. The next three sources are driven by more direct agendas of politicizing the faith and work space, a topic explored in greater detail in Chapter 7.

## The Lilly Endowment

The first funder to grant major attention to theological thinking surrounding work was the Lilly Endowment.[21] Created in 1937 by family members of Eli Lilly, the endowment continues to be made up largely of stock in the Eli Lilly Company. The Lilly Endowment is managed by a board of directors separate from the company and focuses on support for three different funding areas: religion, community development, and education. At one point in 1998, the Lilly Endowment was the largest charitable endowment in the world. As of 2020 the endowment held $21 billion in assets, Because the Lilly Endowment is intentionally inclusive and ecumenical in its support of various religious traditions, parsing out its support of evangelical efforts requires sifting through three large funding initiatives that reached far beyond evangelical organizations. In two programs the concept of "vocation" was front and center: the Lilly Endowment integrates the dual priorities of helping draw people toward both full-time clergy work as well as the broader "theological exploration of vocation." Both programs also targeted higher education.

An early initiative in 1999 named the Program for Theological Exploration of Vocation (PTEV) funded vocational programming in religious-oriented schools, in this case all schools affiliated with the Christian faith. Grants were awarded directly to colleges to design their own programming related to vocation. Over its eight-year existence the program awarded over $225 million to eighty-eight different schools, twenty of which were affiliated with evangelical denominations.[22] After the initial years of the program, private non-religious schools were also admitted to the program, grafted in under an intentionally underdefined conceptualization of vocation. The rationale posted on a website tied the funding to the Endowment's interest in the vitality of religious congregational life: "In order to keep these important religious communities strong and vibrant, a new generation of talented, energetic, creative, and committed pastors and religiously informed lay leaders is needed."[23] Sociologist Timothy Clydesdale's assessment of the PTEV initiative (funded by Lilly) found grantees used the funding in various ways, funding curriculum, internships, service learning, themed residence halls, mentorship, seminary semesters, faculty and staff development, retreats, personality assessments, campus events, and mini-grants handed off to smaller initiatives. Clydesdale highlights "Pullman College," a pseudonym for one of the evangelical schools receiving funding. Pullman dedicated its

Lilly-provided funding to support the addition of a new major in nonprofit management, an "urban semester" away from the university, a collaborative symposia on social justice with a local Catholic university, the addition of new academic minors, and a few new faculty hires. Perhaps most wide-reaching effects for Pullman were efforts to insert "vocational theology" and "nurture a wider awareness of the world's pressing needs" in programming for all first-year students, infusing these themes into orientation week, first-year seminars, residential halls, and retreats.[24]

In 2009 the program formally ended, but a new initiative funded by the Lilly Endowment pulled together nearly all of the PTEV recipients in a new networking organization: the Network for Vocation in Undergraduate Education (NetVUE). NetVUE is formally an initiative of the Council of Independent Colleges that receives support from the Lilly Endowment. NetVUE claims 223 members, including most of the eighty-eight PTEV funding recipients. Their mission is to "enrich the theological and intellectual exploration of vocation among undergraduate students."[25] While NetVUE in some ways replicates PTEV in injecting funding into locally controlled college programs related to vocation, its primary purpose is a membership organization focused on sharing resources, best practices, and providing gathering opportunities for college administrators. Like PTEV and the program that followed, evangelical colleges and programming are just one of many different perspectives involved in the initiative, at times overshadowed by a broader inclusiveness. However, both NetVUE and PTEV saw as part of their mission drawing together and promoting the sorts of faith and work books outlined earlier.

Finally, in 2012 the Lilly Endowment piloted funding support for five campus ministries at larger state schools. Called the Campus Ministry Theological Exploration of Vocation (CMTEV), this program brought vocational programming to a new population of students attending publicly funded universities. The 2015 call for proposals reveals that over fifty-two different ministries have been supported by this endeavor, out of which several dozen are affiliated with evangelical denominations or parachurch organizations. According to the call for proposals, this program reinforced the dual commitment of earlier programs to both full-time clerical vocations and non-religious vocations, observing that an increasing number of college students "want to make a difference in the world and are considering careers in public service and the helping professions," before adding that some of these students are "finding their way to seminary because they sense that the church may be an avenue for living out their call to service."[26] The CMTEV materials celebrate the diversity of the programs established, reporting that some recipients focus on mentorship and internships while others draw students to seminary courses and specialized Bible studies on vocation. This program's funding totaled $4 million from its start to 2015.

In contrast to the other funding sources outlined in this chapter, the Lilly Endowment maintains a seemingly arms-length relationship with the faith and work movement. Interviews with leaders and observation at events suggest they profess the same "remedial theology" of the movement that overcomes compartmentalization and the vocational hierarchy common across religious groups. But their favored language and frameworks for promoting a "theological exploration" remain rooted in a largely ecumenical language of meaning, purpose, calling, and spirituality. All theological particularities are avoided, as well as any references to economics, whether policy, theories, or schools of thought. Observation at a Lilly-led event for their grantees managing local campus ministry vocation grants revealed Lilly's ambivalence went so far as to waver on the use of the word "vocation." "Vocation is scary," the main speaker at the event informed the audience in the first session. "We are unsure what it means, we feel boxed in by the idea that we must choose. It can still be reduced to 'ministry.' Many think of vocations as impinging on lifestyle." Several sessions at the event operated at the broadest levels of generalities regarding religion and spirituality. The main speaker, likely recognizing the diverse demographics of Catholics, Mainline Protestant, and evangelical Protestant denominations that receive their grants, staked out an open-handed notion of "callings" and even the identity of the "caller." "Does the caller have to be God? Can it just be 'me'?" one of the presentation slides provocatively posed to the audience. Several leaders of evangelical ministries—both in the general sessions and then later in smaller group sessions divided by Christian traditions—were critical of this theological vagueness and ambiguity, raising concerns that important doctrinal specifics were being lost. A few energized evangelical college ministry leaders utilized the questions and feedback portion of conference sessions to express their impassioned contempt for this theological vagueness.

The Endowment presents this conceptual underdevelopment as not accidental to its mode of Christian ecumenism.[27]But this facilitates a great amount of autonomy to evangelical ministries to determine how Christian college students might "explore" vocation. Many evangelical ministries use these funds to sponsor lectures and purchase books from many of the leaders in the evangelical faith and work movement—thus ultimately boosting the movement's resources—but, importantly, this was happening on the volition of the ministries themselves. This arms-length approach is surprising given foundations' increasing prioritization of results and measures of effectiveness in recent decades. Part of this can be attributed to Lilly's wider interests in providing resources for general religious vitality in the United States, an objective that is largely indifferent to the particular denominational or theological dimensions of that vitality. As made visible in the next sections, this objective sharply differs from the more politically and economically minded foundations operating within the faith and work space.

## The Acton Institute for the Study of Religion and Liberty

The Acton Institute for the Study of Religion and Liberty was founded in 1990 and predates much of the activity in the faith and work space. The Acton Institute's stated mission follows the perspective of their namesake Lord John Emerich Edward Dalberg Acton in promoting classical liberalism and exploring the "religious underpinnings of a free market and free society." While many think tanks located in Washington, D.C., are more focused on producing policy briefs, the work of the Acton Institute focuses far more on popularizing free market ideas through seminars, summer conferences, white papers, book publications, and production of *The Journal of Markets and Morality*, a scholarly journal. A central part of their stated mission is "educating religious leaders of all denominations, business executives, entrepreneurs, university professors, and academic researchers in economic principles."[28] Acton entered the evangelical faith and work space in the 2010s. On the surface Acton would not be a natural fit for this space: while designed to be religiously ecumenical in mission, their leadership and board of directors are largely Roman Catholic, and a heady Catholicism at that. Their efforts draw on Oxford-educated academics to publish treatises on classical political theory, and their publishing arm regularly resurrects the writings of largely obscure Catholic economic thinkers like Martín de Azpilcueta and Juan de Mariana. Acton leaders at one time regularly rubbed shoulders with intellectuals like Michael Novak and Milton Friedman. However, their highbrow and more theory-driven programming in recent years has been impressively retrofitted to the far more populist, media-centric, branding-savvy culture of American evangelicalism. Several efforts specifically develop theologies of work that align with the organization's overarching economic principles.

The organization commissioned *Poverty, Inc.*, a documentary shown on college campuses and available on Netflix, on the ineffectiveness of government aid for helping developing countries, combined with a more comprehensive six-part DVD series curriculum that promotes free market principles for curing poverty. The 2016 Faith and Work Summit dedicated one of its evenings to a special showing of this documentary and promoted it to attendees throughout the day of programming. The accompanying curriculum targets congregations, small groups, and classrooms. In 2014, Acton released another seven-part short-film series—*For the Life of the World*—which emphasizes broader themes of personal responsibility and engagement with economics, promising in its promotional description to "help you, your friends, church, or organization investigate God's Economy in All Things." The films feature several evangelical authors and seem targeted toward evangelical circles. Acton's 2016 tax filings recount that over 3,000 different programs, churches, and organizations have engaged the *For the Life of the World* in some way. Acton also released four book "primers" of faith and work, each targeted toward a specific Protestant tradition, described in greater detail in Chapter 6. Finally, Acton may have symbolically cemented its place in the evangelical subculture by forgoing its usual high-profile economist or political figure at their 2018 Annual Dinner to instead host pastor Tim Keller as their keynote speaker. The speech contained no specific references to policy or economic systems. Instead, Keller reverted to his general minister-style of speaking and delivered a sermon on how the modern conceptions of work-based identities contrast with grounding one's identity in Christ. Acton Institute president Robert Sirico followed up Keller's lecture with a shorter talk that seemed intended to envelop the discussion of identity within the principles of "ordered liberty" and "limited government" as a means to reach a "new generation that does not remember what totalitarianism really looked like."[29]

Since 2010, the Acton Institute has served as a sponsor and supporter of various conferences and gatherings, demonstrating a savvy ability to integrate itself with one-time events, organizations, and seminaries active in this space. While public tax forms do not disclose the amount of the Institute's contributions to faith and work events, their recurring sponsorship attests to their vested interest in this space. Two events received support from (and in turn provided booth space and sponsor recognition to) from the Acton

Institute: the 2016 Faith and Work Summit and the 2014 Jubilee Professional Conference.

## Kern Family Foundation

No foundation has been more active in the evangelical faith and work space than the Kern Family Foundation. Founded in 1998 in Waukesha, Wisconsin, by Robert and Patricia Kern, the foundation came into existence when the Kerns sold a division of their very successful home-powered generator company, Generac Power Systems. In 2006 the Kerns added to their foundation by selling the remaining shares of their company and depositing significant portion of the profits in the foundation. The Kern Family Foundation reported assets of over $700 million in 2020. The group prioritizes four funding areas: STEM education at the K–12 level, character education at the K–12 level, engineering and entrepreneurial skills at the college level, and "faith, work, and economics." For much of the 2010s, the foundation employed two program directors and a program coordinator to manage their faith, work, and economics program. The Kern Family Foundation also partners closely with economically conservative organizations like the Acton Institute (mentioned above) and the American Enterprise Institute.

The stated mission of Kern's Faith, Work, and Economics program mentions many of the concerns that make up the remedial theology discussed in Chapter 1: they are "inspiring people to view their daily work as a source of personal dignity and a valuable contribution to human flourishing." A preference for free market economic principles is stated more fully in its full mission statement: "Our Faith, Work, and Economics Program seeks to partner with organizations that (1) recognize the economy as a moral system in which people exchange their work and that (2) promote free enterprise grounded in moral character as an effective way to instill dignity, lift people out of poverty, and produce human flourishing."[30] In 2018—the last year for which numbers are publicly available—the foundation handed out ten grants designated for faith and work support, totaling $4.6 million in all. Among the recipients were parachurch organizations, seminaries, religious colleges, and other faith and work groups. Around $2.5 million was designated as support for the Acton Institute's faith and work programming. Prior years have seen higher amounts injected into the faith and work space: over $15.4 million in grants was distributed in 2014 to many of the programs they continue to support annually. Significantly, Kern Family Foundation funding has enabled organizations to create entirely new events and gatherings from scratch, drawing in previously uninvolved faculty members, pastors, and business leaders around conversations concerning work and economics around the country. One of these events is described in greater detail in Chapter 6.

Perhaps the strongest influence of the foundation has been demonstrated in two influential spin-off organizations active in the space. The first is the Made to Flourish Network, which is dedicated to building a network of pastors and "city networks" around faith and work resources.[31] The second is the Oikonomia Network, an organization that partners with twenty different evangelical seminaries and colleges to produce new curricula, majors, and events around the idea of the integration of faith and work.[32] Both organizations strategically target their respective institutions—churches and seminaries—as avenues to promote new frameworks to pastors and religious leaders, who can then take the frameworks to the wider audiences of their congregations. Kern's influence ends up permeating the entire faith and work space. All of the conferences attended for observation in this study featured speakers promoting either Kern's work, the Oikonomia Network, or the Made to Flourish Network. While Kern's political commitments were not always visible at these events, attendees who took up the invitation to become more involved in various arms of Kern's operations would almost certainly encounter an explicit political vision on taking these next steps.

## Freedom Partners, the Koch Brothers, and the Institute for Faith, Work, and Economics

In the early 2010s a new form of support began entering into the faith and work arena: conservative lobbying dollars. Unlike the Kern Family Foundation outlined above, this trail of money appears to be fairly concentrated around a single actor: the Institute for Faith, Work, and Economics, an organization name cleverly abbreviated as "IFWE" in their materials, in reference to the "we" of the church laity. In 2011, IFWE founder Hugh Whelchel grew discontent with the lack of faith and work thinking at a Christian seminary he was leading and instead set out to start a new organization—IFWE. The group started small but took advantage of their location in the northern Virginia suburbs of Washington, D.C., to snatch up a number of well-connected intellectuals in the conservative Washington, D.C., think-tank world. According to Whelchel, the organization's mission is serving as a content provider for "gaps" they observed in the faith and work movement at the time. Their vision is to provide high-level content to other organizations active in this space, filling these gaps. The Acton Institute leaders I interviewed praised IFWE's ability to produce a remarkable number of resources and materials in a relatively short time.

But IFWE is an anomaly in the faith and work space due to its funding and organizational structure. According to Whelchel, much of their fundraising comes from "family foundations" led by Christian business leaders who, having been successful themselves in business, get very excited about the Institute's mission. However, IFWE also serves as one link in a long chain of political and lobbying money passing through various entities. Previous research on such chains have compared them to a set of Russian nesting dolls because of their complex relationships with one another. Fortunately, the manner in which these groups register with the Internal Revenue Service often provides some indication of how various links in the chain function in relation to one another. IFWE itself is a tax-exempt 501(c)3 nonprofit, which by U.S. tax code regulations prevents partisan or lobbying activity. But IFWE also appears to function downstream in a larger chain that includes 501(c)6 and 501(c)4 organizations, both of which are permitted to lobby. At the top of this chain was at one point a 501(c)6 group called Freedom Partners, an organization that garnered a reputation for being run by the executives of Koch Industries. The last public filings for Freedom Partners reported annual revenues of $146 million. Because Freedom Partners, as a 501(c)6, was formally classified as a trade association, the names of donors—formally the organization's "members"—do not have to be disclosed. As a result, there was always widespread uncertainty about Freedom Partners' source of income, an arrangement that generally draws criticisms of infusing political processes with "dark money."

Until being absorbed by other groups in 2019, Freedom Partners regularly passed money to IFWE in at least two ways. The first pathway was by giving money to a 501(c)4 group called EVANGCHR4 Trust. This organization shares their mission statement, trustee control, and mailing address as IFWE, suggesting a tight relationship. EVANGCHR4 Trust then passed funding to any of several different religious 501(c)3 organizations, including IFWE. EVANGCHR4 gave $725,000 to IFWE in 2013, $5.5 million in 2014, and $2.05 million in 2015. The second pathway is far more indirect and has proven difficult to track due to the lack of paper trail. In 2011, EVANGCHR4 took over another existing 501(c)4, called ORRA LLC, which at the time of its termination in 2011 reported $3.8 million in assets, the total of which was granted to EVANGCHR4 Trust.[33] ORRA LLC also received $5.5 million from Freedom Partners and $725,000 from a defunct Koch-related group called TC4 Trust. Unfortunately, there are no public records of where this money ended up.

The money passed to EVANGCHR4 Trust and IFWE appears to fan out through several major streams. EVANGCHR4 Trust, as a 501(c)4, passes several hundred thousand dollars to other conservative 501(c)4 lobbying groups, including the lobbying arm of the Family Research Council, the lobbying arm of Focus on the Family, several pro-life groups, and religious environmental groups dedicated to denying climate change. IFWE, as the 501(c)3 organization in the partnership, in turn passes several hundred thousand dollars in "support grants" to several other 501(c)3 organizations that often are the respective non-lobbying side of the lobbying groups above. *The New Yorker* journalist Jane Mayer, in her investigative work on the Koch family's political influence in U.S. politics, chronicles how 501(c)3 and 501(c)4 organizations (what the IRS calls "social welfare groups") became recipients and carriers of significant political money:

> When Congress created the legal framework for "social welfare" groups almost a century earlier, it never anticipated that they would become means by which the rich would hide their political spending. In fact, to qualify as tax-exempt, such groups had to certify that they would be "operated exclusively for the promotion of social welfare." The IRS later loosened the guidelines, though, allowing them to engage marginally in politics, so long as this wasn't their "primary" purpose. Lawyers soon stretched the loophole to absurd lengths. . . . They also argued that one such group could claim no political spending if it gave to another such group, even if the latter spent the funds on politics.[34]

According to Mayer, the *Citizens United* decision sent an unprecedented surge of political money through these channels. The founding of IFWE falls at approximately the same time that the Koch family coordinated a "national explosion of dark money" into politics, as Mayer recounts: "In 2006, only 2 percent of 'outside' political spending came from 'social welfare' groups that hid their donors. In 2010, this number rose to 40 percent, masking hundreds of millions of dollars."[35]

Importantly, IFWE as a 501(c)3 is not permitted to run ads in elections or engage in political lobbying. This suggests that the Institute's position within the Koch network of funding is better understood as working within what Koch executives have called their "ideological production line."[36] The Koch organization first turned its focus to building up this part of its efforts after a key event in the family's history: David Koch's failed presidential run as the Libertarian Party candidate in 1980. After Koch managed to muster only one percent of the national vote, the Koch organization recognized a dire communications gap in their movement. An effort was needed to translate the think tank-produced ideas promoting libertarian policies "down to the average citizen." "What we needed was a sales force that participated in political campaigns or town hall meetings, in rallies, to communicate to the public at large much of this information that these think tanks were creating," David Koch recounted in a 2011 *Weekly Standard* article. "Almost like a door-to-door sales force that some of the cosmetic organizations have."[37] A cluster of academic programs, legal centers, and issue advocacy organizations bubbled up in the immediate years, dedicated, in Mayer's words, to "winning hearts and minds" to libertarian ideology. In the early 1990s, these efforts spearheaded rallies and ad campaigns to oppose President Clinton's proposed energy taxes. But also on the agenda for Koch leaders was finding ways to bring libertarian ideas down to the level of the masses.

The incorporation of religious organizations into this "sales force" is a relatively new phenomenon. A 2015 piece in *The Public Eye* by journalist Mariya Strauss recounts how the Koch organization has tapped into Christian scholars and groups to resolve areas of "potential tension between the Corporate and Christian Right." Strauss focuses in particular on the work of IFWE fellow Anne Bradley, who regularly delivers lectures and writes articles that attempt to "faith-wash" inequality while making biblical arguments against government aid for the poor.[38] IFWE is not shy about injecting free market thinkers and free market books into the faith and work space. At times their efforts appear only loosely tethered to discussions of work and calling. After dedicating their first three years in the space producing research, the organization moved toward facilitating public speaking engagements for conservative scholars. The organization draws in a wider cohort of conservative scholars—Dr. Art Lindsley, a theologian; Dr. Jay W. Richards, a philosopher and theologian; and the aforementioned Dr. Bradley—to inject more rigorous and systematic conservative economic thought into the faith and work movement. Though none of these scholars was ranked among the most frequent speakers at national faith and work events, they all maintain busy speaking schedules in the larger conservative world.

IFWE sponsors many of the national events mentioned below and also contributes to the Theology of Work project, an organization producing new faith and work commentaries for every book of the Bible. While there are obviously large amounts of funding changing hands around and through IFWE, we unfortunately do not know what portion of this is injected into the faith and work space. However, IFWE has served as sponsor for the 2014 Faith and Work Summit and the 2016 Faith and Work Summit. The influence of this group has also been felt in Whelchel's speaking schedule, which has included the Fourth Annual Christian Business Ethics Conference (2014), the Gospel at Work Conference in Washington, D.C. (2014), and the Biblical Entrepreneurship Conference (2016).

## Sizing Up the Movement Leaders and Their Reach

Like many movements, the faith and work movement has various levels of adherents whose affiliation and identity range from general awareness to regular attendance at events and consumption of the movement's resources. Here, the available data can shine light on the innermost rings of participants: the thought leaders—authors, pastors, professors, successful executives, and startup leaders—who most frequently speak at conferences and shape the types of cultural frameworks promoted at these gatherings. For the thought leaders who agreed to be interviewed for this project, a post-interview questionnaire was distributed to those who participated in the interview, and from this sample ($n = 24$) we can get a basic profile of the leading conference speakers in the movement. A second rung of thought leaders was also identified, based again on frequency of speaking at faith and work events. These numbers can be compared to a general breakdown of the U.S. population and a general breakdown of evangelicalism as a whole (Table 3.2).

This comparison suggests thought leaders at the center of the movement are disproportionately older, whiter, more educated, and more male than the U.S. population, and significantly more male and educated than the general evangelical population. This pattern persists across the first and second rung of leaders. In the total population ($n = 77$) there are sixty men to seventeen women. Educational over-representation also persists.

**Table 3.2** Demographics of Faith and Work Thought Leaders

| Proportion of Total Population That Is . . . | U.S. Population | Evangelicals | F&W Thought Leaders, 1st Rung ($n = 24$) | F&W Thought Leaders, 1st & 2nd Rung ($n = 77$) |
|---|---|---|---|---|
| Male | 49.2 | 42.9 | 91.7 | 77.9 |
| White (not Other) | 73.8 | 73.7 | 83.3 | Not collected |
| Holds bachelor's degree | 27.3 | 20.5 | 100.0 | 97.4 |
| Holds advanced degree | 12.4 | 7.0 | 93.8 | 76.1 |
| Baby-Boomer or older (born before 1965) | 32.9 | 51.0 | 43.8 | Not collected |

These disproportionate representations at the most influential levels of leadership are likely multi-causal, and many of the factors may be exogenous to the faith and work movement itself. Regarding race, many of the white leaders emerged from seminaries and denominational structures that have historically been predominately white. It is unclear how leaders from the black Protestant tradition—which scholars typically see as theologically distinct from white evangelicalism—come to enter this space, though some leaders I interviewed had made this entrance without recounting much challenge. On gender, evangelicals lag behind the U.S. population on views of women working outside the home. Many denominations active in this space also do not allow women to serve in particular leadership roles in the church.[39] Notably, female evangelicals have not lagged behind in the educational gains evangelicals have made across the twentieth century, suggesting this gap is not a product of qualifications.[40] For both racial and gender under-representations, the Faith and Work movement seems to reproduce the imbalances of evangelical leadership that characterize the larger subculture. However, taking these factors into consideration does not offset the reality that faith and work thought leaders speak from a very particular perspective of power and privilege within the contemporary social order. This is discussed more in Chapter 5.

There is no straightforward way to gauge how many people "belong" to the faith and work movement, both due to conceptual ambiguity of what belonging designates, as well as the limitations of existing data. Sociologist Robert Wuthnow also finds many religious special purpose groups do not hold "membership growth" as a salient goal, often not even keeping numbers of members themselves.[41] While the movement shows remarkable growth in organizational and cultural resources, there could very well be a limited group of activists, consumers, and adherents disproportionately consuming these resources. Unfortunately, there are no survey data available on whether an individual has attended a faith and work conference, has read a faith and work book, or views faith and work leaders favorably. A 1992 nationally representative survey probing attitudes between religion and economics found evangelicals exhibited only moderate differentiation from the general population regarding the integration of religious thinking with their work. By and large, evangelicals at that time did not adhere to some very basic ideas of the faith and work movement (outlined more in the next chapter): the universality of callings and vocations, the flattening of the vocational hierarchy between the value of clergy versus laity work, the relevance of religious teaching to work, and the belief that God cares about our work. Assessing the larger findings of the survey, Wuthnow posited that faith for all religious traditions in the U.S. plays a relatively minor role in shaping tangible work behaviors. Religious commitments "still exert a significant influence . . . but that its influence is often mixed, leading to more ambivalence than to informed ethical decisions or to distinct patterns of life."[42] Wuthnow concludes that faith primarily plays a therapeutic role in shaping how a person *feels* about their work. In regard to tangible action or behavior, people of faith "go about their lives pretty much the same as those who have no faith at all."

The 2010 Baylor Religion Survey Wave III provides a more recent assessment.[43] Findings from that survey—displayed in Table 3.3—reveal, on most measures, respondents who self-described as "evangelicals" were more likely to affirm statements that saw their faith integrated with work. Whether these views can be attributed to the influence of the faith and work movement remains an open question, requiring more direct measures of contact with faith and work resources and events. However, it is noteworthy that evangelical respondents in 2010 did not subscribe to one of the central tenets of the movement's teachings: the denial of a vocational hierarchy regarding occupations, discussed more in the next two chapters. As Table 3.3 reveals, 88.1 percent of all respondents agreed or strongly agreed that "people who go into careers like nursing, teaching, or ministry should be admired for that career choice," and this statement is also highly affirmed among evangelical respondents. This presents the possibility that the work-affirming ideas of the faith and work movement may be sharing the stage with other economic

**Table 3.3** 2010 National Survey on Faith and Work Views

| Question | All Respondents (%) | Among Religiously Affiliated (%) | Among Self-Identified Evangelicals (%) |
|---|---|---|---|
| Participated in a discussion group on faith in the workplace in the past month | 14.6 | 16.3 | 29.7 |
| "Sometimes," "often," or "always" view my work as a partnership with God | 47.8 | 55.3 | 80.0 |
| "Sometimes," "often," or "always" see connections between my worship and work | 47.5 | 55.3 | 79.8 |
| "Sometimes," "often," or "always" view my work as a mission from God | 40.4 | 47.1 | 69.6 |
| "Sometimes," "often," or "always" view my work as part of God's plan to care for the needs of people | 51.7 | 59.8 | 80.2 |
| "Sometimes," "often," or "always" pursue excellence in my work because of my faith | 52.1 | 60.4 | 87.2 |
| "Agree" or "strongly agree" that people who go into careers like nursing, teaching, or ministry should be admired for that career choice | 88.1 | 88.7 | 89.4* |

Data source: 2010 Baylor Religion Survey Wave III ($n = 1{,}732$).

* Indicates a lower number would suggest wider adoption of basic evangelical faith and work theology.

ethics that have also deeply penetrated the evangelical populace. I explore these alternative currents in Chapter 8.

My overall assessment of the movement's diffusion is that the movement's offerings disproportionately circulate among a narrower demographic profile within American evangelicalism, one that is located at a particular intersection of economic, institutional, and social factors. Several arguments supporting this assessment will be outlined in greater detail in later chapters. But we can gain some idea of this parochial audience by turning to a demographic survey of the attendees at the 2016 Faith and Work Summit—which may have been the largest faith and work conference to date. As Table 3.4 reveals, attendees once again heavily skewed toward male and higher education populations, while age and racial demographics hover roughly around the wider evangelical proportions. This disproportionately male and overeducated audience is likely the outcome of both endogenous and exogenous

**Table 3.4** Demographics of Faith and Work Conference Attendees

| Proportion of Total Population That Is . . . | U.S. Population | Evangelicals | F&W Conf Attendees ($n = 272$) |
|---|---|---|---|
| Male | 49.2 | 42.9 | 75.3 |
| White (not Other) | 73.8 | 73.7 | 81.4 |
| Holds bachelor's degree | 27.3 | 20.5 | 93.6 |
| Holds advanced degree | 12.4 | 7.0 | 71.3 |
| Baby-Boomer or older (born before 1965) | 32.9 | 51.0 | 49.2 |

factors relative to the movement itself, with the homogenous nature of wider American evangelical leadership—itself predominantly white, male, older, and more educated—likely playing a role in shaping who is showing up in this space. However, we will directly examine both the visible and more latent sorting mechanisms of the movement itself in Chapter 5.

# 4

# The Four Evangelical Theologies of Work

*The religious virtuoso can be placed in the world as the instrument of God and cut off from all magical means of salvation. At the same time, it is imperative for the virtuoso that he "proves" himself before God, as being called solely through the ethical quality of his conduct in the world. No matter how much the "world" as such is religiously devalued and rejected as being creatural and a vessel of sin, yet psychologically the world is all the more affirmed as the theater of God-willed activity in one's worldly "calling."*

—Max Weber, "The Social Psychology of the World Religions"[1]

*Why should you spend your life evangelizing? There are more important things to do in the world.*

—Hans Rookmaaker[2]

*God loveth adverbs; and cares not how good, but how well.*

—Joseph Hall, 1607[3]

## Reprogramming Understandings of the Holy

The syllabus had been handed out, attendance had been taken, and everyone in the class had completed a conversationally generative icebreaker. I was sitting through the first day of a week-long course, "Taking Your Soul to Work," a summer course offered at an evangelical seminary for three hours every morning one week in July. While a handful of apparent graduate student–appearing students—judging by their MacBook Air laptops, stylish messenger bags, and relatively young age—sat near the back of the classroom, the rest of the forty adults sitting around me seemed far outside their normal routines. While the enrollees were somewhat homogenous in all likely having previous college course experience, the icebreaker question—perhaps intentionally—drew attention to

*Saving the Protestant Ethic.* Andrew Lynn, Oxford University Press. © Oxford University Press 2023.
DOI: 10.1093/oso/9780190066680.003.0005

various cultural backgrounds represented by asking all of us to share: what is your name's meaning? Approximately one-third of students hailed from places other than the United States. I also discovered that cultures other than my own seem to invest far more thought in selecting names, needing to quickly consult Google for my own name's meaning.

For several decades this seminary has offered week-long summer courses for laypeople interested in engaging in the academic side of the evangelical faith. Likely due to the location in a relatively mild summer climate in the Pacific Northwest, the program traditionally has no trouble attracting a who's-who of top evangelical scholars to teach the courses, drawing from evangelical colleges and seminaries, as well as larger research universities like Duke and Notre Dame. The six different three-hour-a-day courses offered each week, as well as a daily chapel service, evening lectures, and film showings, all took place in a large three-story building with a spacious open-air atrium, creating a unique summer-camp feel for attendees. A centrally located religious bookstore—well-stocked with both academic and more popular titles—provided immediate reference resources or a place for mindless browsing during downtime. Casual conversations with classmates, scholars, visiting lecturers, and seminary professors occurred throughout the day and often spilt out into the local restaurants and bar scene after the evening lecture concluded, with attendees taking advantage of the long summer daylight hours. Though the seminary is located in the midst of a much larger public campus, the building itself offered a bit of a subcultural enclave. The barista working the morning coffee rush figured out that she and I shared mutual acquaintances in my university's religious studies program (several thousand miles away), while the bookstore workers frequently shared their (rather sophisticated) thoughts on the books I purchased. While the summer program stretches across three months, most courses lasted only a week, and administrators made an effort to "reset" the experience each week as new participants arrive for their courses. These efforts seemed to cater to attendees' limited availability to step away from their regular lives to have a seminary-like experience.

The second part of the course's icebreaker asked the enrolled students to share their occupations. I found I was surrounded by a variety of occupations: schoolteachers taking advantage of summer flexibility, retirees RVing around the country, pastors looking for fresh ideas for their churches, as well as a nurse practitioner, a financial asset manager, and an international consultant, all clearly allocating their vacation time to be here. The occupational diversity was appropriate for the subject matter: work. The lecturer—a near retired professor of the seminary—drew on the character of Jacob in the Old Testament book of Genesis to pose the question, "Whose work matters to God?" Jacob, best remembered in the biblical narrative for his place in the lineage of early Israel's patriarchs, was held up as the worker par excellence. His efforts as a shepherd tending to his father-in-law's goats were deemed significant to God due to the manner in which Jacob carried out his labor. Jacob's work was labeled "kingdom work" (advancing God's kingdom) because it was done out of the virtues of faith, hope, and love—not, it was noted clearly, because his work had an inherently "religious character."

"What makes work 'Christian' is not its religious character but faith, hope, and love," the lecturer concluded, seemingly wrapping up the first portion of the class. Giving us little time to respond to this point, the lecturer moved on to some more substantively ethical dimensions. A slide with the label "Can God call his people to work here?" appeared as the lecturer cued up a bulleted list: work in a nail salon, lead a company that makes $30 million, serve a corrupt prime minister, work to legalize the gaming industry, develop Islamic smartphone apps for Muslims. The tone of the lecturer at this point took on a relaxed open-handedness: rather than pronouncing concise answers to these questions, the lecturer moved into an explanation of why these questions proved so complicated. Taking your soul to work was apparently not as straightforward as simply fulfilling the previously mentioned virtues.

Modern work, the class was told, is "divided." While these divisions are later directly connected to the theological concept of sin, the list presented here would be at home in any business ethics course: an "ecological divide" that facilitates overconsumption beyond the rate of sustainability; an "ownership divide" that overuses scarce resources; a "leadership divide" of political and economic elites creating undesirable outcomes; and an "income divide" framed by statistics on the vast inequality of wealth between the world's richest and poorest populations. The message for the class seemed to be that modern work is "fallen" and complicated and, against what was implied earlier, "taking your soul to work" would require more than cursory applications of moral lessons from ancient texts.

At this point, the second lecturer of the course—a younger scholar whose expertise bridged Christian theology and organizational leadership—jumped up to present his portion of the lecture. His less-senior status, combined with a slightly less formal lecture style, moved the class to a more participatory mode. Supplementing the earlier divisions listed, the lecturer warned of another deep division that was making "one billion people in this world very sick." This division was the "divided self." To get the class more involved, the lecturer requested we react to the two words that appear on the screen and pronounce which one is "holier." We were instructed to shout out our reaction "from our gut instinct" rather than reflect on the answer. The pairs of words were each organized into two columns, forming an easily recognizable dichotomy after all the words appeared. The class complied with the directions and began pronouncing their views on relative holiness on the following pairs: "Sunday service or Monday meeting," "congregations or colleagues," "pastor or politician," "Sunday school or school," "church choir or house chores," "missionaries or managers," "prayer or work," "tithing or taxes," "bread for communion or bread for breakfast," "sermon or speech," "ministers in the church or ministers in a cabinet," "ministry or management," "seminary or business school," "church or city," "worship or work," and "Bible study or case study."

The first few pairs produced instantaneous and unanimous judgments as the students followed their gut instincts: church-related activities were holier than work-related activities. But as we moved through the pairs, slightly more reluctance began to trickle through the chorus of answers. The didactical intention of the exercise soon became clear. On reaching the bottom of the list, the lecturer took a more irresolute tone, pointing to the right-hand column of words, "You know, the Bible actually has a lot of things to say about these things: taxes, management . . . lots of insights, and yet . . ." (pointing now to the left-hand column) ". . . somehow we value these parts more." He posed a question to the class: Why was it so easy to pronounce the church-related activity as "holier"?

After a moment of silence, the class reverted back to the open, comfortable environment established in the icebreaker. Answers tended to be carefully deliberated, non-theological, and almost always tied to personal self-reflection. A woman toward the front of the classroom volunteered the first reaction: "The intention of the right-hand column is not as clear. It's like the difference between a box company and a church: we know more about the church's intentions." Another woman added, "And it may also come down to what we think God cares about more." A male pastor attending the class provided his reflection: "And also, who gets the glory out of the work that we do? For some things, God is getting the glory," as he nodded at the left-handed column. "For others, God is in the periphery." A younger male added, "To follow that, we often forget whose work it is. On the left side, we assume that's God's work. But on the right side we assume that's our work."

After another moment of silence, a student from the far side of the class added, "I just think our intuitive answers are how we have been trained." The lecturer used this observation to transition to his next point: "What is the first moment at which we are programmed to think on left and right sides?" Instead of answering the question, the lecturer explained how he himself developed these views by seeing his father "carry the Bible everywhere he went." "My father thought business was bad and church was good," the lecturer said. Shifting into more theological language, the lecturer observed that our notion of holiness has traditionally tended to equate the sacred with place, persons, or positions. But this was what seemed to obstruct the alternative view—that all work can in fact be holy.

Throughout my week at the seminary, I was able to hear evangelical laypeople process these sorts of ideas. The responses tended to follow the ambivalence expressed above: a reflective openness to being convinced "all work matters to God" alongside a recognition that this idea represented something novel to evangelical ways of thinking. Something about it seemed both familiar and alien. One near-retirement couple sitting near me later recounted that these ideas represented "a new theology" for them. "We're still getting our minds around it," the woman explained to me and others in a small breakout group for the course. "At our home church, the concern is 'are you there every Sunday?' If you're not there every Sunday, you're a problem." The couple admitted that they themselves had been on the wrong end of this heuristic, even when missing church to travel to the seminary program. The message they felt their church instilled was: church first, everything else second. "Maybe it comes down to which comes first: life or the Christian life?" posed the husband. It was not clear that they had an answer to this question. To them, the prioritization of the "Christian life" threatened to elevate church activities as more valuable than all other "life" activities. But denying this hierarchy of activities seemed to present its own dangers.

Another student in the classroom revealed his hesitancy to accept the conclusion of the exercise outlined above: "I experience God much stronger in the activities on the left column over the right column," the student shared at the conclusion of the activity. This assessment was greeted with several affirming nods, suggesting that others could resonate with this point. Could what is holy really be so freely encountered in the realm of the profane? This proposition, for these committed evangelical laity, seemed to cut to the heart of what constitutes the Christian life.

## Awakening to the Crisis of Monday

I witnessed episodes like this one play out again and again in faith and work spaces. The leaders of the movement were not shy about inciting these theological conundrums: their goal was to unmoor American evangelicalism from its dominant orientation to the the world of work. Here, we can begin fleshing out this discovery of a "moral crisis of Monday" that recurs throughout the movement's cultural resources. Many of the people I met in the faith and movement stories told similar stories of waking up to their dangerously bifurcated existence and seeking to overcome this condition. Some recounted this story from the position as a pastor: a popular speaker in the space presents his awakening as recognizing his "pastoral malpractice" of not equipping laity for their day-to-day lives. Others recount confronting this divide as workers. Bob Doll, a senior portfolio manager and Christian who also serves as a popular faith and work event speaker, recounts that he first began to feel a Sunday-Monday divide through the very real geographic divide between his home and work. Amidst working in Manhattan but commuting from Princeton, Doll began to recognize that his daily train ride represented what he identified as the "barrier" between his life and work. Taking a job closer to his home freed him from "living in two different worlds" connected only by train. He credits this geographic rearrangement with triggering his own reckoning with the need to integrate the realms of home and work.

Leaders telling these sorts of stories in many ways function as the movement's "moral entrepreneurs," a term developed by sociologist Howard Becker. Moral entrepreneurs are movement visionaries who pair together the identification of a particular moral crisis or threat with a particular solution proffered through their own teachings or instruction. These leaders then set out to disrupt apathy or indifference to that crisis while also guiding others toward the solution they offer. Represented in this threat is a Christian faith that fails to permeate the everyday activity of laity, a divided or compartmentalized faith that has somehow been compromised with the world. Importantly, leaders are certainly not conjuring into existence a problem that might otherwise bear no effect on actors. This was a crisis that not only resonated with the common beliefs and prevailing experiences among evangelical laity but also reflects a particular phenomenon noted by prior survey research. Surveys of evangelical laity reveal little evidence of a distinctly "evangelical" orientation to work, economic activities, or even economic systems at large. A survey of evangelical college students in the 1980s reveals evangelicals are *more* likely than their secular counterparts to derive satisfaction from the private realm of "friends, family, and hobbies" instead of their work.[4] Interviews with evangelicals in the 1990s suggest that most laity saw little that their faith had to say about their work lives.[5] Faith and work leaders, then, play a key role in labeling this predicament a crisis demanding immediate and deliberate response.

Leaders sought to guide laity toward frameworks that could sacralize and stabilize the world of work. As I argued in Chapter 1, these efforts were birthed out of leaders and laity recognizing the emerging mismatch between the social location that many laity had come to occupy and the theological resources available to navigate this space. Something new was needed. The near-retired couple I spoke with in the above episode rightly recognized that the ideas of the seminary course represented what they called a "new theology." The course was indeed seeking to distance contemporary evangelicalism from the "fundamentalist work ethic" and the revivalist mode of faith associated with Billy Graham to which many laity had grown accustomed. The promoted "remedial theology" served to patch up the otherwise inadequate frameworks of American evangelicalism in order to draw the world of work back beneath the umbrella of a committed Christian life.

## Four Different Theologies of Work: Re-Commissioning, Re-Sacralizing, Re-Integrating, Re-Embedding

This chapter reviews the ideas and frameworks intended to patch up this compartmentalization. Popular books published on evangelical presses from 1940 to 1980 reveal a growing awareness that the Sunday-Monday gap posed a challenge to conservative evangelicalism, as well as establishing an undesirable vocational hierarchy. But the prescribed means of resolving or overcoming this challenge varied widely. The "Protestant ethic" these leaders constructed and promoted in many ways differed from the more classical work ethic of the Puritans. For one, these frameworks lacked anything resembling what Weber called the "doctrine of proof" regarding salvational anxieties.[6] It also was not particularly concerned with channeling industrious and disciplined energies toward labor as a form of cultivating Godly character. Work and economic activity had instead come on evangelicals' radar as a realm that was primarily afflicted with a harmful compartmentalization described earlier. Modern compartmentalization had come to represent a form of "fallenness" that broke from creation's intended design and order, inaugurating a harmful arrangement that afflicted over one billion people in the world with a "sickness," according to the course described above.

Table 4.1 outlines four different frameworks that serve to overcome the Sunday-Monday gap and to make Monday matter. Each has been pursued at different points in the twentieth century and has been captured by books written in the area of interest. While this method of analyzing texts does not allow for evaluations of each framework's relative diffusion, the cultural materials and events observed within the contemporary faith and work movement suggest that all four frameworks still exist within the faith and work space today.

As the latter part of this chapter contends, it is the re-integrating framework that dominates the faith and work movement today. But many tensions and conflicts still remain within faith and work theology. Re-integrators and re-embedders often consciously distance themselves from re-commissioners. Re-commissioners challenge re-embedders as presenting an overly agentic view of work's potential for cultural transformation, which they claim applies to a very limited population of workers. Meanwhile, re-integrators may protest the ecclesial overreach implied by re-embedders (Dorothy Sayers's arguments, outlined below), while re-embedders may criticize the moral passivity of re-integrators and their "adverbial theologies" (a critique explored in Chapter 8). Sometimes, Monday is deemed meaningful and sacred on its own merits; other times, it is not.

## The Re-Commissioners: Faith and Work as Workplace Evangelism

While these four frameworks cannot be easily placed along a chronological timeline of emergence, the first framework engaged here was likely the first to appear on the scene in the twentieth century. This is largely due to the establishment of the first faith and work organization in the twentieth century: the Christian Business Men's Connection, established in 1930 sought "to evangelize and disciple business and professional men for Christ." This

**Table 4.1** Four Different Frameworks for Overcoming the Sunday-Monday Gap

| Framework | (Approximate) First Exemplar Text on Evangelical Press | Injects Religious Concerns into Monday (Denies Compartmentalization) | Valorizes "Special" Vocations Outside of Professional Clergy | Flattens Vocational Hierarchy (Equalizes and Sacralizes All Work) | Confronts Work Sphere with Extra-Organizational Ends |
|---|---|---|---|---|---|
| Re-Commissioning | Broomhall 1969 | YES | — | — | — |
| Re-Sacralizing | Day 1946 | YES | YES | — | — |
| Re-Integrating | Sayers 1941 | YES | YES | YES | — |
| Re-Embedding | Moberg 1965 | YES | YES | YES | YES |

group worked closely with the earlier Gideons group, though the latter largely took up a more general evangelistic effort rather than specific ministry to workers. A similar organization, the Full Gospel Business Men's Fellowship International, was founded in 1951 by Demos Shakarian, a Californian dairy farmer, commercial real estate developer, and Pentecostal evangelist. These organizations were driven by the conversion impulse of early-century fundamentalism: in Moody's language, they were trying to "save all you can." The "Great Commission"—found in the Gospel of Matthew—provides the blueprint for these efforts: "Go and make disciples of all nations . . ." This charge is positioned as central for organizations like the Christian Business Men's Connection: the organization's stated mission today is to "[p]resent Jesus Christ as Savior and Lord to professional men; and to develop Christian business and professional men to carry out the Great Commission." Notably, this framework stands out from the others in *how* it makes Mondays meaningful. While other frameworks radically innovate new understandings of *what* and *how* one works, this framework largely preserves prior orientations toward work. Moody's commission to "save all you can" largely serves as the driving impetus of these efforts. However, the difference between prior fundamentalist approaches and re-commissioning frameworks is the emphasis placed on workplace evangelism, seeing these settings as more than an afterthought for sites where Christians might carry out "Christian work."

Only a handful of evangelical books published between 1940 and 1980 draw on this call to evangelize in the workplace. Alfred James Broomhall (1911–1994), a medical missionary to China, identified workplace evangelism as the central form of lay action in his 1965 book, *Time for Action: Christian Responsibility in a Non-Christian World*, published by Intervarsity Press. Broomhall calls on laypeople to "wake up, think, and act" for "when daylight lasts we must carry on the work of him who sent me; night comes, when no one can work" (John 9:4). The world's "Godless state" and its coming judgment demand action, a call to evangelize the world, according to Broomhall. Christians, then, must recover their "missionary passion" and remember the "unchanging commission." Clearly laypeople in their respective positions are called to take up the same missionary calling Broomhall himself took up. Broomhall voiced skepticism toward "world-changing efforts": "Social service with no spiritual motive is complemented by the title [of calling], but so called 'evangelism by friendship,' by digging artesian wells or improving livestock for the people, is in danger of being just a trick of speech. It can be 'pre-evangelism,' if the presentation of the gospel is its ultimate aim, but 'evangelism without words, without a message, is a contradiction'. . . a missionary is one with a message. Much that passes as missionary work but which is a social service and little more should not take the term."[7]

This theology of work is by far the easiest to tack onto early-century revivalist Protestantism, largely because "work" itself picks up only marginal value in this framework. Workers certainly become charged with a religious task to carry out through their economic callings, so "Monday" is no longer completely unrelated or insignificant to their religious lives. But notably, the underlying premises of the vocational hierarchy is not directly threatened by this framework, as pastors, evangelists, and missionaries enjoy the advantage of (and likely the greater results from) evangelizing full-time without distraction, whereas other laity are constrained in their ability to carry out the Great Commission amidst other work duties. "Secular" vocations, then, are redeemed, but are only redeemed to the extent to which they come to resemble religious vocations. This alters the Sunday-Monday gap in instilling certain "Monday" duties for the laity, but its thin theology of work would later attract criticisms from writers who recognized the failures to transcend the conversionist imperative.[8]

## The Re-Sacralizers: Faith and Work as a Theology of Success

While workplace evangelism efforts made their mark with early organizational growth, another framework worked through the vehicle of several successful business leaders who put their revivalist faith front and center in their public image. This framework was best enshrined in several mid-century books written by a series of more conservative Protestants sharing their personal stories of success and faith. Titles and authors include: *Breakfast Table Autocrat: The Life Story of Henry Parsons Crowell* (1946) by Richard Ellsworth Day; *Fifty Years with the Golden Rule: A Spiritual Autobiography* (1950) by James Cash (J. C.) Penney; *Mover of Mountains and Men* (1960) by R. G. LeTourneau; and *God Owns My Business* (1969) and *Every Christian a Soul Winner* (1975) by Stanley Tam.

The wider "remedial theology" is on full display in both of these accounts, but for Crowell, LeTourneau, and others, their theology of work takes on a supplemental function: valorizing wealth and personal success. As theologian David Miller observes of these and other lay writers, these works stake out a "biblical hermeneutic of the business world" grounded in the day-to-day experience of the business executive.[9] This is in many ways similar to frameworks that "re-integrate" the work experience with spiritual meaning and significance, explored more below. However, the frameworks promoted by these business executives and many who follow them posit a special blessing on the vocations of business leadership. In contrast to more democratizing theologies of work that flatten the vocational hierarchy by declaring *all work* equally valuable to God, this framework in many ways raises the particular callings of the business elite "up" to the level of the clergy. For the cases of Crowell and LeTourneau, this meant positioning their own callings as equally significant with those of prominent "soul savers" of their respective eras: D. L. Moody and Billy Graham, respectively. In some ways, this valorization of a status hierarchy is a byproduct of a sharp business-religion status competition playing out, something explored more in the next chapter. But generally neglected in such battles of status are non-business vocations and callings which are not granted the same consideration as the "called" business leader.

This framework "re-sacralizes" in a number of ways. For one, the managerial tasks of business owner or executive within modern industrial or postindustrial capitalism are granted a particular moral sanctioning by this framework. This is not so much the result of the framework itself carrying pro-capitalist tendencies—although many times it did—but the outcome of casting a religious significance over more influential positions of power in the modern economy. Telling workers with little autonomy, agency, or means of change that their work "matters to God" may leave room for moral ambiguity regarding the moral status of the system as a whole. Telling the same message to those whose job it is to manage and control those workers leaves less room for ambiguity. Religious frameworks invoked in this manner can fulfill what sociologist Pierre Bourdieu identifies as a "consecrating" function: they assume an "ideological function, a practical and political function of absolutization of the relative and legitimation of the arbitrary."[10] Thus this framework, in identifying the faithful industrialist or manager so closely with the faithful church leader, provides a substantial endorsement for the existing economic system and its various roles as part of the "sacred canopy" that is seemingly rooted in nature.[11]

Closely related to this consecrating function is the sacralizing of a particular vocational ranking, mentioned earlier. While Luther argued that all "offices" were equal in God's eyes to take part in his "creating and sustaining activity on earth," the imperatives of the fundamentalist work ethic had provided a new criterion by which vocations can be evaluated: How many nonbelievers can be "reached" through a person's work? With this criterion in place, business leaders rightly recognize that their own resources—whether a large workforce of potential converts, a wide reach in customer base, public recognition as an inspirational figure, or even just their own philanthropic dollars—exceeded that of the average evangelical worker. It seems God "needs" successful businessmen in a unique way, according to many of these writings.

A theology of wealth and success provides the means to impute significance and meaning on economic behaviors, thus permeating the religion-economic divide. The concept of "stewardship" frequently appears within this framework. Business leaders are called to steward their wealth and recognize God's ownership of all things.[12] The business they own becomes "God's business," or one in which God has entered as a business partner, providing ample reason to reconnect work with the transcendent values. Stewardship, for some writers in this era, opened the door to justifying financial success as part of God's plan: ". . . the gangrene of money possession is totally negatived for the man who holds wealth as a stewardship. On this thesis, [another Christian businessman] Russell H. Conwell fired the hearts of thousands who today are commercial leaders with the ambition to 'get rich for the glory of God!' "[13] This framework is not void of ethical parameters for pursuing wealth: the major autobiographical works are filled with anecdotes of deviating from the normal mode of doing business, frequently after either feeling great conviction of conscience or hearing from God directly. Some of this conviction led to basic restructuring of the workplace: LeTourneau's factories incorporated chapels that regularly brought in preachers, choirs, traveling evangelists, and Gideon representatives, providing at least one chapel service a week for his employees.[14] For plastics manufacturer Stanley Tam, the focus of faith was more outward than inward; he included religious tracts in shipments and informed customers of the faith-driven motivations behind certain decisions.[15] Many of these same leaders also take part in many of the "re-integrating" behaviors described in the next framework: the two modes are not at all sealed off from one another. Most re-integrating frameworks, however, have a far wider application to various vocations and roles in the social-economic order; theologies of wealth and "success," in contrast, have limited applicability to those not seen to possess those particular attributes.

## The Re-Integraters: Faith and Work as Full-Life Integration

By far the largest and most commonly voiced evangelical vision of faith and work is a vision to make work "matter" to God through integrating one's faith life *into* work. Of all the frameworks outlined, this one links most closely to the classical Lutheran framework related to vocation: work of any variety can matter to God because, when understood properly, work inherently serves God. At the center of this framework is the deliberate extension of evangelical forms of piety into the workplace in a manner that spans thought and action. The earliest modern text promoting this framework is British novelist Dorothy Sayers's 1941 radio lecture "Why Work?" Sayers's institutional, theological, and geographic location (in relation to American evangelicalism) give good reason to be skeptical of any immediate or direct influence of this work on the American evangelical populace. However, many evangelical writers of the 1960s and 1970s clearly demonstrate familiarity and agreement with the lecture, and even today Sayers's essay is one of the most cited works in the faith and work space. Sayers lays out a criticism of how the church has come to view work, a criticism that others will later apply to the American context: "In nothing has the Church so lost her hold on reality as in her failure to understand and respect the secular vocation. She has allowed work and religion to become separate departments, and is astonished to find that, as a result, the secular work of the world is turned to purely selfish and destructive ends, and that the greater part of the world's intelligent workers have become irreligious, or at least, uninterested in religion." The cause, according to Sayer, is what will become known in many works as the "Sunday-Monday gap": "How can anyone remain interested in a religion which seems to have no concern with nine-tenths of his life?" Individualistic moralism is singled out as reason for the failure: "The Church's approach to an intelligent carpenter is usually confined to exhorting him not to be drunk and disorderly in his leisure hours, and to come to church on Sundays. What the Church should be telling him is this: that the very first demand that is religion makes upon him is that he should make good tables."[16] As evidenced by numerous titles of books written after 1980, this diagnosis of the Sunday-Monday gap is seen as one of the central dimensions addressed by the re-integrating framework.

The central arguments of works falling in this category seek to locate work and labor as closer to the actions and nature of God. Sayers, in both her fiction and the early faith and work essay analyzed here, draws attention to the connection between creating and God the creator: ". . . work is the natural exercise and function of man—the creature who is made in the image of his Creator."[17] Marquette professor of sociology David Moberg makes a similar argument in a 1965 text: "The very first picture of God is that of a worker busy at the task of creation."[18] Writing in 1974, evangelical theologian Udo Middelmann draws a parallel between God's creation to our calling to be creative: "Just as God expressed himself and his character in his creation and in his revelation to man, so the image of God in man must be expressed, must be externalized." Contending with an argument that work is inherently tainted by the effects of "the fall" recorded in Genesis, Middelmann roots work in a pre-fall configuration: "In Genesis 2:15 before the Fall we find this statement: 'The Lord God took the man and put him in the garden of Eden to till it and keep it.' That was creative work. It was not merely a matter of man's survival. It was part of man's original purpose. It tied in with his being creative and imaginative with his being God's vice-regent . . . work is intimately linked with the question of who God is and who man is." Work then provides the opportunity to "externalize the identity we have as men made in the image of God. This then is the true basis for work."[19] Hans Rookmaaker, an art theorist who ran in the same circles as Middelmann, expressed a similar idea about work and identity in 1978: "We should remind ourselves that Christ did not come to make us Christians or to save our souls only but that he came to redeem us that we might be human in the full sense of the word . . . to be a Christian means that one has humanity, the freedom to work in God's creation and to use the talents God has given to each of us, to his glory and to the benefit of our neighbors."[20] As a book affirming secular vocations from 1978 observes, "The God of the Bible is a God who works."[21]

Sayers and a handful of others also draw a connection between labor and Jesus's time on spent on earth. Making the case that "Christian work" must be done with an eye toward excellence, Sayers quips, "No crooked table legs or ill-fitting drawers ever, I dare swear, came out of the carpenter's shop at Nazareth. Nor, if they did, could anyone believe that they were made by the same hand that made Heaven and earth."[22] Field and Stephenson's book of interviews with various Christians on their vocations provides this quote: ". . . it was in his muscle-building trade that Jesus spent all but three years of his working life. The hands which held the whip that drove the crooked money-changers from the temple in Jerusalem had been hardened by years of work with an axe, a saw, and a hammer. Tough, physical labour was not beneath the dignity of the Son of God."[23]

An alternative way of making this case was appealing to the concept of "dominion" from the book of Genesis. This generally draws on the theological thinking of late nineteenth-century theologian Abraham Kuyper and his conception of a creational or cultural "mandate."[24] Two academics involved in science fields provide one of the earliest uses of this concept. Malcolm Jeeves, a cognitive psychologist writing in 1969, championed carrying out scientific endeavors as "sons of God, who created and sustains the natural order which he has given them to study, to enjoy, and subdue. This means that scientific activities are properly regarded as one aspect of the fulfillment of the command given to mankind to subdue the earth (Genesis 1:28)."[25] Oliver Barclay, a zoologist who later became involved in the organization Intervarsity Fellowship, wrote in 1970, "The tasks of advancing knowledge and of subduing the earth been enthusiastically pursued by Christians all down the ages, if their thinking has been truly biblical . . . it is part of the work given to mankind to do." Citing the growth in education that opens fields like science, art, and literature, Barclay declares "all these things are good, because they are the fruits of subduing the earth as God originally commanded us to do."[26] Anglican bishop John Gladwin, writing in 1979, articulates a similar line of thinking: "Work is an aspect of human life as God created it. In Genesis man is given domination in the world and told to fill and subdue the earth. Adam is the tiller of the garden. Work, therefore, is an expression of our nature as people to whom power is entrusted. It is a vocation which fits the Creator's pattern for human life." Work must not be seen as merely paid employment, as such reductionism would "miss the biblical point about our vocation to order and subdue the earth and to express the creativity which God gave us at creation." Instead, a properly balanced Christian life recognizes the "high value of his work in God's calling."[27]

These interpretations all instill work with new significance. Work is repositioned as part of God's vision for his creation and the people he created. Work thus inherits divine meaning and significance. Much like soul-saving revivalism elevated personal evangelism and foreign mission efforts to the highest plane of spiritual value, the re-integrators are now lifting secular work to this plane. In a sense, they are recovering Luther's original view of vocation. One direct consequence of this valorization is an explicit move toward flattening the vocational hierarchy. If secular work is just as valuable to God as religious work, the moral and spiritual status of secular workers becomes equivalent with the status of professional and full-time ministers. The following passages capture those efforts of flattening:

> Let the Church remember this: that every maker and worker is called to serve God in his profession or trade—not outside it. . . . The official Church wastes time and energy, and moreover, commits sacrilege, in demanding that secular workers should neglect their proper vocation in order to do Christian work—by which She means ecclesiastical work. The only Christian work is good work well done. Let the Church see to it that the workers are Christian people and do their work well, as to God: then all the work will be Christian work, whether it is church embroidery, or sewage farming.[28]

> Every Christian layman is in this sense a minister of Christ; this ministry is his basic "other vocation." . . . What happens in church buildings during weekends is important but it is far less important to the Kingdom of God than that which occurs on the working days of the week.[29]

> [interview with layperson] Way out on the top of the list come those who have "vocations"—including no doubt, missionaries and clergy, followed at a short distance by RE teachers, doctors and nurses. Halfway down, we meet those with "ordinary jobs" (such as work for Christian organizations). Then, right at bottom and in serious danger of relegation, are those involved in much more dubious pursuits—pop musicians . . . and barmaids. This division of jobs into vocations and "others" is quite foreign to Scripture.[30]

Some writers were not shy about drawing a firm line between their re-integrating framework and theologies of work that merely promoted evangelism, the re-commissioning framework described above. Sayers is most notable here, drawing attention to a passage in the New Testament (in the book of Acts) where early church leaders delegated benevolence work to others to preserve their own callings: "The Apostles complained rightly when they said it was not meant they should leave the word of God and serve tables; their vocation was to preach the word. But the person whose vocation is to prepare the meals beautifully might with equal justice protest: It is not meant for us to leave the service of tables to preach the word."[31] As an even more direct example of this line-drawing, one book recounts Hans Rookmaaker, an evangelical art theorist, directly criticizing the elevation of evangelism above all other vocation. In a lecture at Oxford that his biographer described as heated and controversial, Rookmaaker allegedly created a stir among evangelical students with the following statement: "Why should you spend your life evangelising? There are more important things to do in the world. . . . I have done twenty-five years thinking, relating Biblical principles to art. You should be willing to do the same in your areas of life and work."[32]

Finally, re-integrating frameworks vary greatly in where they land on the spectrum of inward-meaning and outward-behavioral approaches to addressing the Sunday-Monday gap. Some re-integrate work with the realm of religion without providing much tangible consequence regarding specific activities, ethics, or attitudes. Re-integrating becomes a new vision or perspective on work, primarily internal to the worker without much articulated concern regarding outward consequence. Many texts, however, see the consequence to be *how* one works. High standards become the central ethical imperative:

> What the Church should be telling [the carpenter] is this: that the very first demand that his religion makes upon him is that he should make good tables. Church by all means, and decent forms of amusement, certainly—but what use is all that if in the very center of his life and occupation he is insulting God with bad carpentry?[33]

> Even monotonous daily routines become avenues of joyful service to those who have heard God's call. They no longer perform them as meaningless and empty drudgeries, perfunctorily, carelessly, and as quickly as possible, for they know their contributions promote the work God and the good of mankind.[34]

> Plumbers who give great evangelistic talks but let the water leak are not doing their jobs. They are bad plumbers. It becomes clear that they do not love their neighbor. The meaning of the job is in the love for God and neighbor.[35]

> To be a vice-regent of God over God's creation means to work creatively and to enjoy it.[36]

> In a word, he will seek to carry out his scientific endeavors efficiently, to increase his knowledge and control of the created order and to do this in such a way that he is able to use this knowledge to serve his neighbors more effectively.[37]

> The scientist who is Christian can engage in his works enthusiastically and with an attitude of enjoyment, that of a son enjoying the inheritance given to him by his Father.[38]

Amy Sherman, a contemporary leader in the movement (whose own views are reviewed more in Chapter 8), critically labels this form of faith-work integration an "adverbial" approach: the primary focus is on *how* one does work, with the prescriptive imperative being a laudable adverb (creatively, enthusiastically, diligently, excellently, wholeheartedly, etc.) shaping one's effort to fulfill one's role. This mode of re-integrating drifts back toward the Puritan or classical Protestant "work ethic," as religious identities are primarily channeled as a motivator for taking one's work more seriously and dedicating more energy toward it.

There are also cases where this imperative for excellent work goes hand in hand with the injection of more conventional acts of piety like engaging in prayer, holding company Bible studies, tithing profits (in the case where one is the business owner), or, more broadly, practicing "neighborliness" by showing love for others, whether co-workers, clients and customers, or even competitors. For example, Fish and Shelly, writing specifically for Christian nurses in the workplace, encourages nurses to offer spiritual consolation and pray with patients.[39] Middelmann, in advocating for a variety of ways to practice creativity on the job, concedes that some settings such as assembly lines allow little freedom; the solution for him is to form deeper relationships with others during break times.[40] But such imperatives are presented in a manner that they do not threaten to undermine the central message of work activity holding spiritual value in and of itself: it is spiritual, sacred, part of a providential plan for creation, a charged task for taking dominion, or simply significant to God by its own nature.

## The Re-Embedders: Faith and Work as New Ends for Economic Behavior

A final framework in many ways supplements the re-integrating framework with an otherwise absent ethical component. Re-embedding frameworks all posit ethical standards, ends, or norms that stand outside the workplace norms that workers likely encounter. The label conferred here draws on economic historian Karl Polanyi's observation that market societies tend to disembed economic relationships and exchanges from wider social norms and institutions.[41] In this case, faith and work efforts seek to re-embed the processes and behaviors of one's work life within a wider moral vision, placing it back within a framework of non-economic norms, ends, and social forms. For individual workers, we might think of this re-embedding as instilling the laity with "extra-organizational commitments" that then require negotiating said commitments with settings where these commitments are not naturally at home.[42]

Several texts offer visions of workers being sent out to, in their words, "infiltrate" particular industries or vocations. The ethical vision these infiltrators will promote—the extra-organizational commitments they would bring to their job—are not always clearly articulated, but one would presume that "infiltrators" bring something previously not present in the workplace setting. Political journalist Wesley Pippert, in his more politically oriented book *Memo for 1976*, lays out a vision for evangelicals to be "effective infiltrators" in the "Kingdom of Man." Quoting another Christian ethicist's vision for relating "the gospel" to the social order "in a faithful and saving fashion," Pippert advocates infiltrating society through "the *individual* Christian leavening society, as an independent man of faith bringing a redemptive life style and Word to the family, a particular vocation, social groups and, in a sense, self-consciously infiltrating the PTAs, the YMCAs, corporate structures, governmental processes and other social units. The Church in this case becomes a kind of strategic center sending out agents to help reform the world."[43]

David Moberg and John Gladwin flesh out how this leavening might work: "Our calling is also to be critical of our times. Christians are called to speak prophetically. To hunger and thirst for righteousness means that we shall never just defend the established order of the day. . . . Christians should never be conservative simply for the sake of conformity, of conserving the established order for its own sake. We must be critical. . . . We must be constantly aware of any growing lack of freedom, of the authoritarianism of petty bureaucracy which treats people as things, of any forces which dehumanize . . . never accept the status quo because this is the easiest thing to do or seems inevitable. To take this and to respond to our calling today means that we shall not be afraid to show that we are Christians; not only in saying that we have been saved by Christ, but also in our stand, in our way of life, in our prophetic analysis of the situation." Arguing that nothing is neutral about daily work, Moberg calls Christians to defend their daily activity against the "new spirits of the age."[44] Gladwin sees Christian workers tasked to ask larger questions concerning their roles: "Once more, we are bound to ask the question, does what we are encouraged to do at work help us to learn the patterns of human life in which we serve our neighbor? The question must lead us to criticize the divisive patterns in working life today." This need for questioning also extends to the wider operations of the company: "Christians will be interested in more than the internal operation of a place of work. There must also be concern for what an entire company or business does in service to the wider community. Not all that is offered as a 'service' to the public is genuine service. The way in which a company engages in economic activity in the world market can be either a help or a positive hindrance to the development of needy and poorer communities."[45]

Dorothy Sayers's essay, which advances the foundational vision of re-integrating framework, stakes out a strong opposition to imposing specific ethical dimensions on workers:

> This brings me to my third proposition; and this may sound to you the most revolutionary of all. It is this: the worker's first duty is to serve the work. The popular catchphrase of today is that it is everybody's duty to serve the community, but there *is* a catch in it. It is the old catch about the two great commandments. "Love God—and your neighbor: on those two commandments hang all the Law and the Prophets." The catch in it, which nowadays the world has largely forgotten, is that the second commandment depends upon the first, and without the first, it is a delusion and a snare. Much of our present trouble and disillusionment have come from putting the second commandment before the first. If we put our neighbor first, we are putting man above God, and that is what we have been doing ever since we began to worship humanity and make man the measure of all things.[46]

Sayers's line of thinking reflects theologies of work that imbue the already present ends and logics of work as entirely appropriate to loving and serving God through work. Efforts to re-embed work within extra-economic ends then fall guilty of overlooking the primacy of serving God *through* the work and behaviors in which one already partakes.

Though Sayers subscribed to Anglican theology, such understandings of personal piety often trace back to sources in Lutheran social thought. Martin Luther's theology, with its radical turn against formal religious offices and holy "works" of righteousness, insisted that all offices and vocations were themselves equally qualified as callings to serve God. Yet combined with a certain mode of realism regarding the "orders" that make up this world, Lutheran-inspired pietism can enable a theology of work that severs itself from concerns of reforming broader social arrangements. Meanwhile, notions of re-embedding work are nearly all connected to the theological ideas centered around the work of John Calvin. This form of Protestantism instilled within the laity a more reformist (or revolutionary) impulse that would be translated into their various vocations and callings. This impulse, when translated to a theology of vocation, declared all vocations to share in not only the same sacredness of the priest, but also the same political-ethical imperatives of the prince. Building from Calvinist theological sources, the Puritans of the sixteenth and seventeenth centuries developed a more communitarian understandings of their callings, working for the "common good," as sixteenth-century Puritan William Perkins advocated. This understanding of calling made a significant mark on the early Puritan colonies that settled New England.

But the Lutheran-Calvinism divide is not a perfect fit for explaining the divergences of re-integrating frameworks from re-embedding divide. Centrally, the later emerging Calvinist thought generally referred to as Neo-Calvinism now provides the greatest energies for contemporary efforts to re-integrate work. The most avid promoters of re-embedding framework today, meanwhile, often reach for accounts of justice or the common good that go beyond what is endorsed by Neo-Calvinist voices in the movement. These thinkers are explored more in the final chapters.

## The Faith and Work Movement from 1980 to Today: The Aestheticization of Work

In more recent decades, the re-integrating framework continues to dominate the faith and work space, weaving its way through books, lectures, website materials, podcasts, worship songs, and Bible commentaries. The overarching message of today's movement forgoes the re-embedding, re-sacralizing, or re-commissioning frameworks and instead centers on one pronouncement: your work, *in and of itself, independent of any distinctly spiritualized additives or alterations, matters to God.* Perhaps the most significant development to emerge after the mid-century books is a growing emphasis on the aesthetic nature of work. The earlier rejection of the spiritual vs. worldly dualism of fundamentalism opened space for evangelical writers to flesh out what is called a "theology of creation," which consists of far more affirming views of the world as the "created order" and a far narrower gap between God the creator and the elements of God's creation, which includes humans and their earthly activities. This has allowed for accounts of work that emphasize work's potential for creative acts that conform to God's intended design of the creative order. A remarkable number of themes associated with early nineteenth-century Romanticism are incorporated to make this point. Laity are invited to recognize how their callings are harmoniously located within a higher reality that aligns with the "natural" (or divinely imposed) ordering of the universe. Their daily efforts can then be infused with a creative, lifegiving, cosmic significance predicated on their embeddedness within the higher dimension. Metaphors and symbols related to art, craftsmanship, and agriculture are often invoked to frame the more mundane dimensions of life as fruitful and life-giving. Work is seen to take place amidst a larger redemptive narrative spanning from the creation of the world and its ultimate restoration in the future (referred to in theological language as the "consummation of all things"). These events then serve as the temporal and spiritual "bookends" for our own activity.[47] Leaders speak of the "created order" in which humans find themselves and God's "redemptive mission" for that order, a mission to which they are called to participate through their work.

Andy Crouch, an author, writer, and former editor of *Christianity Today*, represents one of the leading voices in this aestheticization of work:

> Like our first parents [Adam and Eve], we are to be creators and cultivators. Or to put it more poetically, we are artists and gardeners... after contemplation, the artist and the gardener both adopt a posture of purposeful work. They bring their creativity and effort to their calling. The gardener tends what has gone before, making the most of what is beautiful and weed in out what is distracting or useless. The artist can be more daring: she starts with

a blank canvas or a solid piece of stone and gradually brings something out of it that was never there before.[48]

Speaker and writer Kate Harris offered perhaps the most robust theological conception of how work participates in the continuation of the created order. In our interview on the subject, Harris explicitly built onto Crouch's gardening metaphors: "You're taking creation, and then we have a responsibility to make it better. . . God gives grapes and then the human acts upon that as fermentation to make wine, so grapes are good, wine is better." Other leaders enlist Dorothy Sayers's influential essay, discussed above, which promotes duties of approaching work as one's creative or artistic endeavor. While Sayers's essay directly mentions only a handful of occupations like architecture, painting, and carpentry, faith and work leaders confidently expand her directive to all contemporary professions. All work becomes what Sayers called a "sacred" site where "living and eternal truth is expressed." From this claim it follows that, just as "no crooked table-legs or ill-fitting drawers" were ever produced by Jesus's work as a carpenter while on earth, so too, Christian workers' primary duties are to conform to the standards of excellence endogenous to their particular trade or industry.

How did this aesthetic-grounded re-integrating framework gain the upper hand over the other frameworks? Answering this question requires circling back to many of the wider social and cultural factors laid out in Chapter 1. A key part of the story for the emergence of the faith and work movement is white evangelicalism's ascension into the realms of knowledge-economy work and creative-class capitalism.[49] As sociologist Nancy Ammerman observes, the working-class fundamentalists of the early part of the century gave birth to middle-class mid-century evangelical children.[50] A survey from the 1930s suggests that only 7 percent of fundamentalists had a college education, and these comparatively low levels of educational attainment persisted into the 1950s.[51] But things began to shift in the 1960s: whereas only 13 percent of evangelicals thought of themselves as middle class at the beginning of the decade, that number rose to 37 percent by 1972. And as early as the 1980s, white evangelicals appear to have quietly closed the educational gap between themselves and the wider population.[52] Many of the denominations once identified as the "churches of the disinherited" had come to comfortably occupy mainstream middle-class society, enjoying an improved social and economic standing. By the 1980s the educational gap between evangelicals and the rest of the population had become negligible.[53]

Fundamentalism had instilled a separatist orientation toward participation within wider societal institutions. The 1925 Scopes Monkey Trial is frequently cited as the pivotal moment when fundamentalism had severed itself from mainstream American society. Many religious groups that came together beneath the fundamentalist cause had originated from schisms with the socially ascending Methodism and other more established forms of Protestant denominations.[54] Conservative Protestant groups that had made relatively more inroads among non-white populations—the Holiness movement and Pentecostal groups—also disproportionately took hold among working-class populations in the rural South and the Midwest.[55] As these groups witnessed a widening gap between their own values and the urbanizing centers of American culture, they only more deeply entrenched themselves within this separatist subculture. Many groups warned against the dangers of "mammonism" that they saw in the more established forms of religion taking hold among upwardly mobile and urban populations.[56]

But the social ascension of fundamentalism's second and third generation prompted a renegotiation of their orientations to the wider American society. Many laity were now making their way into knowledge economy fields like administration, teaching, engineering, finance, real estate, or work in the public sector.[57] By the end of the twentieth century, evangelical elites had even established footholds in positions of power in the corporate, political, media, and educational worlds, finding entrances into America's elite halls of power.[58] Greater representation within these jobs and careers also placed different sorts of strains and demands on religious laity. Many knowledge economy workplaces have long been organized around work processes that cultivated emotional connection, affectual ties with others, cooperation, and communicative skills.[59] Because these workplaces often engage "whole selves" as a means of normative control, work is not as easily sequestered to a particular sphere or corner of one's life. These workplaces instead exert very particular *pulls* on their workers: to work longer hours, concede more emotional energies on work, and the dedicate longer portions of one's biography to gaining the education and credentials necessary for one's career. Knowledge-economy workers frequently experience these pulls as humanizing and fulfilling: some workers—particularly working mothers—recount their jobs coming to serve as a place of refuge from the demands of family life and other forms of labor that often go unrecognized and unaffirmed.[60]

The framework of "greedy institutions" serves as a helpful heuristic for understanding these work settings, drawing from sociologist Lewis Coser's work. Coser perceives individuals at the intersection of competing organizations and groups vying for energy and time—they "seek exclusive and undivided attention" and "attempt to reduce the claims of competing roles and status positions." [61] Work's "greediness" is likely aided by the diminishment of countervailing pulls on workers through the second half of the twentieth century. Some of this can be traced to the macro trends of what demographers label the second demographic transition, which places more workers in single-person households, free of the competing institutions of familial relationships.[62] Already in the 1970s, evangelicals were showing accelerated decline in fertility rates in comparison to their Mainline counterparts that likely stemmed at least in part from the social ascension trends outlined here.[63] But there were also marked changes in other institutions surrounding higher-educated and creative-class settings: traditional forms of civic engagement in many cases were translated into "loose connections" with voluntary associations, and more binding ties to place and neighborhoods often gave way to the demanding professional trajectories that moved adults through multiple degree locations followed by competitive placement in residency programs or top firms.[64] *Atlantic* writer Derek Thompson's conception of "workism" provides a striking assessment of the end result: work, no longer confronting any challenges to its own greediness, evolves from "a means of material production to a means of identity production."[65]

But for religious laity hailing from traditions affiliated with conservative Protestantism, "greedy work" represents a serious problem. Historically, American evangelicalism has operated as its own greedy institution. A number of theological streams within American evangelicalism emphasized whole-life commitments that simultaneously declared no realm or sphere could possibly remain neutral in relation to the Christian life.[66] First, a more demanding German pietism emphasized a religious devotion that specifically sought to revitalize religious behaviors within everyday life, and this orientation came to inform teachings of "Christian perfectionism" that spread in the United States through the Second Great Awakening. Promoted by nineteenth-century leaders like Charles Finney and Phoebe Palmer, Christian perfectionism subscribed to a more optimistic view of religious converts' capacity to overcome the effects of sin and to be subsequently transformed by an act of sanctification. The consequence of this view was fervent attention granted to one's actions in every realm. Finney's revivals often led to widespread adoption of far more strict prohibitions on personal behaviors, often prompting converted tavern owners to publicly dispose all their supply of alcohol. The later emerging nineteenth-century "Holiness movement" would only institute more restrictions on personal behavior. A second stream was the pre-millennial eschatology that ushered in a more fervent personal ascetism among many conservative Protestants. As historian Grant Wacker observes, anticipation of the pending return of Christ led to anxieties among religious groups that Christ would find them engaged in "worldly" or merely frivolous activities on his return, including attending parades, theater, circuses, or riding in cars on Sundays. This instilled an unceasing surveillance over all of one's activities while remaining "on watch."

Finally, a third source of this whole-life ethos stems from Reformed and Lutheran theology and its calls to be constantly on guard for activities that might take the form of idolatry. Any activity, life sphere, or value that came to function as one's ultimate end was thereby judged spiritually harmful. The evangelical subculture has maintained vestiges of the "whole-life" ethic congealed from such sources. One site in which it remains visible is within the evangelical parachurch world, where specialized ministries and conferences and corresponding experts can be found on nearly all imaginable facet of the "Christian life," whether marriage, parenting, aging, dieting, investing, job coaching, recovering from personal tragedy, budgeting, and—the phenomenon of interest examined here—working. Experts in this realm frame their offerings as providing the invaluable evangelical perspective on the topic at hand, allowing them to differentiate themselves from other offerings.[67] Notably, the parachurch world and most ecclesial settings lack formal means of enforcing a whole-life asceticism on their adherents. A wide degree of latitude and personal discretion is afforded to the evangelical laity. But these theological currents nevertheless preserved a powerful notion that a *serious Christian* is not someone who leaves their faith at the door of other life spheres. These conditions then place a premium on the re-integration framework: it stands to harmonize together that which might otherwise prove intractably opposed. In the context of creative-class evangelicals and those occupying realms of workism, re-integrating frameworks permit the peaceful coexistence of two greedy institutions, promoting affective ties to both work and religion.[68]

Work matters a lot to this population. It is comforting, then, to hear that work matters a lot to God, too. To return to the central injunction of Sayers's essay on work, the task for all Christian workers then becomes the same as the carpenter: to do the equivalent of "making good tables" in whatever field they find themselves. The three alternative evangelical theologies of work—re-comissioning, re-sacralizing, or re-embedding—cannot offer the same means of peacefully bringing these two worlds together.

## Meaningful Work as the Affirmation of "Ordinary Life"

We might conclude this chapter by placing the contemporary faith and work movement in the larger history of Protestantism's changing orientations toward economic activity. As the prior chapters have shown, the contemporary movement has set out to save or, more accurately, reconstruct, an inner-worldly asceticism regarding work that mirrors that of the earlier Calvinists and Puritans. This task centers on recovering theological resources that charge working laity to sacralize and stabilize their participation in the economic sector, rather than subordinate or shirk such responsibilities in light of pressing ecclesial duties. Finding resources for such a directive does not prove to be challenging: faith and work leaders are able to return to the insights of Martin Luther himself. Luther posited all positions on earth can equally "participate in God's creating and sustaining activity on earth." He declared that

> . . . the works of monks and priests, be they ever so holy and arduous, differ not a whit in the sight of God from the works of the farmer toiling in the field or the woman going about her household tasks. . . . [Indeed] the menial housework of a maidservant or manservant is often more acceptable to God than all the fasting and other works of a monk or a priest, because the latter lacks faith![69]

The Calvinists of the sixteenth century and the Puritans that followed them enthusiastically translated this vocational egalitarianism into the emerging world of commercial capitalism. Though Weber likely oversells the degree to which these energies were themselves responsible for capitalist growth, the pursuit of callings and vocations within the economic realm certainly offered cultural resources for disciplined and methodical participation in the economic worlds of this era.

But the earlier review of popular religious books suggested that such mentalities and practices began to confront alternative views among conservative Protestants at the end of the nineteenth century. New theological currents gained a strong foothold within conservative Protestantism, whether the rise of an eschatologically charged pre-millennialism, the spread of Keswick theology, or the primacy of soul-saving as the central imperative of the laity. The inner worldly asceticism of the earlier Puritans was in many ways a bystander casualty of these developments, as the strenuous and methodical energies previously channeled toward labor were channeled toward other matters. Historian Douglas W. Franks provides a compelling account of how these new theological currents ultimately gained the upper hand. Franks contends that the harder edged work ethics of the nineteenth century became more challenging to adhere to as American society entered into the dawning age of industrial capitalism. Many social changes were afoot: the migration of Black populations to Northern cities, greater numbers of immigrants pouring into urban centers, the rise of concentrated corporate power, and the appearance of more radical social movements and ideas from Europe. Traditional commitments to character and self-discipline that could previously ensure the achievement of upward mobility and financial security suddenly seemed less certain. But white conservative Protestants were not ready to surrender assurances of personal blessings and security, which they continued to tie closely to God's providential care for them. In Franks's interpretation, this predicament "multiplied the discontents of middle-class life in industrial America, making for nervous exhaustion in many. It was this exhaustion that the [Keswick] Victorious Life movement promised to relieve—instantly, fully, and without the long, wearying journey implied by the older Calvinist quest for that thing called character."[70] A growing number of books emerged in this era that preached not relentless discipline and strenuous effort but precisely the opposite: a surrendering to God and acceptance of victorious rest conferred by a "second blessing" of the Holy Spirit.[71] Many low-church sects preserved the more emotional and collective experiences that more economically prosperous denominations were leaving behind, deliberately cultivating spaces sequestered from the wider status systems related to race, class, and political economy.[72]

If we fast forward to the mid-twentieth century, it is career-minded white evangelicals who first become keenly aware of the cost incurred by this earlier alteration. They began to recognize their tradition's flight from the world had left far too much of "the world" behind. These evangelicals found themselves desperately wanting to restore what had been jettisoned: a means to spiritually affirm the hours of toil that they were not directing toward the work of the "King's business." New theological frameworks endorsed more favorable views of the created order that could not only restore a particular goodness in "secular" realms, but also sanction a serious duty or charge to participate within them.

But this revised Protestant work ethic of career-focused evangelicals also contained its own novel elements. Social theorist and historian R. H. Tawney summarized seventeenth-century Puritan notions of calling as a "bugle-call" which summons the elect into a "strenuous and exacting enterprise" that takes the form of a "long battle which will end only with their death."[73] The Protestant ethic of the twenty-first century, in contrast, might be better compared to an invitation to cultivate a garden or master a new medium of art. The ends of such activity are not so much preparing for a solemn death but achieving harmony and wholeness in life. The perceived threats to one's calling have also significantly shifted. Whereas the moralizing Puritan leaders were haunted by a depravity-rooted inclination toward idleness or slothfulness, the threat to today's Christian callings is identity disintegration. Proper participation in one's calling then requires overcoming the divided self and a compartmentalized identity that otherwise leaves the economic world severed from one's personal faith.

But while there are noted differences, Protestant ethics old and new may very well be pursuing very similar ends. The contemporary movement's concept of "work"—which seems to be strategically left undefined at times, as discussed in the next chapter—provides a means for career-minded evangelicals to regain what philosopher Charles Taylor calls "the affirmation of ordinary life." This affirmation had been a hallmark of sixteenth-century Puritanism in England and the early American colonies. Taylor narrates the advent of this doctrine as representing a transvaluation regarding the highest vocations within the Christian life: the "highest life" was "no longer defined by an exalted *kind* of activity; it all turns on the *spirit* in which one lives whatever one lives, even the most mundane existence." Writings from this era commanded Christians to undertake their callings "most diligently" and "with most consciousable and dutiful hearts and minds." These writings entailed precisely the sacralizing and stabilizing frameworks that contemporary faith and work movement aspire to recover: an *adverbial* orientation to the mundanities of Monday life. Contemporary faith and work books expend the majority of their energies endorsing a certain spirit or mode of work that allows work to take on the worth and significance perceived by the Puritans.

But injecting such ideas into the capitalist workaday worlds of the twentieth and twenty-first centuries required new adaptations. Faith and work leaders had to lead a charge into an economic realm that had, according to many theorists, long been surrendered to its own logics and ethical frameworks. Sociologist Peter Berger observed in a 1967 text that, in the context of modernity, "religion stops at the factory gate."[74] We might think of religion's re-entrance into the economic sphere as a process of "de-privatization," as religious sentiments, logics, and values are effectively pushed back into a realm conventionally thought to be a-religious or secular.[75] How can this de-privatization be pulled off? Re-integration frameworks and their affirmation of ordinary life offer a compelling way forward. For one, such frameworks certainly exhibit an elective affinity with many elements of workplace culture already common to postindustrial work. The broader cultural ethos of such work environments adheres to what social scientists call "postmaterialist values," which place far more emphasis on needs of self-realization, self-expression, and aesthetic satisfaction.[76] Sociologists Paul Heelas and Linda Woodhead point to changes in managerial and organizational thinking in the 1980s that usher these values into workplaces: work settings begin attending to "the subjective life, emotional well-being, and intimacy" of the modern work experience.[77] Workplaces began taking onboard the task of addressing their workers' *whole selves*—their physical, mental, emotional, and spiritual needs.[78]

In some ways, this brings out the manner in which re-integrating frameworks likely benefit in being ethically underdeveloped. Re-integrating efforts that consecrate work as part of an aesthetic project fall in line with modern forms of workplace control, which generally cultivates intrinsic motivations that "aim to induce people to do what one wants them to do by themselves, as if under the influence of voluntary, autonomous decision."[79] Few employers would oppose a faith system that instructs workers to do the best they can at their jobs. Channeling religious energies into an ethically innocuous mode of "adverbial" orientations also trims away many of the weightier moral directives that characterized earlier "Protestant ethics," whether prohibiting certain practices, condemning mammonism, or promoting charity for those in need. The favored Romantic-inspired themes instead elevate work as a matter of harmony, wholeness, and finding one's natural and intended place in the world. This mode of religion can easily harmonize with the ethical directives already present in many workplaces. Sociologists Luc Boltanski and Eve Chiapello identify a specific set of Romantic-grounded values and qualities that come into vogue in managerial literature in the 1990s:

> Autonomy, spontaneity, rhizomorphous capacity, multitasking (in contrast to the narrow specialization of the old division of labor), conviviality, openness to others and novelty, availability, creativity, visionary intuition, sensitivity to differences, listening to lived experiences and receptiveness to a whole range of experiences, being attracted to informality and the search for interpersonal contacts.[80]

Assurances that work holds an integral place an overarching narrative of creation, then, provides both space and justification for pursuing work in alignment with many values already celebrated within modern workplaces.

This elective affinity also explains the relative unpopularity of the three alternative frameworks. The alternative frameworks may very well continue to struggle getting past the "factory gates" of contemporary workplaces. The re-embedding framework, for instance, introduces external criteria or standards which might incite calls for change in a workplace. Bureaucratically ordered modern workplaces find such ethical commitments to be disruptive to their own ends: as an interviewee in one study of managerial work settings recounted: "What is right in the corporation is not what is right in a man's home or in his church. What is right in the corporation is what the guy above you wants from you."[81] Re-commissioning frameworks, in turn, pose a threat of religious proselytization that threatens cohesion and open-minded pluralism. Even managerial scholars enthused about "workplace spirituality" often warn that such elements are detrimental to organizational functioning.[82] And re-sacralization frameworks may fail to effectively disperse the notion of callings across all occupations and work activities. Workers in more menial jobs may affix God's blessings on their individual advancement *out* of their position and not necessarily perceive God's blessings resting on the work they are already doing.

It is worth revisiting Catholic writer G. K. Chesterton's claim that religion plays a deferential role to capitalism when it is reduced to the "encouragement of small virtues supporting capitalism [and] the discouragement of the huge virtues that defy it."[83] Determining to what degree the faith and work movement manifests a subservience to creative-class capitalism is more directly addressed in the book's later chapters. But in summarizing the preceding chapters, it is worth recognizing the existence of very real humanistic and existential needs to which faith and work resources seem to be responding. The "good news" at the core of the movement should not be overlooked or explained away: many religious laity find great value in the pronouncement that the virtues and ends of work are not in fact at odds with the ultimate ends of their religious identities. In theological terms, leaders of the movement pronounce the same theological breakthrough that Tawney attributes to the earlier Puritans: the possibility of "serving two masters" in a religion where such a thing is strictly forbidden.[84] Yet as was true with the earlier Puritan work ethic, the contemporary message does not necessarily displace virtue with vice or God with mammon. "Work" for these religious laity is generally conceived as going beyond a mere engagement in profit-seeking behavior. The fundamental proclamation more precisely seeks to reframe the ends and activities of "ordinary life" as those ends toward which individuals are in fact Providentially ordered. This effectively reclaims the vocational egalitarianism promoted by Luther: all ordinary lives then become capable of holy and sacred activity regardless of office or position. Mondays, then, become reclaimed for God.

# PART II

# CONTOURS, CONTENDING INTERESTS, AND CONFLICTS

# 5
# Whose Work Matters to God?

On September 23, 1857, a New York businessman named Jeremiah Lanphier distributed a simple flier advertising a noon prayer meeting. "This meeting is intended to give merchants, mechanics, clerks, strangers, and business men generally an opportunity to stop and call upon God amid the perplexities incident to their respective avocations. It will continue for one hour." Lanphier arrived at the designated church at the time advertised, only to find no one there. After several minutes had passed, six businessmen had made their way into the church to pray. Two days later he repeated the routine: the number of attendees was up to forty, all of whom stayed for an hour of prayer. Within a year, over 10,000 people were gathering daily to pray. This became known as the "Businessmen's Revival," which was believed to be at the forefront of the Second Great Awakening. Historians recognize it as a key event that set off what is considered the closest thing to a truly national revival in American religion, placing the activities of religious groups on the front page of secular newspapers for the first time.[1]

The contemporary faith and work movement often points back to this event as part of their historical lineage. The founder and president of the Corporate Chaplains of America describes the "profound impact" Lanphier has had on workplace ministry: "The fact that he was a businessman and not a clergyman broke down the barrier of church and work in a fundamental but elementary way."[2] A 1992 book on laity vocations draws out Lanphier's identity as a businessman: "Thousands met to pray because one man stepped out. . . . Can God do something extraordinary through you?" A 2015 faith and work book also challenges the reader with Lanphier's example: "Who knows what would happen in your workplace if you made prayer a priority?"[3] A 2019 blog article produced by the Center for Faith and Enterprise presented the historical episode as a "case study" providing "important lessons that can be drawn from the success of this movement."[4]

Historians, however, fill in critical details missing from what is commonly recounted by faith and work leaders. The first person who attempted to join Lanphier's movement was sternly turned away: *she* was not a "businessman."

*Saving the Protestant Ethic.* Andrew Lynn, Oxford University Press. © Oxford University Press 2023.
DOI: 10.1093/oso/9780190066680.003.0006

Lanphier saw a woman approaching on the day of the first meeting and rushed to meet her at the door: "Madam, this is a [businessman's] meeting: it is not intended for women. If women come, men will hesitate to come in their working clothes." Another population was also denied access to this gathering: non-white workers. A letter appearing in the *New York Tribune* recounted a similar experience as had by the woman attendee: on attempting to join the prayer meeting, a Black couple were escorted to an empty third-floor room, where "the colored people have good meetings." Disgusted at this relegation to another space and exclusion from the larger group, the pair left.

Many aspects of the faith and work movement have radically changed since the 1857 revival. City-wide prayer meetings, for one, are no longer common. But to what degree has the contemporary movement perpetuated the tight exclusivity of their movement's recognized forebears? Have leaders perhaps preserved this narrow and exclusive understanding of the "businessman's" work and vocation? To explore this question, I was able to draw on several sources of data, from observations regarding the movement leaders themselves, the audiences they tend to draw, the events they tend to coordinate, and the cultural content created. This chapter brings to light one of the central sorting mechanisms I found operating at the movement's most fundamental level: What exactly is "work"? And what populations counts as workers?

In all of the discussions, events, and cultural materials I examined, these questions are never explicitly or systematically taken on: no event speaker or leader interviewed rolled out an explicit typology of the diverse forms of labor practices in modern societies.[5] The definition and boundaries around what counts as work are far more latent, implicitly captured by the moral imperatives delivered, topics addressed (and left unaddressed), event speakers selected (and not selected), and anecdotes commonly given. One central indicator of what counts as work permeates nearly all content produced by faith and work leaders: the moral crisis of Monday or the "Sunday-Monday" gap that drives much of the movement's urgency toward providing interventions. Closely associated with such framing are discussions about "bringing God into the workplace." This brings out a key assumption of the movement at large: work is generally presumed to be not activity routinely taking place in the home, nor is it held to be ubiquitous with life itself. This suggests the "work" drawing the movement's focus dates back to industrial capitalism. It is at this point that work becomes both geographically and relationally centered outside the household. Work instead begins to operate as a separate realm with its own relations, logics, and values that potentially compete with one's home or wider lifeworld. And it is *this* conception of work that leaders saw as needing urgent theological engagement. This conception of course raises many questions about the moral status of work that fails to meet such criteria, and closely related to these questions are the corresponding status of those populations that disproportionately do not participate in such work. This chapter seeks to probe how the cultural and theological content of the movement institutes particular boundaries around its discourse and audience. In doing so, the movement fundamentally provides an answer to the question: Whose work matters to God?

## The Long Life of the "Faith and Businessman" Movement

Answering this question takes us back to the modern movement's origins, which first takes hold among professionally successful Christians. As Chapter 2 explored, conservative Protestants who found themselves among the economic successful were some of the earlier Christian laity to develop new understandings of how faith and work integrate. The recurring motif found within this experience is struggling with the reality that their new-found status and success in "the world" did not translate into any higher status or greater achievement in their religious lives. However much money and prestige they might gain, they would never save the same number of souls as D. L. Moody, Billy Sunday, or Billy Graham. Their discovery and promotion of frameworks to "re-sacralize" their own world of industry offered a resolution to this tension, raising the spiritual status of their own vocations to equal the level of professional clergy.

These early efforts could just as easily be labeled the "faith and businessman" movement. The theological writings and frameworks that emerged within these spaces focused almost exclusively on the plight of the male executive, taking for granted the particular positions of power and influence that these early leaders held in the socioeconomic realm.[6] The Fellowship of Christian Companies International—which still holds a place in the contemporary faith and work movement—composed its initial statement of faith around articulating the calling of the CEO and "his" company. Through at least the late 1980s, the movement's figures, gatherings, and theological frameworks continued to valorize a very narrow mode of work, with the exception being the occasional book on professions like nurses or scientists breaking this mold.

The long shadow of the faith and businessman movement can be attributed to the central anxieties of the "successful" businessmen now effectively serving as the anxieties of a wider spectrum of Christian laity. It continues to be professions who feel caught between their role in a religious congregation and an exogenous status system that find the faith and work movement effectively relieving this tension. Certainly, the evangelical laity I met at faith and work events regularly attested to the persistence of this tension. Christian college students were navigating the degree to which success in their field should be subordinated to soul-saving and church involvement. Business leaders continued to profess worries that their work was treated with suspicion by their own pastors. Entrepreneurs continued to feel like they would have received better reception among their congregations had they become missionaries. The experience of being a second-class Christian, falling on a lower vocational tier, may actually be larger than the evangelical populace: Billy Graham regularly grabbed the highest non-politician ranking in Gallup's most admired living person poll until his death in 2018.[7]

The early business leaders of the movement are then continually recognized for charting a way out of this subordination. The 2014 and 2016 Faith and Work Summits both dedicated several sessions to honoring "pioneers" of the movement, including R. G. LeTourneau, Howard Butt, Pete Hammond, Richard C. Halverson, and Bill Pollard. But even if more professions are now granted the spiritual status previously denied to them, the modern movement is not immune from endorsing new vocational hierarchies. Certain occupations continue to be venerated, whether Silicon Valley tech work, risk-taking startup culture, or corporate executives possessing the mystique of charisma and leadership. A popular evangelical writer and conference speaker made this veneration explicit when leading a session at a week-long conference on entrepreneurship. Speaking to a room of two hundred Christian college students from all over the country, the speaker observed that earlier in his Christian life, full-time missionaries were the most celebrated and honored Christians in the church. But in the 1990s, that shifted to successful megachurch pastors. More recently, it became urban church planters. But after the emergence of faith and work, there was yet another change. "We've now taken the urban church planters off the pedestal," the speaker observed, "because now, it's you guys."[8] These 18- to 22-year-old entrepreneurs were perceived as optimally integrating their work with callings in a manner that yielded the greatest societal impact. Of course, the criteria for this "impact" were not grounded in any particular framework related to distinctly evangelical purposes or objectives. Such cases reveal how the contemporary movement can easily absorb and reproduce the particular status systems at work in broader society rather than flatten the vocational hierarchy. All work matters to God, but their work may matter a bit more.

## Making Creative-Class Work Matter to God

On asking movement leaders "who they normally see in the crowd" when they spoke at events, I found nearly all recognized two major and consistent populations over-represented: men and white-collar professional workers. Many leaders were very cognizant of this homogeneity. "My audiences tend to look a lot like me," one white, male, middle-aged speaker told me. Another male interviewee largely agreed: "We've found women and blue-collar folks have been neglected by the faith and work movement. It's primarily a white collar, white male thing so far."

Though the selective demographics are deeply intertwined, we will first explore class dimensions before turning specifically to gender dimensions. Today, the movement seems to disproportionately attact evangelical laity who have entered into high-demand, identity-intensive career. For those most dedicated to their jobs, this entrance went hand in hand with a looser tethering to other institutions providing meaning and significance. The resulting condition is a higher demand for a "calling" in a social space where fewer meaning sources make themselves available. For workers who approach their careers in this manner, the faith and work movement provides particularly good news: the work that already matters a great deal to you also matters a great deal to God.

Other occupants of advanced capitalist societies do not find themselves in this predicament. Identities and purposes related to non-work spheres remain strong, whether they emerge from intimate relational ties, civic associationism, ethnicity, family, place, or political partisanship. "Monday life" (or at least Monday prior to 5 p.m.) is not tasked to shoulder the burden of meaning and significance on its own. Work may simply be a taken-for-granted dimension of reality—a source of material wealth in most cases—and requires nothing beyond the pragmatic acceptance of its existence as simply a part of life.[9] For others, particularly those with mental or physical conditions that prevent them from formal work and those populations confronting structural obstacles to formal employment, the central tasks and activities occupying their lives may not meet tighter definitions of work. Such individuals are not exempt from the larger *humanistic* need for meaning, but they do not collapse that need on the back of their professional identities. The social ties that come with work may continue to serve as a central source of relationships and a sense of belonging, particularly as other institutions fail to provide such bonds and meaningful relationships.[10] But forming social bonds with co-workers is not the same as finding a "calling" or purpose in work: it is this latter attribute that work scholars see as more prevalent among knowledge-economy workers.

It is not surprising, then, that it is this population that shows up at faith and work events. Nearly all leaders interviewed noted the movement's challenges in making inroads into non-knowledge work settings. This again stems from the larger argument regarding the movement's origins: it was the entrance of evangelicals into knowledge economy and creative-class jobs that made leaders realize their theological cupboard for making sense of such experiences had run bare. But this mobilization around only *particular* types of work becomes accentuated by later trends in the labor market. Many workers today find themselves in a poor position to relate to the faith and work message. While many workers in vocational or artisan trades are able to carry out projects that honor the "make good tables" mandate of Dorothy Sayers, service-economy and even manufacturing workers often occupy impersonal systems of bureaucracy, exploitative work conditions, and industries serving little societal goods beyond returning maximal profits for shareholders. Adverbial theologies to "serve wholeheartedly as if serving God and not man" become difficult in settings where employers turn over their managerial responsibilities to impersonal algorithms to surveil, control, and even terminate workers, whether in Amazon warehouses or on ride-share apps.[11]

Faith and work leaders seem to have two tricks up their sleeve for adapting their message to such contexts. The first is doubling down on the idea of all work positions as places to which the particular Christian is called, thereby pronouncing a divinely ordered *duty* to faithful service. This duty is believed to exist independent of objective conditions of work. Here, one sees traces of the "religion of the proletariat" or "religion of the precariat" that echo earlier Christian moralists shoring up worker loyalties to grueling factory conditions. But these calls to endure grueling toil are rare: the more common tactic is a very subtle shift in precisely what it is about work that is being consecrated as holy and sacred. Leaders pull back from consecrating the *labor* to instead consecrate the relationships featured in the workplace. These relationships may serve as the arena to live out one's faith on Monday, even if the work itself lacks redemptive potential. In our interview, Andy Crouch, generally recognized as one of the promoters of the loftier "creating and cultivating" vision of work, employed this tactic when discussing work on assembly lines or service work:

> Maybe we're building things or we're on an assembly line, or we're assembling a complex object, but there are people standing next to me, people I'm interacting with. And the quality of those relationships is somehow very fundamental. So it's not enough to just be making a great widget, and oddly, you can be making a terrible widget, but if your relationships are deep and real, that's strangely rewarding to people.

Crouch went on in our interview to cite a study of workers in the fast-food industry feeling very fulfilled and happy in their work due to the deep relationships they had with each other. He sees this sociability as an indication of work being performed in the "image of God":

> The image of God lends itself very readily to: what's the quality of relationship I have with my coworker and customer, and are we recognizing each other as persons?

This framing of work still poses faith as a helpful intervention to ameliorate such settings. But this "theology of work" leaves out something central: the work itself. This pivot to the relational context could just as easily serve as a theology of middle school, a theology of military service, a theology of extreme sports, or a theology of cruise ship vacationing. The quality or features of work themselves go unaddressed. Sayer's aesthetic demands for excellent work are also quietly jettisoned, as Crouch approves the production of a "terrible" product. The targeted object of Christian responsibilities has been shifted elsewhere.

I interpreted this pivot as indication that some faith and work leaders were able to sense—but fail to articulate—that their loftier portrayals of work may come into conflict with many different settings or conditions of work in contemporary capitalism. Pivoting toward the relational context in some cases, then, functions as an escape valve for when conventional frameworks come to appear overly idealistic. This shift can also represent a tapping in of the re-commissioning framework where the re-integrating framework gets outmatched: evangelicals are able to revert back to the notion that all *relationships* matter to God when all *work* may not matter. But this pivot performs an important function in circumventing what would otherwise likely appear in these discussions: recognition and evaluation of the features of modern work that might come into conflict the movement's more general pro-work message. Does all paid labor in contemporary capitalism *really* have intrinsic eternal worth? Should workers supervised by faceless algorithms serve these systems as if "serving the Lord and not man"? These harder questions then go unanswered.

Several interviewees actually articulated that the faith and work conversation was seemingly engaging only the more privileged workers of modern capitalism. One leader reported his primary audience to be workers undergoing times of introspection that incited the exploration of bigger questions of "Why am I working, what am I doing this for?" Such big questions are far more at home in knowledge-economy jobs, which exhibit an elective affinity with post-materialist values.[12] Being told one's work matters to God offers an invaluable foundation to ground the wider need of this space for acquiring personal meaning, purpose, and self-actualization. Another leader observed that he primarily saw younger adults gravitating toward the movement due to "a real existential struggle" related to questions of calling and being in the right job. Questions of this sort tend to be taken up in a life stage that only some workers in the contemporary labor market pass through: a college or post-college phase of discerning one's calling, generally at a stage that narrows relational or geographic commitment and thereby grants the worker more agency to undertake vocational discernment. These are the phases in which college ministries and "vocational programming" guided by faith and work resources swoop in to provide pastoral guidance.

Two leaders were even more specific regarding the narrow demographic drawn to the movement:

> My impression [of the movement's focus] has fundamentally been a white middle- or upper-middle-class . . . uhhh . . . problem. Like you know, you talk about first-world problems. Well, that's a first-world problem in a way. Now that's maybe a little too negative. I think it's getting at a real issue, which is this sacred-secular divide in its various manifestations, but for the

> most part I would say the conversation has been either academic—and so largely theoretical—and to the extent that it's been practical, it's been kind of angst about people who are making a bunch of money and spending a lot of time at work worrying about how they are responsible then. To their families and their churches and to that sort of thing.

Another leader observed that the movement attracted an intense concentration of mid-life workers, which were described as going through a period of existential questioning:

> . . . maybe not mid-life crisis, but they'd sort of accomplished what it is they envisioned to accomplish in their career, and then wherever that was feeling flat or feeling empty or they were looking onto the next thing, they were sort of revisiting those same questions: what is the purpose of my work? Does it matter? Is it just for making money?

A second sorting mechanism favoring higher-status workers stems from what issues are simply not discussed in relation to work. During my fieldwork I began to notice a particular datedness to much of the faith and work discourse, which often drifted into traditional "breadwinner" visions of workers employed within what work scholars label "old economy" jobs.[13] In contrast, faith and work conversations fail to address many characteristics associated with the "new economy": rising labor market insecurities, pressures from increasing financialization of corporate environments, the bifurcation of work experiences and labor markets, de-unionization, decreasing stability and benefits-granting work, the rise of the "gig" economy and freelance work, changes in traditional managerial structures, hybrid and nontraditional forms of work-home configuration, the rise of care work, irregular scheduling, workplace surveillance, the threat of automation, participation in informal economies, lower rates of work participation, and wage inequalities related to gender and race. Some session titles at events I attended included "Gender Challenges in the Workplace" and "Rethinking Urban Poverty," but these sessions often lacked any direct engagement with on the ground phenomena. For the 2016 Faith and Work Summit, a description of "new" social trends in their event program attempted to speak to some of this datedness: "In various ways the movement needs to move decisively forward with respect to: women, African-Americans, global voices, the unemployed and badly employed, pre-career youth, post-career 'retired,' specific industries and professions, specific topics, and workplace insights for churchplace."[14]

These omissions likely stem from the personal work experiences of the leadership of the movement, whose age, gender, and education levels have likely confined their work experiences to the old economy labor market. This parochialism effectively walls off the conversation from those populations whose work experience is either characterized by new economy phenomena—migrant workers, temp workers, or gig economy workers—or has been historically excluded from the old economy "breadwinner" model, whether minorities, women, or immigrant populations facing obstructions to employment.[15]

Tightly coupling vocation with formal, paid work also introduces yet a subtle favoring of those participating in these breadwinner forms of work over those devoted to tasks or activities like parenting, volunteering, community organizing, unpaid creative work, monastic life, or missionary work. Particularly those populations engaged in unpaid care work—whether care of children, the elderly, or special needs populations—have not traditionally been considered breadwinners. The Gospel at Work conference described at the beginning of Chapter 3 had a session on "finding peace and contentment in 'staying home' or in working behind the scenes without pay." The session was led by an English PhD student whose short bio reveals she had initially envisioned a career in academia before she shifted to a variety of part-time, off-the-clock, and non-work arrangements. Her bio concludes with the sentence, "She continues to be open to the variety of ways God can use her for Kingdom work . . . but sometimes still wonders, 'Should I get a real job?'" The 2016 Faith and Work Summit, however, did not offer any option like this in their breakout sessions. At one point in the sequence of sessions, the event channeled all attendees to any of six breakout sessions intended to highlight a particular setting where the "church-workplace gap" could be bridged to "make whole-life disciples." All six sessions revolved around paid, formal work. All speakers were introduced by their professional identities in formal paid work, even if they were full-time ministers. In another breakout session, the conference divided all attendees by sector, and here again, "sectors" of work were only those marked by formal, paid work: commerce, technology and science, law, government, education, and arts and media.

## Peacekeeping in a Status Standoff: The Competitive Masculinities of Faith and Work

The previous section laid out the case that the faith and work movement seems to disproportionately resonate or find its way to a certain type or class of worker. Here, I will explore the other attribute that seems to shape who does and does not find their way to faith and work resources: gender. The heavy over-representation of men involved certainly reveals something about the elective affinity between male creative-class work and the offerings of the movement. As Chapter 3 laid out, the demographics of the thought leaders themselves are fairly homogenous—mostly white, middle-aged males with advanced degrees. The gender imbalance is also present in a larger sample of movement leadership: out of the top seventy-seven most frequent faith and work conference speakers, there are seventeen women appearing among sixty men. It is perhaps not surprising, then, that a movement led by male, disproportionately over-educated leaders draws toward itself roughly that same demographic.

Men disproportionately find their way to the faith and work space due to several related factors. A more basic factor may relate to wider conditions of gender and masculinity within contemporary work settings. White-collar male workers are generally believed to have fared far better in the new economy relative to their blue-collar counterparts: white-collar men continue to have access to work that aligns with contemporary conceptions of masculinity. But research on men in white-collar workplaces reveals how particular dimensions of masculine identity continue to shape white-collar work dynamics. One study of thousands of white-collar workers revealed that their work settings often incorporate "masculinity contest cultures" that recognize one mode of "tough" masculinity above all others. Prevalent qualities in these settings include exhibiting a rugged "I have what it takes" demeanor, an elevation of physical fitness (demonstrated at times through extreme hours), and a "put work first" loyalty that decries all commitments that could interfere with work. These qualities are found to be more dominant in male-dominated industries. Women and minorities often start out behind in these competition cultures, viewed suspiciously as not "having what it takes."[16]

The career-dedicated, white-collar worker has historically found himself in an awkward standoff with his evangelical clergy. It is unclear whether the professional's dedication to the achievements of Monday occupies equal footing with his clergy's dedication to the achievements of "Sunday." In settings where soul-saving imperatives still hold legitimacy, the worker's dedication to the marketplace may in fact represent a misdirected use of time and energy. Previous studies of predominantly male Christian business leaders revealed a perceived "turf war" between both clergy and laity, with both groups feeling threatened by the others' judgments, values, and priorities.[17] Weber's classic *Protestant Ethic* even gives mention to this phenomenon in his own time: he observes a class of men characterized by "restless activity" who had "grown up in the hard school of life" and were now "shrewd and completely devoted to their business." Business has become "a necessary part of their lives," they "exist for the sake of their business, instead of the reverse." These men, Weber observes, were no fans of organized religion: "The thought of the pious boredom of paradise has little attraction for their active natures; religion appears to them as a means of drawing people away from labor in this world." Thus, despite capitalism drawing its initial motivational energies from religious energies enacted in the world, Weber sees a different story for the restless, male careerists of his day: "The people filled with the spirit of capitalism today tend to be indifferent, if not hostile, to the Church."[18]

This tension has occupied a persisting place within American Protestant history. Protestant religion in the nineteenth century often found itself sequestered to the "domestic sphere" of family, sheltered away from the realm of business. The long-standing imagery of lay Christian piety was the praying Christian mother, located in the home, safely away from her husband's economic pursuits. One of the achievements of the businessman's revival was the novel introduction of the "Christian businessman" as an image of devout lay piety.[19] Yet anxieties about the feminization of piety and the low participation of men within Protestantism would come to inspire efforts of establishing a "muscular Christianity" at the beginning of the twentieth century, reacting to a perceived effeminate weakness in the church.[20] Among social gospel and mainline denominations, a 1911–1912 Atlanta initiative called Men and Religion Forward pronounced its goal of repopulating churches with "1,000,000 missing men."[21] On the fundamentalist side, conceptions of effective fundamentalist evangelists venerated a similar sort of virulent masculinity that Mainline denominations aspired for: pastors should be able to "pack a punch" for the Lord, as one periodical said.[22] Evangelist Billy Sunday in at least one case made this imperative literal, exchanging blows mid-sermon with a German sympathizer who had been provoked by Sunday's hurled insults toward the German enemy during World War I.[23] Fundamentalist ministers eagerly allied themselves with the businessmen and the sophisticated techniques (as well as financial backing) these populations brought to the cause.

But this eventually invited conflict between these two different forms of masculinity. According to historian Margaret Lamberts Bendroth, the Christian business associations that first formed with the Gideons and then the Christian Business Committee were not interested in painting themselves into the image of the humble businessman at noonday prayer.[24] They instead framed their efforts as a revitalizing intervention urgently needed to correct the church leadership deficiencies, tasking themselves with taking over conservative Protestantism's soul-saving imperative. Their drive for efficiency had little time for doctrinal controversies and saw little justification for letting inefficient leaders monopolize spiritual efforts.[25] A 1936 speech delivered at a San Francisco Christian Business Men's Committees blamed ministers for their "excess program machinery and ineffectual whirring of wheels." The speaker, an investment banker, invoked Moody's vision of the lifeboat tasked to save as many as possible from the "wrecked vessel" of the world. The speaker issued a warning to the clergy that if they could not effectively present the gospel, changes would be made: "The laymen will run the life boats, and you can run the hulk."[26]

Another leader becoming involved in these Christian Business Men's Committees was R. G. LeTourneau. Speaking before a Chamber of Commerce in the 1930s, LeTourneau identified "commercial men's" calling as yielding more results than what was seen among the clergy. "We commercial men have no conflict with preachers," he told the Chamber, before moving to praise the superior opportunities of ministering businessmen who "rub shoulders with people in the world every day" and can "tell them that Jesus Christ is the solution to all our problems." "They can't say of us as they sometimes say of the preachers: 'They get paid for it,' " LeTourneau boasted.[27] These businessmen felt they had resolved any vocational-status standoff issue by one-upping clergy at their own game. A similar confidence was expressed later in the century by William Garrison, an evangelical who spent most of his career practicing law before getting involved in early parachurch efforts of developing lay theology. Garrison is remembered for making the claim to Christian leaders: "God's favorite people are never behind the pulpit."[28]

Some of the leading faith and work efforts of the 1990s articulated the need to rein in a certain type of "business personality" that reflects a competitive masculinity. Movement leader Pete Hammond, working at the time with Billy Graham's ministry organization, identified a central priority of helping pastors understand "the Type-A business person" while at the same time helping the type-A personality understand the pastor. "Billy Graham Evangelistic Association wants to be a bridge to pull these [personality types] together, working with and through the local church," Hammond explained to a reporter for a 2004 article. "Our role in workplace ministry is largely to bridge this gap and provide an environment for healing and understanding."[29] Another quote from the same article spoke of these two groups meeting at the center of a bridge to "put their arms around each other, fall on their knees, look toward God and begin to pray together about how to make an impact in the marketplace." Presumably, had this bridge not been built, these Type-A personalities would remain disengaged or even at odds with their clergy. Championing the abolition of the church's distinct vocational hierarchy (and quietly downplaying expectations of ecclesial involvement) served to remove tensions that career-minded men would otherwise perceive between career and church. A 2016 Faith and Work Summit session seemed to continue this line of thinking by addressing a question that apparently arose at a prior Summit gathering: "How do we get pastor buy-in?" The "we" referred to the faith and work movement leaders and enthusiasts attending the conference, suggesting that this project of earning recognition and legitimacy from their clergy persisted. "They" just needed to see the real value of career-driven laity.

But perhaps this buy-in has already been achieved. Returning to the speaker's pronouncement at the entrepreneur conference mentioned earlier, the church's highest honors of vocation—conventionally reserved for heroic missionaries leaving behind careers, wealth, and family for work abroad—is now conferred upon the entrepreneur. Perhaps, as LeTourneau had anticipated, the layperson really can beat the full-time minister at their own game. And perhaps, reflecting other dimensions of this competitive masculinity, these high-achieving Christian workers have begun carrying out religious and pastoral tasks *within* their workplaces that have allowed them to break free of dependence on congregational or pastoral care. The "I have what it takes" work ethos may continue to minimize dependencies these Christian business leaders maintain on organizations or ministers outside their particular workplace.

## Finding "A Woman's Place" in the Evangelical Parachurch World

The strongest evidence for faith and work resolving a specifically male status anxiety is the significantly lower representation of women in the space, as outlined earlier. The exception here appears to be events and gatherings targeted at college students and very early career young adults: two leaders who mainly worked with that population reported equal male-female gender representation at their events. A national gathering targeting Christian MBAs was slightly tilted toward women over men, an imbalance I also observed among events targeting college students. This early-career (and pre-career) programming often focuses more on discerning vocation and navigating life choice, an offering that may hold appeal to broader audiences. But for events targeting mid-career laity, evangelical women are significantly underrepresented, generally at a 2:1 ratio or higher. As one speaker at the conference remarked from the platform: "We are too male and too pale." A female attendee at the same gathering, in responding to my inquiry about gender representation in the room, amusingly remarked, "Well, these events are the only places I go where there is a long line for the men's restroom but no wait for the women's."

Some of this selectivity stems from the narrow conception of work discussed earlier. A female leader I interviewed pinpointed this as directly steering female laity away from the space:

> You have a whole contingent of people, primarily women, who may not think of themselves as workers in that sense. Yes, they would say caring for children or caring for a home is work, but they also understand implicitly that that's not quite what we're talking about when we talk about work or the workplace. Maybe it's permitted that you opt in, but it's not intended that you're part of that audience.

Another leader observed that many churches have long assumed all ministry related to "work" and "business" are properly located within a church's "men's ministries" programming.

A key factor at play is the absence of the earlier "competitive" standoff, as white evangelical women historically have not sought equality in status with their clergy. This is due to a variety of factors. For one, many evangelical denominations do not ordain women or allow them to preach, rendering hopes of equal status with world-renowned evangelists unimaginable. But the larger gender conservatism of the subculture as it relates to family roles is almost certainly also at play here: the high proportion of both evangelical men and women who believe "a woman's place is in the home" lowers the interests of even those women formally employed to invest in finding meaning in their Monday callings. This is due to many evangelical couples adhering to "complementary sacred callings" with each member fulfilling a distinct role relative to household and economic behavior.[30] Events asserting the value and dignity of work outside the household, then, would hold appeal only to one half of this duo. Katelyn Beaty, a former editor of *Christianity Today*, provides an overview of evangelical attitudes toward women and work in her book *A Woman's Place: A Christian Vision for Your Calling in the Office, Home, and Work*. Beaty finds that many evangelical leaders still overtly present motherhood as a woman's highest calling. Working and career-minded evangelical women—particularly unmarried women—can also experience marginalization within their own congregations, where female breadwinners have never been particularly accepted.[31] This predominantly leaves evangelical women on the sidelines of this status turf war outlined earlier.

My own observations of the faith and work space brought to light the way that a certain adaptiveness was demanded for navigating a space designed by and for a certain type of male worker. A frequent speaker and writer in the space recounts that it was her time out of the paid workforce while parenting children that made her recognize just how inadequate the conversation was for domestic, non-marketplace vocations. She authored a book that attempted to fill some of this void. One entrepreneur who had spoken at several conferences shared that she still felt there was "no place within the Christian church context for female entrepreneurial leadership callings." The church she had spent the most time in "was all about missions, all about ministry, but the only way that you could do ministry and missions is basically, if you're a man." Another female interviewee appeared pained to acknowledge the male dominance of the space. The phrase "it could be worse" was used four times in the span of two minutes:

> Lynn: Is it a male dominated space?
> Interviewee: (long pause) Yeah, it is, um . . . (longer pause) . . . it is, but it could be even worse than it is. Yeah it is, it is. (pause) I mean, it's not unusual for me to be the only female speaker on the docket or one of a

couple. . . . It's not unusual for me to look out at an audience and see more men than women. But that would be the point where I would say it could be even worse. Because I would say, on the whole, when it comes to larger speaking gigs like [specific examples given], my impression, anecdotally, is that it's a 60–40 [male to female] audience, but at [specific name of program she leads] it can even be 90–10. . . so it is male dominated, but it could be worse. . . . So yeah, unfortunately it is a male dominated space, um, but, you know, it could be worse.

A female business professor was subtly reminded of how gendered the space can be when speaking onstage at a national faith and work conference. Her talk took place amidst a lineup of eight rapid-fire presentations on faith and work that each concluded with the moderator coming on stage to pose a friendly follow-up question. All seven male speakers received questions engaging the subject matter on which they spoke. The moderator's chosen question for the female speaker, however, revolved around how she balanced work and family commitments. This was noticed by a handful of event attendees, who registered publicly visible complaints on the event's official smartphone app. But the incident went unaddressed by the event coordinators.

But there is also another factor at work that keeps women's presence in the space to a minimum: the parallel world of evangelical "women's programming."[32] The evangelical conference space, after all, continues to be shaped by a division of labor determined by market segmentation and consumer demand, and here, the very clearly demarcated gender roles of evangelicalism only reinforce how events are catered to niche audiences. Accordingly, women who take up the faith and work topic appear to land far more frequently on stages at women's conference rather than stages within *the* faith and work movement. Linda Rios Brook represents the first figure to blaze this trail, establishing a "Women in the Workplace" mini-conference in 2007 as part of a lead-in to a larger faith and work event. This was at the time one of the first major faith and work events on record. Brook's event dedicated a panel to discussing the challenge of juggling the various roles and tasks assumed by women. But beyond the lingering presence of her 2004 book, *Frontline Christians in a Bottom Line World*, Brooks is no longer active in the faith and work space.

Diane Paddison, a real estate corporate executive-turned-author, represents a more contemporary example. Her writing on faith and work has landed her not at national faith and work conferences but a combination of women's luncheons, women's fraternity groups, and women in the workplace themed events. Paddison's book—cleverly titled *Work, Love, Pray: Practical Wisdom for Professional Christian Women and Those Who Want to Understand Them*—puts forward practical advice for professional women balancing career, family, and church. The book articulates a personal experience that squarely fits within the social pioneer genre mentioned earlier: having successfully emerged from her Harvard MBA and settled into a Fortune 1000 company, Paddison recounts it being incredibly difficult to find a church that could aid her in making sense of her identity and her occupation. She marvels at churches tapping high-powered corporate women to make casseroles while their far less qualified husbands deliberate on church finance committee. "I soon learned that most churches don't quite know what to do with a woman who couldn't attend the 10:00 am women's Bible study because she was giving a presentation in a conference room two thousand miles away," Paddison recounts.[33] Brooks delivers the same assessment in the advertisement for the Women in the Workplace conference: "Working women are the most disenfranchised people group in the American Church," reads a pull quote positioned just below the conference title.[34] Paddison now runs an organization called 4word that aids women in navigating faith, family, and work. A similar organization called Propel also provides support, guidance, and conferences for career-minded evangelical women "called to step out, called to influence, called to lead." Both 4ward and Propel are composed of local chapters around the country that bring women together for networking, book clubs, Bible studies, and social events.[35]

Perhaps what is most telling about Paddison's role in the space—relevant to the competitive masculinity analysis provided above—is that Paddison's book is one of the rare faith and work books that spends very little time lavishing spiritual value and dignity onto secular work. Her first chapter recounts a crucial episode of considering a job offer with a significant pay raise but also the requirement to take her away from her family. The decision does not come down to which position would best allow her to fully participate in God's "redemptive purposes" or follow her God-ordained calling. Instead, Paddison is most concerned about balancing loyalties to family and church with financial security and new career challenges. Another female speaker in this space also speaks to these competing pressures, calling this the "Wonder Woman" challenge of simultaneously serving family, church, and career.[36] But Paddison's perception of competing work tensions is unique: instead of feeling caught between sacred work versus secular work,

Paddison speaks of navigating the "tensions that come up with two incomes, two careers . . . what happens if one of you enjoys success and promotions while the other one struggles?" The fact that few other faith and work books discuss such things may reveal why "women's faith and work" becomes relegated toward programming specifically designed for women: the dilemmas explored are ultimately attributable to the sharply defined gender roles that create far different experiences for career-oriented women in comparison to career-oriented men.

This specialization within woman's programming also has an inverse effect on the faith and work space. Pulling discussions of multi-career households, parenting, and family commitments *into* the space of woman's programming pulls such issues *out of* the wider faith and work space. Individualistic explorations of work are able to more easily venerate high-demand careers premised on what work scholars call "ideal worker norms": expectations that workers can toil long hours, shield their work from all outside responsibilities, and relocate or travel whenever requested.[37] Explorations of calling then take place *not* at the intersection of overlapping commitments and dependencies but instead within a metaphysical arena with only two relevant actors, the caller (God) and the one called (the worker). The wider culture surrounding work in the United States reinforces this notion of the abstracted, Promethean worker with few limits on their time and energies. Work researchers have pointed to how work-intensive norms reinforce gender inequality in the workplace by serving as advancement escalators for those most protected from family caregiving responsibilities. As these ideal workers ascend in the workplace hierarchy, the prevalent framework for worker achievement and worth becomes centered on one's ability to never permit private sphere issues to intrude on work performance and availability. This feat is of course not one that all workers can achieve, particularly those more engaged in family caregiving.[38] But what message does this ascendant ideal worker receive at a faith and work event? Largely the same one that is reinforced by workplace cultures built around ideal worker norms: one's worth as a worker relates closely to one's ability to unimpededly devote oneself to his or her career. But devoutness to career and calling is in many places a premium on insulation from family caregiving responsibilities.

The faith and work movement, as a byproduct of invisible sorting mechanisms and gendered social structures at work in the parachurch space, is able to funnel toward itself a particular type of economic actor while screening out others. Funneled away from this space are women and the family-spousal-career tensions of trying to "do it all." There is, notably, no discussion of the "Superdad" in the faith and work space and *his* challenge of fulfilling all obligations to parenting, caretaking, and church. Such challenges seem to only be deemed relevant to the "Wonder Women" hosting such discussions at alternative conferences.[39] This sorting only reinforces the parochial nature of the faith and work discussion, as it proves difficult to export its cultural frameworks to populations other than white, male, and creative class workers. With these assumptions so deeply ingrained within the faith and work content, it is likely that other spaces in the parachurch division of labor actually follow the same path as women's programming in hosting *their* respective faith and work conversation independently of *the* faith and work movement.

Meanwhile, the faith and work conversation may continue to serve as a primary pastoral setting for those workers whose work lives closely reflect the homo economicus actor most prized by the neoliberal economic order. This circles us back to the fundamental insight of Weber's own account of Protestantism and Christianity: the Protestantism that guides the faith and work movement today, much like that of the Puritans, appears distinctly equipped to produce worker subjectivites that prove to be deeply at home within the current economic order.

# 6
# From the Christian Right to the Corporate Right

*Christian Servants should be examples to all others of obedience and honesty, otherwise they will bring a reproach upon Religion, and brand themselves in the eyes of all as hypocrites. More is expected of them than of those who make no profession . . . if you are faithful in your station, you shall, as well as other men, higher and greater than yourself, obtain the Crown of Life. God places one man in one station and one in another, according to his will. What he requires is, that every man in his particular station, serve Him, and all will be well for time and Eternity.*

—Jas A. Sloan, 1857[1]

*Labor degrades no man. Labor is honorable, because the products of labor feed and clothe the world, and thus conduce to the welfare and happiness of mankind.*

—T. W. Hoit, 1860[2]

## Winning Hearts and Minds for Hayek

*Jesus was a theopreneuer, selling hope and love in his ministry.*

I sat in a room of round tables with the other conference attendees, munching on the complimentary lunch generously provided by the conference organizers. The elusive free lunch, offered at a gathering about economics, of all topics. How did this happen? Two days earlier I had caught a flight to the warm state of Florida, checked into my budget hotel, and explored by foot a very pedestrian-unfriendly part of Orlando. The conference I came to town to attend had popped up on my radar late in my research process: a three-day

*Saving the Protestant Ethic.* Andrew Lynn, Oxford University Press. © Oxford University Press 2023.
DOI: 10.1093/oso/9780190066680.003.0007

conference hosted by the Florida campus of Asbury Theological Seminary. One unusual detail of the event stuck out: the event was free to attend and all the meals were complimentary. This was slightly unusual among my research sites, but my Google queries revealed the conference was a recurring event, seemed to have a legitimate foothold in the world of faith and work, and was generating the expected level of buzz among the thought leaders I had been monitoring on Twitter. It appeared to be the real deal. Being accessible by discount airlines shuttling travelers to the center of Florida's tourism industry made it all the better. A perfect research site.

But while the conference proved in many ways to be a very run-of-the-mill event, this gathering also offered a much clearer view of how politically driven forces carefully shaped and cultivated the faith and work movement. Influences more obscured at other events were on full display here. In retrospect, there was good reason not to be surprised by this. To invoke the proverbial economic platitude, if there is no such thing as a free lunch, a free conference packaged with several free lunches also warrants skepticism. At this particular lunch on the first day, I was in the midst of conversation with other conference attendees when a speaker walked up to a podium on the side of the room. To my surprise, this was a "working lunch": a session not on the program. I grabbed my notebook from my bag to begin taking notes.

The speaker began by lamenting the individualistic "pietistic" church of his upbringing. Invoking themes common within the movement, the speaker criticized how little his "Sunday" faith had to say about Monday outside of working to pay church tithe and maintaining a private devotional life. But notably, the speaker, a Black pastor from a large metropolitan area, gave credit to a somewhat unexpected source for guiding for his escape from this pietistic form of faith. The Kern Family Foundation, a private foundation based in Minnesota, was his lifeline to a new way of thinking. And then, likely reflecting these resources' own theological content, the speaker prescribed a way forward out of the individual privatistic faith. The way forward was business. Jesus's public ministry was upheld as an example of entrepreneurship and business, labeled by the speaker as a "theopreneuer."

This is not a commonly used term in the faith and work movement: a Google search reveals it is not commonly used anywhere. The term was likely coined by either the speaker himself or those within his network. But what it signified was clear: Jesus provides an example of how workers can integrate faith and work through entrepreneurial activities in service to others. Of course, the Bible's descriptions of Jesus's ministry provide no reference to entrepreneurship, and the pricing scheme deployed for the services he offered does not suggest a sustainable business plan. But Jesus represents a theopreneuer by living out his calling within the public sphere. Christians, then, should also live out their callings in the public sphere of the marketplace.

A later talk in the conference revealed more of the underlying intellectual genealogy for this mode of faith and work. The speaker was Christopher Brooks, a figure who wears several hats as an author, Christian radio show host, pastor, and organizational leader in Detroit. The title of the talk he gave at this gathering was "Economic Thinking for City Pastors."[3] After beginning by speaking of the "tough" character of his hometown of Detroit, Brooks spent a great amount of time speaking at the abstract level of economic theory, skillfully incorporating theologians, economists, and political theorists. Brooks's articulation of remedial theology relied on the thought of Hugh Whelchel, the executive director of the Institute for Faith, Work, and Economics discussed below. Brooks drew on Whelchel to juxtapose Martin Luther's theology of work and the own culture in which he grew up: "Let me tell you the type of church that I grew up in. I grew up in a church that said if you couldn't preach or sing, you were only good for writing a check." Later in his talk: "The only way to prove you're serious about serving God is to join a committee that pulls you away from what you're doing." The solution, according to Brooks, was to extend the idea of callings to more than the "five percent of people who work for the local church." Brooks turned to the commandments in the New Testament to love God and love our neighbors. "The greatest tool for loving our neighbors and loving our communities is the gift of work," Brooks relayed. Brooks emphasized the need for integrating faith into other spheres of life several times: "We have a Christian worldview on Sunday mornings but not every day," he lamented. This theology of work was embedded within a more direct impetus to transform inner-city pastors into "community leaders" armed with particular economic frameworks.

Brooks shared with the audience that a Christian think tank called Acton Institute was critical to his formation in connecting faith with larger frameworks, describing his experience attending Acton University (an event designed to immerse clergy and laypeople in free-market and libertarian thought) as personally and spiritually transformative: "I felt like I was going through a born-again experience." Brooks then made the case that ethnic-minority and inner-city pastors must engage economics far more frequently than other pastors: "Because of the unique and ubiquitous challenges that you find in these types of communities, I find that urban pastors think about economics pretty consistently. You know, they're constantly facing things like budget shortfalls, or having to work in bi-vocational ministry . . . high congregation unemployment, the realities of ministering to underserved—and I just want to add here—traumatized communities." Toward the end of his talk, Brooks pushed his message toward developing a "biblical view of government." Overtly political themes began to emerge. Fretting that government can often "play God," Brooks lamented the efforts of government to "exchange liberties" for the "false promise of safety and provision," identifying minimum wage laws and national healthcare as part of these liberty-limiting efforts. Brooks ended his talk by the praising capacity for "strong families," "socially involved churches," and "free market economic thinking" to offset the need for governmental interventions. Brooks then switched to the final slide of his hour-long presentation and a picture of a statesman-like scholar appeared behind him. It seemed Brooks was out of time, so he tacked on only a brief explanation of this:

> We could also spend some time talking about this fellow [projecting an image of Friedrich von Hayek behind him]. If you don't know him, you should. F. A. Hayek. He's a very important figure when it comes to economic thinking. And so I'll stop there.

This was a strange way to end a talk on a number of levels. While Hayek won the Nobel Prize for Economics in 1974, he is not commonly encountered "in the wild" without reason.[4] But the promotion of Hayek and free market economic thinking to a room full of evangelicals reflects the "invisible hands" that worked to shape this and other programming in the faith and work space. The two talks summarized here managed to incorporate the full trifecta of groups unpacked in this chapter: the Kern Family Foundation, the Acton Institute, and the Institute for Faith, Work, and Economics. Likely due to major funding for this event coming directly from Kern, the speakers and attendees at this event regularly interwove the standard remedial theology of faith and work with pro-market and pro-business messages. One speaker identified a New Testament parable as crucial to helping him overcome his "fear" of money and to embrace entrepreneurial thinking. Several speakers took the stage to speak to issues of inequality or under-resourced urban neighborhoods but promoted the creation of new businesses rather than structural changes. Permeating the event was also the valorization of entrepreneurialism. An attendee I spoke with over dinner shared her optimism that the event could help her leave her receptionist job at a local hospital to launch a startup producing religious curriculum for children. Reinforcing these visions of self-guided entrepreneurial efforts, the event concluded with a social entrepreneurship pitch competition.

The seminary hosting and sponsoring the conference is a satellite campus of Asbury Theological Seminary in Kentucky, a century-old seminary established in the Wesleyan tradition. Asbury is one of twenty-one Christian seminaries to receive support from Kern Family Foundation through an initiative called the Oikonomia Network, receiving just over half a million dollars in the most recent year for which financial data are available. The funding was at least partially allocated for the establishment of an "Office on Faith, Work, and Economics" program at Asbury, which then coordinated and hosted this annual conference. The office also undertakes other initiatives at Asbury, creating and promoting a new Doctorate of Ministry focused on faith, work, and economics, shaping new seminary curricula available to the wider seminary, and providing research grants to Asbury faculty and students studying relevant topics. The office also coordinates a small business incubator and several other social entrepreneurship business pitch competitions.

From an idea-dissemination or culture-influence perspective, the Asbury event provided a valuable platform to promote libertarian ideas where they almost certainly do not naturally reside. In sharp contrast to the rest of my fieldwork, the Orlando event drew very few white attendees. In one session of approximately sixty attendees, I appeared to be the only white person in the room. White speakers on the platform were also significantly outnumbered. I asked two people involved in coordinating this conference about the audience demographics, but neither was certain why the event might draw such a high proportion of non-white populations.[5] Regardless of the cause, the event seemed to bring a non-white audience together to hear a significant amount of discussion on community development and responses to poverty that was almost completely built around the ideas of white and European Evangelical thinkers: Abraham Kuyper, Chuck Colson, Andy Crouch, and Hugh Whelchel. Notably absent were any voices from the Black Protestant tradition—neither its more prophetic tradition nor writings that specifically engage race, historically marginalized communities, and historical injustices. Hayekian libertarianism appeared to be filling the space that might otherwise be filled by a far different approach to theology and social ethics.

## The Capitalism War and the New Corporate Right

The cultural frameworks that permeate the faith and work movement can be understood as functioning to serve workers in any number of ways. Up to this point we have explored the movement as providing cultural frameworks that channel religious energies toward sacralizing and stabilizing participation in economic activity. But cultural frameworks related to work also possess a particular sort of political or ideological power. The rise of the faith and work movement opened up a space for politically oriented groups to contend over evangelical laity's orientations toward work, economics, and capitalism more generally. Contention over economic imaginaries could be classified as a new front in the well-worn "culture war" more commonly associated with issues like family, gender, the arts, and education. However, the groups leading the charge are not the same as those groups most active in the culture war. Battle-tested groups like Focus on the Family, the Christian Coalition, or National Right to Life are nowhere to be seen. Instead, a combination of big business interests, private foundations, free market think tanks, and political lobbying groups appear to be advancing a politicized agenda. This conflict also appears to entail different goals or perceived spoils of victory: the groups committing resources to such efforts are not necessarily attempting to propel particular candidates into office or support ballot initiatives. The spoils instead are the hearts and minds of the evangelical: the economic imaginaries that shape their non-formal economic orientations toward their day-to-day lives.

Prior work has labeled the activities of some actors in this space as a pivot from the old guard Christian Right to the new guard Corporate Right.[6] In the sections that follow, I focus on how these Corporate Right actors have particularly taken up residency within the culture-producing space associated with the faith and work movement. Their efforts and resources primarily attempt to elevate particular sacralizing and stabilizing frameworks that can instill belief not only that *work* matters to God, but that the capitalist system in which that work takes place also bears God's favor.

It is worth briefly exploring how religion and other meaning systems serve the ideological interests of economic systems. Religious systems hold a unique capacity to sacralize and stabilize the existing social order and its accompanying social hierarchies, thereby legitimating the social position of those occupying subordinate status within that social order.[7] This function is clearly on display in cases like sermons from the Middle Ages that condemned aspirations of moving up in the social hierarchy as prideful, instead charging the poor of the era to "struggle against the vices peculiar to their social class."[8] In the era of early industrial capitalism, the ideological function of Christianity garnered even greater attention. Many historians of the nineteenth century identify major shifts in both work conditions and the wider cultural order that suddenly put a premium on frameworks that could solidify worker compliance and docility.[9]

How does the faith and work movement fit within this lineage? Are faith and work leaders continuing to churn out updated "spirits of capitalism" that sacralize participation in the economic system? Before turning to this question, it might first help to identify where the faith and work movement does *not* devote its sacralizing energies. First, there are no visible organizations, leaders, or resources in the movement that engage in efforts to make religious interventions in the form of "human resources" or organizational improvement techniques. Movement leaders do not preach the merits of team-building practices, management styles, effective employee retention strategies, or efficient organizational structure.[10] One indication of this neglect in its focus is the movement's only miniscule footprint within the wider "workplace spirituality" movement, a scholarly and practitioner-driven movement which *does* devote the majority of its energies to exploring means of spiritualizing and optimizing organizational performance and practice.[11] Certainly, many faith and work leaders assure their audiences that their offerings will make the work experience better, but this improvement is yielded primarily through intersubjective benefits of applying particular frameworks of meaning.[12] This "improvement plan" is largely agnostic on particular organizational practices, techniques, or structures.

The other omission is any paternalistic messaging exclusively directed toward those at the lowest rungs of the labor hierarchy. This point requires some unpacking: certainly, the faith and work movement provides ample cultural resources for ennobling labor of all varieties, and this message is easily transposable to even the most degrading and alienating forms of labor. That becomes a central topic in next section. But there *is* a void of any content specifically targeting populations perceived as excessively victimized by the modern economic system. In other words, the message of faith and work leaders is that "we" all are toiling and laboring, whether the CEO, the stay-at-home-parent, the pastor, or the call center employee. The universalism of this message could be attributed to a number of sources, including the spiritual egalitarianism of Protestantism that runs all the way back to Luther.

However, my own interpretation, as laid out below, would suggest that this universal message may be driven by the absence of a certain interpretive repertoire within evangelicalism's understanding of modern political economy. As several previous studies of white evangelicalism reveal, many evangelicals are adherents to a mode of individualism that, while common across wider American society, is made more salient by a combination of theological, cultural, and racial factors that intersect with evangelicalism's central populace.[13] One central feature of this individualism is the discounting of influence or causal efficacy of social structures that shape and pattern the basic experiences of opportunity and moral agency. Instead, a preference for individualistic free will and personal responsibility means that even questions of political economy are translated into visions of atomistic individuals pursuing courses of actions largely independent of (and therefore unimpeded by) structural relations.[14]

It then becomes difficult for white evangelicals to preach a message curated for a particular location in the social hierarchy: their overarching interpretation of the social order fails to recognize that such hierarchies exist. Leaders are more likely to adhere to a classless understanding of society as an aggregate sum of atomistic individuals. In this view, we are all simply "laborers" marching off to our respective workplaces on Monday. Moral paternalism toward a particular social stratum then becomes difficult to locate.[15]

## Three Tactics in the New Capitalism War

The actors seeking to politicize the faith and work spare employ three different tactics to effectively win evangelical hearts and minds over to their own preferred frameworks. We will break down each in turn before assessing the general effectiveness of each tactic.

### Lowering the Ethical Floor of Dignified Labor: Dispensing Certainty Amidst Unstable Economic Conditions

*Whatever circumstances you find yourself in, remember that you are working ultimately for your God.*

*Just as God needed Joseph to be in prison, God needs you to be there [at your job] right now.*

> *If you have a job or employment, it's because God has deployed you to it.*
>
> *What matters is not your perfect job but faithful service to the king.*
>
> *God is sovereign over every detail of your life and you don't know how it will work out. It doesn't matter because it all ends up at the feet of Jesus anyway. At the end we will say to the Lord, "To you belongs all the glory, honor, and praise."*

All of these statements come from the faith and work event described in greater detail in Chapter 3.[16] At that gathering, in a packed church of mostly middle-class and professional evangelical laity, speakers preached a message of encouragement and assurance for workers who confront challenges and struggles in their economic lives. Yet because the economic sphere cannot be sequestered from God's purposes, its struggles and challenges, too, must be seen as part of God's intentions. In many ways, these statements of assurance are deeply linked to the re-integrating framework outlined in Chapter 4. After all, part of realizing "your work matters to God" is recognizing that the economic conditions in which you find yourself are not arbitrary arrangements but are divinely ordained. God has "deployed" you there. You can have assurance that your predicament is part of God's sovereign plan. And locating your plight within that plan, then, confers eternal significance onto present experiences, challenges, and opportunities. This opens the door to naturalizing the economic system at large, a separate tactic we will explore below.

Such framing of work—particularly its imputation of eternal weight onto one's economic role and position—accomplishes at least two things. For one, it undoubtedly cultivates personal commitment and discipline toward work. This is essentially what Weber observes of the frenzied Protestant work ethic, which he narrated as "the intensity of the search for the Kingdom of God" which gradually "pass[ed] over into sober economic virtue."[17] With such eternal weight infused upon one's work efforts, the notion of opting out of work altogether would be deemed morally offensive to God himself, if imaginable at all. Labor instead becomes enmeshed within one's spiritual role, identity, and status before God. A 1982 text reprinted and promoted by the Acton Institute makes clear the spiritual importance of labor participation: "God does indeed display, throughout the Bible, great concern for the poor. . . . But the poor God loves are, as is evident from St. Paul's rule requiring work in order to eat, the unwilling poor, those who are in need because they cannot find, or cannot do, work." This presumably leaves a population of the poor who may be disqualified from God's love: those who do not work. "God is no sentimentalist!" the same text goes on to say, before providing a terse summary of Paul's writing in the New Testament: "Work, if you can, or starve!"[18]

But this leads to the second implication: these frameworks elevate the phenomenological experience of work over objective conditions in which work takes place. The phenomenological experience of meaningful work, then, can be effectively abstracted from the conditions under which one enters into work. The "dignity of work" is often celebrated without any indication of whether it is being performed by serfs, wage-laborers, self-employed entrepreneurs, short-term contract workers, members of a collectivist society, or an enslaved workforce. And ultimately, addressing such questions of objective conditions becomes irrelevant: work's significance and dignity may be deemed inviolable and inalienable.

Contemporary scholars of work helpfully label the decoupling of work conditions and work experience the "subjectivist" turn in discussions of meaningful work.[19] This decoupling bears important consequence for all parties invested in worker productivity and engagement: it assigns the strongest causal efficacy in determining worker performance to subjective feelings *rather than objective conditions*. The result is the primacy of workers' subjectivities as the primary avenues for not only assessing the meaningfulness of work, but also the primary avenue for intervening upon, modifying, and improving it. White conservative Protestantism has a long record of dignifying hard labor by way of reducing evaluation to worker subjectivities. This practice became salient in dignifying labor performed under the conditions of slavery.[20] The first two epigraphs of this chapter depict how these tactics were deployed by Christian ministers in the nineteenth century: slavery should not be condemned because all labor is "honorable" and its products "feed and clothe the world, and thus conduce to the welfare and happiness of mankind." "Coercive labor," the same text goes on to add afterward, is no less honorable than any other form of labor.[21] An 1857 pro-slavery religious tract titled *The Great Question Answered; or, Is Slavery a Sin Itself (Per Se?) Answered According to the Teaching of the Scriptures* draws a tight equivalence between the moral worthiness of labor and slavery, arguing that God established both in the book of Genesis, with slavery thought to be established by the curse placed upon Ham. The author sees these decrees so tightly linked that those objecting to racialized slavery would be objecting to labor itself.[22] An 1837 Christian catechism with the subtitle "designed also for the oral instruction of colored persons" sprinkles Scripture references through a passage on the "duties of servants" before summarizing its moral dictates:

> Servants are to count their Masters "*worthy of all honour*," as those to whom God has placed over them in this world: "*with all fear*," they are to *be subject to them*; and obey them *in all things*, possible and lawful, with *good will and endeavor to please them well*, so that there may be no occasion for fault-finding or correction, and let Servants serve their masters as faithfully behind their backs as before their faces.[23]

As these earlier theologies of work reveal, one product the subjective turn is the removal of any "ethical floor" regarding the objective conditions in which work can be meaningful and dignified. In other words, both the problems and solutions of unmeaningful or undignified work become located within the interpretative schemas of workers' minds. This brings to light the unmistakable compatibility of lowering the ethical floor of meaningful work and the free-market, anti-regulation agenda that animates Acton, Kern, and the Koch brothers' larger interests. Steering America's largest religious constituency toward such a theology stands to legitimate an economic system that demands greater docility, flexibility, and fluidity from a labor force. For lower-skilled workers navigating the present economic system, their obligations to dutifully submit to work are not contingent on such work offering protections from market fluctuations, competitive pressures, or stagnant and declining wages. Faith and work theology can then transform a bad job into a "good" job—a job that matters to God—without altering the conditions of that work whatsoever.[24] This perspective then renders superfluous collective organizing or political interventions that might otherwise seek to improve objective conditions, as work is already inherently "good" in and of itself.

## Channeling Evangelicals Away from Progressive Activism

The second tactic employed is perhaps the least conventional of the three. Culture-producing organizations involved in the faith and work organization see their promotion of meaningful work as part of a proxy war against a handful of left-leaning religious figures. Faith and work leaders position faith and work theology as vehicle to shore up greater loyalties to the economic system at large. Success in cultivating these loyalties, according to the logic at work here, then builds resistance to the beckoning call of the "evangelical left" and their anti-capitalist sentiments.

Some context is important here. For several decades, journalists and other observers of American evangelicalism have popularized notions of a certain fragility to the conservative voting patterns of a younger generation of evangelicals. Political analyses since at least 2004 have generated headlines like "Emphasis Shifts for a New Breed of Evangelicals," "Why Young Evangelicals Are Leaving the Church," "Millennials: Why the Young Religious Right Is Leaning Left."[25] Though political scientists and pollsters report this voting bloc actually shows no indication of fragility, there remains among older conservative leaders a haunting sense that the "youth" of the subculture are on the verge of deserting the traditional conservativism of their parents. A revolving list of hot political issues are typically portrayed as the instigators of unraveling the coalition, whether poverty, human trafficking, racial reconciliation, global aid, or climate change. Typically, these accounts include references to a handful of religious left leaders always threatening to poach conservative youth: Ron Sider, Tony Campelo, Jim Wallis, and Shane Claiborne.

Leaders of the organizations discussed above all perceived themselves engaged in a struggle against these left-leaning leaders. Strangely, I never witnessed any of the actual ideas of these left-leaning leaders ever directly engaged: this struggle takes the form of shadowboxing an opponent lurking just out of view. I likely would not have known these figures bore any relevance to the movement had I not asked all the movement leaders I interviewed whom they saw themselves working against. The Acton Institute leaders, in response to this question, named Wallis's Sojourners group, Sider's Evangelicals for Social Action, and the left-oriented Center for Public Justice. Likewise, the director of Kern's Faith, Work, and Economics efforts identified the rise of "social justice mentality" among some Christian colleges inciting the concern that drove Kern's involvement: "So if you looked at the popularity of Jim Wallis, Tony Campolo, or Shane Claiborne, in some ways there's a different argument being made in the case of free enterprise and the moral case for work, rather than saying, effectively, some form of redistribution is the best way to help the poor." Similarly, Kern's director of faith and work programming pointed to an American Enterprise Institute video as reflecting the preferred response to social issues that could avoid the "social justice mentality."[26] This partnership was spelled out more directly in a 2011 *Philanthropy Today* article that recounts Kern's partnership with the American Enterprise

Institute as motivated by worries that younger evangelicals "no longer see the connections between following God and serving others in a free marketplace." The identified danger, as described earlier, was younger evangelicals being "increasingly attracted to leftish arguments for 'social justice' and its resulting dependencies."[27] Kern has funded debates between free market advocates and their favorite nemeses Shane Claiborne and Jim Wallis, including one debate taking place at Wheaton College. These debates—often framed around highly abstract questions like "Was Jesus a capitalist or a socialist?"—are perceived as part of their efforts to fight this leftward evangelical drift.

But *how* faith and work frameworks represent a response to a "social justice mentality" or redistributive social policy is not a straightforward matter. The faith and work movement, after all, deals almost exclusively in the non-formal side of economic frameworks, which is largely sequestered from formal economic views of the system at large. The ever-threatening "evangelical left" leaders, for their part, also produce very little writing on work, purpose, and meaningful callings, creating an awkward mismatch between the content of faith and work literature and more explicitly political texts written by Sider, Wallis, and Claiborne. The leaders of Kern and Acton, however, saw their efforts as serving to syphon off would-be activists by enticing them with God-ordained purposes *through* economic activity. The thinking here is that energy channeled toward Monday "marketplace callings" is energy channeled away from activism that might challenge market functioning more generally. IFWE scholar Anne Bradley, in a 2016 *Washington Times* special section on faith and work, brought her own angle to this effort to syphon off would-be activists. Bradley suggested that Christians should see their economic choices, rather than their voting choices, as the most effective means to bring about the common good and creating change. "Voting with our feet through the market provides countless opportunities for us to use our God-given gifts to help others," she argues.[28] For all these leaders, arriving at a proper understanding of marketplace vocation goes hand in hand with resisting appeals to harness the state and economic policy to pursue social justice or the common good.

## Sacralizing Laissez-Faire Capitalism

Finally, as seen by the inclusion of Hayek in the earlier described presentation, faith and work leaders on occasion inject free-market and laissez-faire economic ideas into the standard faith and work message. In general, these efforts mirror the earlier cases in evangelical history of "business Christianity" or "Christian libertarianism" that have always occupied certain corners of American Protestantism.[29] The most easily recognizable sign of this addendum being made is the subtle latching of the word "economics" onto the end of the more conventional "faith and work" label. Other phrases also appear far more often in this "faith, work, and economics" space: "the role of business in society," "biblical economics," and the ever-so-popular word "freedom." On this front, the three organizations of interest commonly draw on each other's work while also weaving in resources from the American Enterprise Institute. Both Kern and IFWE often promote what the Acton Institute has labeled its faith and work "primer" series, published on the Acton-directed Christian Library Press. Each primer is written by a well-known author from a particular Protestant tradition or denomination: at present they have published these works for Baptists, the Reformed tradition, Wesleyans, Lutherans, and Pentecostals. These primers are not surfacy or pop-devotional works: the writers are all recognized as reputable systematic theologians deeply informed on their own tradition. Acton's think tank headiness shines through these works in their impressive citation lists of sociologists, economists, and historians dotting the pages and filling longer-than-normal bibliographies. But this academic level of writing is complemented by skillful marketing and packaging, particularly at faith and work events. All of the books' covers are filled with glowing reviews by faith and work leaders, denominational heads, and even widely influential figures like Rick Warren.

Setting these works side by side reveals a shared pattern: the commissioned authors lay out the familiar remedial theology of the movement but with the inflection of that author's respective tradition. Prominently featured is a dismissal of the vocational hierarchy and any sacred-secular divides that threaten to devalue everyday work. The authors then are able to declare work itself as sacred and intended by God, falling squarely in the re-integrating camp of theologies of work. Generally, notions of creation and redemption are developed that open up a space for lay Christians' participation in God's activity and intention for the world through their work, with Kuyper's creational mandate either lurking in the background or explicitly embraced, depending on the respective tradition. Authoritative thinkers are generally called upon to back up many of these arguments: Jonathan Edwards, John Wesley, A. W. Tozer, etc. But from there, the primers weigh in on specific political issues.[30] Perhaps the most consistent element is an effort to sacralize work as an opportunity to participate in the generative and creative aspects of contemporary capitalism, and here, a familiar cast of free market economists emerge from the wings to take center stage: Thomas Sowell, Michael Novak, Milton Friedman, and Friedrich Hayek. From there, the books effectively stitch together a grab bag of political and social issues while patching them into the earlier theological doctrine of work.[31] Governmental aid programs, environmental regulation, and economic regulations are the usual targets. Interestingly, identity politics are completely absent from these books, as is any discussion of race, historical injustices, immigration, or postindustrial changes in the labor market. This is a more classical Cold War conservatism that bears all the marks of 1950s–1980s *National Review* fusionism. Frequently, one sees Marvin Olasky's Bush-era "compassionate conservatism" dusted off and offered up as an alternative to "planning" and redistribution. Other times, a stern warning is issued against visions of social improvement that do not ultimately rely on individual regeneration as the only pathway to true social change, a throwback to the Grahamism outlined earlier.

A similar presentation of "faith, work, and economics" runs through a glossy thirty-one-page pamphlet for the "Economic Wisdom Project," a program of Oikonomia, which articulates Kern's commitments to economic ideas alongside remedial theology. The relatively short pamphlet lists a remarkable number of "recommended resources" that could be divided into two categories: popular evangelical writers (Dallas Willard, Tim Keller, Katherine Alsdorf, Os Guinness, John Stott) and social and economic conservative thinkers (Hernando de Soto, Michael Novak, Marvin Olasky). Also promoted are resources from the American Enterprise Institute and the Acton Institute, a synthesis of messaging also reflected in Kern's YouTube Channel offering resources for their Oikonomia project.[32] Oikonomia has sponsored over one hundred seminary professors to attend Acton University and many times draws on Acton-affiliated authors and fellows for their own conference speaking lineup.

Made to Flourish is the other Kern-created organization active in the faith and work space, this one aimed at supporting churches and building regional groups of leaders to foster faith and work discussions. For a time, the Made to Flourish networks were hosted within the Acton Institute before being split off as its own organization. The organization has conducted "learning communities" in twelve cities and now boasts of localized "city networks" of pastors in twenty-six cities. Made to Flourish's website also seemed to position faith and work as an entry point to laissez-faire capitalism and libertarian political philosophy. Books promoted on the website included: *The Virtues of Capitalism: A Moral Case for Free Markets*; *Money, Greed, and God: Why Capitalism Is the Solution and Not the Problem*; and *Poverty and Wealth: Why Socialism Doesn't Work*. Unfortunately, I was not able to observe any Made to Flourish local gatherings to see what role these ideas play in their events, but archived e-newsletters sent out to the network's members (pastors and community leaders) promoted new releases of Acton's faith and work primers and encouraged attendance at Acton University, described as "a great opportunity to go deeper in the 'economics' portion of faith, work, and economics integration."

Finally, the work of the Institute for Faith, Work, and Economics stands on its own for its explicit economic messaging. There is little ambiguity regarding the Institute's intended purposes in the faith and work space: their efforts have been described by critics as "faith-washing" free market economics. Compared to the other groups described here, they seem to feel less constrained by the need to package their economic and political views around the standard remedial theology of work, instead often cutting to the chase and promoting libertarian ideas independent of any specific work content. An earlier Institute initiative led to a very public clash in the pages of *Christianity Today*. An IFWE-produced video called "I, Smartphone" (intended as a tribute to the classic libertarian essay, "I, Pencil") championed the pursuit of self-interest and the powers of the invisible hand to coordinate activities through markets. An Asbury University business professor, writing in *Christianity Today*, criticized the video and the organization for uncritically deifying the free market while ignoring economic externalities and harms incurred by global capitalism. IFWE, in response, assembled various statements from many scholars affiliated with their organization—and some scholars affiliated with Acton—to defend the video and the virtue of markets.[33]

In my interview with leaders of these organizations, the Acton Institute's leaders were perhaps the most open about their economic messaging. Acton Institute programming director Jordan Ballor tied Acton's presence in the faith and work back to the organization's founding mission: "Our two founders were disturbed by the lack of economic knowledge—just very little exposure to fundamental ideas—among the clergy, and the result being that when the clergy speaks to these topics, whether from the pulpit or publicly, it was usually misinformed or kind of unconsciously embraced a left-wing or government focused kind rather than being responsible about the place of free enterprise, entrepreneurship, and so on." Acton's intentions echoed the intended purposes listed on their nonprofit tax filings: their mission was to create materials that "target current and future religious, business, and community leaders" to "promote an understanding of market principles" that "encourages the economic freedom that creates opportunity for all." The faith and work movement seemed to have come on their radar as a new potential vehicle for pursuing these ends.

Leaders of Kern-backed initiatives were more reticent of pushing particular political agendas. The director of Kern's own faith and work programming—which initially served as the funding source from which Oikonomia and Made to Flourish originated—followed Acton's lead in openly narrating their battle with redistributism and a "social justice mentality." But other leaders did not see their efforts as part of this project. Tom Nelson, director of Made to Flourish, explicitly distinguished his organization's vision as less partisan than that of Acton or the Kern Foundation itself: "We're not pushing some ideology, we're not pushing some school of economics." The vision instead was to "help pastors think carefully about their responsibility in the collective flourishing of people." Greg Forster, director of the Oikonomia project and former director of Kern's faith and work programming, put emphasis on helping seminary professors overcome a lack of economic education. Forster was quite adamant that Oikonomia's work was not engaged in morally defending capitalism itself, clarifying that he had even stopped invoking the term "capitalism" in his work to avoid unhelpful ideological battles. But neither Nelson nor Forster provided any acknowledgment of or reflection on their respective organizations' promotion of exclusively conservative and libertarian economic thinkers.

Hugh Whelchel, executive director of IFWE, viewed his organization's heavily politicized messaging somewhat differently. The first hour of our interview was entirely about his passion for the standard remedial theology of faith and work with no reference to politics. However, on being directly asked about his organization's relationship to larger Koch lobbying efforts, Whelchel confirmed IFWE's close relationship to the parallel 501(c)4 sister organization and the Koch network more widely. For Whelchel, the only real objection to be identified as "part of the network" was that the Koch brothers were not known to be Christians. "Particularly on that [501]C4 side, we believe there's nothing wrong with coming alongside people that—now, once again, we realize that they're not believers, and at some point, we understand that we have a loose alliance with them. It's not a firm partnership, that's why we're not, quote, part of the network, unquote." But setting aside these differences, Whelchel did not seem to raise objections to the characterization that his efforts were part of the Koch organization's "sales force" for popularizing libertarian ideas. The only objection he raised to this characterization was insisting that IFWE was committed to conservative social values that were not always shared by the Koch brothers themselves.[34]

## Assessing Wins and Losses in the Capitalism War

Fully evaluating the effectiveness of this battle for "hearts and minds" requires far more data on the faith and work movement than what is presently available. My own assessment is that each of the three tactics reviewed here—lowering the ethical floor of work, diverting religious left activism, and popularizing laissez-faire political views—have achieved remarkably different outcomes. For the first tactic, the subjectivization of the dignity of work is by far the most foundational aspect of nearly all faith and work materials and every event I attended, so on this front, the Corporate Right's efforts appear maximally successful. In fact, politicized efforts on this front might be redundant to the movement at large: the faith and work movement marches with lockstep unity in declaring that *all* work matters to God and possesses inherent dignity. The commitments to an individualist ontology only reinforce the subjectivization of work's meaning and significance, perhaps magnified by the Romantic-grounded message of harmony and integration. The one-and-one relationship between worker and God takes place on a cosmic plane where conditions of work and political economy appear irrelevant.

Effectiveness on the second tactic—diverting young adult laity from the clutches of the religious left—also appears to be successful, at least on the surface. The evangelical voting bloc on the whole appears to show no signs of fissures in national or state elections, and more specific to the faith and work space, I did not encounter anyone who was promoting a "social justice mentality." But the necessity of these efforts, too, might be put to question. While evangelical religious left leaders may receive a hearing at seminaries and among pockets of progressive evangelicals, these leaders have never actually drawn a particularly large constituency. The politicization of evangelicalism since the 1970s likely ensures that this constituency remains relatively small, as the tighter linkage between evangelicalism and conservative politics likely constrains the number of progressive-minded laity that continue to identify with evangelicalism. Defectors from political evangelicalism appear far more likely to exit evangelicalism altogether. These dynamics ensure that the "market share" for cultural products produced by evangelical left leaders remains limited. We thus arrive at a similar assessment as the first tactic: the desired outcome has been achieved, but perhaps not because of any particular effort pursued within the faith and work space.

On the third tactic, however, the outcome is far more complex. It is important to note that the actors who lead efforts to inject economics into the space have *themselves* assessed their success to be somewhat limited. All the leaders of the organizations mentioned here—with the exception of IFWE—have voiced skepticism that their efforts have been particularly effective. The Acton Institute's Ballor shared that their "economic agenda" might not be a good fit for this arena: "There's definitely been a boom in what I would call faith and work, which is more about the individual experience than what I would say is about structural change or structural critique and engagement." As recently as 2014, Forster recounted a similar challenge: the basic faith and work integration piece had produced "strong buy-in" much faster than anticipated, but the "economic connection" piece pushed by Kern appears to be a "hard road" yielding a less immediate buy-in.[35] Nelson, in our interview, also recounted that pastors find it more challenging to grasp the economic piece of their educating efforts: "Frankly, I think the biggest question I have as a pastor is: 'I get the faith and work thing, but I don't get the economic thing.'" Perhaps IFWE's leadership does not identify this same challenge because their efforts are more loosely tethered to work in the first place. The organization's very intentional knowledge-disseminating mission grants them an exceptional level of freedom in this battle for hearts and minds, as they appear more willing to rewrite the rules of engagement wherever needed.

What all of these efforts are likely up against is the fundamentally subjectivist and personal aspect of white American evangelicalism. They are essentially facing off against Grahamism, the mode of evangelicalism identified earlier that favors pre-millennial eschatology, soul-saving, and individual regeneration. The results are a mixed bag: Grahamism likely contributes to the success of their first tactic, while simultaneously limiting the success of the third tactic. As summarized earlier, white evangelicals are not particularly apt to think about social structures, even if the "economics" addendum to their faith and work theology largely aspires to deify or naturalize these structures. This might suggest that the rather unusual end of Christopher Brooks's talk described earlier actually captures how these messages struggle to find a place in the larger faith and work conversation: leaders struggle to make room for Austrian economics in the remedial theology that ultimately revolves around personal experience and individual faith. A two-sentence shout-out to the wisdom of Hayek at the end of an hour-long presentation is the end result. Vocation and Von Mises, as it turns out, are not a match made in heaven.[36]

But perhaps the most complex part of arriving at a solid assessment of these efforts' effectiveness is a component of the movement that showed up again and again in my field notes and interview transcripts: the vast majority of lectures, talks, conference themes, session themes, curriculum, books promoted, sermon series, Bible commentaries, worship songs, podcasts, and workshops conducted in the faith and work space *contain absolutely no content* related to economic policy or the functioning of markets more broadly. What shows up again and again is the basic presentation of remedial theology—the adverbial theologies, the challenges of Monday, the leveling of vocational hierarchy, etc.—that was repeated ad nauseum in all the cultural materials I reviewed, with the rare exceptions being the materials recounted in this chapter. Of the five national conferences I attended, the Asbury Seminary conference was the only exception in its promotion of specifically political content: the other four conferences did not articulate or promote any direct political or economic agendas. Seventeen other gatherings and events observed also contained no visible political messaging. Interviews with leaders of faith and work organizations—even those organizations leading the capitalism war—were not economically or politically charged conversations: these leaders also just wanted to talk about remedial theology and generally could speak for 30–45 minutes on work without mentioning any element of formal economics. In all cases, where economic views were discussed, it was the result of my explicit prompting and invitation to do so. Additionally, against the possibility that perhaps political commitments were purposefully masked behind an innocuously packaged remedial theology, no interviewed leaders took any issue with my direct questioning on their political and economic agendas. They in fact appeared to be entirely *uninterested* in my probing, seeming to react as if I had pushed them far outside their general talking points or area of expertise.

This would lend credence to the insights of organizational leaders of Acton, Kern, and IFWE: they do indeed find themselves swimming upstream in terms of appending a political message onto the movement's message. These leaders may be achieving their greatest success in instrumentalizing the faith and work space as an on-ramp to their more explicitly political programming, such as attracting new attendees to the Acton Institute's summer seminar, getting pastors to order books praising the virtues of markets, or following IFWE's conservative commentary on public policy. But in the faith and work movement space itself, these efforts had continual difficulty unmooring evangelical laity from their individualistic orientation to economic systems and their behavior within them.

# 7
# From Culture Wars to Cultural Stewardship

> *Christian asceticism, at first fleeing from the world into solitude, had already ruled the world which it had renounced from the monastery, and through the church. But it had, on the whole, left the naturally spontaneous character of daily life untouched. Now it strode into the market-place of life, slammed the door of the monastery behind it, and undertook to penetrate just that daily routine of life in the world, but neither or nor for this world.*
>
> —Max Weber, *The Protestant Ethic and the Spirit of Capitalism*[1]

> *. . . the idea of duty to one's calling prowls about in our lives like the ghost of dead religious beliefs.*
>
> —Max Weber, *The Protestant Ethic and the Spirit of Capitalism*[2]

## "You Have to Be in the Room"

Attending faith and work events took me into all kinds of venues, from old churches to seminary classrooms to hotel banquet halls. These spaces are generally very similar, adequately serviceable, and entirely unremarkable. But it was an event entitled (all too appropriately) "Disruption" that diverged from these other conference-hopping experiences. I arrived at a restored railyard-building-turned-modern-office-building in the West Chelsea Historic District of lower Manhattan, only a block away from the High Line. Located on the third floor was my destination, the Center for Social Innovation, a chic co-working and event space. "Elegant yet rustic, colorful yet industrial," touted the venue's website, a description I would not contest. It was clear the architects had prided themselves in preserving the building's original open industrial feel, with several garage-door-style room dividers, furniture made from repurposed materials, and liberal usage of Edison light bulbs. In the

*Saving the Protestant Ethic.* Andrew Lynn, Oxford University Press. © Oxford University Press 2023.
DOI: 10.1093/oso/9780190066680.003.0008

more open areas, inspirational quotes in disparate typefaces adorned the walls, casting their motivational energies over whatever occupants undertook their innovative labor in the space. On entering I hung my jacket on a rustic looking wall that bore a plaque explaining its origins as repurposed wood from an old nunnery.

The event was part of a larger series, the ninth annual Entrepreneurship and Innovation Forum, sponsored by the Center for Faith and Work, an organization housed at Redeemer Presbyterian Church in Manhattan. This was one of the many annual faith and work events launched in the early 2000s that quickly generated a regular following. The lead-up email had promised a "weekend together taking a look at how disruption leads to innovation." A small event program patched together quotes from Peter Drucker and the Book of Isaiah amidst a speaking lineup of largely business start-up founders and a few popular faith and work authors. The second day featured two of the most popular thinkers in the faith and work movement: Katherine Alsdorf and David H. Kim. Alsdorf played a fairly ceremonious role in the proceedings, coming on stage only to welcome the crowd and describe the wider reaching efforts of the Center for Faith and Work. But in her concise summary of the Center's work, Alsdorf employed the theme of disruption to summarize three major interventions made by the faith and work movement. "We have disrupted the Sunday morning church model. We have disrupted the hierarchy of vocations. And we have disrupted how theology enters into everything we do."

It was the first night's lecture that captured one of the more central elements of the faith and work movement. The evening's keynote speaker was Michael Lindsay, a president of an evangelical seminary. While an academic and college administrator might at first appear out of step with the event's entrepreneurial focus, Lindsay's promised expertise illuminates one of the most central dimensions of this gathering: the "stewarding" of cultural power. For nearly a decade, Lindsay had been interviewing elites in leadership across societal sectors—business leaders, politicians, nonprofit executives, presidents of foundations and universities, influential religious figures, etc. His end goal was conducting over five hundred interviews. While he is by trade and training a cultural sociologist, this project seemed designed and executed to produce knowledge relevant to "leadership studies" or the trade-book CEO-guru-type writing.[3] The research seemed predicated on the assumption that leaders possess the capacity to identify and to articulate the keys to their success—their best insights, practices, and techniques—and these factors, when viewed in the aggregate, could reveal otherwise unknown wisdoms for those aspiring to replicate their success.

Lindsay's talk was framed to speak directly to the theme of disruption. Titled "The Crucible of Crisis," the talk delivered a "Gospel-centered approach" that can appropriately respond to circumstances of crises and organizational struggles. Crises, Lindsay told the audience, were opportunities for self-renewal for great leaders, opportunities for being part of "the change." But "great leaders" were also presumed to be in charge, not just riding the ship through the storms, but actually steering it. As Lindsay pronounced near the beginning of his talk, "To affect change, you have to be in the room." Based on who Lindsay interviewed, workers who are considered "in the room" are those who work in boardrooms, C-suites, and legislative rooms in government. Those listening were effectively being charged to occupy these higher positions of power within organizations across society. Lindsay relied on insights collected from his interviews to set out three principles for leading organizations through crisis.

Lindsay's research was impressive in its breadth: I was personally puzzled how this project had not yet achieved canonical status alongside the leadership classics like *In Search of Excellence*, *Good to Great*, or *The Seven Habits of Highly Effective People*. But there is also a larger puzzle here: a president of an evangelical college—one founded by a Baptist minister to train missionaries—now contends to be one of the world's leading experts on effective organizational leadership. And now, here he was coaching his own tribe on how they too could serve as high-status leaders by imitating America's most powerful elites. There also seemed to be a tension operating at a basic level of the event's theme: were Christians part of disrupting the social structures that defined an uncertain world, or were they being charged to effectively reproduce such structures, with themselves now standing atop of them? There was also an unquestioned premise that the "rooms" of power bearing significance in the past would serve as the same spaces of power in the future. Christians wanting to exercise lasting influence and impact through their leadership, then, had no choice but to climb predetermined ladders that grant access to these rooms. So what precisely is the nature of the "disruption" being promoted here?

This chapter maps out central aspects of the faith and work movement that directly speak to American evangelicalism's engagements with societal institutions and positions of power more broadly. Actors in this space display varying degrees of awareness regarding this aspect of faith and work thinking. Lindsay himself proves entirely aware of what his research offers to high-status Christian audiences: a Christian orientation to power. "The antidote to the pernicious effects of power," he relayed to the evangelical publication *Christianity Today* in a 2014 interview, "is not giving up power. It is using power sacrificially."[4] We again encounter an adverbial ethic. This chapter examines what it means for evangelical laity to hold secular (or extra-ecclesial) positions of power "sacrificially," or as it is more commonly presented, as a means of renewing or redeeming culture. This inquiry requires unpacking the larger historical context of this particular wing of the faith and work movement, its key leaders, and an underlying theological shift in evangelical thinking that shapes these actors' engagement with not only work, but with power, politics, and culture at large.

We might begin by examining the larger context of the Disruption event itself. The Center for Faith and Work that sponsored the event was birthed out of Redeemer Presbyterian Church, a theologically conservative church planted by Tim and Kathy Keller in 1989. The church saw rapid growth soon after its launch in 1989 and eventually expanded to four campuses across Manhattan, today attracting about five thousand congregants weekly. In 2002, leaders of the church established the Center for Faith and Work, at that time led by Alsdorf. Around this same time, Keller began converting many of his sermons and main ideas into books that would greatly raise his profile in the evangelical subculture. His 2008 book, *The Reason for God*, reached as high as the seventh spot on the *New York Times* nonfiction bestseller list.[5] Books on topics like suffering, marriage, prayer, church-planting, and social justice soon followed. Though Keller lacks the boisterous soundbyte-generating tendencies of other famous pastors, he has made a mark in non-religious national media and the wider evangelical subculture, largely due to the success of Redeemer Presbyterian Church and his rising popularity as a bestselling religious author. He has appeared on several cable news shows to discuss religious topics, has been the subject of numerous *New York Times* pieces, has written op-ed columns for the major newspapers, and has even been featured in an episode on NPR's program *This American Life*. The latter recounted that he is sometimes identified as the "yoda" of evangelical church-planting, as Redeemer is credited for helping plant dozens of other churches. The evangelical subculture typically see this as part of Keller's most valuable skills: he has a proven record of planting and leading a traditional church belonging to a theologically and socially conservative denomination (the Presbyterian Church of America) in an urban environment known for secularity, cosmopolitanism, and largely liberal political views. But amidst these achievements, Keller in 2014 teamed up with Alsdorf to write *Every Good Endeavor: Connecting Your Work to God's Work*. The book is likely the single most cited faith and work book in the movement, with citations showing up in nearly all the events I attended while doing fieldwork.

The Center for Faith and Work should be viewed in the context of its very particular social and geographical location. Redeemer Presbyterian Church in its earliest days was largely a collection of younger professionals who met together in a small group supported by Campus Crusade. Today, three decades later, it still maintains this distinctly professional and career-focused profile. As Keller and Alsdorf observe in *Every Good Endeavor*, their church is uniquely young (average age is thirty-three), largely early in their careers, and 70 percent are single. A church consultant working with the congregation at one point hypothesized this was the largest proportion of single persons of any church body in the world. *Every Good Endeavor* describes these laity as "seriously career-minded," working in fields like law, arts, finance, business, education, healthcare, technology, government, architecture, and advertising. In our interview, Keller recognized these demographic factors likely enhanced the church's ability to draw people toward work-focused ministries. He recounted the Center's coming to recognize that their nine-month intensive course on vocation demands so much of its students that it would be nearly impossible for all but the single, career-driven, early career workers to participate. Keller compared these offerings to a "Marines"-like training for "the few and the proud" of the congregation. While there are no measures of how much time the average Redeemer congregant spends at work each week, their demographic profile would suggest their average work hours were some of the highest in the country.[6] Alsdorf at one point in our interview made reference to overwork as both a feature and a central challenge of the ministry: pulling certain types of workers together for regular meetings often proved nearly impossible due to their demanding work schedules and other commitments.

All of these contextual factors bring out the unique population that Redeemer serves. Manhattan stands out for its concentration of high-tech, knowledge-base, and creative-content industries.[7] Workers across all industries appear to work more hours than in another city in the country: the Census and American Community Survey suggests that New Yorkers dedicate on average 49.08 hours to working and commuting each week. A study produced by the New York Comptroller broken down industry by industry suggests that New Yorkers even outwork those working in precisely the same professions in other cities. New York financial workers spend an average of four extra hours in the workplace, while lawyers, accountants, and auditors all put in an extra three hours a week in comparison to workers in other cities.[8] The area around Redeemer's initial church location is also exceptional for demographic reasons: the measures of creative-class workers in this neighborhood—those in educational, professional, managerial, artistic, and technology fields—suggests 72 percent of those living in the surrounding census tract are creative-class workers, compared to 26 percent in service-class work and 2 percent in the working class. The New York metro average of creative-class workers is only 35.9 percent.[9] The area has also become one of the wealthiest and highest-educated zip codes in the country. Median household income checks in at $111,334, and 78 percent of the population have college degrees, numbers that put it in the 98th percentile—a "super zip"—in a nationwide ranking of zip codes.[10] A *Forbes* study ranked it as the ninth most expensive real estate market in the country.[11]

In many ways, the Center's efforts to tailor Christian beliefs and practice to this population resembles what evangelicals have long done in contextualizing their message for "missions work." But now, instead of contextualizing to a culture on the other side of the world, the faith is being contextualized to the high-end professional sectors of Manhattan. The Center's ideas have also been rapidly disseminating out into other churches and evangelical laity far beyond Manhattan. The Center aids other churches and faith and work organizations in establishing their own nine-month intensive course, modeled on the Center's proven success. There seems to be a demand for a version of this "in the rooms of power" evangelicalism that could speak to the sorts of evangelicals that either occupied or aspired to occupy such positions. Kim and Alsdorf have both become highly demanded speakers in the faith and work speaking circuit, with Keller's involvement likely tempered only by his greater commitment to speaking on a larger range of topics.

## White American Evangelicalism's Evolving Orientation to Culture

While the faith and work movement's primary objective is altering the economic imaginaries of evangelical laity, this task goes hand in hand with revising how evangelicalism orients itself to the dominant institutions of American society. Such an undertaking is aided by the long-standing bricolage-like nature of American evangelicalism in relation to wider culture: the theological streams and movements that came together to form evangelicalism in prior centuries contained a range of orientations toward mainstream institutions or "the world" at large. The remedial theology of the faith and work movement seeks a particular alterations that, while sharply contrasting with some of the more dominant orientations of the subcultural spac today, are not necessarily novel to the longer evangelical tradition. This move could be compared to arranging a deck of cards in a particular order: evangelicalism contains any number of cultural orientations that can be arranged and ordered in any number of ways. Different eras and different groups promote some orientations while demoting others. What faith and work leaders have set out to do is bring a very particular cultural orientation to the top of the deck: a culture-affirming, world-embracing orientation that I call Kuyperian humanism.[12]

To fully understand this undertaking, we might first briefly survey which cultural orientations have occupied the "top card" status in the past. Beginning with the emergence of pre-millennialism and Moody's more individual-focused revivalism in the late nineteenth century, much of white evangelicalism gravitated toward a stance of cultural separatism. This orientation in many ways served as a reactionary response to intellectual and social currents perceived as threats to faith: theological modernism, the rise of "Social Christianity," the growing influence of Darwinian and evolutionary thinking, and the surge of European immigrant groups—many of them Jewish or Roman Catholic—who came to occupy the country's urban-industrial centers. This orientation became more institutionalized in nationally organized revivals and conferences in the 1870s. American religious historians generally see this reactionary strand of white conservative Protestantism crystallizing with the 1925 Scopes Monkey Trial, though many scholars challenge interpretations that portray the emerging fundamentalism as taking up strongholds exclusively in marginalized and backwood sectors of American society.[13] The important part of this story for our own purposes is that fundamentalist religious leaders regularly decried major cultural institutions and the crass worldliness thought to be running amok within urban centers.[14] The separatism they preached was grounded in the pursuit of purity and a drive to avoid contamination from the ways of the world.

While the rise of neo-evangelicalism in the 1940s charged the laity to become "ambassadors" in the wider American culture, this development by and large perpetuated an overall indifference to the achievements of secular American institutions. This neo-evangelical orientation toward these institutions might be best characterized as slightly modifying the prevalent "cultural separatism" in favor of "cultural detachment." Engaging institutions was always primarily framed as a strategic means of achieving the ends of Grahamism, discussed more in Chapter 2. But evangelical theology of the era gave little reason for Christians to invest in the ends of those institutions in and of themselves. Ambassadors functioned similarly to missionaries, primarily tasked with injecting something exogenous to a setting rather than investing in that setting's welfare.

The real challenge to cultural separatism and cultural detachment appeared in the form of the Christian Right. Religious leaders of the 1970s saw the dominant cultural orientations as directly impeding their task of transforming evangelicals into a dependable voting bloc. Leaders worked to demote cultural separatism in favor of a culture war. Cultural institutions, viewed through this mode, came to serve as both sites of spiritual battles as well as the spoils awarded to the winner of such battles. Leaders framed these battles as an ecumenical traditionalism taking on a vast set of institutional and cultural forces are believed to be conspiring against Christianity and traditional values. Yet the call to action was not toward a self-purifying separatism or a lifeboat-minded urgency of soul-saving, but instead a charge to seize control of dominant institutions—to "take back" society for God, as most succinctly expressed by adherents to Christian nationalism. This orientation drove Christians to the ballot box as the means of winning battles against oppositional forces.

These cultural orientations—separatism, detachment, warring—have never been entirely exclusive to one another. But we can utilize these orientations as descriptive ideal types in order to bring out the unique trajectory of a subset of voices in the faith and work movement. Their preferred orientation toward culture is not separatism, detachment, or warring, but instead a more affirmative view that narrows the space between church and world, sacred and secular. As Lindsay's presentation argues, evangelicals should climb the ladders of power as part of their God-ordained callings and vocations. This affirming orientation toward culture then yields any of several broader calls to steward or renew culture in a manner that works in harmony with the predetermined goals of dominant cultural institutions.

For the past seventy years, pockets of evangelical leaders have drawn on the ideas of Dutch theologian and political leader Abraham Kuyper to construct a more affirming account of culture that warrants the laity's affirmations and careful attending to cultural institutions. Understanding how Kuyperian thought came to inform the contemporary faith and work movement requires tracing the intellectual genealogy of Kuyper's thought and influence as they wove their way through denominations and institutions that gave shape to twentieth- and twenty-first-century American evangelicalism.

## Abraham Kuyper's Influence on American Evangelicalism

Abraham Kuyper (1837–1920) is not a household name across evangelical landscape today. But during the twentieth century, Kuyperian strands of thought left a distinct mark on the white evangelical parachurch organizations and educational institutions that continue to shape the subculture.[15] Kuyper's influence always operated in the background of the far more visible efforts of Graham or Fallwell, carrying out a "quieter but far more rigorous intellectual revival" in the religious schools and seminaries associated with Reformed theology, as historian Molly Worthen observes.[16] It was in the latter half of the century that Kuyperianism broke out of this enclave by way of more popular writers and speakers, who were fervently battling for hearts and minds in the evangelical populace. The faith and work movement in many ways represents one major front in this larger battle.

Kuyperianism is associated with Protestant theology known as "Neo-Calvinism," a larger school of thought which first took hold in the Netherlands in the 1870s. It was the decades immediately after this period that saw the highest levels of Dutch immigration to the United States, many of whom brought their Neo-Calvinist views with them. Kuyper himself visited the United States in 1898, delivering Princeton's Stone Lectures before receiving an honorary degree from Princeton Seminary, touring the Midwest, and meeting with President William McKinley. But Neo-Calvinism and Kuyperianism did not immediately find itself facing off against the other strands of American conservative Protestantism: the ideas primarily resided in Dutch-settled areas of the Midwest, particularly within colleges and denominations based in Grand Rapids and Holland, Michigan. Neo-Calvinist ideas made their biggest impact in Princeton Seminary, shaping many of the intellectuals who would eventually take up posts in the more conservative Westminster Seminary following the fundamentalist-modernist battles of the 1920s. Schools like Westminster and Calvin College would in turn exert significant influence through the development of a transposable intellectual product that would eventually work its ways through nearly all evangelical educational institutions. This intellectual product was the notion of a Christian "worldview."[17]

Kuyper's lectures at Princeton 1898 contained the basic germ of a Christian worldview, asserting:

> God's holy ordinances shall be established again in the home, in the school, and in the state for the good of the people; to carve as it were into the conscience of the nation the ordinances of the Lord, to which the Bible and Creation bear witness, until the nation pays homage again to God.[18]

According to philosopher David Naugle, Kuyper had come to realize that if sin and subordination to God produced a particular persuasion or pattern across the whole spectrum of life, it only made sense that the life obedient and subordinated to God also diffused across all of life.[19] Kuyper likely learned some of his worldview thinking from a Scottish theologian named James Orr. But importantly, Orr saw worldview as a necessary *defensive* response to anti-Christian thinking within nineteenth-century German thought: Christianity's intellectual foes had purportedly already taken the form of a *Weltanschauung*, which contained a view of life as an ordered whole. Orr believed only the "comprehensive method" of Christianity would mount an adequate defense. Kuyper, however, came to champion this "comprehensive vision of reality" as something generative and positive, capable of serving as a foundation on which a larger social order might be built. Anything short of comprehensiveness would mean conceding intellectual real estate to one's intellectual foes, a concession judged unacceptable to Kuyper: "If the battle is to be fought with honor and with hope of victory . . . then it must be felt that in Modernism the vast energy of an all embracing *life-system* assails us, then also it must be understood that we have to take our stand in a life-system of equally comprehensive and far-reaching power."[20] Not only does this prove to be a serviceable means of taking on competing intellectual systems—whether modernism, Marxism, or materialism—but it also reinforces the *impossibility* of any dimension of reality to somehow be purely "secular" or outside God's will or interests. This will come to play an important role in faith and work thinking, as Kuyperian thought has little tolerance for conceding the realm of "Monday" to another life-system or worldview.

The immediate impact of this comprehensiveness is that it allows Christians to engage secular forms of knowledge, art, literature, philosophy, and science. As historian James Turner notes, this more inclusive understanding of which disciplines or arenas warrant Christian concern would breathe new life into conservative Protestant intellectualism, which had arguably been left dilapidated by fundamentalist anti-intellectualism. Beginning in 1950, *The Reformed Journal*, produced out of Grand Rapids, served as a central hub for scholars writing from broadly Neo-Calvinist outlooks that spanned not only academic topics but also short stories, poems, hymns, and sermons.[21] As worldview orientation gradually spread to other denominations and traditions, other hubs of evangelical Christian intellectualism were able to declare greater compatibility between faith and knowledge originated from non-religious sources.

One of the most significant conduits for taking Kuyperianism to wider circles was philosopher Cornelius Van Til. Van Til began his studies at Calvin College in Grand Rapids before transferring to Princeton, where he would eventually join the faculty. After ongoing conservative-modernist feuds among Princeton faculty, Van Til would join theologian J. Gresham Machen and other conservative faculty in starting Westminster Theological Seminary. Van Til's arguments for presuppositional epistemology—which had its roots in Kuyper—fanned out into mid-century evangelicalism, diffusing through various Christian colleges, theologians, and popular writers. Francis Schaeffer, a student at Westminster who studied with Van Til, became an important theological and organizational leader in this era, establishing an alternative living community called L'Abri in Switzerland that saw among its many visitors a number of influential evangelical thinkers. Schaeffer popularized Van Til's conception of a Christian worldview, portraying the Christian worldview as at war with the humanistic, relativistic, and scientific worldviews of the time. Schaeffer came to influence several evangelicals who wrote on faith and work in the twentieth century, including Os Guinness, Hans Rookmaaker, R. C. Sproul, and Udo Middelmann. Observing this diffusion across the wider evangelical subculture, historian George Marsden in 1987 pronounced "the triumph—or nearly so—of what may be loosely called Kuyperian presuppositionalism" within the evangelical intellectual world.[22]

This orientation achieved its greatest penetration into the core of evangelical leadership by way of theologian and ethicist Carl Henry. Henry helped found the National Association of Evangelicals and went on to serve as chair of the association's commission on social action in the 1950s. Henry located in Kuyper the more reform-oriented impulse of the American evangelical heritage that had been diminished by fundamentalism and reactions to Social Christianity. Henry in 1948 was already pushing back against the urgent pre-millennial soul-saving, asking if the present global crisis was truly the terminus of Western culture, or perhaps if Christians still had time to "reintroduce into earthly history—before the advent of Christ—depths of meaning, as at the highest reaches of medieval culture." This represented Henry's concerted efforts to inch evangelicalism away from the cliff of apocalypticism and cultural fatalism and back toward a richer appreciation for humanist values found in the Renaissance.[23] Henry rooted his views in the work of Machen, who had served as a respected intellectual voice in the 1920s.

Here it must be noted that the ideas of Kuyper prove remarkably malleable and have been melded into a wide range of political and cultural agendas. To index a few streams of Kuyperianism: the concept of worldviews has come to the aid of many political and cultural traditionalists who demarcate sharp lines between a traditional way of thinking and threats posed by encroaching scientism, secular humanism, postmodernism, and evolution.[24] "Worldview education" has become a perennial feature of Christian education, both K–12 private schools, homeschool curricula, and in Christian colleges. R. J. Rushdoony built upon Van Til's worldview thinking (while also incorporating another Dutch Reformed thinker, Herman Dooyeweerd) to found the modern Christian Reconstructionist movement, a theocratic-leaning political movement. Advocates of "theonomy"—a vision of installing Old Testament laws as contemporary societal laws—also produced "worldview treatises" in the 1980s, blueprints on how every sphere of society could be "Christianized" and rid of oppositional views.[25] In a different setting, theologians in the Dutch Reformed Church of South Africa drew on the doctrine of sphere sovereignty (described below) to build a theological defense of apartheid, keeping at bay more prophetic voices that challenged racialized institutions and white supremacy.[26] Several Christian thinkers have constructed from Kuyper a theological grounding for neoconservatism and Reaganism: this includes Chuck Colson, John Bolt, and many scholars clustered around the Acton Institute.[27] Philosopher Nicholas Wolterstorff draws on Kuyper to stake out more progressive calls for justice, peace, social reform, and liberation from oppression.[28] More recently, historian George

Marsden prescribes an updated Kuyperianism to navigate contemporary questions of religious pluralism in the public square.[29]

Kuyperian ideas have also inspired several evangelical leaders supporting or working in congruence with Donald Trump. In the weeks following the contentious 2020 presidential election, Billy Graham's son Franklin Graham turned to Kuyper to ground his continual advocacy of restoring America's Christian values while blaming election fraud for Trump's loss.[30] Earlier in the Trump era, Secretary of Education Betsy Devos would cite Kuyper's cultural mandate as guiding her motivations for her support of Christian education and support for private schooling. Another leading conservative of the Trump era was Missouri senator Josh Hawley. Hawley identified Kuyper as the inspiration for his form of Christian nationalism that he pits against progressive causes like Black Lives Matters, marriage equality, LGBTQ rights, and the more progressive economic policies of Vermont senator Bernie Sanders.[31]

## Kuyperian Humanism as a Means of Making Peace with Culture

Against this backdrop of these very politicized "varieties of Kuyperianisms," it is perhaps surprising to find that faith and work leaders turn to Kuyper almost exclusively for *cultural* orientations rather than political agendas. A fuller explanation for this will be unpacked below, but certainly at play is the particular demographic profile described earlier. These evangelicals ultimately seek alternative cultural strategies that offer a more harmonious relationship with their social location, in this case creative-class professionals bearing college degrees and likely living in creative-class neighborhoods with higher levels of cultural and religious diversity. It is for this population that the other cultural orientations surveyed above—separatism, detachment, or warring—prove far less accommodating. Kuyperianism humanism, in contrast, offers resources and justifications to embrace education, the arts, technology, artisan trades, science, and humanities as sites and carriers of God's redemptive purposes.

This humanism served as the central ingredient behind the re-integrating framework explored in Chapter 4. Here, we can examine in more detail the three major resources from Kuyper that support re-integrating frameworks. All three resources extend from a foundational piece of Kuyper's project, which is the denial of sacred–secular, purity–impurity, and spiritual–material dualisms in the world. As Richard Hofstadter observes, American fundamentalism had in the early twentieth century become essentially Manichean, perceiving a conflict between good and evil in all arenas. It embodied the "paranoid style" of politics that saw history itself as "a conspiracy, set in motion by demonic forces of almost transcendent power" that drives groups to reach beyond the usual methods of politics toward "all-out crusade." For fundamentalists, these warring crusades were largely spiritual, responding to the "Satanic" powers working behind the various perceived threats. But this established a sharp disdain for the worldly or "secular" foes of these battles, feeding into the world-averting emphasis that pulled fundamentalism away from worldly institutions.[32]

Kuyper leaves no room for such a perspective. He instead constructed from Calvinist theology a "theology of creation." This framework affirmed all of created reality as God's handiwork, rather than elevating a "sacred" swath of reality ascribed to a special spiritual or eternal realm and thereby judged superior to other dimensions.[33] This bears significant consequences for the Protestantism that follows Kuyper's lead: German ethicist Georg Wunsch compares Kuyperianism to Thomism (dominant in medieval Catholicism) in its "great unified conception" which "enabled the Christian to be active in the world with good conscience and without a break between the Christian-ethical and the worldly ideals."[34] What this challenges, then, is fundamentalism's propensity to view the "world" as secular, profane, fallen, impure, or, in the pejorative descriptor often assigned to it, "worldly." Theologies of creation instead deny that there is a profane "world" standing in opposition to the spiritual realm. All dimensions of reality are then ascribed a unity rooted in a divinely ordained order. Christians, then, cannot oppose any sector of the world, for "no single piece of our mental world is to be hermetically sealed off from the rest." This view is lent support by a Kuyper quotation most often cited by faith and work leaders: "There is not a square inch in the whole domain of our human existence over which Christ who is sovereign over all, does not cry: 'Mine!' "[35]

This positive view of creation then leads to the notion of "sphere sovereignty," a concept that appears only briefly in an 1880 lecture by Kuyper but is extensively developed by other Neo-Calvinists. Kuyper sees reality as divided into spheres or domains, and each of these spheres contains its own authority and order, as ordained by God. Because no aspect of culture and society is inherently profane or beyond redemption, Christians are called to bring all orders of society "under Christ's sovereignty." Most Kuyperian thinkers do not equate this task with bringing spheres under *ecclesial* control or necessarily instrumentalizing the formal powers of the state: bringing the orders of society under Christ's sovereignty means seeing that they are ordered *toward their intended creational design*. Christians are thus called "not to destroy it or simply impose another structure alongside [a particular sphere], but to unlock the power that lies hidden within it."[36] Such action not only protects each sphere from the improper over-reach of the state—which Kuyper sees as a separate sphere tasked with its own self-maintenance—but also reflects a prelapsarian order of creation, that is, a dimension of creation not tainted by creation's fall to sin. Spheres are thereby able to reflect God's rule and order, independent of formal state control.

Three major implications or related concepts are tied to this theology of creation and the notion of sphere sovereignty. The first is the concept of common grace. Through this grace, God has "curbed the operations of Satan, death and sin" to preserve an "intermediate state of cosmos" for the human race. Grace, then, is not uniquely possessed by the church, but has been dispensed across creation: indeed, "creation would self-destruct" were it not held together by this divine favor. Kuyper finds in Calvin a deep linkage between creative intentions and the world, as the world holds worth due to "the virtue of its capacity as God's handiwork and as a revelation of God's attributes." For Kuyper, this "puts an end once and for all to contempt for the world, neglect of temporal and under-valuation of cosmical things."[37] This undermines fundamentalism's conspiratorial dispositions: all entities outside the church are not so much conspiring against it, but may instead be ordered by a "divine favor."

The second implication is a specific ethical charge or commission that is derived from this divine order. This extends beyond the revivalist soul-saving of fundamentalism. A remarkable amount of faith and work theology is built upon the "cultural mandate," an interpretation of Genesis 1:28 promoted by Kuyper and several other Dutch Calvinists. This mandate sees the creation narrated in Genesis as God handing over to humans the duty to "fill the earth" by participating in their own creative acts, to create and cultivate culture. The callings and duties of Christians, then, expand far beyond conversionism toward a wide variety of cultural, social, and political causes, many of which Kuyper himself developed further in his writings and lectures. The cultural mandate becomes an applicable framework for "secular" work. Evangelical leader Chuck Colson assures Christians in his book *How Now Shall We Live*: "God cares not only about redeeming souls but also about restoring his creation. He calls us to be agents not only of his saving grace but also of his common grace. Our job is not only to build up the church but also to build a society to the glory of God."[38]

Finally, Kuyperian humanism's third contribution made perhaps the most significant imprint on American evangelicalism, particularly in its relation to faith and work. While pre-millennialism has since the nineteenth century occupied the dominant view of eschatology among most conservative Protestant denominations, Kuyper's eschatology effectively drove a wedge into the heart of American evangelicalism. Due to Kuyper's institutional location far outside the United States, his Neo-Calvinism theology was insulated from the influence of John Nelson Darby, Lewis Sperry Chafer, H. A. Ironside, and C.I . Scofield that slowly took hold among white conservative Protestantism with the emergence of fundamentalism.[39] The semi-enclaved nature of Reformed Dutch immigrant communities also likely contributed to this insulation. Whereas dispensationalism and pre-millennialism established strongholds at Wheaton and Dallas Theological Seminary in the early decades of the twentieth century, Reformed Schools held strong to the post-millennial eschatological views of John Calvin and other earlier Reformation thinkers. Kuyper's cultural mandate was a key resource for keeping at bay the gloomy "lifeboat theology" of D. L. Moody and other evangelists who held little hope for redeeming or renewing American society. Kuyper's vision holds out hope that some aspects of creation have themselves maintained their intended and ordered purposes even amidst the radical social disruptions that conservative Protestants might perceive to undermine those purposes.

Faith and work leaders rarely discuss their abnegation of pre-millennialism, nor do they acknowledge the gulf that exists between their own eschatological views and those of Moody, Billy Sunday, Billy Graham, Tim LaHaye, and much of the rest of the evangelical world.[40] But their eschatology provides a significant boost to theologies of work by discarding the assumption that all of the world and all its activities will "pass away" when Christ returns, a belief that perpetuates a vocational hierarchy rooted in valuing the spiritual over the material.[41] My own sense is that faith and work leaders recognize that pre-millennial eschatology represents Grahamism's central affront to their own efforts: pre-millennialism reduces workplaces to mission fields for soul-saving, but beyond that, the laity can only be charged to "man their stations" while awaiting the return of Christ.[42] Neither re-sacralizing nor re-embedding frameworks can be assimilated with this view, and re-integrating frameworks are reduced to a grim submission to mundane toil while awaiting heavenly relief.[43] Kuyperian "worldview" thinking, meanwhile, permits a far richer appreciation of "worldly" culture while quietly discounting separatist attitudes toward the world.

All three of the resources described here—as well as the larger theology of creation—flow through faith and work theology. Kuyperian humanism thus offers a valuable bridge to move white conservative Protestantism from a world-rejecting or world-flying asceticism and toward an inner-worldly asceticism that can reunite religious energies with duties of work and labor. As Chapter 4 recounted, such themes began appearing in faith and work books in the mid-twentieth century. The earlier described "Disruption" event featured a lecture by David H. Kim that explicitly introduced Kuyper's concept of sphere sovereignty. Pursuing one's calling was described as the process of Christians stepping up in the face of contemporary challenges to "leave their stamp" on something. The way to do this, according to Kim, was recognizing how one's work connected to God. "We end up separating God's glory from what our hands do," Kim warned, calling this a form of "spiritual amnesia." But the right call to which Christians respond pulls them toward "worshiping God" to bring about the vision of God's glory in particular spheres. Kim drew several circles on the white board to make his point: family, religion, government, economics. Kim identified each of these spheres with a particular essence and purpose: economics creates opportunities, government brings about justice, families nurture, etc. "If these spheres don't provide these things, the spheres begin to collapse." Callings, then, are seeing that these spheres continue to reflect God's glory by ensuring these spheres serve their right functions. In Kim's words, callings are "getting to do what one is created to do" in working for God's glory in these spheres.

To return to the earlier point, the faith and work movement appears to turn to Kuyper for a very specific reason. Leaders are not looking for a political vision or political theology that might aid them in translating their religion into political preferences or policy positions, nor are they particularly interested in Kuyper as a means of grounding a vision of restoring a "Christian" nation. What they instead take from Kuyper is a particular orientation toward wider society. Kuyperian humanism provides a means of making peace with the larger cultural and economic institutions of American society and Christians' position within it. Evangelical laity could find in Kuyper a calling to work *within and through* cultural spheres and the institutions that shape them. As Kim elaborates in our interview:

> [Faith and work are] part of God's larger orchestration. As we look at Scripture, God invites his people to participate in this larger work of renewal. What that looks like in each industry and office—there's no prescription for that. So how do you begin to give people the eyes to see the invitation that God gives us throughout the day that for the most part we ignore or can't perceive.

The call to participate in renewal bears significant cultural consequences. Instead of either separating from or warring against secular institutions, evangelicals can engage and, in fact, even preside over them. Kim was the only interviewee who brought up the politicization of evangelicalism without my prompting, and he specifically drew distance between his own perspective and the "triumphalist vision of Christianity" that he associated with the "culture war perspective." Faith and work were depicted as an alternative path from the better-known culture-warring Christianity. Keller, in a similar vein, portrays participation in these institutions as an opportunity to work for the good of those institutions and wider society. In our interview, Keller rooted this in Kuyper's cultural mandate :

> Ruling the world as God's image bearers should be seen as stewardship and trusteeship. God owns the earth, but he has put it under our care to cultivate it. It is definitely not a mandate to treat the world and its resources as they are ours to use, exploit, and discard as we wish . . . the word "subdue" indicates that even in its original, unfallen state, God made the world to need work.

Kim and Keller are both presuming a certain amount of agency and influence for the workers who might implement such a message. And based on the demographics outlined earlier, they have good reason to do so: the primary audiences they speak to are generally career-driven professionals climbing the ranks of industries like media, fashion, and finance. Specific events designed for entrepreneurs also bring in an audience of workers who have remarkable control over both their time usages on Monday as well as the ultimate fruits of their labor. Keller, in particular, is quite aware of the very specialized audience finding his message, and in our interview, he voiced some wariness of other organizations replicating his own church's efforts. Other faith and work leaders in turn have recognized how these notions of "cultural renewal" or "cultural stewardship" appear to best serve workers in higher-status careers or in positions of cultural influence. One coordinator of a major faith and work conference voiced skepticism regarding the "redemptive language" and its applicability beyond urban professional spaces like Redeemer Presbyterian Church, saying in our interview:

> So much of this redeeming culture stuff comes from Keller. I love Keller. But I think his whole redeeming culture thing was a pastoral application to his congregation, many of whom are those super high performers, who are asking themselves: "How does being an investment banker make sense?"

Judging the redemptive framework to be "not pastorally helpful for most people," this leader asserted that such frameworks serve only "a very niche group of Christians who even have the means and capability of 'redeeming culture.'"

Combining this assessment of the Center for Faith and Work's intended audience with Kim's deliberate distancing from the culture war yields a compelling thesis: at least some portions of the faith and work movement aspire to serve as an off-ramp to the culture war. Adopting Kuyperian humanism offers religious laity a means of occupying creative-class and high-status settings by making peace with those settings and their endogenous ends. Certainly, Kuyper's influence in American evangelicalism spans beyond this particular demographic—particularly through the concept of worldview and its popularity within Christian education—but the world-affirming Kuyperian humanism outlined here appears to have far less diffusion within the wider evangelicalism landscape.

We might think of Kuyperian humanism as the theology of the "thriving" side of the thriving-embattled dialectic that has been used to describe American evangelicalism. The faith and work leaders that I talked to do not perceive themselves to be particularly beleaguered or threatened by societal institutions, nor do the many lawyers, MBAs, entrepreneurs, seminarians, business owners, educational administrators, and philanthropy-sector workers I met at the events. No one I interviewed spoke in terms of actively battling secularism, progressivism, or humanism. My time in the field—coming at a time when there was no shortage of political battles being fought over workplace issues—revealed a pocket of evangelicalism that also appeared insulated from the beleaguered mindset that arguably defines the evangelical populace as a whole.[44] In particular, faith and work adherents do not seem to see their fate hanging in the balance with every two- and four-year national election cycle, nor do they see their freedom to live out their faith commitments under threat by governmental over-reach. The vast majority of faith and work speakers, events, and writings I encountered made no reference to any such threat or anxiety. They seemed to exhibit exceptionally high trust in the dominant institutions of society, particularly secular institutions of higher education, which they themselves graduated from and now usher their own children toward. This creates an ambivalent reaction to conservative rallying cries around the "betrayal of elites" or the urgent need to "save" society from those leading dominant institutions, as faith and work audiences appear to have secured their own places of power within those same institutions.

Part of this story certainly comes down to class position within the broader political economy of American society. As a predominately white, college-educated population residing in knowledge-economy hubs, faith and work adherents would be far less likely to see their social status threatened by events surrounding the 2008 financial recession, the two-term presidency of Barack Obama, the inflow of immigrant populations alongside increasing racial and ethnic diversity, or the continual effects of free trade and globalization.[45] This sense of stability may then be pulling them out of step with the sense of persecution and precarity that dominates other religious conservatives. To highlight one episode where this was put display, in 2016, popular evangelical blogger and author Lore Ferguson Wilbert shared with her followers on Facebook an article in *The Atlantic* overviewing evangelicals' unwavering support for President Trump with Wilbert's added commentary: "Evangelical Christians need another model for culture and political engagement . . . and one of the best that I am aware of has been articulated by the artist Makoto Fujimura, who speaks about 'culture care' instead of 'culture war.' " Fujimura is a frequent speaker at faith and work events: several interviewees I spoke with praised his insights on culture and the arts. Fujimura draws directly on the social thought of Kuyper.

But it is again important to recognize that Kuyperian humanism primarily alters the world of Mondays and not necessarily the world of election days. Regarding election days, while existing data are limited, faith and work leaders and their adherents appear to remain largely conservative or, at the least, more right of center.[46] Surveys of higher-educated evangelicals—the laity most likely to engage faith and work resources—suggest they remain fairly loyal Republican voters. This is not, then, a political realignment that converts long-standing culture warriors into eager supporters of progressive candidates and political causes. It is more accurately a shift in how Christians relate to mainstream American culture and participation in mainstream institutions more broadly. At least for the world of Mondays, evangelical laity encountering faith and work resources are able to step away from militaristic culture war orientations and instead dedicate themselves to their own roles and positions of power within the institutions at the center of American society.

## Adverbial Theology and a De-Ethicized Kuyperianism

As discussed above, Kuyperian humanism and Neo-Calvinist theology have proved capable of grounding a diverse set of political and ethical orientations, ranging from Dominionism and conservatism to a justice-oriented Christian progressivism. Yet in the hands of faith and work leaders, Kuyper's ethical and political prescriptions are significantly tempered. Much of this can be attributed to the elevation of sphere sovereignty as Kuyper's key political-social vision. The promoted understanding of calling then becomes a directive to "unlock the power that lies hidden within" different spheres," as Kim described it. To work in unison with this discovered goodness then represents the essence of a Christian calling. This rather muted ethical vision heavily tilts Kuyperian humanism in favor of preserving the status quo and even naturalizing the existence and functioning of major social structures.[47] Outside of Reformed circles, Kuyper's social thought is most closely associated with a particular case of this: leaders of the Dutch Reformed Church of South Africa rooted their theological justifications for racial apartheid and white supremacy in Kuyper's thought. In that case, theologians drew on the theology of creation and the Scriptural case of the Tower of Babel to naturalize existing racial segregation. Kuyper's critiques of "modernism" were then turned against those who protested such arrangements.[48]

A similar ethical underdevelopment or imprecision characterizes much of the faith and work space. Events that promised to "help you think and live differently in the workplace" and think through the question "how does the gospel change my work?" delivered relatively few tangible answers to such questions. Speakers would forgo ethical prescriptions to instead subtly drift back toward evangelicalism's proselytization impulse: "We're living now for the sake of eternity . . . let us work hard to show the gospel as attractive, work hard to ordain the gospel, work hard to advance the gospel," said the speaker at the end of the event recounted in Chapter 3. Stories that followed this statement recounted business owners and medical workers who recognized they could export their efforts into other countries as vehicles for evangelism. Event attendees I spoke with at the Disruption event recounted instructions from leaders to think through their respective fields and the ways in which the fields exhibited "brokenness," a theological term that refers to the persisting effects of sin that emerged in the wake of Adam and Eve's initial disobedience in the garden of Eden. But this abstract theological concept seemed to come up short in yielding a substantive ethical framework or commitment to social practices to respond to persisting brokenness. Event attendees were more likely to fall back on vague commitments to a general benevolence in one-to-one interpersonal relationships, likely circling back to an underlying imperative of evangelizing others.

A panel discussion at the Disruption event featuring Christian start-up leaders captured some of this tension. These laity perceived a religiously grounded imperative to be more cooperative and benevolent than others in their field. But this wasn't perceived as easy. "You're required to have this killer drive [as an entrepreneur] . . . you find yourself saying 'We want to kill Facebook!' all the time." Another executive lamented the ultra-competitiveness of New York City in particular: "This city can get the best of us sometimes . . . it is challenging on a daily basis." When the panel was asked to articulate what possibilities exist for resisting ultra-competitive startup culture tendencies, the speakers expressed a grim realism."Can we lead and create this collaboration . . . but still protect ourselves?" one panelist asked, seemingly in a non-rhetorical manner. Some of this reflected the trickiness of a "disruption"-themed event that was animated by sphere sovereignty thinking: the values at home within the entrepreneurial sphere were precisely those that conquered market share, "killed Facebook," and left little standing in the wake of one's success. But something about the Christian calling seemed to introduce unease toward this drive to disrupt and destroy. "There's a way to win with an ethical product or having a better service," one panelist contended. "Disruption is a good thing . . . if it shows what God can accomplish." Another panelist revised the earlier destructive by adding a more positive interpretation: "You could take down Facebook . . . with a more efficient product!"

The underdevelopment of ethics in the faith and work space almost certainly stems from some broader factors within American evangelicalism.

Precisely what ethical commitments *should* evangelical start-up leaders inject into these various "spheres" of work? Do these professionals bear particular responsibilities and duties to workers, customers, or marginalized populations? Other faith traditions provide concise answers to these questions: designated offices within the Roman Catholic Church and many Mainline Protestant denominations routinely issue documents and statements that map out developed visions of economic justice, capitalism, free markets, the dignity owed to workers, the relationship between the market and the state, as well as reflections on consumption and sustainability.[49] Islamic moral teaching maintains a tradition of resisting particular capitalist values: parts of the Islamic world today continue to prohibit charging of interest on certain types of loans and transactions.[50] But leaders in the faith and work movement have few ethical teachings within their tradition to which they might appeal.[51]

In interviews with leaders, I posed the question of how a hypothetical faith-and-work-integrated worker would look different from a Christian worker who failed to re-integrate their faith with their work. Leaders almost universally cited differences in subjective orientations to work:

> Purpose. That's the whole difference, right. The idea that once you get this idea about faith and work, it gives perfect purpose, it gives significance through work . . . you're going to spend a lot of time through your lifetime working in those four areas [family, church, community, vocation, mentioned earlier in the interview] but just take the vocational, that's going to be a huge chunk of your time. And if you don't see that as being significant . . . that's connected with what God is doing in the world, it becomes secular.

Another leader appealed primarily to internal change, slow to acknowledge there would be *any* visible difference, even between a Christian versus a non-Christian worker:

> You might not see anything different, even in a non-Christian. Non-Christians have incredible gifts and can be people of great character, they do outstanding work. So we need to be careful when we talk about this. The difference is primarily more internal than external, realizing, "Why am I working, what am I doing this for?" And that hopefully issues forth in the way they take care of their work, do their work, the ethics behind it, why

> they do certain things and don't do certain things . . . all those things should be hallmarks of how Christ shows up in their work.

One leader initially spoke in terms of both internal and external effects:

> I think there's an impact personally on the worker and externally on the world. Personally, I find an increasing number of people who live in this [integrated] worldview increasing[ly] grow in their imagination . . . it feels like their world is always getting bigger, right? Where there's just such a constant awareness of inputs or maybe inspirations for creativity . . . the world keeps getting bigger and bigger and that brings a lot of excitement, joy . . . and a continual lens that I'm part of a much bigger thing.

But this same leader's understanding of "external" effects moved toward abstract values of creativity rather any ethically distinct activities:

> Externally, you know the fruit of that or outgrowth of that, if you're the kind of person that sees connectivity everywhere you see possibility. You tend to be more creative . . . creative in terms of problem-solving, being able to innovate, being adaptive, you know, all those traits of leadership. And so sometimes that makes a big impact of the next grand idea and you redeem humanity . . . but I think it's probably manifest more in how you engage with your workers, draw gifts out of other people, relate interpersonally, relate with the work itself, how you engage frustration.

All the leaders interviewed were also asked to identify some "go-to examples of faith-work integration." A few gave more robust answers that entailed specific ethical practices and even workplace alterations implemented by faith-integrated executives. Others named well-documented cases of Christian business leaders. But by and large, the leaders responded to the question by pivoting back to the "changed heart" vision, rather than laying out examples of altered behavior:

> To me, the best examples would be those who have kind of a settled heart and a peace about what they're doing, are doing their work with excellence, and are doing it with an open hand.

One of the thought leaders who had been speaking on faith and work for over two decades admitted to having no go-to examples:

> "Whewwww . . . you know, I rarely talk about people. I talk about principles, I talk about things I've done—some successful, some mistakes. Ummm . . . (laughs). Nope, you got me. I'm gonna make a note; I need to develop some good examples. I'm sure there are tons out there; I just haven't given it much thought.

There is a definite favoring of the *how* over the *what* in these visions: the leaders do not appear entirely confident that the integrated-faith worker is *doing* anything that is substantively new or distinct in comparison to the non-integrated worker. There is an unmistakable resonance here with the earlier Puritan notion of callings which exalted not specific *kinds* of activities and conduct but a particular *spirit* by which one undertakes activities.[52] The primary transformation celebrated from these perspectives is a worker's internal awakening to how his or her work aligns with God's creational purposes and is thereby part of something bigger.

But this orientation essentially reinforces the movement's ethical underdevelopment. What is most common is a very loose and vague ethical addendum to the central message of the re-integrating framework: "Your work matters to God . . . so do it diligently, faithfully, wholeheartedly, reverently, etc." But with no distinct ethical commitments or principles also amended to this directive, the faith and work movement often ends up channeling religious energies into maintaining stability and the reproduction of existing economic and social structures. As Chapter 4 explored, adverbial frameworks, when embraced by those at the top of the socioeconomic structures, quickly become another form of re-sacralizing frameworks by cloaking the wider larger economic system within a divinely ordained legitimacy. This is due to the inseparable relationship between the day-to-day activities of economic elites and their crucial function within larger economic structures: to frame a CEO's "Monday world" of preparing for quarterly earnings call as part of his or her sacred calling indirectly consecrates the functions and operations of the respective firm and likely the structures of corporate capitalism more broadly. A de-ethicized Kuyperian humanism's taking hold among high-status evangelical elites then invites closer examination of whether this portion of the faith and work movement is largely serving to legitimate the wider structures of capitalism.

## Examining Faith and Work as a Conduit of Accommodationism

Recognizing the propensity of adverbial ethics to inspire deeper commitments to established practices and economic structures brings us to the question of accommodationism.[53] Accommodationism to the economic order is not the same as accommodationism with modernity, nor is it necessarily an indication of a broader and more uniform shift toward secularism. For one, to "accommodate" with the structures of contemporary capitalism does not necessarily represent a process of secularization or *dis*enchantment, particularly if the capitalism encountered preserves elements of its own enchanted religion—workism, for instance—or spiritualized self-understandings such as those promulgated by workplace spirituality efforts. This process might be better thought of as assimilation within a more dominant social or cultural order that entails the adoption of that dominant order's values, beliefs, and practices.

One means of assessing the faith and work movement's role in assimilative processes would draw on longitudinal survey data of laity who report engaging the movement's resources or events, assessing their endorsement or rejection of dominant economic mentalities and structures. But with no such survey data available, we are still able to trace an important institutional story of shifting inter-religious organizations that makes visible particular dynamics of accommodation. This evaluation is aided by sociologist John Schmalzbauer's previously mapped out processes by which evangelical and Catholic laity entered into higher education and media fields in the latter decades of the twentieth century. Schmalzbauer's work follows the same trajectory as the one of central interest here: the recurring patterns of religious groups that travel from "the margins to the mainstream" of a social order.[54]

A valuable finding from Schmalzbauer's study is the institutional pathways by which religious groups complete their journey into the dominant or mainstream society. His examples come from American Catholic professionals: for decades, the American Catholic subculture featured institutions that supported particular professions while also instilling distinctive means of engaging in particular fields and professions. Journals like *Catholic Historical Review* and professional associations like the Catholic Psychological Association and the Catholic Economic Association served this role. But the final stage of moving into the mainstream was exiting (and many times letting fall into disrepair) those subcultural institutions: professionals would come to favor full participation within particular fields and their corresponding a-religious associations and organizations. Assimilating high-status Catholics effectively "burned the boats" of the groups and associations that had served to transverse the gulf between earlier Catholic marginalization and the mainstream social positions they eventually occupied.

Applying Schmalzbauer's model to the case of the evangelical faith and work movement yields suggestive insights about both the past and the future of the movement, particularly as it relates to the central question of aiding evangelicals in making peace with their location within creative-class culture. The first insight is that the current movement's "success" may represent the quiet demise of a prior wave of evangelical groups that were engaged in the same mission. Contemporary leaders and their organizational efforts rarely recognize the manner in which their efforts in many ways displaced what were once well-established organizations already speaking to the integration of faith and work. Some of these organizations gathered together amidst the "first wave" of evangelical faith and work events that originated in the 1990s. The "marketplace ministries" of the Billy Graham Evangelistic Association, the evangelical professional associations in specific trades, the associations and directories of Christian businesses modeled on trade associations, and many other "Christian businessman" groups had all secured a leading position in constructing theologies of work that could make Mondays meaningful for their constituencies.[55] Yet is also not difficult to see that these earlier groups were far more rooted in distinctive beliefs, practices, and priorities that have comprised evangelical identity. The initial faith and work "organizations"—going back to the 1930s—were essentially daily prayer meetings seeking to incite revival and soul-saving. Organizations that sprung up in the wake of such meetings continued to promote a re-commissioning framework. All of the efforts associated with Billy Graham's efforts in the space preserved this mission. Even well into the 1970s and 1980s, the organizations on the ground added only minimal ethical injunctions to the re-commissioning framework: they promoted some "proven principles" of Scripture for leadership and business while channeling energies toward evangelizing customers and workers. These groups championed employee Bible studies and workplace prayer groups, generally led by the faith-and-work-enthused executive.

While some of these older groups found their way to the cultural mandate and other Kuyperian ideas, these groups were not as confident to pronounce the sacredness of work in and of itself. Obedience to specifically biblical imperatives were still key to making work sufficiently "Christian." A select number of these older groups continue to exist, but their role in the subculture has become largely usurped by many of the later-emerging faith and work groups that now boast affiliation with top-ranked colleges, seminaries, parachurch ministries, and influential evangelical congregations. Calvinist and Neo-Calvinist themes like theologies of creation often serve to soften the distinctly Christian aspects of a Christian calling. Work is deemed inherently "Christian"; the Christian is called merely to undertake it with greater fervor, as Dorothy Sayers prescribes in her influential essay on work. These later groups also got a leg up on prior groups by proving more responsive to changing economic currents like the rise of Silicon Valley start-up culture, the growing prevalence of post-material values, and the dominance of urban settings in shaping the knowledge economy. Earlier groups, meanwhile, appeared more affixed to the "Christian businessman" model of the mid-century corporate firm. To draw on Schmalzbauer's model, perhaps the initial cohort of assimilating organizations has already been scuttled by the wider evangelical subculture in favor of these newer groups.

But this of course leads to the question of the faith and work movement's own obsolescence or shelf life, and whether its ultimate "success" will also usher in its demise. This question will be taken up in the next chapter in relation to factors that are largely exogenous to the movement itself. But Schmalzbauer's study allows us to probe how endogenous features of the movement may factor into the movement's future. Other cases of religious embourgeoisement and entrances into mainstream society seem to reveal recurring patterns of assimilation. Here, we can gain insights by examining Mainline Protestant denominations that now sit at the top of the present U.S. socioeconomic hierarchy. Mainline denominations, on average, draw some of the highest-status constituencies across all American religious groups. Of the eight Christian denominations with the highest proportions of college-educated adherents, seven belong to the Mainline tradition. Similarly, Mainline denominations typically draw wealthier adherents: five of the top seven wealthiest Christian denominations are Mainline denominations.[56] Mainline Protestantism has long been at home among white-collar and knowledge-economy elites, whether U.S. presidents, Ivy League college presidents, Rotary club members, or industry executives.[57] Their political attitudes and voting patterns also largely mirror the broader white, upper-middle-class populace, suggesting a comfortable relationship with their social location.[58] Generalizing solely from this demographic profile, these

Mainline denominations may accurately represent the "respectable church of respected classes," in Niebuhr's words.[59]

But the history of Mainline Protestantism records two familiar phenomena: a gradual embourgeoisement process as lay populations move from lower classes into the respectable middle classes and the advent of a "theology of the laity" that would confer spiritual significance upon non-clerical vocation and work. To review the first phenomenon, denominations like Methodism underwent an embourgeoisement process in the latter half of the nineteenth century, preceding white evangelicalism's own entrance into middle-class settings by roughly one hundred years. And emerging in the decades after this embourgeoisement were a set of theological ideas and corresponding organizations that elevated familiar-sounding themes. These efforts have gone under different names: the "theology of the laity" or the theology of everyday life. It is illuminating to hold up the evangelical faith and work movement against this Mainline phenomenon. In fact, if certain liberties are permitted in selecting comparable points of development, there is a remarkably consistent *sixty-year lag* between Mainline developments in a theology of the laity or work and evangelical efforts replicating the same developments within the faith and work space.

To briefly survey these: in 1906, social gospel advocate Walter Rauschenbusch, in a speech entitled "Wanted: A New Kind of Layman," first made the case for a new type of ethically driven layperson who, rather than merely saving souls or retreating to monasteries, would "carry the determination to live consecrated lives into the workshop and office." Explicitly addressing the Sunday-Monday gap, Rauschenbusch envisioned Christian workers experiencing "that glorious consciousness of serving God in the totality of their lives."[60] Roughly sixty years later, evangelical leader and *Christianity Today* cofounder Carl Henry issued his own "vocational call" to Christian workers in his 1964 work, *Aspects of Christian Social Ethics*. Henry criticized the earlier "fundamentalist movement" for reducing workplace responsibilities only to evangelism and personal moralism. In Henry's vision, the Christian worker was to "penetrate into the social structure" and thereby transform it by serving God and neighbor at work. Jumping back to Mainline developments, several precursor gatherings of lay-directed "Life and Work" groups culminated in the formal gathering of the "Life and Work World Conference" at Oxford in 1937. This gathering aimed at supporting lay-led study and action regarding social, political, and economic problems. Right on cue, 1997 was the year of the initial gathering of leaders from forty-five different evangelical marketplace ministry organizations. It was this gathering that thrust ecumenical faith and work efforts onto the radar of Billy Graham's ministry organization and secured support for future gatherings. Returning to the 1950s, a surge in efforts among Mainline Protestant leaders to infuse Christianity into workplaces—led by mainline scholars like J. H. Oldham, Howard R. Bowen, and Elton Trueblood—managed to capture the attention of *Harvard Business Review* and *Fortune* magazine, which heralded a perceived surge in religious activity in the workplace That era bears an uncanny resemblance to evangelicalism's faith and work surge in the 2010s, as outside funding sources hit their high mark and conference coordination proliferated. Finally, returning one more time to Mainline developments, a 1954 World Council of Churches assembly gathered theologians began to consider a "third-way," bottom-up vision of social change that identified numerous sites of power, with several leaders seeing promise in MBAs and "responsible leaders of enterprise." The commission's final report called for a vocation of "participatory industry" in which "the actions of any man in the work process" are to become "a fitting part of an undivided pattern of human relationships."[61] By most counts, progressive voices within evangelicalism have not achieved a similar justice-oriented account of vocation in the 2010s. However, a more left-leaning community-developing arm of evangelicalism—the Christian Community Development Association, constructed around the thought of Civil Rights leader John Perkins—first introduced a "Market Solutions for Community Transformation" mini-conference in 2014. These events, while still incorporating a healthy dose of entrepreneur-praising neoliberal language, offer a gathering point for justice-minded business owners and investors to contribute to the empowerment of under-resourced and marginalized communities.[62]

Drawing on Schmalzbauer's model of assimilation, one could then ask: Did these Mainline efforts and groups also fall into disrepair as Mainline laity secured their places in the higher socioeconomic careers and positions of American society? The answer here is mixed: several efforts do appear to bottom out and dissolve, while others undergo significant transformations.[63] Ecumenical groups like the World Council of Churches largely abandoned their "life and work" focus after 1954. Such explorations were eclipsed as these groups turned their focus to either more abstract theological questions or coordinating political responses to world issues. Some denominational leaders who continued exploring theologies of the laity up through the 1970s transitioned into more scholarly (and non-affiliated) "leadership studies" and workplace spirituality efforts: a handful of these leaders helped found the Academy of Management's subsection on Management, Spirituality, and Religion and now primarily work in academic fields of organizational studies and leadership.[64] Other Mainline workplace efforts are housed in chaplaincy ministries that reside more closely within particular industries rather than a particular religious body. Though Mainline seminaries make occasional gestures at developing lay-oriented resources devoted to theological praxis, these efforts far more frequently favor engaging social and political issues—generally issues engaged by way of conventional political behaviors—over navigating one's "Monday" life. An initiative at Andover Newton Theological School called the Andover Newton Laity Project, which was founded in 1974 to address the challenges of vocation in specific fields and occupations, folded after only a few years.[65] One surviving effort in the seminary space is the Workgroup in Constructive Theology, housed at Vanderbilt Divinity School, that has coordinated the publication of a book series called "Christian Explorations of Everyday Living," published by the Evangelical Lutheran Church's official publishing house, Augsburg Fortress Press. One of these books—*Working* by theologian Darby Kathleen Ray—is specifically devoted to work.[66] Other topics engaged by the series include playing, shopping, eating and drinking, parenting, traveling, and dreaming.

There is also little evidence that Mainline laity come into contact with theological frameworks promoted by their church that might apply to their Monday lives. Only 18 percent of Mainline Protestants report participating in a discussion group about faith in the workplace, compared to 24 percent of evangelical adherents. Only a narrow portion of Mainline Protestant laity report hearing a sermon or being part of a group discussion concerning social responsibilities of corporations (16 percent, compared to 14 percent of evangelical laity). A higher percentage of weekly-attending Mainline laity participate in formal political activities in comparison to evangelical adherents (55 percent to 45 percent, respectively), supporting popular conceptions of a politically engaged "Saturday" faith of activism. But there is little evidence that these commitments to the political activity of Saturday translates into advancing particular religious values within the realm of Monday.[67]

This of course raises the question of whether this trajectory of Mainline Protestant efforts might provide some indication of the future of the evangelical faith and work movement. Deriving any sort of confident predictions would fall far beyond the aspirations of this project. We should also grant careful attention to the disparate processes and outcomes of evangelicalism's own embourgeoisement, which are likely still being understood by religion scholars. But perhaps the central reason to exercise caution in such comparisons is that both traditions feature multiple sites of influence promoting economic orientations, with theology of work or theology of laity serving as only one of many theological offerings. Recognizing this heterogeneity, the next chapter takes up the question of current and future trajectories of the faith and work movement within the broader context of other contending economic orientations vying for power within the evangelical space at large.

# 8
# On Roads Not (Yet) Taken

*I fear, wherever riches have increased, the essence of religion has decreased in the same proportion. Therefore I do not see how it is possible, in the nature of things, for any revival of true religion to continue long. For religion must produce both industry and frugality, and these cannot but produce riches. But as riches increase, swell pride, anger, and love of the world in all its branches. . . . Is there no way to prevent this—this continual decay of the pure religion?*

—John Wesley, "Thoughts on Methodism," 1787[1]

The preceding chapters have captured the contemporary faith and work movement as an effort to renegotiate and revise evangelicalism's orientations to the economic realm, particularly in relation to work. What becomes clear when surveying contemporary efforts is the long shadow of fundamentalism and its own "work ethic," as Chapter 2 outlines. But the faith and work movement is not the only effort to make "Monday" matter for conservative Protestants. This chapter attempts to survey the points of intersection and commonality, bringing out a wider range of Protestant ethics adjacent to the contemporary faith and work movement. Many of these alternatives become visible in contexts where the faith and work movement exhibited key moments of contingency and contention regarding precisely *how* work would be rendered religiously significant. Importantly, to remain consistent with the approach undertaken in prior chapters, this survey of other economic orientations continues to emphasize the "non-formal" views of economic laity. This means continuing to set aside the formal economic prouncements and treatises produced by Protestant denominations or theologians, which generally favor abstract sets of ideas or policy positions related to capitalism regulation, labor conditions, and political economy. Instead, this analysis draws on cultural frameworks that speak to economic roles and activities that appear to engage everyday actors on the ground. The

*Saving the Protestant Ethic*. Andrew Lynn, Oxford University Press. © Oxford University Press 2023.
DOI: 10.1093/oso/9780190066680.003.0009

main currents of thought surveyed, then, are those that seem to resonate with similar lay needs for conferring significance on Monday and day-to-day "lived religion."

We can revisit the categories from Chapter 1 to sort some of the major contenders for other economic orientations or economic imaginaries relevant to laities' day to day lives. Table 8.1 locates several movements or theological traditions that promulgate some sort of "Monday ethic" within the American Protestant landscape.[2] Though previous chapters have emphasized the variegated nature of the faith and work movement's cultural orientations to economics and work, this table, for reasons of simplicity, has located the movement by its most central dominant strand, the re-integrating framework that seeks to pronounce the sacredness of work in and of itself, independent of any particular ethical or spiritual additives. This simplification then finds the faith and work movement joining a crowded space in the "sacralizing and stabilizing" category that also includes the classical (Puritan) "Protestant ethic" surveyed by Weber and the more establishment-oriented views of Mainline denominations. We also find a growing branch of Dominionism in this category, which has made remarkable inroads within evangelicalism in the past two decades. Though not identified on this chart, this category would also hold the strategic attempts of the "Corporate Right" to inject pro-capitalist and free market ideas into the faith and work movement.

But flanking this crowded sacralizing and stabilizing category are the two other explored categories of orienting to the economic sector. On one side of the sacralizing and stabilizing category are the subordinating and shirking category, the category that continues to hold the heirs of the soul-saving, other-worldly Grahamism. The fundamentalist work ethic

**Table 8.1** Categories of "Protestant Ethics" and Their Orientation to the Economic Realm

| **Subordinating and Shirking** | **Sacralizing and Stabilizing** | **Subverting and Straining** |
|---|---|---|
| "Fundamentalist Work Ethic" | Classical "Protestant Ethic" | Sectarian and Separatist Groups |
| Grahamism | Mainline Protestantism | Communitarian Faith and Work |
| | Re-integrating Theologies of Work (Faith and Work Movement) | |
| | Dominionism | |
| | Prosperity Gospel | |

that served as the antecedent to Grahamism is also placed here. These efforts preserve the centrality of spiritual and ecclesial activities like soul-saving and inward-facing piety at the expense of providing theological content relevant to Monday and economic activities. Other movements and currents fall within the third category identified, the "subverting and straining." Here we find two efforts or currents. The first is a rather hodgepodge grouping of "sectarian" or separatist religious groups that imbue Monday life with religious responsibilities but in a manner that creates points of tensions and conflict with the wider economic system. For these groups, worries over Monday somehow becoming sequestered from religious identities have little resonance. Falling alongside this grouping is a subsection of the faith and work movement that has yet to be discussed: those leaders and efforts championing the re-embedding frameworks discussed in Chapter 4. These leaders—identified here as "communitarians"—harness the same concerns of the broader faith and work movement to steer evangelical laity toward ethical commitments and actions that should be imposed on the economic sphere. However, their guiding vision and approach occupy a distinct space that warrants a more focused exploration, undertaken below.

Prior chapters have already explored the faith and work movement's relationship to Mainline Protestantism, Grahamism, the older Christian Right, and the well-funded politicization efforts of the Corporate Right. This final chapter now fleshes out relationships and points of intersections with these remaining "contender" orientations for imbuing Monday with significance: sectarian, Dominionist, Prosperity Gospel, and communitarian orientations. These movements and traditions reviewed confer a broad range of meanings on Monday: Monday becomes, respectively, a realm of service performed in conformance with communal values, a realm of defeating and displacing one's spiritual foes, a realm for laying claim to God's assured material blessings, or a realm for serving the common good of wider society. While the analysis that follows is primarily intended to be comparative, each section below also probes the historical intersections with the faith and work movement to bring out the historical contingency of the faith and work movement itself. Each of these, then, in some way represents "roads not (yet) taken" by the faith and work movement.

## Faith and Work among Its Contenders: Sectarian, Dominionist, Prosperity Gospel, Communitarian

### Sectarian Separatists: Anabaptists, Low-Church Sects, Labor Churches, and Quakers

It is worth surveying several Protestant groups that forged radically different paths than the Puritans and Calvinists closely studied by Weber. These churches did not participate in what R. H. Tawney narrates as "the abdication of the Christian Churches from departments of economic conduct and social theory long claimed as their province." This allowed them to avoid what Tawney observes as the "uncritical acquiescence of values that uncritically conferred ethical values on pecuniary gain."[3] These groups instead occupy a position closer to what scholars label a religious "sect." Sects see themselves in tension with their surrounding sociocultural environment and create "subcultural deviance or tension: difference, antagonism, and separation."[4] Perhaps what is most interesting about these particular cases is that no religious group here could be labeled "anti-work" or deeply opposed to inner-worldly asceticism: all of these groups broadly endorsed the classical work virtues of disciplined effort, thrift, and industriousness. Some groups in fact gained recognition among their contemporaries for famously cultivating such virtues among their laity. But these groups sent their adherents into capitalist work settings bearing theological frameworks that greatly tempered their acceptance of the surrounding economic order or their assigned place within it.

The sectarian camp would include several groups in the Anabaptist tradition that draw on a long historical lineage of engaging the economic sphere with suspicion and prudence, generally mediated by authoritative mechanisms within the church itself. An early church document from 1568 commanded church members not to engage in buying and selling without the counsel and prior knowledge and consent of the brotherhood and elders.[5] This communalist orientation to business dealings in many ways continues today among Anabaptist groups, though not without difficulty. As one Mennonite scholar observes, this communalism fit much more naturally at its place of origin—European peasant agricultural societies—than it does in contemporary capitalism.[6] Nevertheless, Mennonites have continued to approach business as endeavors to a means of contributing to the community. A 2000 cover story of the weekly publication *The Mennonite* warned of the dangerous pull on Mennonite business owners to enter into contractual relationships with those who do not hold to Mennonite values, thus possibly making it difficult to fulfill their commitments to distinctive values. These seemingly high-demand commitments have not obstructed many Mennonites from entering professional and business careers, including positions of leadership in major corporations. Today, the tradition continues to rely on discipleship within their local communities to ward off the pulls and allure of the surrounding materialist culture.[7]

Studies of contemporary Mennonite entrepreneurs reveal an overarching affirmation for entrepreneurial and industrious behaviors at the local level. But laity are expected to keep these behaviors integrated within local communal relationships while avoiding an overly acquisitive materialism. Likely following from this imperative, individual economic enterprises serve as an integral part of Mennonite community and symbolize an adherent's dedication to serve and love others in the community. But increasing profits and business expansion generally entails doing more business with members outside the community, interactions that generate judgment and suspicion from those within the church. Successful business owners report feeling alienated and misunderstood by their local churches, paralleling the "perils" of success experienced by upwardly mobile conservative Protestants. Anabaptist entrepreneurs will occasionally sell their businesses when they perceive their economic success threatens either their own lifestyle commitments or their relationship with church and family. "I saw that the business was running away with me," explained one Amish entrepreneur who sold a highly profitable, thirty-person construction company. "I saw that the business was interfering with my relationships with my family and church, and so I had to make a choice." After giving up the profitable enterprise he started a harness shop that employed only himself and his two sons.[8]

Several sect-like churches from the nineteenth century also constructed similar oppositional orientations toward their surrounding economic systems. Many of those churches have been lower-class, "low-church" congregations—the "churches of the disinherited," following Niebuhr—which far more commonly draw upon uneducated clergy from the church's own population for leadership, thereby reinforcing a working-class ethos in the congregation. Several of these groups—Wesleyan Methodists, Free Methodists, Stillwell Methodists—split off from Methodism over doctrinal or church governance disagreements. Their defection created groups and networks of Methodists that did not experience the same embourgeoisement of mid-nineteenth century Methodism.[9] Several African American Methodist groups like the Church of God in Christ, dissatisfied with their treatment in white-controlled churches, also splintered off from Methodism around the beginning of the eighteenth century.[10] In the United Kingdom, the Primitive Methodists represented a workers-led splinter group seeking to preserve the more revivalist elements that they felt were being lost as Methodism gained middle-class respectability.

These groups' location within the working-class social strata made them natural allies to labor causes born from changing work conditions in the nineteenth and early twentieth centuries. Both Free Methodists and the Salvation Army were on the frontlines of urban labor organizing and conflict at the turn of the century, condemning corporate monopolies, assisting Chinese and Japanese immigrant workers, and caring for striking workers on the picket lines.[11] This dynamic also played out in non-urban areas: Liston Pope's classic work *Millhands and Preachers* surveys the different reaction of religious leaders to a 1929 miner's strike in Gaston County, North Carolina. Pope observes that those churches supporting the workers were the leaders of Pentecostal, Holiness, and Wesleyan churches.[12] Of course, these churches and their leaders were rarely engaged in reflexively constructing a "theology of work"; they were more often confronting an inability to sequester economic matters from spiritual matters due to the immediate material needs of their members. But in other cases, sectarian churches saw the forces of industrialization as spiritual impurities requiring an ascetic resistance: such developments were decried as leading to impersonal social relations, unchecked pursuit of profit, and a materialism that detracted from a life of holiness.[13]

Finally, in addition to Mennonites and low-church sect groups there is also the very complex case of the Quakers, a group that German theologian Ernst Troeltsch saw as defying his dichotomous categorization of church and sects. Industrious Quakers in England were at the forefront of the Industrial Revolution, with Quaker iron mill owner Abraham Darby recognized as one of the leading innovators in modernizing iron production. Quakers of the seventeenth and eighteenth centuries would enter into particular trades and businesses with specific interests of serving the public good, whether producing affordable cooking pots for working-class families, making chocolate with medicinal purposes, or producing beverages that could serve as alternatives to alcohol. They also devoted considerable amounts of profits to the betterment of the working poor, whether through supporting relief work or building housing for their own factory workers. Local Quaker Meetings imposed formal and informal modes of oversight on members who were engaged in economic enterprises. Similar to the Anabaptists, they preached caution of business owners "running beyond their depth, and entangling themselves in a greater multiplicity of trade and business than they can extricate themselves from, with honor and reputation."[14] Those discovered to be manufacturing weapons or even winter coats for the military ran up against the group's avowed pacifism: their owners were summoned to the Meeting to give account of their dealings. But Quakers had fewer qualms about a properly run business in comparison to Anabaptists: they became associated with high ethical standards and trustworthiness, which served to fuel greater economic success. The group's eventual social ascension into a more respectable middle-class faith is generally seen to have weakened their theologically rooted economic ethic, reflecting the common pattern observed by John Wesley and others.[15]

## Interactions with the Faith and Work Movement

Sectarian groups' orientations to work and economics have borne minimal impact on the faith and work movement. There is good reason for this: most evangelical leaders advocating for theologies of work across the twentieth century were consciously seeking to escape the insularity and separatism of fundamentalism that incited withdrawal from the wider economic-cultural order. Thus, no voices in the faith and work movement have ever endorsed communal oversight of commerce and trade, moral condemnation of economic prosperity, skepticism toward impersonal market relationships, a preference for communal ties in business dealings, identification with labor over and against owners and capital, or a transvalued status system that valorized those at the bottom of the capitalist order. In fact, on all these fronts, the faith and work movement is far more likely to adhere to precisely the opposite position. Postwar evangelicalism's steady gains in education and status are likely responsible for widening the gap between the faith and work movement and the remnants of sectarian tendencies in certain low-church denominations. For one, the steadily gaining educational and occupational prestige among white evangelicals—combined with a broader exodus of working-class adherents from religious communities since the 1970s—has granted many evangelical churches insulation from firsthand experiences of precarity and labor unrest, a privilege not afforded to earlier fundamentalist churches. Even denominations birthed from splintering "sects" from larger denominations—such as Holiness, Wesleyan, and Pentecostal groups—have largely failed to exert counter-pulls against the gradual assimilation into the more comfortable and affluent middle class.[16] Enduring racial and ethnic divides in evangelical congregations also firm up this insularity from significant labor issues, shielding many homogenously white congregations from those populations more likely to experience labor market precarity or the more sedimented labor market stratification. But there is likely an additional structural factor keeping sectarian thinking at bay: the dominant model of funding parachurch efforts (like faith and work events) tightly binds organizational activities to the guiding interests of the donor class, a phenomenon that dates back to at least D. L. Moody's ministry and the establishment of business-funded urban ministry efforts.[17] This alignment contributes to the faith and work space reflecting the dispositions and perceived needs of those who occupy the "thriving" arenas of capitalism. Such arenas typically fail to be strongholds for sectarian orientations that minimize participation within dominant societal institutions.

## Dominionism

Other subsections of American Protestantism approach the economic realm with a unique orientation that warrants consideration here. This subsection not only implores religious adherents to bring their faith into the marketplace: they want adherents to take it over. Historian Sara Diamond's work traces the economic visions of Dominionist theology: drawing on the same Kuyperian themes elevated by contemporary faith and work movement, Dominionist leaders deliver a call to "return American to its Christian roots." Dominionists of various stripes adopt the idea that "Christians, and Christians alone, are biblically mandated to occupy all secular institutions until Christ returns."[18] The dominant form of Dominionism in American religious history is a branch called Christian Reconstructionism led by R. J. Rushdoony. Rushdoony was deeply inspired by Kuyper's notion of sphere sovereignty, from which he developed a vision of theonomic rule that turns back to the juridical laws of the Old Testament. Reconstructionist leaders have always had complex ties to wider evangelical theology: for one, they are adamant critics of the soul-saving revivalist individualism that dominated twentieth-century evangelicalism. Leaders at times found more resonance with the Christian Right, seeing themselves as the inspiration for Falwell's Moral Majority and appearing on television shows hosted by Christian Right leaders Pat Robertson and D. James Kennedy.[19] However, Reconstructionists sharply diverge from many evangelicals due to their endorsement of post-millennialism over pre-millennialism, rejecting the notion that history can only regress until Christ's return.

Since the 1990s, this Reconstructionist branch of Dominionist theology has lost ground to another branch of Dominionism, which simply goes by the more general name of Dominionism. This group, too, reads Kuyper and follows his sphere sovereignty approach to warrant a transformational takeover of the structures of society.[20] Dominionists stitch themselves into the Reconstructionist history following Kuyper and Rushdoony, but they make several important turns after the 1970s. According to theologian Peter Wagner's history, Dominionists incorporate several Pentecostal figures and a set of independent charismatic churches, as well as the Chinese House Church Movement and the Latin American Grassroots Church Movement. Today, the most visible form of this later, more charismatic Dominionist arm is the New Apostolic Reformation.[21] One study of this movement estimates that three million Americans attend Dominionism-driven New Apostolic Reformation congregations.[22] The New Apostolic Reformation dates back to the 1970s, when two religious leaders—Bill Bright, founder of Campus Crusades for Christ, and Loren Cunningham, founder of Youth With a Mission—recounted receiving an identical prophetic message from God in 1974. This message was: society is made up of seven different mountains that must be "brought under the headship of Christ." Kuyper's spheres and the concept of sovereignty operate in the background here. Lance Wallnau, a popular prophetic figure associated with the movement, is quoted by Wagner: "If the world is to be won, these are the mountains that mold the culture and the minds of men. Whoever controls these mountains controls the direction of the world and the harvest therein."

Important to our story, one of the seven mountains is business. Seven Mountain theology subscribes to "displacement theology," which discards the concept of "common grace" that allows Christians to partner together with non-Christians through a shared interest in working toward the good of society. Instead, religious individuals are conferred a favored status that warrants taking control of the institutions within the business sector while displacing current leaders. The movement relies on an "apostolic" understanding of power, which they see as a point of disagreement with churches that confer power and authority upon "groups" (identified as deacon boards, boards of trustees, presbyteries, and general assemblies); they have instead turned to apostolic individuals who exhibit signs of conferred spiritual authority. These individuals are charged to engage the individuals and forces currently occupying the mountains in "spiritual battle," wrestling away power from Satanic forces currently controlling the mountains. Dominionist leaders openly identify these teachings as defecting from broader American evangelicalism in several ways, particularly related to eschatology and cultural influence. Os Hillman (mentioned below) and Wagner consciously reject the "hearts and minds" relational model of cultural change that dominates white American evangelicalism. They instead speak of "elite power structures" or nations as their desired targets, at times citing sociological theories of culture change. "Winning souls is important," asserts Hillman in a webinar on Seven Mountain theology. "However, that alone won't change culture. [We] must avoid 'rapture theology.'"[23]

The cultural influence strategy of Seven Mountain theology has made impressive inroads among evangelical institutions. A 2012 book by Gabe Lyon called *The Next Christians: Seven Ways You Can Live the Gospel and Restore the World* championed seven "channels" through which culture could be influenced by Christians, reproducing much of Hillman's arguments for cultural influence. This framework would go on to serve as the background vision for Q-Ideas, Lyon's influential leadership gatherings which regularly draw together influential evangelical leaders and pastors. In May 2020, the Southern Baptist Convention sought to enlist its congregations to pray for the "seven centers of influence in America" in coordination with the National Day of Prayer. While neither of these institutions explicitly identifies with wider Dominionist or Reconstructionist theologies, organizational leaders seem to be replicating the underlying strategy of influence.

## Intersections with the Faith and Work Movement

Both New Apostolic Reformation and Seven Mountain Prophecies played a central role in early faith and work movements. This is largely the product of something for which Dominionists are rarely given credit: they effectively invented the faith and work conference, leading the "first wave" of events described in Chapter 3. The Dominionist theology promoted at the earliest events was minimal: materials and recaps from the first organized faith and work conference suggest the event largely promoted a re-commissioning framework in seeing workplaces as strategic places of evangelism. But in the early 2000s, Dominionist theology and cultural visions became more prevalent. Os Hillman, head of the Atlanta-based group Marketplace Ministries, coordinated the first "Church in the Workplace" conference in downtown Atlanta in January 2007, targeting Christian pastors and workplace leaders. The conference featured Wagner, popular Christian author Henry Blackaby, and Kent Humphreys, a faith and work leader who was then leading the Fellowship of Companies for Christ International. Hillman's website recounts three more conferences that followed this 2007 gathering, each one becoming more vocal in their commitments to Seven Mountain and Dominionist theology. But after a 2010 event in Atlanta, the influence of Dominionist theology appears to lessen in the faith and work space. Dominionists leaders largely vanish from the faith and work conference circuit, while Dominionist charges to cultural transformation seems to be displaced by more popular Reformed understandings of Kuyper's cultural mandate, which notably lack commitments to displacement theology or apostolic notions of power.[24]

This abrupt usurping of Dominionism at first appears puzzling: having "invented" the national faith and work conference, why did Dominionist leaders then fail to maintain their central role in the movement? Dominionists had no shortage of networks and social ties connecting to organizations and individuals. Hillman reports his daily devotional reached 190,000 subscribers by 2011, and early rosters of attendees demonstrated a broad inclusion of evangelical parachurch organizations. More impressively, Hillman's efforts from the beginning had an unmatched symbolic legitimacy in the backing of Billy Graham and his ministry association. All of Hillman's books, websites, and conference literature proclaim Graham's endorsement of the workplace as the location for "one of the next great moves of God." Involvement by well-known evangelical scholars and authors also boosted legitimacy. Yet their unique political-cultural agenda becomes difficult to locate within the faith and work space after the 2010 Atlanta conference. Hillman himself, when asked in our interview, had no explanation for this development: Hillman cited his own deliberate shift away from the work arena toward the culture arena, focusing his energies on a different "mountain" to be captured.[25] Another faith and work leader familiar with Hillman's efforts suggested that Hillman's gatherings were simply outgunned by groups making better use of newly emerging technology in the early 2010s.[26]

My own conjecture, based on assessments of popular speakers and leaders at the early Dominionist conferences, is that the larger faith and work movement underwent a subtle but consequential status upgrade—based on prestige markers related to education levels, geographic proximity to knowledge economy hubs, and occupational prestige—that bore consequences for movement leadership during these decades. Whereas Pentecostal theology typically occupies Protestant denominations with the lowest levels of educational attainment, Reformed groups like the Presbyterian Church in America (P.C.A.) are composed of the highest-educated evangelical laity. It is not surprising, then, that Reformed currents of the movement gained a stronger hold among the knowledge-economy, highly educated laity in which most of faith and work movements came to reside. Dominionist leaders, in contrast, lacked the needed educational credentials or subcultural legitimacy that holds sway within urban centers of influence, at least among white evangelicals.[27] But regardless of the precise explanation, this first wave of faith and work leaders deposited their most lasting influence in the publication of faith and work books written by not only Hillman, but also Peter Wagner, Ed Silvoso, Kent Humphreys, and Linda Rios Brook. These books continue to show up on bibliographies of faith and work books endorsed by actors and organizations across the movement.[28]

## The Prosperity Gospel

There is a long tradition in the American context of religious belief or values promising material rewards and achievement. This weaves through early Puritan preaching on the reward of good character while becoming the target of Wesley's hand-wringing over increasingly affluent Methodists eventually leaving their faith behind. It also famously makes its way into Andrew Carnegie's "Gospel of Wealth" thinking. Such beliefs are today most centrally located in the rapidly growing Prosperity Gospel movement. According to historian Kate Bowler, the Prosperity Gospel positions faith as the mechanism of power that unleashes spiritual forces and translates words into material reality. Faith, then, is "palpably demonstrated" through the acquisition of wealth and health.[29] Prosperity Gospel beliefs then offer to supercharge Monday with spiritual significance by linking work with spiritual and material blessings: acquiring such blessings represents a special calling and opportunity afforded to clergy and laity alike.

Today, surveys suggest 17 percent of the American public adheres to Prosperity Gospel beliefs. Three of America's largest twelve congregations preach the Prosperity Gospel message. But Prosperity Gospel beliefs tend to take hold among a demographic profile quite different from those attracted to the faith and work movement.[30] A 2006 Pew Forum of Pentecostals reveals that individuals with higher incomes and education are *less likely* to embrace Prosperity Gospel beliefs.[31] A Christian research firm found in a 2017 study that 69 percent of Protestant churchgoers believe "God wants me to prosper financially," but this belief is held by a greater percentage of Black Protestants (84 percent) and Hispanics (68 percent) than white Protestants (63 percent). The racial divide is even greater among those who agree with the statement "To receive material blessings from God, I have to do something for God." Here, 44 percent of Black respondents and 34 percent of Hispanic respondents agreed, compared to 17 percent of white respondents. For all beliefs measured, the denomination most likely to agree was Assemblies of God or Pentecostals; Lutherans always came in last.[32] A 2014 Pew study suggests 51 percent of U.S. Hispanic Protestants and 54 percent of U.S. Hispanic Catholics agree with the statement "God will grant wealth and health to believers who have enough faith." Several other studies have shown Black Protestant adherents are the most likely of any religious group to subscribe to Prosperity Gospel beliefs.[33]

## Intersections with the Faith and Work Movement

Faith and work leaders make remarkably few references to Prosperity Gospel leaders or teachings, whether positive or negative. This may reflect an earlier movement splintering in the faith and work movement that tacitly funneled Prosperity Gospel adherents to a more self-contained wing of the "Christian business" world. The Full Gospel Business Men's Fellowship International was founded in 1951 by Demos Shakarian, a Californian dairy farmer, commercial real estate developer, and Pentecostal evangelist. Shakarian was already heavily networked with Pentecostal leaders of the era, and his business fellowship came directly out of a conversation with evangelist Oral Roberts.[34] He went on to help plant the ministry of Pentecostal minister John Osteen, whose better-known son Joel Osteen took over in 1999 on John's death. In the postwar years this fellowship was successful in taking Pentecostal practices of healing "mainstream," inviting laity to lunches and dinners in hotel ballrooms—thought to be less threatening than churches—where many experienced healing experiences for the first time. The group grew steadily in size and influence: by the 1980s they reported having 2,646 chapters where 700,000 people met regularly each month. A gathering in 1956 featured Vice President Richard Nixon as keynote speaker. Today the group reports chapters in 140 different countries, though the organization's vitality was hindered by leadership battles and internal lawsuits soon after Shakarian died in 1993. Three splinter groups have come from Shakarian's group: the International Fellowship of Christian Businessmen, the Business Men's Fellowship, and the Full Gospel Business Men's Fellowship of America. There is also some crossover between Shakarian's organized events and charismatic leaders who would go on to influence the Dominionist movement outlined above.

There is no noticeable interplay between these Shakarian-descended groups and the faith and work space today. There are, however, analogous teachings and principles. Faith and work movement leaders commonly package and sell their teachings in a manner that promises "results" for successful faith-work integration. *Experience the Powerful Advantage of Integrating Your Faith and Work* is one example of a book subtitle that effectively signals this. Assurances of success were particularly common in the earlier "faith and businessman" era of the movement, which generally championed running one's companies by biblical or godly principles. Even Billy Graham weighed in, singing praises of several Christian businessmen in a 1954 essay written for the Chamber of Commerce's national publication. Graham asserted these businessmen demonstrated having "God as a working partner" means inserting "integrity into their organizations, sincerity into their sales, and spiritual and monetary profits into their hearts and pockets."[35] For Graham and others speaking in this vein, it would be largely unimaginable that entering into a "partnership" with God would yield anything other than success. The faith and work leaders of this earlier era are still quoted and awarded platforms in the movement today. Among today's leaders, several interviewees, when asked how a faith-integrated worker differs from a Sunday-morning-faith worker, cited improved productivity as a byproduct. Thus, despite leaders keeping their distance from figures and ideas formerly associated with the Prosperity Gospel, this does not stop them from tracing their own assured pathway between faith and success in work, reflecting a phenomenon also observed among creative-class evangelicals by sociologist Gerardo Marti.[36] Workers are instructed to approach their careers dutifully: if faith is properly integrated, enhanced performance and outcomes will follow.

One interviewee, writer and popular speaker Kate Harris, voiced criticism of the movement's overemphasis on success, which she saw being promoted at the expense of adequately discussing limitations and constraints. Workers' day-to-day realities often get papered over within the grander creation-to-consummation narrative, she told me. "What's in between these [creation and consummation]," Harris observes,

> is the life we're actually living, which is the disorienting thing for us. "I want this good thing to happen but all these bad things are happening." "I want to be successful, but I keep being disappointed." I think the thing Christianity offers that nowhere else offers is a way to contend with that. It's the tension of: you die to yourself and that brings life. Christ dies and that brings life to the world.

Harris's discussion of constraints and a life-through-death theology stands out in the faith and work space. The possibilities of failure are rarely discussed, and a proto-Prosperity Gospel inherited from the earlier faith and businessman still dispels possibilities of an "unsuccessful" Christian business. The majority of messaging instead speaks from a more optimistic, solution-centered perspective. This positive framing is likely also a product of the underlying entrepreneurial posturing of the thought leaders themselves. Because of their institutional independence, most of them must effectively "sell" their symbolic wares to a wider audience in the form of speaking, consulting, writing, and teaching. This condition tends to favor those offerings that sell a more positive Monday, one permeated with not only meaning and significance but also success. Perhaps the sharpest point of contrast with the Prosperity Gospel movement appears when faith and work leaders directly address a wider range of jobs and occupations. On these points, many speakers move toward a more stoic affirmation of toilsome work as intrinsically good, independent of economic returns.[37]

## Communitarianism

The final strand examined differs from the prior three in that it is entirely endogenous to the evangelical faith and work movement itself. However, the ideas outlined here represent a "road not (yet) taken" due to the larger movement's ambivalence and subtle resistances to these voices. These frameworks depart from the sacralizing and stabilizing category to instead impose exogenous norms, ends, and practices upon the work. "Communitarian" evangelicals thus represent the faith and work movement's sole entry in the "subverting and straining" category. I have employed the label "communitarian" to reflect their frequent references to the "common good." Some books advocating this approach to work include: Amy Sherman's *Kingdom Calling: Vocational Stewardship for the Common Good*; Steven Garber's *Visions of Vocation: Common Grace for the Common Good*; a more textbook-like text published by Intervarsity Press called *Business for the Common Good: A Christian Vision for the Marketplace*; Tom Nelson's *Work Matters: Connecting Sunday Worship to Monday Work*; and Tim Keller's *Every Good Endeavor*. Three of the most frequently cited faith and work books in the space ground their turn to the common good in the political philosophy of communitarianism, citing the need for the restoration of vocation identified in Robert Bellah et al.'s *Habits of the Heart*.[38] Taking seriously Bellah et al.'s charge to restore "secondary languages" of moral commitments, these faith and work leaders look to reinsert into work the biblical notions of justice and compassion.

One leader who makes the most direct appeal to such principles is scholar and writer Amy Sherman. Sherman posits a high bar for what it means to practice "vocational stewardship," writing in her book *Kingdom Calling*: "A central premise of this book is that the average middle-class (or wealthier) Christian in America has been blessed with much from God—skills wealth, opportunity, vocational position, education, influence, networks. We are, in short, prospering. The purpose of all these blessings is simple to state and difficult to live: we are blessed to be a blessing."[39] This sort of messaging has earned Sherman a particular reputation in the faith and work space: another speaker at a conference informally referred to her as the "one who does the social justice thing." Sherman is one of the few leaders in the faith and work space who actively distances her own faith and work message from the more common re-integrating framework, saying in our interview:

> I think what happened to me was coming to the recognition that if we really want to see significant structural transformation in our communities . . . ,[Christians] would need to advance the flourishing of the city in and through their daily work and vocations. So for me, the motivation for getting involved in the faith and work movement has been less about

> "Oh let's help people find deep meaning in their work," although I do want that for people. It's been much more practical, about "I want to see cities change, I want to see justice advanced, I want to see critical social problems addressed effectively by the church." And that's not going to happen until bankers, architects, engineers, and everybody else actually see their vocation as an avenue through which they can advance kingdom foretastes like justice and health and wholeness and beauty.

Sherman and other communitarian voices are advancing what I earlier labeled the re-embedding framework: work is framed as having ends wider than the worker's or the organization's own success. It is Sherman, in fact, who first provided the "adverbial" label for theologies of work that merely task laity to work more diligently or faithfully. Workers are instead charged to see work as means to serve the wider ends of society. Sherman's ethical vision builds from biblical notions of justice and *shalom*, a Hebrew word designating "universal flourishing, wholeness, and delight." *Kingdom Calling* works through the Bible to locate three components of justice: rescuing the poor, innocent, and helpless from grim realities; establishing equitable and fair relationships among the weak and strong; and restoring wrongdoers to the wider community. Sherman's concept of *shalom* also draws out four dimensions: peace with God, peace with self, peace with others, and peace with creation. The ethics of work then becomes navigating some affirmation-worthy elements of one's work while resisting others. Sherman articulated this in our interview by delineating two ethical questions: "In our work, how can we affirm that which is *shalom*-enhancing in our sector? How do we identify and resist that which is *shalom*-decaying or resisting?"

The faith and work space in some ways proves very open to the communitarian message. For one, Sherman likely keeps the busiest travel schedule of any of the leaders I interviewed. She is involved in multiple faith and work organizations, is formally employed by a think tank in a different state than where she lives, speaks frequently at retreats and churches, and even appears as a featured talking head in a professionally produced film series created by the Acton Institute.[40] Common good language is also often interspersed with the cultural-redemption and "transformational" views of Keller and Redeemer Presbyterian Church, which Sherman cites as having a significant influence on her thinking. But the communitarian push of Sherman and other leaders has trouble making meaningful dents in the faith and work space. For one, these visions often fall in conflict with the dominant re-integrating frameworks' interests in affirming the virtues and practices that are endogenous to the realm of Monday. This is a rift that goes all the way back to Dorothy Sayers's original essay on work. Sayers judged churches' pressure for work that serves the common good to indicate a failure in appreciation for the goods already achieved by workers' trades.

But this tension in many ways runs much deeper. The faith and work movement's primary orientation of venerating the inherent goodness of work undertaken within a capitalist system leaves little room for values that might run against that system. As Southern Baptist historian David Sapp observes of his own religious tradition,

> Southern Baptists, along with other religious groups, might be expected to have difficulty in critiquing economic values, since they actually have fostered many of the values which undergird capitalism. A basic emphasis of Max Weber's classic study *The Protestant Ethic and the Spirit of Capitalism* was that modern capitalism is a social expression of the Calvinist doctrine of "calling." This doctrine grew it in the "work ethic" which had strong influence in Southern Baptist life. As one result of this emphasis, the acquisition of inordinate amounts of money and the practice of piety have come to be seen by some Southern Baptists as natural partners. Those who would fault the churches for their lack of a prophetic voice on economic issues must remember that the churches helped teach Americans that diligence was pleasing to God and that prosperity was his blessing. Those same churches may find it hard to sound another note from the gospel which says that hard work is narcotically addictive and that too much wealth is a powerful temptation to idolatry.[41]

Sapp's observations offer clarity to why the "sacralizing and stabilizing" category has become so crowded among Protestant perspectives: it is rare that "Protestant ethics" are able to critique a system purportedly built on "*the* Protestant ethic." Communitarian evangelicals, then, find themselves occupying an otherwise uncommon—and perhaps unsustainable—position. Many times, their own ethical vision seems to clash with the Kuyperian approaches to culture explored earlier. Sphere sovereignty, after all, can easily come to provide an affirmation for the autonomy and goods already operating within different spheres. As Sayers argues, respect for such goods requires keeping at bay the oversight of the church or the imposition of any exogenous ethical criteria.This challenge is exacerbated by the dearth of robust ethical frameworks through which evangelicals view questions of economic justice or political economy more broadly. It also leaves many evangelical leaders vulnerable to those voices on the Corporate Right that present the fruits of competitive capitalism *as* the common good.

Leaders in the faith and work space often inadvertently contribute to this problem by seeking to bracket wider systemic or structural contingencies of the economic realm, which effectively reifies them as natural parts of economic experiences. The influential book *Your Work Matters to God* employs such an approach in jettisoning bigger economic questions from the get-go:

> The right question is not which economic system would be the closest to a biblical ideal. That's an interesting question, but is really a problem of economic theory. Economics enters into this discussion, but economics deals with problems as they exist in an overall system, whereas most of us are trying to deal with problems at our own individual levels, in our own lifestyle. Economics bears on our situation, but what we need is a practical approach to lifestyle.[42]

This tacit acceptance of the status quo often leaves a very narrow range of autonomy to workers to integrate exogenous ethical criteria that serve the common good. Questions of structural injustices related to racial disparities or inequality are quietly shuffled away from consideration: these are sequestered from the "practical approaches" judged to be of use to everyday workers.

To Sherman's credit, her writing and speaking are saturated with tangible examples of ethically infused visions of work: a house-cleaning firm working to provide more accommodating hours for workers, a dance studio owner using performances to bring attention to conflict in Uganda, an inner-city business owner trying to employ the unemployed in his church, a fashion designer who incorporates eco-friendly materials. In my interviews with leaders, Sherman's familiarity with such cases proved exceptional. But these examples subtly favor a certain type of economic actor: workers and actors with exceptionally high levels of agency in their jobs, generally small business owners, entrepreneurs, or CEOs who can personally direct firm attention and resources. How these moral charges might apply to a wider range of workers goes unexplored. Ultimately, the evangelical communitarian vision seems to replicate many elements of the voluntary or nonprofit sector. "Do gooders" are presumed to work in hyper-agentic settings somehow operating outside of the organizational or competitive pressures of the contemporary economic landscape. Evangelical communitarianism thus represents a far more truncated ethical vision of vocation than those promoted by earlier Puritans or the more prophetic preaching of nineteenth-century revivalists. Both of these earlier groups interspersed personal responsibility with prophetic calls for social reform.[43]

* * *

To conclude, it is worth speaking to the future of the faith and work movement in view of the larger landscape laid out above. The two most salient sociological factors shaping the future of the economic orientations of American evangelicalism are likely exogenous to the faith and work movement. The first are the economic structures that will shape the future of the labor market and common work experiences. To date, the diffusion of the contemporary faith and work movement has proven limited by its parochial conception of work, one that—while rarely explicitly defined—disproportionately resonates with higher-status managerial and creative-class evangelicals. While this message was forged within settings tailored to the challenges of Christian businessmen, it has now found a receptive audience among a wider swath of workers possessing strong and affective bonds to their jobs and careers, including nurses, teachers, artists, and writers. But the movement's success as a subcultural insurgency effort likely remains dependent on the prevalence of a labor market providing such opportunities. Any number of changes in work conditions among evangelical laity could move more laity away from conditions in which the faith and work resources prove helpful, whether a greater loosening of worker ties to white-collar work, the continual decline of labor force participation, or growing scarcity of "good jobs" that offer stable settings facilitating deeper commitment and loyalties. Meanwhile, economic changes could easily drive a greater number of evangelical laity toward religious resources that provide far different interpretations and frameworks for making sense of one's experience, including those that reduce work's centrality within individuals' conception of their identity and sense of worth.

Economic conditions themselves may also prove consequential to how evangelicals orient themselves to their work. As made visible by John Schmalzbauer's study of religious groups assimilating to dominant culture, the successful social ascension and incorporation of evangelicals can easily lead to a paradoxical situation in which the faith and work movement's success also represents its own obsolescence over time. Promoting resacralization frameworks—or, as discussed in prior chapters, re-integrating frameworks to those in elite socioeconomic positions—raises the possibility of the movement serving as its own gravedigger as it shuttles evangelicals from subcultural institutions centered on evangelical distinctives into full admission within mainstream societal institutions. In preaching the virtues and merits of economic behaviors achieved independently of "Sunday" activities, faith and work leaders may see their message become superfluous to the wider career-centric ethos of creative-class capitalism. We might return to Niebuhr's classical analysis of socially ascendant religious groups generally venerating those "peculiar virtues" already residing within the class strata that group comes to occupy.[44] For the social ascending middle-class Methodism of the nineteenth century, Niebuhr identifies those virtues as honesty, industry, sobriety, thrift, and prudence. This time, it is the virtues in creative-class capitalism that are given a theological gloss. Creativity, an aesthetic approach to work, and callings falling in harmony with supra-individual purpose now take on greater value.

But setting aside the cultural-economic interplay of the movement, the future will also almost certainly be shaped the steady growth and prevalence of "political evangelicalism." This term—described more in Chapter 1—refers to the increasingly homogenous political constituency that have made their way to evangelicalism, effectively rendering evangelicalism a group defined more by political views rather than theological dispositions. Since roughly the time of the 2008 recession, political evangelicalism has largely followed wider conservative currents in elevating anti-immigrant, authoritarian, and nationalist values to the center of its political vision, gravitating toward a paleo-conservatism constructed around cultural anxieties related to race, national identity, and immigration. Due to this book's central focus on economic orientations among the evangelical populace, the political dimensions of evangelicalism have made only spot appearances. But political evangelicalism likely stands to simultaneously reshape not only the constituency categorized as evangelical but also the economic imaginaries to which that constituency subscribes. For one, the growing energies around political evangelicalism will likely deepen distrust toward the institutions that shape creative-class settings, whether the media, higher education, the arts, the financial sector, or tech companies. This will likely narrow the proportion of the evangelical populace that takes interest in adverbial ethics seeking to steer lay energies toward serving these institutions' ends and well-being. Political evangelicalism instead represents a return of a more conspiratorial orientation to the world that prevailed within earlier fundamentalism. From that perspective, such institutions are viewed as hostile and threatening, not only to the larger social order, but also to the maintenance of a white Protestant majority in the United States.

On another front, political evangelicalism appears to alter the criteria for figures, ideas, and organizations granted admission into evangelical spaces. Because criteria have shifted from theological to political beliefs, theological perspectives that in the past would not make it past the subculture's gatekeepers are now granted free rein within the evangelical space. Two particular economic orientations surveyed above—Dominionism and Prosperity Gospel teaching—have made tremendous gains in the era surrounding Trump's 2016 and 2020 presidential campaigns. Dominionist leader Lance Wallnau's veneration of Trump as God's chosen "chaos candidate" made deep inroads into the discourse of Christian Right and directly shaped the language of campaign rallies featuring Trump himself alongside more traditional Christian Right leaders.[45] Dominionist frameworks also mobilized what political scientist Damon Berry called "prophecy voters": religiously motivated supporters of Trump who saw their support as a means to vanquish evil forces in alignment with the teachings of the New Apostolic Reformation.[46] Prosperity Gospel teachings also gained new legitimacy in political evangelicalism through Trump's close association with well-known Prosperity Gospel teachers like Paula White and Kenneth Copeland.

This reconfiguration of leaders and legitimate theological beliefs is reinforced by a reconstitution of the populations that make up evangelical populace. Political scientist Ryan Burge has demonstrated that the coalescing of political evangelicalism has led to higher levels of evangelical self-identification among conservative voters with lower levels of religiosity and even conservatives affiliated with Roman Catholic and Mainline Protestant denominations. These more politicized inflows have occurred with—and numerically offset—the exodus of other laity bearing weaker affiliations with the Republican Party.[47] A similar phenomenon has taken place among non-white populations that now draw upon the evangelical label to signal their affiliation with political beliefs independent of affiliation with any historically defined evangelical denomination or the lineage of white evangelicalism. These changes in evangelicalism's constituency make room for a far wider range of economic orientations than those found among white evangelicals in the 1990s.

This reconfiguration poses a perplexing challenge to the current faith and work movement: its current resources are specifically catered to "save" or recover an inner-worldly asceticism purportedly demoted in favor of fundamentalism's world-rejecting asceticism. But for many adherents to political evangelicalism, "the world" has always mattered a great deal, whether as a battleground for spiritual warfare or as an arena for receiving God's promised material blessings. To many of these constituencies, the dangers of somehow over-prioritizing soul-saving or missionary work are not directly relatable. This leaves little need for a "remedial theology" aimed at rooting out the remnants of Grahamism. Some churches incorporated by political evangelicalism—particularly non-white congregations and those promoting Prosperity Gospel—also minister to populations located outside creative-class spaces, who may find little resonance with the aestheticization of work or an affirmative message about economic structures more broadly.

Perhaps the best hope for the faith and work movement going forward—and the economic orientations of evangelicals more broadly—would be the retrieval of a far broader set of "Protestant ethics" found in the history of American Protestant Christianity. While the contemporary movement prides itself in productively *adding to* resources for making Monday meaningful, movement leaders often fail to recognize the manner in which they may be reducing moral and spiritual resources that have historically served as Protestant responses to work. Some of these resources appear to get swept away by blanket dismissal of the "pietistic paradigm," judged guilty of promoting subordinating and shirking orientations toward economic activity. But the earlier Puritans made a spiritual case for subordinating work: a sixteenth-century teaching by Puritan pastor John Cotton warned that the result of making one's labor the "chiefest good" from which happiness is derived would only lead to selfish materialism.[48] Chronologically closer to contemporary evangelicalism were those religious groups of the nineteenth and twentieth century that formed solidarity with low-status workers and offered an alternative space of refuge for populations conferred with lower status by the dominant economic and social structures of their time. Such religious groups included some of the sectarian groups mentioned earlier, including Wesleyan, Free Methodist, and Salvation Army groups that provided support and coordinated collective action among laborers. These groups found ways to preserve modes of resistance to the totalizing economic forces that threatened to encroach upon their congregants' well-being and ways of life.

These "Protestant ethics" sharply contrast with the thrust of faith and work messaging. There are notably no celebrations of the "real worship" of Monday over and against conventional religious involvement. For those Protestants, it was not the church that was to be dispensed out across the economic world, but that the economic world that must be supercharged with ecclesial purpose. These groups thus devoted few resources to constructing Sunday experiences—sermons, worship songs, and corporate practices—that enthusiastically slingshot workers back out to their true Monday "callings." Within the contemporary Protestant landscape, there is good evidence that non-Anglo Protestant churches often continue to create communal bonds or collective identities that resist some of the excessive pulls of capitalism and careerism. Not all of this is by choice or theological intention: many attendees of these churches face legal or licensing challenges to pursuing careers of high status or achieving upward mobility. They instead turn to their roles and callings fulfilled through church activity.[49] Evangelicals hailing from historically white denominations would likely find in such communities some of the older "Protestant ethics" that continue to respond to demanding work conditions by providing places of refuge, support, and solidarity in the face of pressures and volatility.

With these other Protestant ethics in view, the faith and work movement's aspirations to tightly affix workers' sense of identity and purpose to their occupations and formal, paid labor warrant scrutiny. As sociologist Robert Nisbet observes, it was Protestantism that first "sought to reassimilate men in the invisible community of God" before capitalism, coming on Protestantism's heels, "sought to reassimilate them in the impersonal and rational framework of the free market."[50] This latter assimilation has always maintained some semblance of earlier religious forms: in Weber's words, the draw toward finding "duty in one's calling" continues to "prowl about in our lives like the ghost of dead religious belief."[51] But there is today a growing recognition of unmet needs for deeper social connections and forms of solidarities that might be anchored *outside* the economic sector or individualistic pursuits of careerism. Given these conditions, efforts of mining Luther, Calvin, and other early Protestant thinkers for their work-glorifying doctrines may be misdirecting theological resources toward shoring up capitalism's assimilative project at the expense of other ecclesial functions.

An alternative way forward would be constructing an evangelical economic ethic or theology of "work" that more deeply ties one's identity and purpose to a particular religious community. This holds the potential to ground callings and vocations within forms of solidarity and sociality that do not replicate or reinforce the social relations or logics favored by economic structures. Such forms have historically served to mitigate the mental and physical anguish inflicted by work experiences, whether among factory workers, transient workers, precariously employed workers, or those neglected by the labor market entirely. Instituting such a focus in no way entails a dualistic mode of thinking that relegates work to an areligious or irreligious sphere. Nor does such an economic ethic fail to speak to the world of "Monday." It would in fact instill lay callings and vocations that more deeply embed everyday worlds with greater spiritual and transcendent values, resolving precisely the dehumanizing conditions that Weber saw as plaguing the modern world. At a time when so many institutions have become fractured by political, social, and racial divides, there is an enduring need for callings that draw people toward forms of social relations not determined by status, wealth, or achievement. The neglect of such callings is precisely what stands to haunt all modes of religious life that prove resilient and adaptable to the ever-churning structures of the global economic order.

# Acknowledgments

This project was supported by the Institute for Advanced Studies in Culture at the University of Virginia, the Office of Undergraduate Research at UVA, and a Lake Institute Research Advancement Award from the Indiana University Lilly School of Philanthropy. Several organizations went out of their way in providing access to resources: Alderman Library at UVA, the Christian Study Center at UVA, the Consortium of Christian Study Centers, the Acton Institute, the Latourneu Center for Faith and Work, and Seattle Pacific University. I'm also indebted to many people who answered my inquiries and/or connected me with resources, including Amanda Battaglia, Cynthia Strong, Trish Owen, Ken Myers, Karen Marsh, Fitz Green, Bill Wilder, Drew Trotter, Jon Hart, David Blanchard, and Bill Reimer. Several interviewees also went above and beyond their participation in the project by providing additional helpful resources: Katherine Alsdorf, David Miller, Amy Sherman, Shirley Roels, and Os Hillman.

I am grateful for the ongoing conversations and substantive feedback I received from various colleagues and friends throughout the writing process: Stephen Assink, Kassandra Barbee, Joel and Kathryn Dart, Luke Jones, Matt Haggerty, Peter Hartwig, Phil and Amy Lykosh, Margarita Mooney Clayton, David and Diana Morris, Sarah Mosseri, John Nolan, Andrew Thornton, Garrett Trent, Jesse Robinson, Timothy Rutzou, Brad Vermurlen, Kyle Williams, and Christopher Yates. Additionally, Charles Cotherman, Allison Kelley, Wes Markofski, Charles Mathewes, Adam Seligman, and Robert Wuthnow all provided substantive feedback on various forms of the project as it morphed from dissertation to book proposal to book manuscript. A group of scholars came together to read and respond to the entire book manuscript with generous and very helpful feedback: here I thank Daryn Henry, Joseph Davis, Tony Tian-Ren Lin, Eugene McCarraher, Samuel Perry, Matthew Hedstrom, Brandon Vaidyanathan, and T. J. Jackson Lears. Thanks to John Muether for scrupulously reading and indexing this very long manuscript. I am grateful to Cynthia Read, Theo Calderara, Paloma Escovedo, and the many others at Oxford University Press who assisted through the production process. Of the many books and articles trifled through during the research phase, the experience of stumbling upon and then becoming absorbed within the pages of Sarah Hammond's dissertation left me with both a deep appreciation for her scholarship as well as a reminder of the very human side of the scholarly vocation. I am very grateful for all that she contributed to this subject area and feel honored to draw on her excellent work.

This book was born out of an earlier dissertation project. My dissertating journey was blessed by ongoing support and encouragement from too many colleagues, professors, and friends to possibly mention here, but surviving graduate school, without question, "takes a village," and I am grateful for all who supported me through that life phase. I want to thank my dissertation advisor James Davison Hunter for providing patient and encouraging guidance throughout this project as it took many twists and turns. Thanks as well to my committee for their guidance throughout its development: Nichole Flores, Allison Pugh, Isaac Ariail Reed, and Adam Slez. I am grateful for the assistance of Sarah Corse and Brad Wilcox for methodological guidance and Jeffrey Olick for opening my eyes to sociology's perpetual wrestling with questions of meaning. In finishing the dissertation I am indebted to Emily Hinkel for her professional copyediting and feedback and Dallas Floyd for being an over-the-top friend who read an entire dissertation just for fun. I also want to express a special thanks to my research assistant Isabella Hall for providing invaluable assistance in navigating methodological issues, analyzing data, curating sources, and providing general encouragement for the project through its many ups and downs. Thanks are also owed to the many people who assisted with travel and lodging during my "attend all the conferences all around the country" phase, so thanks to all who made that era a little easier: Jaime Amrhein, Katie Comeau, Olivia Gabbay, Nathan and Ashley Gammie, Dana Gusky, Shawn Kelley, Ryan Ricketts, Samuel Rund, Joshua and Betty Li Simpson, Graham and Angela Webster-Gardiner, Michael Webster-Gardiner, and Taylor Vierrether. I would also thank many in that same group as well as family and friends who tolerated my endless travel and writing schedule that at times seemed to have no end. The irony of perpetually overworking on a project about the centrality of work was not lost on either myself or the many around me.

In recognition of this shared plight, this project is dedicated to all who are engaged in making meaning out of time-intensive projects in which they find themselves engaged, whether in paid labor or otherwise. This extends to the many movement leaders and practitioners who took part in this study. My hope is that nothing in the preceding pages be read as a dismissal of the genuine quest for meaningful work and contributing to projects and people that will outlive us. All of our vocational pursuits—whether bringing about order, pursuing peace, providing care, rendering justice, or creating beauty—represent the best of our efforts of "effectively pointing, even if it is with a trembling finger, to the existence of peace or justice," as philosopher Chantal Delsol so eloquently puts it. May this book in some way serve all who are gesturing toward something transcendent with their day-to-day labor.

APPENDIX

# Research Methods

This study seeks to examine the interaction of ideas with institutions, individuals, and resources that together propel a particular cultural conversation forward. At the center of this study is discursive and ideational content: the frameworks, shared moral meanings, moral vocabularies, metaphors, narratives, and beliefs surrounding purposeful and meaningful work for evangelical lay workers. Yet, this cultural content does not exist in a vacuum, nor is it constructed ex nihilo in the minds of particularly creative individuals. It is instead created, refined, propagated, and legitimated through the vehicles of cultural institutions and movement actors. These actors are referred to as movement leaders, drawing on the social movement theory also shaping this analysis.

Keeping all of these elements central to the analysis guided the following research methods approach. The first section below outlines the specific methodological challenges of studying a space of largely deinstitutionalized actors who acquire legitimacy and influence in various ways. After building a tentative framework of what defines an evangelical thought leader, I turn to the reasoning behind selecting specific cases within the evangelical thought leader realm. An overview is then provided of the two dominant qualitative methods employed: interviews with thought leaders, and participant observation at movement events. Following this, I outline various measures of movement resources, including use of surveys, measuring financial resources, and quantitative book production.

## Challenges in Conceptualizing and Studying Movement Leaders

This study presents faith and work movement leaders as foundationally "entrepreneurs" in several senses. They are first of all institutional entrepreneurs in not occupying a durable institutional setting—an established structure within a university or church, for instance—but instead moving in and out of different settings, at times configuring bricolage structures from existing institutions, while other times constructing entirely new institutions. Examples of this behavior would be the formation of new conferences, nonprofits, and consulting enterprises, or in the case of bricolage structures, building networks of college professors or themed "conference tracks" at more established annual events. Following sociologist Paul DiMaggio's notion of cultural entrepreneurship, these actors are masters of creating new organizational forms that they then control and govern.[1] While these new forms may deviate from existing structures, they are also at times capable of contending with (and invasively infiltrating) established institutions.[2] These leaders are also often entrepreneurial in the colloquial sense of establishing their own organizations and supporting their efforts through providing for-pay services. The most common form of this economic entrepreneurship is developing the ideas and insights of a popular book into an organization that provides a menu of services for individuals and organizations. Drawing on sociologist Howard Becker's insights, this economic entrepreneurship is tightly coupled with their role in producing new moral typifications of a particular problem, as this typification process leaves actors in excellent position to remedy the moral problem with their services.

Thought leaders' entrepreneurial activity can be best understood as that of actors in a particular field contending for various types of resources, whether symbolic or material. Some of these resources are not fixed or static: actors in a field may generate new resources for which they then contend to possess and control. While interviews with thought leaders were crucial to illuminating the cultural content of the faith and work movement, the settings in which these leaders were active offer their own emergent properties for the movement itself. These events offer everyday workers immersive, socially intertwined experience within a social gathering built around shared identities, vocabularies, and narratives. For movements built around "critical communities" articulating alternative frameworks and understandings, these environments are crucial for study for two reasons: for socially reinforcing what Peter Berger and Thomas Luckmann call a "plausibility structure" to solidify these frameworks as credible and real, and for cultivating emotional energies around the shared frameworks and identities.[3] Thus my study of the movement integrated the experience of the environments themselves as a crucial part of describing the respective universes the movements inhabit.

## Constructing a Sample of Thought Leaders for Interviews

The deinstitutionalized and decentralized nature of the movement initially presented a challenge to constructing a representative sample of thought leaders that could best provide insights into the cultural frameworks promoted by the movement. As mentioned above, the movement lacked any central authorities that could deem authority and legitimation to some actors as central players in the movement. This boundary fuzziness challenged any sort of probability-based sampling strategy. Several non-probabilistic sampling strategies were also judged inadequate. Without defined boundaries or legitimating authorities designating movement leaders, convenience sampling would run the risk of only picking off a corner of the movement and over-generalizing it as representative. Relying on snowball sampling would largely run the same risk: this was confirmed by my interview question of whom the leaders identified as "allies in their efforts," as I found they tended to draw a much smaller sub-circle within the wider movement. To overcome this challenge, I employed what is designated as a criterion purposive sampling strategy.[4] Compared to other purposive sampling strategies, criterion methods work to offset researcher bias by subjecting the sample construction to empirical reality, rather than selecting "influential" or "typical" cases a priori, borrowing insights from Pierre Bourdieu and Loïc Wacquant on how particular fields can be studied.[5]

A central figure was selected to provide a foothold in the faith and work world, based on preliminary research. After monitoring discourse online on Twitter and faith and work blogs, having informal conversations with actors within the space, and flipping through various bibliographies on faith and work resources, I intuited that Manhattan pastor and popular writer Timothy Keller, though a more recent joiner to the movement, was likely one of the most cited and influential thinkers in the field. Keller leads Redeemer Presbyterian Church, a large, multi-site congregation in New York that attracts a population of educated, professional, and creative workers, described in more detail in Chapter 7. Though retiring in 2017, Keller gave sermons on topics related to work many times over the long tenure of his career. His real influence in the national conversation began with

Redeemer's establishment of the Center for Faith and Work in 2010. The Center's yearly national conferences—combined with Keller and co-writer Katherine Alsdorf's 2012 book *Every Good Endeavor: Connecting Your Work to God's Work*—propelled the ideas of Keller, Alsdorf, and the Center beyond their congregation to a national audience. The Center also employed pastor David Kim, who spoke widely and served as editor of the *New International Version Faith and Work Bible.* All three of these leaders participated in the study.

Since Keller's Center had coordinated seven annual faith and work conferences with varied speaking lineups, the selection of Keller as the center point immediately generated a list of 15–20 individuals active in the space. These individuals offered a potential starting point for mapping out a wider universe of "thought leaders," as here I began looking for other gatherings, conferences, luncheons, seminars, seminary classes, campus ministry initiatives, and retreats where such individuals made appearances. Faith and work leaders frequently speak at events with many other panels and speakers: collecting the names of speakers from all locatable events events quickly expanded the list of potential thought leaders into triple digits. In the interest of working toward who was leading the national movement, I imposed three criteria for evaluating whether an event these individuals appeared at represented a "national" faith and work event. These criteria were the following: (1) the event was publicized and open to the public; (2) the event spanned more than one day, signaling it is worthwhile investment for non-local attendees to travel to; and (3) the event featured two or more figures who have spoken about faith and work at more than one event that meets the first two criteria. This third criteria can teeter toward a circular definition: national faith and work events are defined by those events that feature national faith and work speakers, a category in turn defined by those who speak at such events. However, events that managed to meet the first and second criteria but not the third were evaluated against one another, and in this manner several events achieved "national" status when shared speakers were spotted across events. Of course, the second and third criteria on their surface appear quite arbitrary: what is it about adding that second notable speaker and perhaps a Friday night session to a full Saturday slate that propels an event to national status? These are obviously analytical heuristics that, as demonstrated below, are necessary (and helpful) to make this thought leader space accessible to empirical study.

Once the national event criteria were established, sixty-one events were identified as meeting these criteria of "national Evangelical faith and work event." The final event included in this list took place in March 2017, representing the cutoff point for fieldwork. Though no beginning date was imposed for consideration in this sample, the first conference to meet these specifications occurred in 2006. Some of this may reflect a methodology that relied on the internet to list old conferences: conferences before 2006 may not have had any web presence that can be excavated today. However, in assembling the recorded historical narratives of faith and work leaders and researchers who have written on this particular space, I became fairly confident that no conference prior to 2006 met the specification of "national conference," as the practice of hosting a national faith and work conference is itself a relatively recent innovation. I also corresponded with the earliest coordinator of national events (Os Hillman), who was well networked in this world during the early era at which national events emerged: he believed his own coordinated events were the first of their kind.

Combining all the advertised speakers and session leaders who appeared at these sixty-one events produces a list of 385 different thought leaders in this space. This heterogeneous incorporation of speakers across events is largely a product of how faith and work events are constructed: once a coordinator secures a respected author or pastor to speak on the topic, the rest of the lineup can be filled with more general theologically minded speakers or local professionals who can draw on their own experience. Adding poets, musicians, artists, and even local politicians to conference lineups also contributes to the heterogeneity of this list. The large majority of faith and work speakers, then, are not on the "speaking circuit" and lack national profiles. Speakers who are recognizable outside evangelical circles are also notably rare.[6]

Ranking this list of 385 speakers by number of national events for which they appeared in the speaking lineup produced a ranking of leaders. A natural cutoff occurred below those who had spoken at less than three national conferences: therefore, the top 29 most frequently speaking leaders were deemed the most influential thought leaders, all of whom had spoken at three or more events. Table A.1 lists those speakers, along with identifying those who agreed to participate in the study.

Three additional pools of people were also interviewed: first, a convenience or opportunistic sample that seemed to offer something unique to the space not well represented by the thought leader sample. These included: a ministry leader who applied entrepreneurship principles to community development; a female leader (significantly underrepresented in this space) who spoke on motherhood as a calling and vocation; two small business owners who had been recognized for incorporating unusual "Christian" practices in their managerial models; and a systematic theologian whose writing on faith and work was well known despite his lack of public speaking presence in this space. Another pool of interviewees were also added: those holding influence and power over resources flowing into this space. In doing early fieldwork and monitoring online discourse, it became clear that the faith and work space contained several organizations in it with disproportionate resources and influence—whether financial or symbolic—that nearly all the other interviewees would mention regularly. These organizational leaders, then, exert far more will on the faith and work space and its frameworks than others. I designated these figures "resource leaders," drawing attention to their capacity to control and steward resources for the movement. Here I interviewed six individuals, five of whom worked to lead some of the major funding sources present in the space, and an additional figure who led up a charge to produce a new Bible commentary on work, a project with significant symbolic power. Table A.1 lists these supplemental interviewees, those who did not meet the criteria established for being a "thought leader."

Finally, my observation at events brought me into contact with several other leaders who could speak authoritatively on some dimensions of the faith and work space but, for varying reasons, were not good candidates for the formal interview script used for the study. These conversations, however, were instrumental in helping ensure I had not overlooked key leaders, historical moments, resources, or gathering in the move space at large. Five authors or organizational leaders filled this role: Matt Bloom of Wellbeing at Work, Jon Hart of Praxis Labs, Os Hillman of TGIF Ministries, Paul Stevens of Regent College/Institute for Marketplace Transformation, and Alvin Ung of Barefoot Leadership.

One other note about sample construction: the criterion purposive sampling approach produced a list that not only surprised me as the researcher but would likely surprise most actors in the movement. This unexpectedness reflects the intentions behind constructing a sample according to objectively established criteria, as the movement can often be artificially limited to dense clusters of leaders who operate only with a particular pocket of the movement. Another surprise was the emergence of a handful of figures on the list who

**Table A.1** Faith and Work Thought Leaders, Resource Leaders, and Supplemental Interviewees

| Thought Leader Ranking and Indication of Study Participation (Participants $N = 24$) | | | |
|---|---|---|---|
| **Name** | **Affiliated Organization*** | **# of National Conference Speaking Engagements Meeting Criteria** | **Participated in Study?** |
| Tom Nelson | Made to Flourish | 12 | Y |
| Katherine Alsdorf | Center for Faith & Work (Redeemer Presbyterian Church) | 9 | Y |
| Henry Kaestner | Sovereignty Capital | 8 | Y |
| Bob Doll | Nuveen Access Management | 8 | Y |
| Greg Forster | Oikonomia Network (Trinity International University) | 8 | Y |
| Skye Jethani | Independent author (formerly Christianity Today) | 7 | Y |
| Tim Keller | Center for Faith & Work (Redeemer Presbyterian Church) | 7 | Y |
| David Miller | Faith & Work Initiative (Princeton University) | 7 | Y |
| Steven Garber | Washington Institute on Faith, Vocation, and Culture | 7 | Y |
| Scott Rae | Biola University | 7 | Y |
| Amy Sherman | Sagamore Institute | 7 | Y |
| Greg Gilbert | Gospel at Work | 5 | Y |
| Anthony Bradley | The King's College | 5 | N |
| Chris Brooks | Evangel Ministries/Moody Theological Seminary | 5 | Y |
| Rudy Carrasco | Worldwide Partners | 5 | Y |
| Mark Washington | MBA Ministries (Intervarsity) | 4 | Y |

(*continued*)

**Table A.1** Continued

| Thought Leader Ranking and Indication of Study Participation (Participants $N = 24$) | | | |
|---|---|---|---|
| **Name** | **Affiliated Organization*** | **# of National Conference Speaking Engagements Meeting Criteria** | **Participated in Study?** |
| Charles Self | Assemblies of God Theological Seminary | 4 | Y |
| David Kim | Center for Faith & Work (Redeemer Presbyterian Church) | 3 | Y |
| Peter Greer | HOPE International | 3 | Y |
| Andy Crouch | Christianity Today (Executive Editor) | 3 | Y |
| Michael Lindsay | Gordon College (President) | 3 | Y |
| Bill Peel | Center for Faith & Work at LeTourneau University | 3 | Y |
| Dave Evans | Stanford University | 3 | Y |
| Ashok Nachnani | Gospel at Work | 3 | Y |
| Sebastian Traeger | Gospel at Work | 3 | Y |
| Y. Marc Belton | Wisefellows Consulting | 3 | N |
| Sherron Watkins | Independent Speaker (former Enron Vice President) | 3 | N |
| J.D. Greear | The Summit Church | 3 | N |
| Phil Vischer | Independent Speaker (Founder of Big Idea Productions) | 3 | N |

**Resource Leaders Participating in Study ($N = 6$)**

| **Name** | **Affiliated Organization** |
|---|---|
| Chris Robertson | Acton Institute |
| Jordan Ballor | Acton Institute |

| | |
|---|---|
| Shirley Roels | NetVUE (Affiliated with Lilly Endowment Efforts) |
| David Cunningham | Campus Ministry Project on Theological Exploration for Vocation (Supported by Lilly Endowment) |
| Josh Good | Kern Family Foundation |
| Will Messenger | Theology of Work Project (Faith & Work Bible Commentary Effort) |

**Supplemental Interviewees ($N = 5$)**

| **Name** | **Affiliated Organization** |
|---|---|
| Kate Harris | Washington Institute on Faith, Vocation, and Culture |
| Wayne Grudem | Phoenix Seminary |
| Hugh Whelchel | Institute for Faith, Work, & Economics |
| Cheryl Broetje | Broetje Orchards |
| Wendy Clark | Carpe Diem Cleaning |

*Affiliated organization was accurate at time of interview.

receive surprisingly little mention by other actors in the space. Their frequency of conference speaking suggests they may simply be known as the go-to experts when conference coordinators assemble speaking lineups. But it is also worth noting that these criteria of sample construction eliminated three parachurch-ministry spaces that, had they been included, might have steered analysis in a different direction. All three spaces produce frameworks related to faith and work that are directed toward American evangelicals.

The first is the most surprising omission: none of the most frequently sought conference speakers were also active in the Business as Mission movement. This movement has a somewhat ambiguous historical origins but generally points to a birth out of the "Lausanne Movement," a series of International Congresses on World Evangelization (initially led by Billy Graham) gathering in Switzerland (1974), the Philippines (1989), and Cape Town (2010). One of the arms of activity emerging from this gathering was an "Issue Group" of thinkers dedicated to exploring workplace ministries and how business enterprises might take the lead in sending missionary efforts in places where missionaries might otherwise have trouble gaining access. Today, the Business as Mission movement has a much more global footprint than the very American-centric faith and work movement, likely reflecting its underlying global interests as well as its birthplace outside the United States. Some movement leaders have embraced a more comprehensive vision of "faith-work integration" that ends up mirroring the faith and work movement; other leaders have stayed more centered on the original vision of using business as a carrier for mission work.[7] As a general summary, this wing of American evangelicalism coalesces around making Mondays spiritually significant through importing a passionate, globally minded zeal for "re-commissioning" laity to spread Christianity.

The second omission of leaders are those located just on the edge of the events and space studied: those who represent the continuation of the earlier "faith and businessmen" focus. These include the contemporary forms of some of the earliest established organizations: the Fellowship of Christian Companies International, Christian Business Man Connection as well as newer groups like Marketplace Chaplains USA, the Barnabas Group, C12, and Fusion Leaders. These groups now largely cater their events to CEOs and those in executive business leadership. They hold regional and national events, coordinate local chapters of meetups, and generally speak a familiar language of "bringing God" to work, though work is almost always "business" at the level of C-suite leadership in this context. This space includes: an organization calling itself a "Christian Business Peer Advisory Group," the Christian Executive Leadership Forum, Priority Associates, Christian Leadership Alliance, and the networks of chapters and organizations that are associated with the earlier groups mentioned. I have included these organizations in the list of organizational growth in Chapter 3. While these groups occasionally purchase booths and sponsorships at national faith and work events, their leaders are seemingly not tapped to speak. They also appear to cleave together in their own subcultural space, many times sponsoring each other's' events. One interviewee for this project mentioned that at least some of these organizations value a degree of marginalization and sequestration from the movement at large as a means of ensuring anonymity for executives who do not publicly identify as Christians.

Finally, a third space is excluded that proves rather difficult to define: this space's events blend together motivational speakers, a very general understanding of "leadership," and some executive-targeted thinking about work and faith. An example would be an organization called "Truth at Work," which sponsored several conference events called "America's Best Hope." While Truth at Work is clearly an evangelical organization, the pool of speakers their events draw together is markedly different from the faith and work movement.[8] Well-known sports figures like Tom Crean (a college basketball coach) and Tony Dungy (a former NFL coach) have shared stages with executives from Chick-fil-a and Hobby Lobby, companies well known for very public religious liberty battles. Anne Graham Lotz, daughter of Billy Graham and enthusiastic supporter of Donald Trump's 2016 presidential campaign, has also been a featured speaker, as well as Karen Pence, then the first lady of Indiana. These events have at times incorporated several highly ranked faith and work thought leaders who were included in my sample, but no speaker that exclusively spoke at such events met the qualifications for inclusion in the sample.

## Conducting and Analyzing Interviews

Understanding the cultural frameworks at the heart of this movement required prioritizing the discourse of thought leaders, both through formal interviews as well as through participant observation at event gatherings. Interviews were intensive, semi-structured script-guided conversations that probed their organization's mission and audience, how faith is integrated into work, assessment of the larger movement, and ethical questions regarding integrating faith into economic settings. Interviews were conducted in person when possible; when not possible they were conducted over Skype or phone. These interactions were recorded and then transcribed. Interview duration ranged from 35 minutes to 95 minutes. The interview questions were specifically created to access the meaning-making processes, metaphors, symbols, narratives, and mental maps of the interviewees. Particularly because so many of the participants were already "in print" regarding these topics, the interview process sought to probe the subject matter at a deeper level whenever possible. For this I drew on researcher Jeffrey Berry's best practices for interviewing "elites" within a movement: coming into interviews deeply familiar with the interviewee's work, having questions prepared to probe some of the information that might otherwise not be accessible to the researcher, and digging deeper in cases where interviewees seemed to be only delivering talking points or the party line on certain subjects.[9] This meant asking for clarification when popular clichés were used, at times asking for the origins of a particular view or idea, and even occasionally holding up the participants' views to alternative views in the movement and inquiring about the difference. The final set of questions employed also pressed participants into cognitive processes of problem-solving and adapting a previously delivered claim into a particular context. The general tone of these interactions was energetic and lively, though at times the more conceptual questions produced a shift in the interaction from neatly scripted responses to longer pauses for careful deliberation and reflection on the questions.

Responses were analyzed and coded for recurring emergent themes that spanned answers and participants. Analysis focused specifically on frameworks, concepts, and ideas that were not as accessible in the public speaking and writing of the participants. A central priority in the analysis was preserving the conceptual framework of the participants themselves, rather than translating it one-for-one into more formal theoretical frameworks, whether that be more formal economic thinking (Chicago School understandings of markets, for example) or sociological theories on contemporary work (the precarity of modern work, for example). Prioritizing inductive analysis allowed for emergence of common themes, codes, and frameworks that were only post hoc connected to more systematic modes of thinking when appropriate.

Relying on interview data of movement elites to study the production of cultural frameworks put this project at the intersection of two different conventions in qualitative sociology: studies of social movement leaders, which almost always identify movement leaders by name, and studies of particular populations, which generally do not. While I briefly considered affording all leaders anonymity, this proved largely impossible when interviewees needed to be contextualized with their own published work and public speaking: identifying any of the latter by name would implicitly identify the interviewee. I also began to recognize that some of the more developed frameworks and ideas shared by the interviewees in our interviews were very much their own "cultural products"—comparable to composed songs or works of art—that, at a very practical level, are the means by which these thought leaders derived their livelihood. Obscuring the authorship of these frameworks and ideas seemed at odds with the ethical imperatives of scholarly research, which works to minimize any harm—including professional harm—inflicted on research participants. Particularly where I feel the interviewee is articulating original ideas, I have identified him or her by name. However, in that same interest of minimizing harm, I have anonymized interviewees when quoting any statements that might possibly be perceived as criticism of other leaders, the faith and work space as a whole, or the evangelical subculture at large.

## Observations at Events

Interviews were supplemented with participant-observation at twenty-three separate faith and work events. Evaluating the particular size, influence, and overall significance of any conference is far from straightforward. However, such evaluation was necessary due to budget and time limitations that required being selective in choosing field sites representative of the larger movement. In my own selection of events, then, I relied on the themes of sessions and the number of recognizable thought-leaders to determine which conferences seemed more central to the construction and dissemination of the faith and work messaging. Early interviewees were also quite generous in providing recommendations of what conferences and events were most central, at times providing historical context and backstage information on conference planning and the coordinators' own strategy.

Gaining access to gatherings proved to be fairly straightforward in most cases. The gatherings and events I attended were openly advertised well ahead of time and open to anyone caring to register for them. Gatherings ranged from one-day to five-day affairs, with registration fees ranging from free to several hundred dollars. The interactive time between conference sessions and the more socializing-oriented moments enriched my experience of the events in numerous ways. These interactions gave further insight into the movement itself from the eyes of the event attendees. I was able to take note of some of the social dynamic questions laid out above while also gauging inconsistencies, tensions, or pushback from those who were sitting through sessions with me. Conversation topics were mostly fairly casual, and my general inquisitiveness as a researcher was frequently matched by an equally enthusiastic curiosity about my project. But these conversations were helpful: many interlocutors expanded my knowledge of other speakers, events, and resources that would have otherwise remained invisible. A few provided anecdotes from past events I was not able to attend. I also had the opportunity to speak informally to many event speakers between sessions, including individuals who did not qualify for the more selective "thought leader" status but could still contribute to my knowledge of the movement.

There is little question that some aspects of conferences demand deviating from more conventional ethnographic practices: silently sitting in an audience watching a single speaker does not yield the rich accounts of person-to-person dynamics that might characterize other ethnographic studies. However, participant-observation in the broader setting produced a substantial contribution to understanding the topic at hand. The size, composition, and quality of interactions of the attendees were the most concrete features made accessible by personal attendance. Not only did this clue me into the racial, gender, and age demographics of the attendees, but the patterns and quality of interactions frequently revealed whether attendees knew each other previously, what sorts of networks linked attendees together, and the general demeanor of interactions, whether they be characterized by a cool professionalism or warm familial bonds. Gauging the tribal-ness of the attendees for many of the events was most crucial: Do people come every year? Do they speak of past events fondly and chart out their plans for the next gathering? Or, alternatively, do attendees engage the sessions more individualistically and with more of a consumerist mentality of coming to be "fed" certain knowledge and insights? Also important to observe were questions related to how these events fit into wider work commitments, whether they seemed to be a break from work or whether they were experienced as deeply integrated into one's workplace.

The most illuminating "programmed" element of these events was the time of open questions that followed most lectures, panels, or workshops. This gave me a sense of the group's collective mood and response regarding the presented material, whether positive, skeptical, dismissive, overwhelmed, or unsure. Of course, the questions voiced in these settings were heavily shaped by the norms of respect for invited speakers, larger social relations of race and gender, and perhaps particular group dynamics that kept dissenters from approaching the microphone. Most questions were pragmatic in nature, many grounded in the particular social role of the questioner asking for guidance in applying an idea or concept to a specific episode in his or her own life. Occasions where questioners voiced substantive dissent against the speakers' ideas were rare, and those cases generally spurred me to chase down and follow up with the questioner later to dig into what motivated the dissent. Hearing these reactions to the "official" material falls far short of a "reception study" of the movement's efforts, but it does speak to the degree to which attendees found the basic ideas plausible, compelling, and reflective on their own experiences.

Participant observation produced several notebooks full of field notes, as well as photos of PowerPoint slides, jotted down references in the margins of event programs, and handfuls of business cards from eager interlocutors and new connections. The field notes were generally preserved alongside print materials I received at the events: programs, advertisements, workshop handouts, and advertisements for future events. All of these materials were drawn upon as cultural artifacts in capturing the personal experience of attending the conference. In cases where an online recording of the talk is available, I drew on both my own notes and the online recording to piece together exact quotes from the speakers.

Event participant-observation began in May 2014 and ended in September 2017. The forms of these events were not at all the same: some were luncheons and evening talks, others spanned several days at a time. If counting individual "sessions" and "events" that occurred within multi-day conferences, I observed over seventy-two different individual sessions related to faith and work while in the field—whether a lecture, breakfast, luncheon, panel, workshop, or class session. Five of the larger gatherings constituted national faith and work events, as defined by the earlier methodology. These gatherings are identified in Table A.2.[10]

Supplementing these five national gatherings were observations at seventeen additional gatherings and events.[11] These other events were not focused on drawing the same sort of general "faith and work" audience. Except where noted, these events were ecumenical in nature but inclusive of evangelical audiences (and many times featured evangelical speakers). Seven events were national in scope of attendees but focused on specific audiences. This included: two weeks of lay-oriented summer courses related to vocation at an evangelical seminary; a five-day national gathering of evangelical college students pursuing entrepreneurial careers; a three-day conference of campus ministry leaders who received grants for vocational programming for college students; a three-day conference of workshops and presentations on management and spirituality scholarship; a three-day gathering of Christians from various occupational sectors creating vocational materials for their respective fields; a theology of work session at a denomination-specific evangelical theology conference; and a breakfast session of Christian management scholars gathered at a professional management conference. Ten other observed events offered more standard faith and work content but catered to local audiences: five faith and work luncheons targeting university undergraduate students; three faith and work luncheons targeting MBA students; one non-denominational Evangelical church service kicking off a faith and work sermon series; and one panel discussion led by New York corporate executives speaking on the topic of Christian leadership. Combining both the events listed in Table A.1 and the ones described here, I observed events or gatherings across ten major cities: Memphis, New York, Indianapolis, Richmond, Dallas, Los Angeles, Raleigh, Anaheim, Orlando, and Boston.

Observation at events provides insights on how activists and attendees respond to and negotiate with the ideas presented by conference speakers, many times online, on conference apps, or informally in conversation. On top of this, during my fieldwork I monitored online activities of around ninety organizations and leaders involved in the movement by following them on Twitter. This exposed me to the ongoing conversations and debates occurring among interviewees and those in their network. Frequently this stream of activity would bring to my attention recordings of events I was not able to attend: from this I watched approximately twenty-five recorded conference sessions to supplement my fieldwork. This recorded content often came from the same events attended above but from previous or subsequent years to my own attendance.

## Drawing upon Printed Texts, Online Materials, National Surveys, and Other Data

Quantitative measures were drawn upon to gauge the organizational strength and resources that the movements had at their disposal. Building on basic insights from social movement theory, movements require a variety of resource inputs to advance their cause and mobilize others.[12] These resources can be material—such as money, supplies, physical space—or organizational, which gives attention to how existing networks, organizations, and organizational infrastructure can serve the organization's interests. I have

Table A.2 Major National Events Observed, May 2014 to September 2017

| Date | Event Name | Coordinating Organization | Location |
|---|---|---|---|
| 5/30–31/2014 | Entrepreneurship & Innovation Forum | Center for Faith & Work (Redeemer Presbyterian Church) | New York, NY |
| 11/10/2015 | Market Solutions for Community Transformation | Christian Community Development Association | Memphis, TN |
| 4/19–20/2016 | The Asbury Project | Asbury Theological Project | Orlando, FL |
| 9/23–24/2016 | Gospel at Work Conference | Gospel at Work | Richmond, VA |
| 10/27–29/2016 | 2016 Faith & Work Summit | Center for Faith and Work at LeTourneau University | Dallas, TX |

drawn upon quantitative measures of resources in order to chart the steady growth of both movements of interest, both in recent decades but also in the larger timeframe of the twentieth century. I have specifically drawn on the following three areas of resource growth:

**Organizational Creation**: For the faith and work movement, basic analysis of when relevant organizations were founded produces a general timeline of when various organizational actors came online. This was used to map out the general timeline of when the faith and work movement developed.

**Funding and Organizational Structure**: Several organizations in the faith and work space have generated attention for corporate and political financial backing. I drew on publicly accessible 990 tax forms—required tax filings for public nonprofits—to trace out relationships and money trails that traveled across multiple fiscal agents. Where cited, I also drew on previous research and journalism .

**Administered Surveys**: In addition to these evaluations of resources, I have also incorporated data from two surveys created or co-created specifically for the project. All thought leader interviewees were given a survey of basic demographic information and a few substantive multiple-choice survey questions for response. The latter were taken from national surveys in order to provide comparisons between the sample of leaders and a nationally representative sample. For the faith and work movement, another survey was co-designed with event coordinators at the 2016 Faith and Work Summit. The final product was a 16-question survey with five questions pertaining to non-event related topics: basic demographics, aspirations for the faith and work movement for the future, helpful influences for faith-work integration, identifying one's greatest passion for faith-work integration, etc.

**National Surveys**: Existing data sets were also drawn upon where polling and survey data on "meaningful work" could be accessed. More data were available here for the faith and work movement: to gauge idea dissemination and adoption I incorporated the following data sets: 1992 Economic Values Survey, the 2010 Baylor Religion Survey Wave III, and a 2011 Public Religion Research Institute News Survey.[13]

## Book Production: Quantitative Production Measures, Qualitative Themes Study

Defining "evangelical faith and work book"—in order to both gauge production trends and construct a sample for qualitative study—was the first step in incorporating book production into the project. The genre or category of a faith and work book is somewhat ambiguous, and boundaries around this category can be rather porous. Books on subjects such as leadership, day-to-day lay ministry, evangelism, gender, or personal piety topics like relationships may bear relevance on work but present the potential for categorical slippage without a precise definition. Books on ethical issues related to specific professions such as issues in the healthcare industry, science, or even the practices of governing are also difficult to categorize. Three different methods were employed to overcome these challenges.

To provide a wider count of "faith and work" books published across the twentieth century, a global database of published materials in 72,000 libraries worldwide (worldcat.org) was consulted to assess books that receive the corresponding subject categorization for faith and work books. Finding that most contemporary faith and work books (those written by the thought leaders identified above) are categorized as "Work—Religious Aspects—Christianity," a chart of books produced in that category was created. The second and third methods revolved around a curated database of 1,648 books in the "Work and Faith Collection," a physical collection of books maintained by Seattle Pacific University's University Library. This is the largest maintained database and collection of faith and work books available. I worked with the reference librarian who oversaw this database to gain digital access to the full catalog of books maintained in this library. The reference librarian also provided an explanation of how the collection is maintained and updated. A memorandum of understanding and "endowment agreement guide" provides guidance for the library's stewardship of the collection, which has its own annual budget for maintenance. The collection is built, maintained, and shaped by the work of a "standing committee" of evangelical scholars and leaders who carefully select which new books will be added each year. Some of these figures are recognizable authors and conference speakers, though none was in the sample of thought leaders interviewed. The committee's priorities for adding to the collection are defined in the collection's scope note: "Materials to be included will be substantive in nature and/or of scholarly value and related to Christians in Business and other professions." A chart of the year of publishing of these books was included in Chapter 3 to show a steady upturn since 1970, with the peak of production around the late 1980s.

The third method took additional steps to gauge book production for works specifically directed toward evangelical laity. Without this third method, the list includes books written across Christian traditions and even sociological and historical works parsing the relationship between religion, economics, and theology, which would not constitute the "evangelical faith and work" books of interest here. To sort out books that are most likely written for evangelical laypersons (as opposed to academics, historians, or adherents in other traditions), this list was narrowed to books published by evangelical publishers. Categorizing these publishers was relatively straightforward: the publisher either self-identified as "evangelical" or self-identified with a denomination historically associated with American evangelicalism. In cases where the publisher had merged or gone out of business, historical data on publishers were consulted to ascertain the identity of the publisher at the time of the relevant book's publication. Chapter 3 contains the resulting chart of books printed on evangelical publishers. While data on readership or perhaps denominational endorsement would have more directly spoken to intended and achieved audiences for these books, publishers provided a useful proxy for at least the former. Several experts working in Christian book publishing were also consulted, who provided general support for the idea that publishers have played a gatekeeping role: only certain theological beliefs and certain topics were permitted to appear in books published by these presses.

Moving to the qualitative study of book production, this third method provided the foundational basis for constructing a sample of evangelical faith and work books published from 1940 to 1980. The start-date was selected in correspondence with two factors: the data set itself did not include any books from evangelical publishers prior to 1941, and the founding of the first evangelical faith and work organization—a central point in all existing histories of American Christianity faith and work—was 1930. With histories of American fundamentalism positing the 1920s seminary battles and 1925 Scopes Monkey Trial as a central point in the production of American Protestant Fundamentalism, 1940 offers as good a point as any to begin charting the subject of interest here: developments of evangelical theologies of work emerging from the neo-evangelical and evangelical efforts of the interwar years. The stop-date of 1980 was chosen for both historical and practical reasons. First of all, while comprehensive inclusion of all evangelical faith and work books prior to 1980 was a manageable universe of texts, the surge in production after 1980 makes comprehensive study of this universe far more difficult, with production rates increasing to 10 to 15 new books a year during the 1980s. Historically, this cut-off also allowed for immersion within the world of American evangelical public theologies and cultural engagement prior to the rise of the Christian Right, a movement that was only just beginning to establish a foothold in the final years of this period. While this may insulate the sample from the significant economic shifts of the 1980s associated with Reagan-era neoliberalism, books surveyed past 1980 seemed to echo the same themes as those produced in the earlier pierod. Closing the Sunday-Monday gap, locating inherent dignity in work, and flattening the vocational hierarchy remained the central themes of these books. There is strong evidence these basic themes persist even in the faith and work books published more recently. Perhaps the only exception would be the move toward more aesthetic and Romantic-inspired themes, discussed in Chapter 4.

The window of 1940 to 1980 produced a list of forty-nine works that appeared on evangelical publishers and were selected by the Seattle Pacific University Library committee for inclusion in the collection. This list was also checked against bibliographies generated by several other "bibliographical authorities" in the movement to find possible omissions in Seattle's collection. This included: a list of references and significant texts by Greg Forster, head of the Oikonomia Network; a bibliography produced by Gordon-Conwell Seminary in association with their faith and work center; a bibliography generated by the "Business as Mission" arm of the Lausanne Committee on World Evangelism; and several lists produced by the Theology of Work project, an organization that has assembled biblical scholars and other leaders in this space for the production of their faith and work Bible commentary. These lists confirmed the Seattle Pacific collection as the most comprehensive: no book identified in these other bibliographies did not also appear in the Seattle Pacific collection.

Drawing on a grounded theory approach, these texts were coded for organically emerging themes related to the relationship between "work" and religion. This process was split between myself and a research assistant. "Work" could cover any sort of economic activity or involvement in the labor sphere: particularly with the books probed from the earlier era (discussed below), work was defined in the broadest way possible, aspiring to include any form of paid or unpaid, formal or informal labor. Seattle's own inclusion process became apparent through this coding exercise: not all books contained explicit discussion of work. The scope note for the collection provides the most likely explanation for this: a "medium priority" for book inclusion was "foundational Christian worldview" books that may "support" faith and work. Several books clearly laid out sophisticated views of cultural engagement and ethical dimensions of Christian lay life, but with no content specifically on work, these books were judged not to contribute to any of the four cultural frameworks discussed in Chapter 4.[14]

Constructing this 1940 to 1980 sample in this manner had a significant shortcoming: if evangelical theologies of work in fact represent a "remedial" and intervention effort by modern movement leaders, these books may represent a post hoc attempt of constructing an intellectual genealogy of those ideas deemed valuable and formative to faith and work movement leaders today. In other words, it was likely these works would not capture the alternative theological orientations against which today's leaders were reacting. This lowered the odds that any books would capture the "before" picture of evangelical theology in this later time period sample: it is more likely the books selected for the Seattle collection could very well represent a selective "greatest hits" collection of those who best aligned with the canonizers' own views. However, this aspect of the list actually proved useful for probing variations across the twentieth century *within* theologies of work: four major codes or themes emerged from these works that served as the basic structures of the four cultural frameworks. But additional steps would need to be undertaken to get at the orientations for which modern faith and work theology provides the interventionary remedial alternatives. A comparison across the same era would theoretically be possible, but there were two methodological challenges: one, there are challenges in attempting to verify the historical *absence* or neglect of a subject in books where, in theory, it might appear (such as lay theology books that one would presume would discuss work and Monday life but do not). Second, there was no way to possibly construct a comparable sample of books that did theology of work "poorly," for a lack of a better descriptor. On a very basic level, there may be no "poor" evangelical theology of work books post-1940. Though interviewees voiced their disagreement with more pietistic, or other-worldly-minded thinkers, they rarely named names, and individuals earning their criticism did not produce books on work written for lay people. For these reasons it made more sense to wade back in time to the previous era to excavate views on work that might warrant the later intervention efforts.

Constructing any sort of representative sample of produced faith and work books from 1889 to 1929 era was found to produce several challenges. For one, both the historians of the faith and work movement and the bibliography-makers cited earlier do not cite any lay-oriented texts on faith and work from that era. While there are some books produced during this era that appear on the Seattle collection list, they are not lay-directed theology texts in any sense. Thus, to locate the theology of work discourse for this era, the criteria of inclusion was opened considerably to any lay Protestant-focused book that provided any substantive commentary on work, labor, or economic activity, with, again, the widest possible understanding of those terms. Since few "evangelical" publishers existed during this era, I drew upon available catalogs from the following presses, both associated with Moody Bible Institute in Chicago: Bible Institute Colportage Association and Fleming H. Revell Company. While this produced a sample of books drawn from only two publishers over the duration of the era, they were not only the most central revivalist-fundamentalist presses, but also some of the only two presses to span the era, as mass-producing affordable lay books was a largely uncharted practice for conservative Protestant groups prior to Revell's efforts.[15]

Books published in this era routinely featured their publisher's catalog in the back of the book, so these catalogs proved fairly easy to access. I constructed a convenience sample of relevant texts by scanning catalogs from five-year gaps across the era. The Bible Institute Colportage Association did not begin publishing until 1894, so for the earlier part of the era I relied heavily on Revell's publishing activities. In the interest of honoring the very deliberate cultural insularity and separatism of fundamentalists, several fundamentalist periodicals were relied upon as subcultural gatekeepers for products (and ideas) holding cultural legitimacy among the emerging fundamentalist subculture of the era. All books selected for inclusion appeared in advertisement listings or review sections in conservative and fundamentalist periodicals of the era, such as the *Sunday School Times* (founded 1859), *Moody Bible Institute Monthly* (founded 1900, formally called the *Institute Tie* and the *Christian Workers Magazine*), and *King's Business* (founded 1910).[16]

Despite their focus on books for the laity, books devoted exclusively to work, labor, or even economics were nearly nonexistent. However, of approximately fifty books that appeared to perhaps touch on economic issues, twenty books were discovered that directly addressed topics of interest. These texts were obtained or accessed online and then coded for themes in any passages related to work, economics, secular callings, labor, industrial relations, money, professions, or any reference whatsoever to "office," "workshop," or "occupation." Relevant passages were summarized in Chapter 2 which provide some insights into how the discourse explored the topic of work during this era.

## Disclosure Statement Regarding Potential Conflicts of Interest

This research was directly or indirectly supported by the Lilly Endowment through three separate channels. First, my travel, lodging, and meals at the gathering of campus ministry leaders (briefly mentioned in Chapter 3) was funded by their Campus Ministry Theological Exploration for Vocation program, a subsidiary organization with which the Lilly Endowment contracts to manage their campus ministry efforts. This funding was the result of college ministry leaders affiliated with my educational institution, on knowing my scholarly study of the topic, inviting me to attend this event as their "student" guest. Second, early in my research process I received a modest research grant award from the Lake Institute of Faith and Giving, a program coordinated within the Lilly Family School of Philanthropy out of Indiana University. Finally, the Lilly Endowment provided funding for a research initiative housed at the University of Virginia that supported the postdoctoral position under which this project was developed into a book manuscript. In none of these cases was I required to coordinate with (or even communicate with) anyone directly employed by the Lilly Endowment; in nearly all cases, the intermediary organizations with which I directly interacted had only cursory knowledge of my project and were not granted any form of editorial oversight over findings, analysis, or publication of research.

# Notes

## Introduction

1. Studs Terkel, *Working: People Talk about What They Do All Day and How They Feel about What They Do* (New York: Pantheon Books, 1974), p. xi.
2. Daniel Rodgers, *The Work Ethic in Industrial America, 1865–1917* (New Haven, CT: Yale University Press, 1973).
3. Julie Battilana, "Agency and Institutions: The Enabling Role of Individuals' Social Position," *Organization* 13, no. 5 (2006): 653–676.
4. David W. Miller, *God at Work: The History and Promise of the Faith at Work Movement* (New York: Oxford University Press, 2007).
5. See Jason Hackworth, *Faith Based: Religious Neoliberalism and the Politics of Welfare in the United States* (Athens: University of Georgia Press, 2012).
6. Gretchen Purser and Brian Hennigan, "Cleaning Toilets for Jesus," *Jacobin*, June 30, 2017, https://www.jacobinmag.com/2017/06/work-to-welfare-unemployment-christian-right-jobs-for-life.
7. The notion of the precariat is developed in Guy Standing, *The Precariat: The New Dangerous Class* (New York: Bloomsbury Academic, 2011). For a discussion of Methodism as the "religion of the proletariat," see E. P. Thompson, *The Making of the English Working Class* (London: V. Gollancz, 1963).
8. Bethany Moreton, *To Serve God and Wal-Mart: The Making of Christian Free Enterprise* (Cambridge, MA: Harvard University Press, 2009). For a greater discussion of Sunbelt evangelicalism, see Darren Dochuk, *From Bible Belt to Sunbelt: Plain-Folk Religion, Grassroots Politics, and the Rise of Evangelical Conservatism* (New York: W. W. Norton, 2011). Translating economic pursuits into acts of "service" also has a longer history among Mainline Protestant industrial leaders in the early twentieth century. See Richard M. Huber, *The American Idea of Success* (New York: McGraw-Hill, 1971). However, this was not a discourse that appears to have made inroads among evangelicals involved in the faith and work movement.
9. For a range of views on the faith and work movement's relationship to workplace spirituality, see: Miller, *God at Work*; James Dennis LoRusso, *Spirituality, Corporate Culture, and American Business: The Neoliberal Ethic and the Spirit of Global Capitalism* (New York: Bloomsbury Academic, 2017); and George González, *Shape-Shifting Capital: Spiritual Management, Critical Theory, and the Ethnographic Project* (Lexington, KY: Lexington Books, 2015). Workplace spirituality researchers and scholars are divided on how evangelicalism-rooted theologies of work fit into the workplace spirituality world. Some scholars disfavor religious traditions that drive adherents toward proselytization, which they see as posing a threat to a pluralistic

workplace, bringing with them zealotry and exclusivism. Other scholars believe a more peaceful assimilation is possible. For discussion of this potential conflict with other spiritual identities and practices in the workplace, see Robert A. Giacalone and Carole L. Jurkiewicz (eds.), *Handbook of Workplace Spirituality and Organizational Performance* (New York: M. E. Sharpe, 2003).

10. A key dimension of the argument presented here is that the *evangelical* faith and work movement has developed from a distinct social and historical background that diverges from the wider ecumenical faith and work movement. As a result, my account of the faith and work movement differs from several other existing works that tend to trace a more ecumenical movement that spans a wider realm of American Christianity, often including even Roman Catholics. Histories of this wider phenomena appear in Pete Hammond, R. Paul Stevens, and Todd Svanoe, *The Marketplace Annotated Bibliography: A Christian Guide to Books on Work, Business, & Vocation* (Downers Grove, IL: Intervarsity Press, 2002); Os Hillman, *Faith@Work: What Every Pastor and Church Leader Should Know* (Cumming, GA: Aslan Publishing Group, 2004); Miller, *God at Work*; Neal C. Johnson, *Business as Mission: A Comprehensive Guide to Theory and Practice* (Downers Grove, IL: IVP Academic, 2009); and Robert L. Mitchell, *A Walk in the Market: My Story of the Fellowship of Companies for Christ International* (Halsey, OR: Milestone, 2013).
11. The term "white American evangelicalism" or "white evangelicalism" is used here when speaking of those denominations, figures, or organizations that have historically been associated with—and led by—white populations and that fall within the Anglo-evangelical tradition dating back to the eighteenth century. This narrower phenomenon is thereby distinguished from the broader developments of "American evangelicalism" and "conservative Protestantism" that feature Latino, Black, immigrant, and multicultural constituencies. While the movement of interest studied here originates from white evangelical Christianity, I have omitted the "white" modifier when referring to the contemporary faith and work movement in recognition of the non-white voices and organizations that currently reside within the movement. More discussion of this terminology is laid out below.
12. See, for example, Kevin Kruse, *One Nation Under God: How Corporate America Invented Christian America* (New York: Basic Books, 2015); Gerardo Marti, *American Blindspot: Race, Class, Religion, and the Trump Presidency* (New York: Rowman & Littlefield, 2020); and Kristin Kobes Du Mez, *Jesus and John Wayne: How White Evangelicalism Corrupted a Faith and Fractured a Nation* (New York: W. W. Norton, 2020).
13. One of the most comprehensive theological and historical review of faith and work ideas is Douglas Woolley, "Theology of Work and Its Practical Implications," unpublished thesis, Carlson Institute for Church Leadership. Accessed online: https://douglaswoolley.com/essays-seminary/ch31_theology_of_work.htm#_Toc164426981.
14. Christian Smith, *American Evangelicalism: Embattled and Thriving* (Chicago: University of Chicago Press, 1998), 119.
15. Robert Orsi, "Is the Study of Lived Religion Irrelevant to the World We Live In? Special Presidential Plenary Address, Society for the Scientific Study of Religion,

Salt Lake City, November 2, 2002," *Journal for the Scientific Study of Religion* 42, no. 2 (2003): 169–174. This focus on lived religion deliberately sets aside both formal religious statements from denominational leaders as well as books written by religious ethicists or faith-affiliated economists, with such resources only being referenced in places where actors cite them or indicate being influenced by them.

16. The leaders and organizations at the center of this study were selected for their active role in what sociologist Robert Wuthnow calls the institutionalized form of culture production. See Wuthnow, *Meaning and Moral Order: Explorations in Cultural Analysis* (Berkeley: University of California Press, 1987), 15. More information on this selection process is outlined in the Appendix.
17. Ron Eyerman and Andrew Jamison, *Social Movements: A Cognitive Approach* (University Park: Pennsylvania State University Press, 1991), 55.
18. For explorations of evangelical scholarship granting greater attention to the role of Latinos, African Americans, Native Americans, and Asian Americans in religious forms that either incorporate the term "evangelical" or resonate with similar theological beliefs, see Andrea Smith, *Native Americans and the Christian Right: The Gendered Politics of Unlikely Alliances* (Durham, NC: Duke University Press, 2008); Peter Goodwin Heltzel, *Jesus and Justice: Evangelicals, Race, and American Politics* (New Haven, CT: Yale University Press, 2009); Felipe Hinojosa, *Latino Mennonites: Civil Rights, Faith, and Evangelical Culture* (Baltimore, MD: Johns Hopkins University Press, 2014); Todne Thomas, *Kincraft: The Making of Black Evangelical Sociality* (Durham, NC: Duke University Press, 2021).
19. National surveys have also tracked that a growing proportion of evangelicals are not white: Pew Research Center's survey suggest 26 percent of evangelicals identified as non-white in 2014. See: Pew Research Center, *Religious Landscape Survey*. Accessed online: https://www.pewforum.org/about-the-religious-landscape-study/
20. A case study in this dynamic of white donor interests shaping the parachurch realm appears in Ronald C. White, "Youth Ministry at the Center: A Case Study of Young Life," in *Re-Forming the Center: American Protestantism, 1900 to Present*, ed. Douglas Jacobsen and William Vance Trollinger, Jr. (Grand Rapids, MI: Eerdmans, 1998), 361–380.
21. The movement also internalizes much of the individualist social ontology that prior have tied to uniquely white evangelical spaces. See Christian Smith, *American Evangelicalism: Embattled and Thriving* (Chicago: University of Chicago Press, 1998); Michael O. Emerson and Christian Smith, *Divided by Faith: Evangelical Religion and the Problem of Race in America* (New York: Oxford University Press, 2000); James Davison Hunter, *To Change the World: The Irony, Tragedy, and Possibility of Christianity in the Late Modern World* (New York: Oxford University Press, 2010), Omri Elisha, *Moral Ambition: Mobilization and Social Outreach in an Evangelical Megachurch* (Berkeley: University of California Press, 2008). For discussion of ways this may uniquely exclude and marginalize non-white voices, see Eric Tranby and Douglas Hartmann, "Critical Whiteness Theories and the Evangelical 'Race Problem': Extending Emerson and Smith's *Divided by Faith*," *Journal for the Scientific Study of Religion* 47, no. 3 (2008): 341–359. While not receiving direct mention

from faith and work leaders, norms of whiteness and the larger individualist social ontology have garnered criticism from several books appearing on evangelical presses in the past few decades: Soong-Chan Rah, *The Next Evangelicalism: Freeing the Church from Western Cultural Captivity* (Downers Grove, IL: InterVarsity Press, 2009); Richard Twiss, *Rescuing the Gospel from the Cowboys: A Native American Expression of the Jesus Way* (Downers Grove, IL: InterVarsity Press, 2015); Simon Chan, *Grassroots Asian Theology: Thinking the Faith from the Ground Up* (Downers Grove, IL: InterVarsity Press, 2014); and Jemar Tisby, *The Color of Compromise* (Grand Rapids, MI: Zondervan, 2019).

22. Political scientists J. Tobin Gant and David Searcy draw on Pew Data to show that religious adherents in conservative Lutheran, Presbyterian, and Reformed denominations continue to be significantly less likely to self-identify as "born-again" or "evangelical" in comparison to other groups classified as Evangelical. See Gant and Searcy, "Organizational Divisions within the Evangelical Tradition," in *The Evangelical Crackup? The Future of the Evangelical-Republican Coalition*, ed. Ryan L. Claassen and Paul Djuge (Philadelphia, PA: Temple University Press, 2018), 109–123.
23. Foy Valentine, quoted in Kenneth Woodward, "Born Again!," *Newsweek*, October 25, 1976, 68.
24. Darren E. Sherkat, "Religious Intermarriage in the United States: Trends, Patterns, and Predictors," *Social Science* Research 33, no. 4 (2004): 606–625. Older data on the insular friendship network and limited intermarriage across evangelical denominations is found in Rodney Stark and William Bainbridge, *The Future of Religion* (Berkeley: University of California Press, 1985),
25. I have combined affiliation measures and measures of theological beliefs due to shared technique of conferring the "evangelical" label on respondents independent of respondents' own self-identification. This permits researchers to identify and label "unintentional" evangelicals—those who may meet certain theological and behavioral criteria of being "evangelical-like" while not necessarily considering themselves "evangelical." "Intentional evangelicals," in contrast, are what Marsden has called "card-carrying evangelicals," who do in fact explicitly embrace the identity. This intentional-unintentional distinction is taken from Robert H. Krapohl and Charles H. Lippy, *The Evangelicals: A Historical, Thematic, and Biographic Guide* (Westport, CT: Greenwood Press, 1999), 11. One important facet of some post hoc methods is deliberate categorical exclusion of the relatively high percentages of Roman Catholics, Orthodox Christian, Black Protestant, and New Age adherents who will, if given a choice, identify as "born again" or otherwise indicate they are evangelicals. For greater discussion of these issues, see Conrad Hackett and D. Michael Lindsay, "Measuring Evangelicalism: Consequences of Different Operationalization Strategies," *Journal for the Scientific Study of Religion* 47, no. 3 (2008): 499–518.
26. While historians employ the term "evangelicalism" to describe the revivalist Protestantism of George Whitefield and various denominations prior to the nineteenth century, I have reserved the term only for post-1940 groups in the interest of descriptive precision and to reflect conventional practices in sociology of religion. Protestants who represent the antecedents of these post-1940 groups are referred

to as conservative Protestants, revivalists Protestants, or in cases where they staked out the conservative side of the fundamentalist-modernist divides of the early twentieth century, fundamentalists. To provide slightly more detail on the "evangelical" lineage—here dealing largely but not exclusively with white evangelicals—this lineage begins within the conservative wing of American Protestantism that begins breaking off from wider American Protestantism amidst the Second Great Awakening. Revivalist Charles Finney embodies some of the basic fissures of this break, as Finney and the revivalists who follow him planted the seeds of a bifurcated Christianity that demotes some social issues as "appendages" to the real priority of "conversion of sinners" and the "general revival of religion." This nascent bifurcation foreshadows conservative Protestantism's gradual drawing away from social reform efforts as soul-saving, and preparation for Christ's return becomes the central religious disposition and priority. "Revivalist" Protestantism gradually sheds its concerns for wider social reforms as it crystalizes around revivalist leader D. L. Moody's organization and network-building. Moody's established network from the 1870s to 1890s serves as the hub for publishing, educating, and preaching efforts that will eventually take the form of fundamentalist Protestantism, which becomes most pronounced as a religious identity in the 1910s and 1920s after its "coming out" from Mainline Protestant denominations and seminaries. It is from ecumenical efforts built out of this fundamentalism that associations and networks emerge in the 1940s that were first associated with neo-evangelicalism or later, simply, evangelicalism. I have also employed the rarely used term of "Grahamism"—named after Billy Graham—to identify what is perhaps the dominant channel of postwar evangelicalism that retains many aspects of a more moderate fundamentalism. In summary, the major eras of the conservative Protestant lineage are as follows: the nineteenth-century revivalist Protestantism (1870–1890), fundamentalist Protestantism (1890–1940, though Chapter 2 cuts off this era at 1930 for methodological reasons), which then gave way to postwar and contemporary evangelicalism (1940–today). I have also sought, where relevant, to demarcate those groups that sat on the sidelines of the fundamentalist-modernist debate and largely defected from the "two-party" version of Protestant history. Their orientations to economics and work are often at odds with "theological individualists," as they speak in terms of both individual salvation and social reform, preserving Finney's more balanced perspective. These include sectarian groups such as Primitive Methodists and other Methodist sects, the Church of God, early African American religious denominations, and many Pentecostal and Holiness groups. Historian Donald Dayton argues these groups have been overlooked as carriers of the nineteenth-century evangelicalism that came to form the groups of the twentieth century. See Donald W. Dayton and Robert K. Johnston (eds.), *The Variety of American Evangelicalism* (Knoxville: University of Tennessee Press, 1991). For a similar effort of including groups overshadowed by the fundamentalist-modernist divides, see Molly Worthen, *Apostles of Reason: The Crisis of Authority in American Evangelicalism* (New York: Oxford University Press, 2014). I have included these groups to the extent that they found access to the major institutions and networks of power that bore influence on the revivalist, fundamentalist, and postwar evangelical subculture.

27. Books published on presses that identify as evangelical presses are categorized as evangelical books. Authors active in evangelical parachurch ministries or organizations—InterVarsity Campus Ministries, Christianity Today, etc.—are categorized as evangelical authors. This avoids imposing doctrinal or political litmus tests on materials, instead appealing to other institutions to serve as subcultural gatekeepers. When needing to categorize a college, publisher, or periodical with clear denominational affiliation, I have consulted the list of denominational members of the National Association of Evangelicals and a foundational piece in the sociology of religion: Brian Steensland, Lynn D. Robinson, W. Bradford Wilcox, Jerry Z. Park, Mark D. Regnerus, and Robert D. Woodberry, "The Measure of American Religion: Toward Improving the State of the Art," *Social Forces* 79, no. 1 (2000): 291–318. But these resources prove less helpful for categorizing fundamentalist books originating in an earlier historical period: in these cases, I relied upon historical works for accounts of the author's biography and scanned it for affiliations with fundamentalist or, alternatively, more modernist denominations and associations. I have noted the rare cases where a figure seems to have bridged the chasm and kept affiliations with both types of groups.
28. Jose Casanova compares several cases of what he calls the "deprivatization" of religion amidst this era. See Casanova, *Public Religions in the Modern World* (Chicago: University of Chicago Press, 1994).
29. Michael Hout and Claude Fischer, "Why More Americans Have No Religious Preference: Politics and Generations," *American Sociological Review* 67, no. 2 (2002): 165–190; and Putnam and Campbell, *American Grace*, 91–133.
30. Ryan P. Burge analyzes how evangelicals view labor unions, Obamacare, Black Lives Matter, Trump, and other political phenomena and how these evaluations substantially deviate from the views of the wider population. Reacting to the substantial deviation from another group, Burge concludes: "It's clear that white born-again Protestants operate in their own world." See Burge, "Did Evagnelicals Become More Moderate in 2018?" *Religion in Public Blog*, January 28, 2019. Accessed online: https://religioninpublic.blog/2019/01/28/did-evangelicals-become-more-moderate-in-2018/.
31. For reflection on politically motivated entrances and exits to evangelicalism that seem increasingly detached from any theological beliefs or motivations, see Ryan Burge, "Think Evangelicals Are Dying? Depends on How You Define Evangelical," *Religion Unplugged* (February 10, 2021). Accessed online: https://religionunplugged.com/news/2021/2/10/think-us-evangelicals-are-dying-out-that-depends-how-you-define-evangelicalism.
32. George Gallup, "Carter Found the Clear Favorite among Evangelicals," *The Washington Post* (September 9, 1980). Accessed online: https://www.washingtonpost.com/archive/politics/1980/09/07/carter-found-the-clear-favorite-among-evangelicals/d14dd751-64a6-46ea-8fb1-4d878b46be0b/. An election-day poll revealed white evangelical voters had moved toward Reagan by the time of the election, with 63 percent of white evangelicals voting for him. See A. James Reichley, "Religion and Political Realignment," *The Brookings Review* 3, no. 1 (1984): 29–35.

33. Gerardo Marti, *American Blindspot: Race, Class, Religion, and the Trump Presidency* (New York: Rowman & Littlefield, 2020), 251.
34. There are several potential misreadings of the labeling of the post-1970s phenomenon of evangelicalism–Republican Party fusion as "political evangelicalism" (for a comparable deployment of this term, see Robert Wuthnow, "'No One Loves the Bible More Than Me': The Ironic Continuities of Political Evangelicalism," in *The Evangelical Crackup? The Future of the Evangelical-Republican Coalition*, ed. Ryan L. Claassen and Paul Djuge (Philadelphia, PA: Temple University Press, 2018), 259–263.) For one, at no point in the history of evangelicalism was the constituency entirely apolitical, nor was alignment with conservative and reactionary politics a novel phenomenon that originated in the 1970s. For a review of some of the earliest forms of reactionary political voices emerging among white conservative Protestants, see Matthew Avery Sutton, "Was FDR the Antichrist? The Birth of Fundamentalist Antiliberalism in a Global Age," *Journal of American History* 98, no. 4 (2012): 1052–1074. Support for a more chauvinistic style of authoritarianism or nativist forms of national identity—two elements that came to the forefront of American evangelicalism with their enthusiastic support for the election of Donald Trump—also has a history within conservative Protestantism circles. See Ralph Lord Roy, *Apostles of Discord: A Study of Organized Bigotry and Disruption on the Fringes of Protestantism* (New York: Beacon Press, 1953), Betty A. DeBerg, *Ungodly Women: Gender and the First Wave of American Fundamentalism* (Minneapolis, MN: Fortress Press, 1990), and Margaret Lamberts Bendroth, *Fundamentalism and Gender, 1875 to the Present* (New Haven, CT: Yale University Press, 1993). However, while recognizing these historical continuities with earlier modes of conservative Protestantism, the "political evangelicalism" of the post-1970s era manifests several key attributes that, in prior eras, never achieved the hegemonic status seen today. For one, studies show that evangelicalism was a constituency with some of the lowest rates of political engagement through the 1950s and 1960s, which posited some distance between the evangelical identity and support for political parties or behaviors. See Robert Wuthnow, "The Political Rebirth of American Evangelicals," in *The New Christian Right*, ed. R. Liebman and R. Wuthnow (Hawthorne, NY: Aldine, 1983), 167–185. Relatedly, white evangelical leaders active in that era would commonly refrain from endorsing electoral or policy solutions in response to "threats" to the nation's well-being, instead falling back to the need for individual and national transformation at a spiritual level. Political scientist John C. Green observes that white evangelicals through the larger part of the twentieth century have incorporated a number of orientations to political institutions, one of which he labels a "quiescent politics" that endorses detachment and separation from political institutions. The most distinct aspect of the post-1970s political evangelicalism may be that this quiescent orientation has not only been entirely usurped by other orientations, but has now become almost unimaginable from the standpoint of what is now associated with the term "evangelical." See Green, "Seeking a Place: Evangelical Protestants and Public Engagement in the Twentieth Century," in *Toward an Evangelical Public Policy: Political Strategies for the Health of*

*the Nation*, ed. Ronald J. Sider and Diane Knippers (Grand Rapids, MI: Baker Books, 2005), 15–34.

35. While faith and work resources do not seem to function as substitute goods or off-ramps for politics for the larger populace of creative class evangelicals, there are some movement leaders who draw on faith and work themes as a means of rejecting the "culture warring" mindset of political evangelicalism, moving instead toward the framework of "cultural stewardship." This is discussed in greater detail in Chapter 7.
36. The politicization of evangelicalism likely solidifies support for such political leaders by reconstituting the constituency of evangelicalism: defectors to politicization effectively "exit" the category of evangelicalism, either by abstaining from self-identification or in disaffiliating with particular denominations. Meanwhile, politically motivated "entrances" inject new adherents loyal to the political cause. Both of these phenomena would reinforce a strong consensus of support for certain political leaders while providing no similar boost in support for theological or organizational leaders not engaged in highly visible forms of politics. Another result of these sorting mechanisms is the decreasing relevance of doctrinal or theological factors operating in the evangelical space. Whereas in the past, Arminians might have faced off against Reformed traditions, or conversion-focused revivalists might be contending against more Kuyperian-minded "transformationalists," such matters may be losing salience in a space increasingly shaped by political evangelicalism. This loosening of doctrinal particularities would explain the relative ease in which political evangelicalism was able to embrace Prosperity Gospel Pentecostals and pockets of Latino Protestant Christians who stood with evangelicals in support of President Trump. Few leaders expressed concerns regarding these groups' relatively distinct theological commitments, instead embracing them as valuable political allies.

## Chapter 1

1. Jakki Kerubo, "A Reflection on the Faith and Work Conference," *Center for Faith and Work Blog*, April 15, 2018, http://52.54.157.119/blog/formed-to-work-for-the-glory-of-god.
2. Max Weber, "The Social Psychology of the World Religions," in *From Max Weber: Essays in Sociology*, trans. Hans Heinrich Gerth and C. Wright Mills (New York: Oxford University Press, 1948), 267–301. This essay is the translated introduction to a series Weber had earlier published under the title "Die Wirtschaftsethik der Weltreligionen."
3. James Davison Hunter, *Evangelicalism: The Coming Generation* (Chicago: University of Chicago Press, 1987); Robert Wuthnow, *God and Mammon in America* (New York: Free Press, 1994).
4. Wade Clark Roof and William McKinney, *American Mainline Religion: Its Changing Shape and Future* (New Brunswick, NJ: Rutgers University Press, 1987); and Robert Wuthnow, *The Restructuring of American Religion: Society and Faith since World War*

*II* (Princeton, NJ: Princeton University Press, 1988). Closure of the education gap was aided by the exit of many working-class adherents from religious congregations beginning in the 1970s, which overall raised the average educational attainment level of regular church attenders in the United States. See Robert Putnam and David Campbell, *American Grace: How Religion Divides and Unites Us* (New York: Simon & Schuster, 2010). Studies employing a looser criterion of "evangelicals" (see methodology discussion below) at times reveal that an education gap remains between evangelicals and the wider American population, but such studies may include a larger representation of non-white evangelicals, whose educational attainment levels, while lower, are more accurately attributed to historical factors. For discussion, see Rebekah Peeples Massengill, "Educational Attainment and Cohort Change among Conservative Protestants, 1974–2004," *Journal for the Scientific Study of Religion* 47, no. 4 (2008): 545–562.

5. John Schmalzbauer, *People of Faith: Religious Conviction in American Journalism and Higher Education* (Ithaca, NY: Cornell University Press, 2003).
6. Andrew Cherlin, *The Marriage-Go-Round: The State of Marriage and Family in America Today* (New York: Vintage Books, 2010), 70.
7. Ron Lesthaeghe, "The Second Demographic Transition in Western Countries: An Interpretation," in *Gender and Family Change in Industrialized Countries*, ed. Karen Oppenheim Mason and An-Magritt Jensen (New York: Oxford University Press, 1995), 17–52. Research on conservative Protestant populations reveals that these trends have had observable effects across religious groups. See Samuel Perry and Cyrus Schleifer, "Are the Faithful Becoming Less Fruitful? The Decline of Conservative Protestant Fertility and the Growing Importance of Religious Practice and Belief in Childbearing in the U.S.," *Social Science Research* 78 (2019): 137–155.
8. Paul Heelas and Linda Woodhead, "Homeless Minds Today?," in *Peter Berger and the Study of Religion*, ed. Linda Woodhead, Paul Heelas, and David Martin (New York: Routledge, 2001), 43–72.
9. Richard Florida, *The Rise of the Creative Class: And How It's Transforming Work, Leisure, Community, and Everyday Life* (New York: Basic Books, 2002).
10. An insightful account of how greedy institutions shape identities and lifeworlds can be found in Lewis Coser, *Greedy Institutions: Patterns of Undivided Commitment* (New York: Free Press, 1974).
11. Robert Wuthnow, *Poor Richard's Principle: Recovering the American Dream through the Moral Dimension of Work, Business, and Money* (Princeton, NJ: Princeton University Press, 1996); Luc Boltanski and Eve Chiapello, *The New Spirit of Capitalism* (New York: Verso, 2007); and Lyn Spilman, *Solidarity in Strategy: Making Business Meaningful in American Trade Associations* (Chicago: University of Chicago Press, 2012).
12. Iannaccone's own work primarily examines fundamentalism's relationship to the "Protestant ethic" in terms of formal economics, an analysis that complements the examination of "non-formal economics" undertaken here. See Iannaccone, "Heirs to the Protestant Ethic? The Economics of American Fundamentalists," in *Fundamentalism*

*and the State*, ed. Martin E. Marty and Scott Appleby (Chicago: University of Chicago Press, 1993), 345–366.

13. I am drawing the idea of imaginary from Charles Taylor, who develops his own concept of "social imaginary" from Benedict Anderson. See Taylor, *Modern Social Imaginaries* (Durham, NC: Duke University Press, 2003).
14. Weber, *From Max Weber: Essays in Sociology*, 321.
15. Robert Wuthnow proposes that religious frameworks generally intersect with economic activity in any of three ways: compartmentalization, harmonization, or conflict. Wuthnow's typology has parallels to the typology laid out below, though Wuthnow's typology is more naturally situated from the point of view of the religious adherent or religious system reacting to the economic system, whereas the typology below works from the perspective of the economic system itself as it interacts with particular religious or meaning systems. This shift in perspective more effectively brings to the forefront of analysis the functions and consequences of various orientations, sketching out the more diachronic processes that might be catalyzed by a "conflictual" or "compartmentalized" orientation. See Wuthnow, *Poor Richard's Principle*, 1996.
16. These three orientations, respectively, align with Albert Hirschman's typology of exit, loyalty, or voice. Hirschman's conceptualization of exit, however, does not directly capture an actor's pragmatic but disinterested state of consent *within* an environment while being emotionally or cognitively disengaged and solely there for utilitarian reasons. Thus, subordinating and shirking orientations represent a wider range of frameworks, from those that promote formal exit to those that advocate the most minimally engaged manner of remaining within a work setting.
17. Dorothy Sayers, "Why Work?," in her *Creed or Chaos?* (New York: Harcourt, Brace, 1949), 46–62.
18. *Starting on Monday: Christian Living in the Workplace* (1987); *First Thing Monday Morning: Reminders for Keeping God in Your Work Week* (1988); *The Monday Connection: A Spirituality of Competence, Affirmation, and Support in the Workplace* (1991); *God on Monday* (1996); *God's Week Has Seven Days: Monday Musings for Marketplace Christians* (1998); *Loving Monday: Succeeding in Business Without Selling Your Soul* (1998); *First Thing Monday Morning* (1998); *The Other Six Days: Vocation, Work, and Ministry in Biblical Perspective* (2000); *Church on Sunday, Work on Monday: The Challenge of Fusing Christian Values with Business Life* (2001); *Seven Days of Faith: Every Day Alive with God* (2001); *Where's God on Monday?: Integrating Faith and Work Every Day of the Week* (2003); *After Sunday: A Theology of Work* (2004); *Mastering Monday: A Guide to Integrating Faith and Work* (2006); *Work Matters: Connecting Sunday Worship to Monday Work* (2011); *The Monday Connection: On Being an Authentic Christian in a Weekday World* (2012); *Monday Morning Atheist: Why We Switch Off God at Work and How to Fix It* (2012); *Monday Matters: Finding God in Your Workplace* (2012); *Church for Monday: Equipping Believers for Mission Work* (2019).
19. The nine faith and work books with identical titles: *Thank God It's Monday* (1982); *Thank God It's Monday* (1990); *Thank God It's Monday: Making Business Your Ministry*

(1996); *Thank God It's Monday!: A Toolkit for Aligning Your Life Vision and Your Life Work* (1998); *Thank God It's Monday: Ministry in the Workplace* (2001); *Thank God It's Monday: Celebrating Your Purpose at Work* (2003); *Thank God It's Monday: How to Take God to Work with You* (2004); *Thank God It's Monday: Everyday Evangelism for Everyday People* (2014); *Thank God It's Monday: Sunday's Not Enough* (2015).

20. Karl Marx, *The Grundrisse*, ed. and trans. David McLellan (New York: Harper & Row, 1970), 124–126.
21. Paul Willis, *Learning to Labour: How Working Class Kids Get Working Class Jobs* (New York: Columbia University Press, 1978), 186.
22. Mark A. Shibley makes a compelling case that evangelicals are far more "world-affirming" than culturally conservative. See Shibley, "Contemporary Evangelicals: Born-Again and World Affirming," *The Annals of the American Academy of Political and Social Science* 558, no. 1 (1998): 67–87.
23. Max Weber, *The Protestant Ethic and the Spirit of Capitalism*, trans. Talcott Parsons (New York: Routledge Classics, 2004), 101.77.
24. While this lack of access to participation in the formal economy seems to deter interest in the faith and work movement, it does not seem to have the same effect for engagement with the Prosperity Gospel, which professes its own variant of the American dream and materialist values. As Chapter 9 explores, the Prosperity Gospel attracts almost the inverse demographic profile as the faith and work movement. For more on demographics of the Prosperity Gospel, see Tony Tian-Ren Lin, *Prosperity Gospel: Latinos and Their American Dream* (Chapel Hill: University of North Carolina Press, 2020).
25. Marry Patillo-McCoy, "Church Culture as a Strategy of Action in the Black Community," *American Sociological Review* 63 (1998): 767–784.
26. See Helen Rose Esbaugh and Janet Saltzman Chafetz, "Agents for Cultural Reproduction and Structural Change: The Ironic Role of Women in Immigrant Religious Institutions," *Social Forces* 78, no. 2 (1999): 585–612; Elaine Howard Ecklund, "Models of Civic Responsibility: Korean Americans in Congregations with Different Ethnic Compositions," *Journal for the Scientific Study of Religion* 44, no. 1 (2005): 15–28; and Carolyn Chen, *Getting Saved in America: Taiwanese Immigration and Religious Experiences* (Princeton, NJ: Princeton University Press, 2014), 111–145.
27. Christian Smith argues that American evangelicalism maintains its unique subcultural strength due to its drive to create clear distinction and tension with other outgroups; see Smith, *American Evangelicalism: Embattled and Thriving* (Chicago: University of Chicago Press, 1998), 189–119. This subcultural strength may very well then be lessened by the loss of one side of this dialectic among the "thriving evangelicals" that gravitate toward faith and work spaces. I discuss this issue more in Chapter 8.
28. Because "embattled evangelicalism" and "thriving evangelicalism" are primarily cultural orientations rather than a particular product of economic positionality, evangelicals occupying creative-class settings are not in any way immune from those cultural, political, or racial currents that can place them in the "embattled camp." This particularly relates to the possibilities of status anxieties related to race and culture

transcending economic position. On this topic, see Diana C. Mutz, "Status Threat, Not Economic Hardship, Explains the 2016 Presidential Vote," *Proceedings of the National Academy of Sciences* 115, no. 19 (2018): E4330–E4339.

29. George Marsden, *Fundamentalism and American Culture* (New York: Oxford University Press, 2006), 210–211.
30. Derek Thompson, "Workism Is Making Americans Miserable," *The Atlantic* (February 24, 2019), https://www.theatlantic.com/ideas/archive/2019/02/religion-workism-making-americans-miserable/583441/.
31. I am drawing on the conception of religion here developed by Robert Bellah, who in turn leans on the work of Alfred Schutz's concept of symbols as offering meanings rooted within "higher" realities. See Bellah, *Religion in Human Evolution: From the Paleolithic to the Axial Age* (Cambridge, MA: Harvard University Press, 2011).
32. "The rationalization of the world, the elimination of magic as means to salvation, the Catholic had not carried nearly so far as the Puritans (and before them the Jews) had done. To the Catholic the absolution of his Church was a compensation for his own imperfection. The priest was a magician who performed the miracle of transubstantiation, and who held the key to eternal life in his hand. One could turn to him in grief and penitence. He dispensed atonement, hope of grace, certainty of forgiveness, and thereby granted release from that tremendous tension to which the Calvinist was doomed by an inexorable fate, admitting of no mitigation." Weber, *The Protestant Ethic*, 71. From Weber's essay on religion and salvation: "The religious virtuoso can be placed in the world as the instrument of God and cut off from all magical means of salvation. At the same time, it is imperative for the virtuoso that he 'proves' himself before God, as being called solely through the ethical quality of his conduct in the world. No matter how much the 'world' as such is religiously devalued and rejected as being creatural and a vessel of sin, yet psychologically the world is all the more affirmed as the theater of God-willed activity in one's worldly 'calling.'" From Weber, "Social Psychology of the World Religions," in *From Max Weber*, 291.
33. Max Weber, *General Economic Theory* (Mineola, NY: Dover Publications, 2003), 366.
34. Weber, *The Protestant Ethic*, 123.

## Chapter 2

1. Weber, "Social Psychology of the World Religions," 289.
2. Details of this account taken from Matthew Avery Sutton, American *Apocalypse: A History of Modern Evangelicalism* (Cambridge, MA: Belknap, 2014). Interestingly, a Google search reveals Biola University in 2016 completed their largest fundraising campaign in the school's history, of which $75.2 million is designated for brick and mortar facilities.
3. Quoted in William L. Burton, *Protestantism and the Cult of Prosperity: Social and Economic Ideas Prevalent in the Protestant Churches, 1919–1929* (Madison: University of Wisconsin, 1958).

4. This distinct understanding of history and time among fundamentalist thinking is explored in greater detail in Susan Friend Harding, *The Book of Jerry Falwell: Fundamentalist Language and Politics* (Princeton, NJ: Princeton University Press, 2000).
5. Details of this account drawn from Eric Hobsbawm, *Primitive Rebels: Studies in Archaic Forms of Social Movement in the 19th and 20th Centuries* (New York: W. W. Norton, 1959); Liston Pope, *Millhands and Preachers: A Study of Gastonia* (New Haven, CT: Yale University Press, 1942); Rolf Lundén, *Business and Religion in the American 1920s* (New York: Greenwood Press, 1988); and Wayne Flynt, *Southern Religion and Christian Diversity in the Twentieth Century* (Tuscaloosa: University of Alabama Press, 2016).
6. Sutton, *American Apocalypse*, 4. For a similar assessment, see Nancy Ammerman, "North American Protestant Fundamentalism," in *Fundamentalism Observed: Volume 1*, ed. Martin E. Marty and R. Scott Appleby (Chicago: University of Chicago, 1991), 2–3; and Josh McMullin, *Under the Big Top: Big Ten Revivalism and American Culture, 1885–1925* (New York: Oxford University Press, 2015), 3–8.
7. Nancy Ammerman's study of fundamentalism in the 1980s suggests that, at her time of study, the church vs. world dualism was still prevalent among American fundamentalists. See Ammerman, *Bible Believers: Fundamentalists in the Modern World* (New Brunswick, NJ: Rutgers University Press, 1987), 205–209. Economics and work were matters that were assigned to the realm of "the world," and therefore had little religious significance.
8. John Calvin, *Commentary on the Psalms* (Edinburgh: T&T Clark, 1845), 107.
9. Quoted in Daniel Rodgers, *The Work Ethic in Industrial America, 1865–1917* (New Haven, CT: Yale University Press, 1973), 8.
10. George Marsden, *Fundamentalism and American Culture* (New York: Oxford University Press, 2006).
11. See James Davison Hunter, *American Evangelicalism* (New Brunswick, NJ: Rutgers University, 1983); Christian Smith, "Introduction: Rethinking the Secularization of American Public Life," in *The Secular Revolution: Power, Interests, and Conflict in the Secularization of American Public Life*, ed. Christian Smith (Berkeley: University of California Press, 2003), 1–98.
12. Robert T. Handy, *A Christian America: Protestant Hopes and Historical Realities* (New York: Oxford University Press, 1971), 84.
13. George Thomas, *Revivalism and Cultural Change: Christianity, Nation-Building, and the Market in the Nineteenth Century United States* (Chicago: University of Chicago Press, 1989).
14. *Old Pine Farm, or, The Southern Side: Comprising Loose Sketches from the Experience of a Southern Country Minister, S.C.* (Nashville, TN: Southwestern Publishing House, 1850), 20–21. Quoted in Carl R. Osthaus, "The Work Ethic of the Plain Folk: Labor and Religion in the Old South," *The Journal of Southern History* 70, no. 4 (2004): 745–782.
15. Finney spared few words for those in his time who were failing to pay back their debt, which at times was known to trigger bank failures and financial panics. "I cannot have confidence in the piety of any man who is not conscientious in the payment

of his debts . . . I believe it is right, and the duty of all churches and ministers to exclude such persons from the communion of the church . . . I do not see why they should be suffered to come to the communion table any more than whoremongers, or murderers, or drunkards, or Sabbath breakers, or slaveholders. There must be a great reformation in the church upon this subject, before the business class of ungodly men will have much confidence in religion." Quoted in Noll, "Protestant Reasoning about Money and the Economy, 1790–1860: A Preliminary Probe." in *God and Mammon: Protestants, Money, and the Market, 1790–1860*, ed. Mark Noll (New York: Oxford University Press, 2002), 75–98

16. Christopher Evans, *The Social Gospel in American Religion: A History* (New York: New York University Press, 2017), 2.
17. George Marsden, *Fundamentalism and American Culture* (New York: Oxford University Press, 2006)
18. Sutton, American *Apocalypse.*
19. A fuller discussion of this is found in Sutton, *American Apocalypse*, and Marsden, *Fundamentalism and American Culture.*
20. Ernest Sandeen, *The Roots of Fundamentalism: British and American Millenarianism, 1800–1930* (Chicago: University of Chicago Press, 1970).
21. The "Higher Life" and Keswick movements claim influence on a remarkable number of authors reviewed in the next section, including Andrew Murray, F. B. Meyer, R. A. Torrey, S. D. Gordon, and A. T. Pierson.
22. These observations are made by historian Robert Maples Anderson specifically in reference to early twentieth-century Pentecostalism. However, Anderson's larger argument draws a strong linkage between the spread of Kewswick theology—particularly in its views of baptism in the Holy Spirit—and the birth of modern Pentecostalism. See Anderson, *Visions of the Disinherited: The Making of American Pentecostalism* (Eugene, OR: Wipf & Stock, 1992), 239.
23. Quoted in George Marsden, *Understanding Fundamentalism and Evangelicalism* (Grand Rapids, MI: Wm. B. Eerdmans, 1991), 21.
24. Peter Goodwin Heltzel, *Jesus and Justice: Evangelicals, Race, and American Politics* (New Haven, CT: Yale University Press, 2009), 42. See also Randall Balmer and Lauren F. Winner, *Protestantism in America* (New York: Columbia University Press, 2002), 61–62.
25. Edward J. Blum, *Reforming the White Republic: Race, Religion, and American Nationalism, 1865–1898* (Baton Rouge: Louisiana State Press, 2015), 137.
26. See Marsden, *Fundamentalism and American Culture.*
27. Numbers taken from Joel Carpenter, *Revive Us Again: The Reawakening of American Fundamentalism* (New York: Oxford University Press, 1997).
28. All information taken from Carpenter, *Revive Us Again*, as well as Revell's own history page, accessed online: http://bakerpublishinggroup.com/revell/about-revell.
29. Fundamentalists did not always back up their militant rejection of liberal theology with expulsion of its protagonists from its own institutional resources. The September 1920 (Volume XXI) cover of *Moody Bible Institute Monthly* represents the extreme ossification of the chasm vision of the debate with an illustration of two cliffs separated

by a chasm. The left cliff is labeled "the faith which was once delivered unto the saints" while the right is labeled "Modernist theology." The words "No Middle Ground—Only a Chasm" appear above the gap between the two cliffs. But Revell published a remarkable number of social gospel writers at the same time that its sister organization's periodical—*Moody Bible Institute Monthly*—decried those authors as deeply flawed, dangerous, and heretical. Revell's website lists both historically significant fundamentalist and modernist books it published amidst this era. Often, issues of *Moody Bible Institute Monthly* would list modernist authors side by side with fundamentalist authors in their advertising for books with no editorial commentary, even when the same issue was deeply critical of the same modernist author elsewhere in the publication. Robert Speer—whose writing shows up below—was able to bridge the two groups for much of his life, writing and working with the early-century revivalists while lining up against some of the prominent fundamentalist leaders in the 1920s. SeeBradley J. Longfield, *The Presbyterian Controversy: Fundamentalists, Modernists, and Moderates* (New York: Oxford University Press, 1991). Some of these persisting overlaps likely stem from the comparable demographic features.

30. For an account of fundamentalism's establishment in the North and in cities like Chicago, see David Harrington Watt, "Fundamentalists of the 1920s and 1930s," in *Fundamentalism: Perspectives on a Contested History*, ed. Simon A. Wood and David Harrington Watt (Columbia, SC: University of South Carolina, 2014). Marsden (2006) argues that the "backwoods, rural, and uneducated" depiction of fundamentalists owes its prevalence to the descriptions produced by journalist H. L. Mencken after the Scopes Monkey trial and failed to realistically depict the scope and fuller influence of the movement. Evans (2017) provides an account of the geographic origins of the social gospel movement, which had strongholds in the Midwest and North early on. Wenger (1974) compares the biographies of forty prominent leaders from each camp to conclude that modernist leadership on average held a greater number of advanced degrees, but geographic footprints of each camp largely mirrored the U.S. population and U.S. churchgoing population at the time. Wenger, looking at the era between 1918 and 1933, sees fundamentalism's greater numeric strength east of the Mississippi and north of the Mason-Dixon line where, in his read, modernism "posed a strong threat." He found Pennsylvania to be a particularly strong fundamentalist stronghold, based on subscribers and donors to a national fundamentalist periodical and the state of origin for many students enrolling in Bible colleges. See Robert E. Wenger, *Social Thought in American Fundamentalism, 1918–1933* (Eugene, OR: Wipf & Stock, 1974).

31. For an overview of wealthy donors supporting fundamentalist efforts, see Douglas Carl Abrams, *Selling the Old-Time Religion: American Fundamentalists and Mass Culture, 1920–1940* (Athens: University of Georgia Press, 2001); Kim Phillips-Fein, *Invisible Hands: The Businessmen's Crusade Against the New Deal* (New York: W. W. Norton, 2009); and Timothy Gloege, *Guaranteed Pure: The Moody Bible Institute, Business, and the Making of Modern Evangelicalism* (Chapel Hill: University of North Carolina Press, 2015). Fundamentalists were accused of promoting a business-friendly and covertly business-funded anti-progressive politics as early as the 1920s. See Gottlieb Hafner, "Premillennialism—A Danger to the Church?" *Moody Bible*

*Monthly* 22 (December 1921): 712. "Modernists" were also no strangers to the realm of wealthy donors. In the early social gospel era, the movement received a boost when a wealthy widow impressed with the radical anti-wealth preaching of George Davis Herron endowed a "Chair of Applied Christianity" for Herron at Iowa College (later Grinnell College). See Susan Curtis, *A Consuming Faith: The Social Gospel and Modern American Culture* (Columbia: University of Missouri Press, 2001). Abrams (2001) also recounts the Rockefellers' support of Harry Emerson Fosdick's church in New York City and the University of Chicago's seminary. In some cases these theological modernists advanced politically conservative agendas that aligned with donors' interests.

32. For respective discussions of each, see Evans, *The Social Gospel in American Religion*, and Wenger, *Social Thought in American Fundamentalism*.
33. For overviews of groups that were left on the sidelines of the two-party fundamentalist-modernist divide, see Donald W. Dayton and Robert K. Johnston (eds.), *The Variety of American Evangelicalism* (Knoxville: University of Tennessee Press, 1991); Douglas Jacobsen and William Vance Trollinger, Jr. (eds.), *Re-Forming the Center: American Protestantism, 1900 to Present* (Grand Rapids, MI: Wm. B. Eerdmans, 1998); and Molly Worthen, *Apostles of Reason: The Crisis of Authority in American Evangelicalism* (New York: Oxford University Press, 2014).
34. Carl R. Osthaus, "The Work Ethic of the Plain Folk: Labor and Religion in the Old South," *The Journal of Southern History* 70, no. 4 (2004): 745–782.
35. Clyde Barrow, *Universities and the Capitalist State: Corporate Liberalism and the Reconstruction of American Higher Education, 1894–1928* (Madison: University of Wisconsin Press, 1990), 25.
36. Alan Trachtenberg, *The Incorporation of America: Culture and Society, 1865–1893* (New York: Hill and Wang, 1982).
37. Daniel Bell, *Work and Its Discontents* (Boston: Beacon Press, 1956).
38. Rodgers, *The Work Ethic*, 22, 28.
39. For a discussion of traditional work ethics and their intersection with emerging managerial ideologies, see Reinhard Bendix, *Work and Authority in Industry* (New York: Wiley, 1956); and Bell, *Work and Its Discontents*. Other observers still see the "Weber-Tawney" understanding of Protestant ethics continuing to exert influence over the American free enterprise system well into the twentieth century, though perhaps more as a part of industrial era ideology rather than actual worker motivation.
40. See Phillips-Fein, *Invisible Hands*; Matthew Tallman, *Demos Shakarian: The Life, Legacy, and Vision of a Full Gospel Business Man* (Lexington, KY: Emeth Press, 2010); Gloege, *Guaranteed Pure*; Kevin Kruse, *One Nation under God: How Corporate America Invented Christian America* (New York: Basic Books, 2015); Darren Grem, *The Blessings of Business: How Corporations Shaped Conservative Christianity* (New York: Oxford University Press, 2016); and Sarah Ruth Hammond, *God's Businessmen: Entrepreneurial Evangelicals in Depression and War* (Chicago: University of Chicago Press, 2017).
41. George Marsden detects a similar favoring of themes among fundamentalists in the later decades of the nineteenth century. He posits that at least 75 percent of

fundamentalist talk and writing focused on the themes of popular piety, simple Bible study, and soul-winning.

42. Some book categorizations captured underlying publishing and teaching priorities. An 1886 advertisement for one publisher divided up works into the following six categories: On the Holy Spirit, On Prayer, On Christ's Return, On Helps in Bible Study, and The Deeper Christian Life. An 1894 "Selected List of Recent Books" in the *Sunday School Times* divided books into four categories: History, Biography, Missionary; Religious Counsel and Devotion; Nature-Study; and Fiction. A 1914 periodical separated their book listings into: Missions, Second Coming, Prayer, and Soul-Saving. While it certainly seems imaginable that books about economics, vocation, and work might slip in under these categories, this was rarely the case. The subjects of work, occupations, business, lay vocations, and economic activity—as well as wider questions of industrial labor, political economy, or economic policy—were almost completely absent from book listings, book descriptions, book reviews, and the content of the books themselves.
43. One of the most prevalent places where work referred to lay functions of proselytization or ministry was in the titles of the periodicals themselves: *The Christian: A Weekly Record of Christian Life, Christian Testimony, and Christian Work*; *Record of Christian Work*; *The Christian Work/The Christian at Work*; *Christian Workers Magazine*; *King's Business*; and *The Christian Work and Evangelist* (a merger of two publications that later became just *Christian Work*) all referred to ministry workers, not workers in an economic or political economy sense.
44. One of the most famous cases of appropriating economic and business terms for this era is the work of Bruce Barton, whose 1925 book *The Man Nobody Knows: The Discovery of the Real Jesus*, was a bestseller. However, Barton's work received an ambivalent to cold response among fundamentalists, who were unimpressed with his largely heterodox theological beliefs. See Douglas Carl Abrams, *Selling the Old-Time Religion: American Fundamentalists and Mass Culture, 1920–1940* (Athens: University of Georgia Press, 2001).
45. Henry Frederick Cope, *Levels of Living: Essays on Everyday Ideals* (New York: Fleming H. Revell, 1908).
46. James I. Vance, *The Young Man Foursquare* (New York: Fleming H. Revell, 1894), 9–10.
47. Robert E. Speer, *A Christian's Habits* (New York: Association Press, 1911). Another text praising and upholding Franklin's frugality and discipline is Orison Swett Marden, *Economy* (New York: Thomas Y. Crowell, 1901).
48. Speer bridged both conservative and liberal sides of this era of Protestantism, initially having a religious experience in the 1890s and joining up with Moody's work, but decades later facing off against John Gresham Machen in rifts over Presbyterian missiology. See Longfield, *The Presbyterian Controversy*.
49. Hugh Black, *Work* (New York: Fleming H. Revell, 1903), 227.
50. Ibid., 227.
51. Frederick Brotherton Meyer, *A Good Start* (New York: Thomas Y. Crowell & Co., 1897), 76.

52. Perry Wayland Sinks, *Popular Amusements and the Christian Life* (Chicago: The Bible Institute Colportage Association, 1896), 111 .
53. Marsden notes that Moody favored portraying the infilling of the Holy Spirit as specifically providing "power to serve," preserving a tighter connection between his Keswick influences and his active revivalist efforts. Had this power been channeled toward the economic sphere, the general orientation would still have preserved what Weber describes as inner-worldly asceticism. However, channeling this power toward ecclesial and evangelistic efforts (and in some cases, social reform) redirects energies that might otherwise be devoted to one's economic labor.
54. Frederick Brotherton Meyer, *The Future Tenses of the Present Life* (New York: Fleming H. Revell, 1892), 27.
55. Frederick Brotherton Meyer, *Words of Help for Christian Girls* (New York: H. M. Caldwell, 1897), 28.
56. Frederick Brotherton Meyer, *Saved and Kept: Counsel for Young Believers* (New York: Fleming H. Revell, 1897), 30.
57. Meyer, *Saved and Kept*, 35.
58. Frederick Brotherton Meyer, *Christian Living* (New York: Fleming H. Revell, 1892), 42.
59. See Rodgers, *The Work Ethic.*
60. Hannah Whitall Smith, *The Christian's Secret of a Happy Life* (New York: Fleming H. Revell, 1883), 31.
61. Quoted in Marsden, *Fundamentalism and American Culture*, 59.
62. Cyrus Ingerson Scofield, *The New Life in Christ* (Chicago: The Bible Institute Colportage Association, 1915). Scofield aims his criticism at Charles Sheldon's proposed ethical orientation of asking "What would Jesus do?" in his famous 1896 novel *In His Steps.* Sheldon's ethical framework granted questions of work and labor a significant place in his biblical ethics. While Sheldon's later promotion of Christian socialism would itself be problematic for fundamentalists of the era, Scofield's interaction with Sheldon's thoroughly biblicist, Jesus-centered "work ethic" captures in one episode much of the larger argument laid out here: fundamentalist writers systematically rooted out from their own tradition the theological resources that would have otherwise preserved the notion that work "matters to God." In the 1970s, faith and work leader Robert Mitchell recounted rediscovering and being inspired by Sheldon's 1896 text, which served as a source of guidance for him as he founded the Fellowship of Christian Companies International. See Robert L. Mitchell, *A Walk in the Market: My Story of the Fellowship of Companies for Christ International* (Halsey, OR: Milestone, 2013). For more on Sheldon, see Gary Scott Smith, *The Search for Social Salvation: Social Christianity and America, 1880–1925* (Lanham, MD: Lexington Books, 2000).
63. Andrew Murray, *Money: Thoughts for God's Steward* (New York: Life, 1900).
64. Frederick B. Meyer, *Light on Life's Duties* (Chicago: Fleming H. Revell, 1895), 110.
65. Meyer, *Light on Life's Duties*, 90.
66. Cortland Myers, *Money Mad* (New York: Fleming H. Revell, 1917), 32.

67. Henry Frederick Cope, *Levels of Living: Essays on Everyday Ideals* (New York: Fleming H. Revell, 1908), 20.
68. Robert Elliott Speer, *The Stuff of Manhood: Some Needed Notes on American Character* (New York: Fleming H. Revell, 1917), 171.
69. Cyrus I. Scofield, *The New Life in Christ* (Chicago: The Bible Institute Colportage Association, 1915), 64.
70. Meyer, *Light on Life's Duties*, 88.
71. Meyer, *Cheer for Life's Pilgrimage*, (New York: Fleming H. Revell, 1897), 57–58.
72. Samuel Dickey Gordon, *Quiet Talks on Service* (New York: Fleming H. Revell, 1906), 46–47
73. Ibid., 47.
74. Howard Walter Pope, *What Every Christian Needs to Know: A Course Study in Personal Work* (Chicago: The Bible Institute Colportage Association, 1904), 42.
75. Reuben Archer Torrey, *Personal Work: How to Work for Christ* (New York: Fleming H. Revell, 1901).
76. William A. Hill, "The Stewardship Library," *The Baptist* 3, no. 51 (1923): 1599.
77. Myers, *Money Mad*, 82.
78. Murray, *Money: Thoughts for God's Stewards*, 35.
79. John Horsch, *Modern Religious Liberalism* (Scottdale, PA: Fundamental Truth Depot, 1921), 136–137.
80. This idea of churches as "exchangers" providing wealth-to-souls "currency" conversion for the laity also appears in the 1915 essay "Our Lord's Teaching on Money," written by Arthur T. Pierson, which appeared in *The Fundamentals* essays. Interestingly, assigning ecclesial bodies as the sites where otherwise unredeemed wealth can be dedicated for eternal purposes locates the individual believer in a dependent and somewhat subservient position in relation to his or her ecclesial body, something that drew Martin Luther's ire in the Protestant Reformation.
81. Gordon, *Quiet Talks of Service*, 152.
82. Howard Pope, *What Every Christian Needs to Know: A Course of Study in Personal Work*, 181–182.
83. Pope, "A Remarkable Career," *American Messenger*, 80, no. 7 1922): 104.
84. Orrin Philip Gifford, *Honest Debtors: Some Sermons and Addresses* (Philadelphia: The Judson Press, 1922), 37.
85. Charles Dickens, *David Copperfield* (New York: Charles Scribner's Sons, 1899), 390.
86. Quoted in Marsden, *Fundamentalism and American Culture*, 131.
87. Statement appears in "Editorial," *King's Business* 8(2) (February 1917): 99.
88. J. H. Ralston, "What Other Editors Are Saying, Church and Industry," *Moody Bible Institute Monthly* 22, no. 3 (November 1921): 664.
89. Charles R. Erdman, "The Church and Socialism," in *The Fundamentals: A Testimony to the Truth, Volume XII*, ed. R. A. Torrey (Chicago: Testimony, 1915), 108–119. For analysis of the sharp change in tone between Erdman's softer, more spiritualized condemnation of socialism and the later 1950s Cold War–inspired condemnation, see T. Jeremy Gunn, *Spiritual Weapons: The Cold War and the Forging of an American National Religion* (Westport, CT: Praeger, 2009).

90. Black, *Work*, 16.
91. Horsch, *Modern Religious Liberalism*, 304.
92. Editorial Notes, "Church and Industry," *Moody Bible Institute Monthly* 22, no. 2 (October 1921): 597.
93. Erdman, "The Church and Socialism,"114.
94. Mark Noll, *The Scandal of the Evangelical Mind* (Grand Rapids, MI: William B. Eerdmans, 1995), 107.
95. Max Weber, "Religious Rejections of the World and Their Directions," in *From Max Weber: Essays in Sociology*, 325.
96. While Moody and other leaders clamped down on overly exuberant and emotional behaviors in their worship services, leaders like Meyer were by and large supportive of some of the early revivals that featured spontaneity and "hysteria." See Robert Mapes Anderson, *Visions of the Disinherited: The Making of American Pentecostalism* (Eugene, OR: Wipf & Stock, 1992), 38, 44.
97. Gottlieb Hafner, "Premillennialism—A Danger to the Church?" *Moody Bible Monthly* 22 (December 1921): 712.
98. Archibald McClean, *The Primacy of the Missionary and Other Addresses* (Saint Louis, MO: Christian Board of Education, 1921), 11.
99. Alfred Griswold, *The American Gospel of Success* (unpublished PhD dissertation, Department of History, Yale University, 1934), 38.
100. Robert Wauzzinsk, *Between God and Gold: Protestant Evangelicalism and the Industrial Revolution, 1820–1914* (Cranberry, NJ: Associated University Presses, 1993).
101. Allan J. Lichtman, *White Protestant Nation: The Rise of the American Conservative Movement* (New York: Grove Press, 2008), 28.
102. See George Thomas, *Revivalism and Cultural Change: Christianity, Nation-Building, and the Market in the Nineteenth Century United States* (Chicago: University of Chicago Press, 1989); and Daniel Walker Howe, "The Market Revolution and the Shaping of Identity in Whig-Jacksonian America," in *The Market Revolution in America: Social, Political, and Religious Expressions, 1800–1880* ed. Melvyn Stokes and Stephen Conway (Charlottesville: University Press of Virginia, 1996), 259–281.
103. Several histories of Protestant thinking on business and capitalism in the early twentieth century make no references to fundamentalist views, reflecting the general neglect of writing or thinking produced by fundamentalist leaders. These include: Gerald F. Cavanagh, *American Business Values in Transition* (Englewood Cliffs, NJ: Prentice-Hall, 1976); John C. Bennett, "Protestantism and Corporations," in *Judeo-Christian Vision and the Modern Corporation*, ed. Oliver F. Williams and John W. Houck (Notre Dame, IN: University of Notre Dame Press, 1982); Oliver F. Williams, "Introduction," in *Judeo-Christian Vision and the Modern Corporation*, ed. Oliver F. Williams and John W. Houck (Notre Dame, IN: University of Notre Dame Press, 1982); Rolf Lundén, *Business and Religion*; Abend, *The Moral Background*. This neglect also shapes Weber's otherwise valuable observations of American Protestant churches in his lesser-known essay, "Churches and Sects in North America," in *From Max Weber: Essays in Sociology*, 302–322. These narratives largely center the more

establishment-oriented forms of white Conservative Protestantism, which featured the likes of industrial elites like Andrew Carnegie, John D. Rockefeller, many religious Rotary Club members, and Ivy League business ethics professors. Historian William Burton provides a valuable counter-example to these works by constructing a tripartite typology of American Christianity: fundamentalism, conservative Protestantism, and social Christianity. Burton's analysis is then able to parse the relatively distinct orientations of fundamentalist leaders. See Burton, *Protestantism and the Cult of Prosperity*. The historians who position fundamentalism as the vanguard class of consumer-capitalism often fail to draw distinctions between fundamentalism and the more established forms of conservative Protestantism, the latter of which generally operated at a distance from fundamentalists and sectarian groups that preserved sensationalized forms of worship services and apocalyptic anxieties.

104. Works indexing fundamentalists' deployment of modern technological, marketing, and consumerist means of spreading the gospel and organizing their ministries include Lundén, *Business and Religion*; Abrams, *Selling the Old-Time Religion*; John Curran Hardin, *Retailing Religion: Business Promotionalism in American Christian Churches in the Twentieth Century* (College Park: University of Maryland Press, 2011); and Gloege, *Guaranteed Pure*.
105. Abrams recounts a fundamentalist ministry leader in Grand Rapids claiming he had calculated the exact price of soul-saving to be $1.60 per soul, based on his ministry's operating costs in relations to souls saved. See Abrams, *Selling the Old-Time Religion*.
106. Lower-status church communities often served as important sites of autonomous culture that were set against the prevailing status system and social order that might be endorsed by mainstream religion. See Flynt, *Southern Religion*, 255. Liston Pope provides an account of low-status millhands establishing this autonomous space in the holiness churches they attended. See Pope, *Millhands and Preachers*. This phenomenon reflects many of Weber's sociological observations about the relation between religion and social strata in his classic essay, "Social Psychology of the World Religions."
107. A similar thought is concisely expressed in Margaret Lamberts Bendroth, *Fundamentalism and Gender, 1875 to the Present* (New Haven, CT: Yale University Press, 1993), 79.
108. See Wenger, *Social Thought in American Fundamentalism*, 212–226, for a very concise outline of political orientations one can derive from fundamentalist thought.
109. An editorial cartoon of the era communicated this mode of proposing "political solutions" with a drawing of a suit-wearing "employer" shaking hands with an overall-clad "employee," both encompassed by a circle with the words "In Christ." The caption is confident in this configuration for resolving labor unrest: "Within this circle no social problem is incapable of solution." See also Wenger, *Social Thought*, 212–226.
110. Burton, *Protestantism and the Cult of Prosperity*, 384.
111. Carpenter, *Revive Us Again*, 116–119. One of the central challenges of assessing fundamentalism's cultural orientation is the different manners in which one may interpret the fundamentalists' creation of a vast network of conferences, publications,

publishing houses, seminaries, colleges, Bible leagues, mission boards, temperance groups, Sabbatarian groups, rescue missions, and other organizations in the late nineteenth and early twentieth centuries. Should this fount of organization creation be categorized in Tocquevillian terms as forms of associationism, there is certainly an argument that fundamentalism was a robust generator of civic associations and networks of voluntary societies well into the twentieth century.

112. This phrase comes from Thekla Ellen Joiner, *Sin in the City: Chicago and Revivalism 1880–1920* (Columbia: University of Missouri Press, 2007), 35.
113. Robert H. Glover, "Harvest Time in Worldwide Missions," *Moody Monthly* 22, no. 7 (March 1922): 904–905.
114. Appears in the May 1909 issue, "Editorial Notes," *The Institute Tie* 9, no. 8: 733.
115. A column in the January 1918 *King's Business* publication out of Biola College condemned pastors promising a "lasting peace" as an outcome of the present war. "There will be no universal and lasting peace until the Prince of Peace, our Lord Jesus, comes and takes the reins of government . . . all this will simply be a precursor and preparation for the glorious day that is surely coming." Editorial, *The King's Business* 9, no. 1 (1918): 3.
116. The only economist to leave his mark on the lay-targeted books of the time was Roger Babson, who published both economic and church administration books at Revell. Babson's work is unapologetically pro-capitalist, comparable to the far more widely read Bruce Barton of the same era. However, most fundamentalist periodicals seemed to be far more interested in his church administration ideas over his thoughts on capitalism and economists. Fundamentalists also seemed to have a shortage of properly vetted economists at their disposal during this era, leaving them reliant on their own in-house expertise. The result, as argued in this chapter, was that pastors and religious writers needed to first spiritualize the sins of their adversaries in order to respond to them in the religious register they knew best.
117. This framing of Bolshevism as having at its disposal a well-known list of complicit parties appears in an address delivered to the 1921 graduating class of Moody Bible Institute, republished as Joseph Taylor Britan, "Religious Foundations of National Life," *Moody Bible Institute Monthly* 22, no. 3 (1921): 652–654. The antidote to such threats is identified as the "supernatural power of Christ."
118. Another example of this tight blending together of atheism, communism, and modernist theology appears in a *King's Business* editorial criticizing the thought and work of Norman Thomas, who represented a dual threat of being both a liberal Presbyterian minister and a Socialist candidate for US president: "Modernism opens the door to Socialism. Norman Thomas, Socialist candidate for President, spoke in many modernist pulpits in his recent campaign. Socialism leads to communism, and communism is virtually atheism." Stewart MacLennan, "Crumbs from the King's Table," *King's Business* 24, no. 2 (1933): 50.
119. Hammond, *God's Businessmen*, 85.
120. The term "Grahamism" has been used on occasion by historian Martin E. Martin to refer to twentieth-century evangelicalism structured around Billy Graham. However, it likely remains an unconventional usage due to potential confusion with

another semi-religious movement, the Grahamism of the nineteenth century that came to describe adherents to the teachings of Presbyterian pastor (and namesake to the famous cracker) Sylvester Graham, a leader who had some influence on Charles Finney. It is nevertheless invoked here to better identify Billy Graham's influence and symbolic legitimacy within American evangelicalism, an influence has at times been so ubiquitous that his efforts and persona are equated with the evangelical identity itself.

121. "Engaged orthodoxy" is a term incorporated in the analysis of evangelicals by Christian Smith. See Smith, *American Evangelicalism: Embattled and Thriving* (Chicago: University of Chicago Press, 1998).
122. John Schmalzbauer, *People of Faith: Religious Conviction in American Journalism and Higher Education* (Ithaca, NY: Cornell University Press, 2003), 28.
123. Historian Dan D. Crawford makes a compelling argument that religious historians have oversold Graham's break with the moderate forms of fundamentalism that came before him, a broader claim that corresponds with the narrower assertion made here that twentieth-century revivalism as manifested by Graham failed to alter the basic economic and cultural orientations of prior forms of fundamentalism. See Crawford, "The Idea of Militancy in American Fundamentalism," in *Fundamentalism: Perspectives on a Contested History*, ed. Simon A. Wood and David Harrington Watt (Columbia: University of South Carolina, 2014), 36–54.
124. Billy Graham, *World Aflame* (Garden City, NY: DoubleDay & Company, Inc, 1965), 144.
125. Michael Emerson and Christian Smith, *Divided by Faith: Evangelical Religion and the Problem of Race in America* (New York: Oxford University Press, 2000), 47.
126. Gottlieb Hafner, "Premillennialism—A Danger to the Church?" *Moody Bible Monthly* 22 (December 1921): 712.
127. Darren Grem, *The Blessings of Business: How Corporations Shaped Conservative Christianity* (New York: Oxford University Press, 2016), 58.
128. Rick Warren, *The Purpose Driven Life: What on Earth Am I Here For?* (Grand Rapids, MI: Zondervan, 2002), 284.
129. Ambivalence about Graham and wider revivalist evangelicalism from a Reformed perspective can be found in the pages of *The Reformed Journal*, published from 1951 to 1990. See James D. Bratt and Ronald A. Wells (eds.), *The Best of the Reformed Journal* (Grand Rapids, MI: William B. Eerdmans, 2011). This ambivalence and resistance are also discussed in greater detail in Chapter 7.
130. For review of religious traditions that did not subscribe to the pre-millennial eschatology of Grahamism, see Donald W. Dayton and Robert K. Johnston (eds.), *The Variety of American Evangelicalism* (Knoxville: University of Tennessee Press, 1991); and Molly Worthen, *Apostles of Reason: The Crisis of Authority in American Evangelicalism* (New York: Oxford University Press, 2014),
131. See Gloege, *Guaranteed Pure*; Kruse, *One Nation Under God*; Grem; and Hammond, *God's Businessmen*.
132. Douglas Carl Abrams describes the fundamentalists' response to Barton's book as uncharacteristically muted, but most fundamentalists who engaged the book

lambasted its liberal theology. See Abrams, *Selling the Old-Time Religion*, 44–46. Spiritual Mobilization, meanwhile, took pride in its distancing from fundamentalism: "Although several thousand predominantly Protestant clergymen subscribed to its magazine, *Faith and Freedom*, the libertarian idealism of Spiritual Mobilization usually repelled religious fundamentalists and political liberals. James C. Ingebretsen, its president in the latter half of the 1950s and Fifield's successor in 1959, explained that Spiritual Mobilization was unique with its 'liberal' theology and 'conservative' politics." See Eckard V. Troy, Jr., "Spiritual Mobilization: The Failure of an Ultraconservative Ideal in the 1950s," *The Pacific Northwest Quarterly* 61, no. 2 (1970): 79.

133. See Markku Ruotsila, *Fighting Fundamentalist: Carl McIntire and the Politicization of American Fundamentalism* (New York: Oxford, 2016), 64; and Rousas John Rushdoony, *Christianity and Capitalism* (Vallecito, CA: Chalcedon Foundation, 2000). Reconstructionist writer Gary North, in several of his books, has continued this line of argument concerning capitalism's origins in Scripture.
134. Henry Charles Carey, *Manual of Social Science: Being a Condensation of the Principles of Social Science*, ed. Kate McKean (Philadelphia: H. C. Baird, 1864), 372.
135. Michael J. McVicar, *Christian Reconstruction: R. J. Rushdoony and American Religious Conservatism* (Chapel Hill: The University of North Carolina Press, 2015), 119. See also Phillips-Fein, *Invisible Hands*.
136. Study cited in Iannaccone, "Heirs to the Protesant Ethic?"
137. This contender against Grahamism would occasionally find help in Billy Graham himself, who openly supported Nixon before coming to regret his explicit endorsement of a presidential candidate.
138. Robert Wuthnow, "The Political Rebirth of American Evangelicals," in *The New Christian Right*, ed. R. Liebman & R. Wuthnow (Hawthorne, NY: Aldine, 1983), 167–185
139. Jerry Falwell, "Ministries and Marches," in *American Religion, American Politics: An Anthology*, ed. Joseph Kip Kosek (New Haven, CT: Yale University Press, 2017), 174.
140. Tim LaHaye, *The Battle for the Mind: A Subtle Warfare* (Old Tappan, NJ: Fleming H. Revell, 1980), 202.
141. Robert C. Liebman, "Mobilizing the Moral Majority," in *The New Christian Right*, ed. R. Liebman & R. Wuthnow (Hawthorne, NY: Aldine, 1983), 52.
142. "We wouldn't have to [get involved] if politicians would confine themselves to government, economics, and national defense." LaHaye, *The Battle for the Mind: A Subtle Warfare*, 202.
143. While the earlier phases of political evangelicalism—the Christian Right and the Moral Majority movements of the 1970s–1990s—may have neglected economic orientations, this omission may have been entirely circumstantial. The more recent wave of political evangelicalism has in fact incorporated theological sources with far more bearing on economic activity. Two particular streams—prosperity gospel teaching and Dominionist theology—represent viable contenders against Grahamism: both effectively override subordinating and shirking orientations by channeling religious energies toward, respectively, a Providentially blessed

materialism or securing economic power as part of an eschatological drama. As Chapter 8 explores in greater detail, these viable alternatives to *both* Grahamism and the faith and work movement will likely play a significant role in American evangelicalism's future orientations to the economic sphere.

144. Perhaps the most sophisticated challenge to Grahamism came from the scholarly leaders surrounding Graham—Harold Ockenga and Carl Henry—who strove to widen the evangelical engagement of ethics and economics in a manner that would equip the evangelical laity with more robust frameworks for engaging "the world." Henry, in particular, was explicitly conscious of the persisting elements of fundamentalism that obstructed serious engagement with questions of labor and industrial relations. Chapter 7 looks at how these leaders' more Kuyperian-influenced evangelicalism would eventually serve as the foundational theological current for the faith and work movement. Yet setting aside some select pockets of influence, the scholars surrounding Graham proved no match for Grahamism, which had the advantage of a decades-old inertia that far predated the neo-evangelical moment. At a more rudimentary level, the scholars were no match for Billy Graham himself: Graham's crusades were well publicized in national media, attracted hundreds of thousands to stadiums, and earned Graham regular appearances on talk shows as well as private audiences with U.S. presidents. But no similar level of access and influence was passed to Henry and Ockenga, whose influence was limited to a substratum of Christian educational institutions. Outside of those pockets, Grahamism reigned supreme. By the 1970s and 1980s, both Henry and Ockenga voiced disappointment that the popularized work of Hal Lindsey and Tim LaHaye managed to rekindle the sensationalized and frenzied apocalypticism they had hoped to drive out of evangelicalism. See Matthew Avery Sutton, *American Apocalypse: A History of Modern Evangelicalism* (Cambridge, MA: Belknap, 2014), 263–264.
145. Richard Ellsworth Day, *Breakfast Table Autocrat: The Life Story of Henry Parsons Crowell* (Chicago: Moody Press, 1946), 59.
146. Ibid., 6.
147. Valborg A. Gundersen, *Long Shadow: The Living Story of a Layman and His Lord* (Minneapolis, MN: Beacon Publications, 1966). For discussion of Gundersen, see Greg Chatterley, "From Norway to Carol Stream: Ethnic Protestant Foundations of White Evangelicalism," Conference Paper from *AAR Annual Conference, Evangelical Studies Unit* (November 2018).
148. Grem, *The Blessings of Business*.
149. All details drawn from R. G. LeTourneau, *Mover of Men and Mountains: The Autobiography of R. G. LeTourneau* (Chicago: Moody Press, 1967).
150. A similar phenomenon also seemed to play out among the small cohort of postwar evangelical scholars who also become unusually reflexive of their status in their field relative to their status in their religious tradition. Neo-evangelical leaders Carl Henry and Harold Ockenga chose to pursue PhDs from Boston University and the University of Pittsburgh, respectively, after judging their theological training at fundamentalist schools to be inadequate. Edward Carnell, a theologian who followed Ockenga as Fuller Theological Seminary president, reached a similar conclusion

about his theological training at fundamentalist-led Westminster Seminary and went on to earn doctorates from both Harvard Divinity School and Boston University. These leaders often framed their educational ambitions as a deliberate withdrawal from the parochialism of evangelicalism in order to gain a greater hearing for evangelical ideas. Carnell justified the pursuit of his degrees in response to so few high-status scholars engaging his earlier writings: "There is a parochialism in evangelicalism from which I must withdraw. I want to command the attention of Tillich and Bennett; then I shall be in a better place to be of service to evangelicals. We need prestige desperately." See Carl F. Henry, *Confessions of a Theologian: An Autobiography* (Waco, TX: Word, 1986), 137. These leaders forged their own dissent from Grahamism in seeing their professions as spiritually valuable in and of themselves, thereby releasing them from duties to distinctly evangelical activities and organizations. This mirrors cases like LeTourneau's pivot away from street-corner evangelism, as their own callings were judged to be equally valuable to soul-saving efforts. But these scholars had at their disposal particular theological resources that allowed them to be far more articulate in how they affirmed their professions. The central theological resource—neo-Calvinist Kuyperian theology—is discussed more in Chapter 7.

## Chapter 3

1. Quotation taken from William Bond, Minutes of the Christian Laymen's Crusade Meeting Held at Benjamin Fraklin Hotel, November 1, 1941. Quoted in Sarah Ruth Hammond, *God's Businessmen: Entrepreneurial Evangelicals in Depression and War* (Chicago: University of Chicago Press, 2017), 76.
2. Text taken from Monday Switch website. Accessed online: https://mondayswitch.com/monday-morning-atheist/.
3. Christian Smith, *American Evangelicalism: Embattled and Thriving* (Chicago: University of Chicago Press, 1998), 119.
4. John D. McCarthy and Mayer N. Zald, "Resource Mobilization and Social Movements: A Partial Theory," *American Journal of Sociology*, 82, no. 6 (1977): 1212–1241.
5. Ron Eyerman and Andrew Jamison, *Social Movements: A Cognitive Approach* (University Park: Pennsylvania State University Press, 1991),
6. David Miller's history of the wider Christian faith and work movement (spanning Mainline and even Catholic groups) also attests to the critical role that special-purpose groups played as carriers of the movement's ideas. See Miller, *God at Work*.
7. These histories include: Hammond, Stevens, and Svanoe, *The Marketplace Annotated Bibliography*; Hillman, *Faith@Work*; Johnson, *Business as Mission*; and Mitchell, *A Walk in the Market*. The only academic book on this topic is Miller, *God at Work*.
8. Miller, *God at Work*.

9. An anecdote from a book on the history of the Fellowship of Companies for Christ International captures just how sudden this growth was. The author recounts hearing a speaker at a 1980 conference: "He shared that he had expected to go to the library, pull down some books on running a company for Christ, and develop talks, but he was shocked to find that there were no materials on the bookshelves. None!" See Robert L. Mitchell, *A Walk in the Market: My Story of the Fellowship of Companies for Christ International* (Halsey, OR: Milestone, 2013). For comparison's sake, one faith and work text published in 2006 claims there were at the time 288 new faith and work books published each year.
10. Publishers themselves were contacted about the availability of historical sales numbers for books but unfortunately neither sales numbers nor past catalogs were preserved in any accessible form.
11. Al Hsu, "Evangelical Tribalism: The Big Sort or the Breakfast Club?" August 02, 2010. Accessed online: https://www.patheos.com/resources/additional-resources/2010/08/evangelical-tribalism-the-big-sort-or-the-breakfast-club.
12. Robert Mitchell recounts multi-day gatherings for the Fellowship of Christian Companies International in February 1980, September 1980, October 1980, and February 1983. Mitchell compares these gatherings to "trade association"-type gatherings that brought together their members for encouragement and fellowship. His historical account is broadly in agreement with the narrative presented here: these earlier gatherings did not attract individuals that had not previously been engaged with the particular association in the manner that Os Hillman's late 1990s gatherings did. Hillman's early gatherings were also distinct in drawing professional clergy and church leaders as attendees in addition to full-time workers.
13. Information that follows was taken from several of Hillman's books as well as a phone interview with Hillman, 10/31/2016.
14. An advertisement for the conference is available online: http://65058.inspyred.com/images/LydiaNewsletter1.pdf.
15. Conference details of the 2008 gathering can be accessed online: https://web.archive.org/web/20080501122426/http://www.marketplaceleaders.org/pages.asp?pageid=42065.
16. Charisma Staff, "Apostolic Pioneer C. Peter Wagner Goes on to Glory," *Charisma News*, October 21, 2016. http://www.charismanews.com/us/60747-apostolic-pioneer-c-peter-wagner-goes-on-to-glory.
17. A 2011 newspaper article discussing both movements' connection with then-presidential candidate Rick Perry describes adherents as having a "growing fascination with infiltrating politics and government" as well as "climb[ing] the commanding heights" of seven cultural institutions in order to "lord over society. "Forrest Wilder, "Rick Perry's Army of God," *The Texas Observer*, August 3, 2011. Accessed online: https://www.texasobserver.org/rick-perrys-army-of-god/
18. See Brad Christerson and Richard Flory, *The Rise of Network Christianity: How Independent Leaders Are Changing the Religious Landscape* (New York: Oxford University Press, 2017).

19. Information taken from Faith at Work Leadership Conference website: http://faithandworklife.org/events/.
20. Information taken from Work as Worship website: https://web.archive.org/web/20121105010203/http://www.workasworshipconference.org/.
21. Several forms of financial support from the Lilly Endowment provided support for research that went into this book. These forms of support are discussed more in the Appendix.
22. Details on this program taken from Timothy Clydesdale, *The Purposeful Graduate: Why Colleges Must Talk to Students about Vocation* (Chicago: University of Chicago Press, 2016).
23. Information taken from Lilly Endowment website: https://web.archive.org/web/20160221013030/http://lillyendowment.org/religion_ptev.html.
24. Clydesdale, *The Purposeful Graduate*, 67.
25. Mission statement and details taken from NetVue's website accessed online: https://www.cic.edu/programs/netvue
26. Call for proposals and news release for program accessed online: https://web.archive.org/web/20170429161007/http://lillyendowment.org/pdf/CAMPUSMINISTRY15.pdf
27. An internal assessment report funded by the Endowment recounts the initial gatherings of grantees intentionally provided little guidance on the nature of funding. The Endowment's vice president for religion is recounted as telling attendees at ministry events, "The 'theological exploration of vocation' is meant, first of all, to be an honest inquiry. What does Lilly mean by the 'theological exploration of vocation'? The honest answer is this: we don't exactly know. That is what we hope you will help us figure out." Report accessed online at: http://www.resourcingchristianity.org/sites/default/files/transcripts/research_article/DavidCunningham_A_Plentiful_Harvest_Essay.pdf.
28. Mission statement accessed online: https://www.acton.org/about/mission
29. Allyson Wierenga, "Rev. Tim Keller on How the Modern Identity Presents Problems for Life and Business," *Acton Institute PowerBlog*, October 24, 2018. Accessed online: https://blog.acton.org/archives/104334-rev-tim-keller-on-how-the-modern-identity-presents-problems-for-life-and-business.html.
30. Accessed online: http://www.kffdn.org/meaningful-work/.
31. Information about Made to Flourish accessed on organization's website: https://www.madetoflourish.org.
32. Information about Oikonomia Network accessed on organization's website: http://oikonomianetwork.org/about/.
33. Another researcher, Lisa Graves, describes the relationship between ORRA LLC and EVANGCHR4 as "mysterious" because there seem to be no publicly accessible files on ORRA LLC. See Lisa Grave, " Josh Duggar-Led Group Funded via Koch Brothers Freedom Partners Operation," *The Center for Media and Democracy's PR Watch*, August 22, 2015. http://www.prwatch.org/node/12914.
34. Jane Mayer, *Dark Money: The Hidden History of the Billionaires Behind the Rise of the Radical Right* (New York: Random House, 2016), 305.

35. Mayer, *Dark Money*, 305.
36. Mayer, *Dark Money*, 304.
37. Quotation and other descriptions of the Koch's efforts found in Matthew Continetti, "The Paranoid Style in Liberal Politics," *The Weekly Standard*, April 4, 2011. https://www.weeklystandard.com/matthew-continetti/the-paranoid-style-in-liberal-politics.
38. See *For the Least of These: A Biblical Answer to Poverty*, edited by Bradley and Lindsley. This volume includes an introduction by American Enterprise Institute president Arthur Brooks and Acton Institute president Robert Sirico. Whelchel provided me with a complimentary copy of this work and all other IFWE works cited here.
39. Robert Putnam and David Campbell, *American Grace: How Religion Divides and Unites Us* (New York: Simon and Schuster, 2010). A previous study of evangelical elites arrived at roughly the same gender imbalance among its sample of evangelical elites as found here (though remarkably, that study admits to over-sampling for females at times). See Michael Lindsay, *Faith in the Halls of Power: How Evangelicals Joined the American Elite* (New York: Oxford University Press, 2007). I discuss the absence of female leaders more in Chapter 5.
40. Kraig Beyerlein, "Specifying the Impact of Conservative Protestantism in Educational Attainment," *Journal for the Scientific Study of Religion* 43, no. 4 (2004): 505–518.
41. Robert Wuthnow, *The Restructuring of American Religion: Society and Faith since World War II* (Princeton, NJ: Princeton University Press, 1988), 100–131.
42. Robert Wuthnow, *God and Mammon in America* (New York: Free Press, 1994), 5.
43. Baylor University, *The Baylor Religion Survey, Wave III* (Waco, TX: Baylor Institute for Studies of Religion, 2010). For a more expansive presentation and interpretation of the 1992 data, see Wuthnow, *God and Mammon in America*.

## Chapter 4

1. Weber, "The Social Psychology of the World Religions," in *From Max Weber: Essays in Sociology*, 291.
2. Quoted in Linette Martin, *Hans Rookmaaker: A Biography* (Downers Grove, IL: Intervarsity, 1979),150.
3. Joseph Hall, *The Works of the Right Reverend Father in God, Joseph Hall, D.D.* (London: C. Whittingham, 1808), 85.
4. James Davison Hunter, *Evangelicalism: The Coming Generation* (Chicago: University of Chicago Press, 1987).
5. Wuthnow, *God and Mammon in America*.
6. Scholars have long identified this to be one of the weakest dimensions of Weber's thesis, as historical reviews of Calvinism's orientation to disciplined economic activity largely appeared to bear little connection to questions of soteriology or predestination. See, for example, Jeffrey R. Watt, *The Consistory and Social Discipline in Calvin's Geneva* (Rochester, NY: University of Rochester Press, 2020), 188–190.

7. A. J. Broomhall, *Time for Action: Christian Responsibility in a Non-Christian World* (London: Inter-Varsity Fellowship, 1965).
8. Evangelical ethicist and Christianity Today cofounder Carl Henry recognized the shortcomings of "fundamentalist" efforts related to work as early as 1964: "It must be granted that the fundamentalist movement sought to impart spiritual overtones to occupational activity. Every believer was to identify himself as a Christian by refraining from morally questionable work—such as the liquor traffic and gambling enterprises (even if permitted by law). Certain tasks such as public school teaching were singled out as offering fuller scope for indirect witness or secondary service to the Church. If possible, moreover, Christians were to find fellowship as workers in organizations like the Christian Business Men's Committee, to the Christian Business and Professional Women's Club, and so on. They should bear glad witness about the forgiveness of sins to be found through Jesus Christ; they should avoid laziness on the job, and shoddy business ethics; they should maintain a reputation for integrity, punctuality, courtesy, co-operation, dependability, and diligence . . . [citations of several Scripture references] . . . Still, fundamentalism did not comprehend all work as divine vocation, as spiritual service to God and man. The subject of 'divine vocation' was table talk only in the parsonage or at missionary society headquarters." Henry goes on to promote a mix of "re-integrating and "re-embedding" frameworks.
9. Miller, *God at Work*, 57
10. Pierre Bourdieu "Genesis and Structure of the Religious Field," *Comparative Social Research* 13, no. 1 (1999): 14.
11. Berger, *The Sacred Canopy: Elements of a Sociological Theory of Religion* (New York: Random House, 1967).
12. From Day's writing on Crowell: "The teachings of the Rush Street Bible Class on the subjects of person and property were in sharp conflict with ideas which Mr. Crowell had for years entertained. He always felt that believers were under obligation to *live* as Christians; but when it came to such things as time and treasure, these were his *personal* possessions. The class summarily blasted this view; not only are you as a Christian under obligation to *live* unto God, but everything you have *belongs* to God. Nothing is excepted! Bank accounts, stocks, bonds, real estate—even the Belleek China in one's home is the property of the Lord, and the Christian does not own a single thing in fee simple absolute. Even his time is bought and paid for! The believer is utterly impoverished; he is simply a trustee for Deity in all that he is and has. The whole case is summed up in the Bible term 'steward.'" From Richard Ellsworth Day, *Breakfast Table Autocrat: The Life Story of Henry Parsons Crowell* (Chicago: Moody Press, 1946), 183, emphasis in original).
13. Ibid., 203.
14. Grem, *The Blessings of Business*.
15. Stanley Tam, *God Owns My Business* (Camp Hill, PA: Horizon House, 1969).
16. Dorothy L. Sayers, "Why Work?," in *Creed or Chaos?* (New York: Harcourt, 1941), 46–62.
17. Ibid., 53.

18. David Moberg, *Inasmuch: Christian Social Responsibility in the 20th Century* (Grand Rapids, MI: Eerdmans, 1965), 147.
19. Udo Middelmann, *Pro-existence: The Place of Man in the Circle of Reality* (Downers Grove, IL: Intervarsity Press, 1974), 21, 22, 34.
20. Hans Rookmaaker, *Art Needs No Justification* (Downers Grove, IL: Intervarsity,1978), 20.
21. David Field and Elspeth Stephenson, *Just the Job: Christians Talk about Work and Vocation* (Downers Grove, IL: Intervarsity, 1978), 14.
22. Sayers, "Why Work?," 57.
23. Field and Stephenson, *Just the Job*, 15.
24. I lay out the fuller influence of "Kuyperian humanism" on the faith and work world in Chapter 7.
25. Malcolm Jeeves, *The Scientific Enterprise and Christian Faith* (Downers Grove, IL: Intervarsity, 1969), 14.
26. Barclay wrote under a pseudonym: A. N. Triton, *Whose World?* (Downers Grove, IL: Intervarsity, 1970), 44–45.
27. John W. Gladwin, *God's People in God's World: Biblical Motives for Social Involvement* (Downers Grove, IL: Intervarsity, 1979), 166.
28. Sayers, "Why Work?," 58.
29. Moberg, *Inasmuch*, 148.
30. Field and Stephenson, *Just the Job*, 19.
31. Sayers, "Why Work?," 57.
32. Linette Martin, *Hans Rookmaaker: A Biography* (Downers Grove, IL: Intervarsity, 1979),150.
33. Sayers, "Why Work?," 57.
34. Moberg, *Inasmuch*, 146.
35. Rookmaaker, *Art Needs No Justification*, 39.
36. Middelmann, *Pro-existence*, 36.
37. Jeeves, *The Scientific Enterprise*, 24.
38. Jeeves, *The Scientific Enterprise*, 26.
39. Sharon Fish and Judith Shelly, *Spiritual Care: The Nurse's Role* (Downers Grove, IL: Intervarsity, 1978)
40. Middelmann, *Pro-existence*.
41. Karl Polanyi, *The Great Transformation: The Political and Economic Origins of Our Time* (Boston: Beacon Press, 2001).
42. I have borrowed this term from studies of organizational whistleblowers. That literature is particularly attuned to when a moral framework brings one into tension with his or her workplace. The re-embedding framework attempts to illuminate similar situations, though conflict is not a foregone conclusion: one may also find ways to harmonize their extra-economic commitments with the workplace or to transform the workplace.
43. Wesley Pippert, *Memo for 1976: Some Political Options* (Downers Grove, IL: Intervarsity Press, 1976), 31–32.
44. Moberg, *Inasmuch*, 249.

45. Gladwin, *God's People*, 169.
46. Sayers, "Why Work?," 60.
47. Andy Crouch, *Culture Making: Recovering Our Creative Calling* (Downer Grove, IL: Intervarsity Press, 2008), 120.
48. Crouch, *Culture Making*, 97.
49. While the contemporary faith and work movement does not exclusively reside within religious traditions associated with white evangelicalism, this rise in social and occupational status is distinctly applicable to demographically and historically white religious groups.
50. Nancy Ammerman, "North American Protestant Fundamentalism," in *Fundamentalism Observed: Volume 1*, ed. Martin E. Marty and R. Scott Appleby (Chicago: University of Chicago Press, 1991), 41.
51. John H. Hendricks, "Religious and Political Fundamentalism," Ph.D. diss., University of Michigan, 1977. Additional observations of evangelicalism's socioeconomic change over time are found in Wade Clark Roof and William McKinney, *American Mainline Religion: Its Changing Shape and Future* (New Brunswick, NJ: Rutgers University Press, 1987).
52. Wuthnow, *The Restructuring of American Religion, 187.* Studies that do not differentiate fundamentalism from evangelicalism continue to find that conservative Protestantism is associated with lower educational attainment levels: see Alfred Darnell and Darren E. Sherkat, "The Impact of Protestant Fundamentalism on Educational Attainment," *American Sociological Review*, 62, no. 2 (1997): 306–315. However, in studies where fundamentalism and evangelicalism are separated, evangelicalism's gap behind the wider population becomes negligible. See Christian Smith, *American Evangelicalism: Embattled and Thriving* (Chicago: University of Chicago Press, 1998) and Kraig Beyerlin, "Specifying the Impact of Conservative Protestantism on Educational Attainment," *Journal for the Scientific Study of Religion* 43, no. 3 (2004): 505–518. Another mediating factor, however, is race and ethnicity: if American evangelicalism is widened beyond white populations—something not done here to key in on the historical trajectory unique to white populations—the present constituency of evangelicalism still lags behind in educational attainment, largely due to structural factors that perpetuate inequality along racial lines in the United States.
53. The 1970s also saw the beginnings of the exodus of non-college-educated population from all religious groups. While 30 percent of the non-college-educated population attended church weekly in 1970, this rate dropped steadily in the decades since, landing at around 20 percent in 2010, thus contributing to the relatively higher rates of education among the religiously affiliated. See Robert Putnam and David Campbell, *American Grace: How Religion Divides and Unites Us* (New York: Simon and Schuster, 2010), 231–259. College-educated evangelicals of the 1970s and 1980s, on the other hand, were highly likely to remain evangelicals beyond their college years, which boosted the educational footprint of evangelicalism as a whole for decades that followed.

54. Donald Dayton, "Roots of Pentecostalism," *Pneuma* 2, no. 1 (1980): 3–21. For critical attitudes of the Church of God toward Methodism, see Mickey Crews, *The Church of God: A Social History* (Knoxville: University of Tennessee Press, 1990), 12–18.
55. George Thomas's study of the final decades of the nineteenth century suggests that fundamentalism held stronger footholds in rural counties and in counties with greater reliance on agrarian over industrial labor, perhaps reaffirming the "sheltered enclave" view of fundamentalism. However, several studies support George Marsden's argument that the common "backwoods, rural, and uneducated" depiction of fundamentalists owes its prevalence to the descriptions produced by journalist H. L. Mencken and failed to realistically depict the scope and fuller influence of the movement, particularly in later decades. Fundamentalists held strongholds in many cities in the Midwest, such as Chicago. See David Harrington Watt, "Fundamentalists of the 1920s and 1930s," in *Fundamentalism: Perspectives on a Contested History*, ed. Simon A. Wood and David Harrington Watt (Columbia: University of South Carolina, 2014), 18–35. Robert Wenger compares the biographies of forty prominent leaders in both the fundamentalist and modernist camp to conclude the geographic footprints of both camps largely mirrored the U.S. population and U.S. churchgoing population at the time. Wenger, looking at the era between 1918 and 1933, sees fundamentalism's greater numeric strength east of the Mississippi and north of the Mason-Dixon line where, in his read, modernism "posed a strong threat." Wenger found Pennsylvania to be a particularly strong fundamentalist stronghold, based on subscribers and donors to a national fundamentalist periodical and the state of origin for many students enrolling in Bible colleges. See Robert E. Wenger, *Social Thought in American Fundamentalism, 1918–1933* (Eugene, OR: Wipf & Stock, 1974). Robert Mapes Anderson finds the South to be a far greater stronghold for the growth of Pentecostal denominations through the early decades of the twentieth century. See Anderson, *Visions of the Disinherited: The Making of American Pentecostalism* (Eugene, OR: Wipf & Stock, 1992).
56. Crews, *The Church of God*, 12–18.
57. John Schmalzbauer, *People of Faith: Religious Conviction in American Journalism and Higher Education* (Ithaca, NY: Cornell University Press, 2003).
58. Michael Lindsay, *Faith in the Halls of Power: How Evangelicals Joined the American Elite* (New York: Oxford University Press, 2007). A study comparing occupational prestige for religious traditions across the closing decades of the twentieth century finds that affiliation with conservative Protestantism had no independent effect on occupational prestige measures. See Ralph Pyle, "Religious Stratification: Have Religious Group Socioeconomic Distinctions Declined in Recent Decades?," *Sociology of Religion* 67, no. 1 (2006): 61–79.
59. Eva Illouz, *Cold Intimacies: The Making of Emotional Capitalism* (Malden, MA: Polity, 2007)
60. Arlie Russell Hochschild, *The Time Bind: When Work Becomes Home and Home Becomes Work* (New York: Holt Paperbacks, 2000),
61. Lewis Coser, *Greedy Institutions: Patterns of Undivided Commitment* (New York: Free Press, 1974), 6.

62. Ron Lesthaeghe, "The Second Demographic Transition in Western Countries: An Interpretation," in *Gender and Family Change in Industrialized Countries*, ed. Karen Oppenheim Mason and An-Magritt Jensen (New York: Oxford University Press, 1995), 17–52.
63. Michael Hout, Andrew Greeley, and Melissa J. Wilde, "The Demographic Imperative in Religious Change in the United States," *American Journal of Sociology* 107, no. 2 (2001): 468–500. For detailed analysis of fertility rates, see Samuel Perry and Cyrus Schleifer, "Are the Faithful Becoming Less Fruitful? The Decline of Conservative Protestant Fertility and the Growing Importance of Religious Practice and Belief in Childbearing in the U.S.," *Social Science Research* 78 (2019): 137–155.
64. Robert Wuthnow, *Loose Connections: Joining Together in America's Fragmented Communities* (Cambridge, MA: Harvard University Press, 1998). Wuthnow labels the dominant middle-class institutions prevalent today "porous" and thereby more conducive to the "flow of goods and information and even people" while involving high levels of uncertainty and demanding adaptability. Paul Heelas and Linda Woodhead provide an alternative assessment of many of the same phenomena, narrating recent trends as the "softening" of institutions that made fewer authoritative demands on people. This, too, facilitates a similar porousness. See Heelas and Woodhead, "Homeless Minds Today?," in *Peter Berger and the Study of Religion*, ed. Linda Woodhead, Paul Heelas, and David Martin (New York: Routledge, 2001), 43–72.
65. Derek Thompson, "Workism Is Making Americans Miserable," *The Atlantic* (February 24, 2019).
66. Chapter 7 examines the manner in which the thought of Abraham Kuyper now serves as the central source this whole-life ethic among evangelicals who have found their way to Kuyperian understandings of their faith. Kuyper's likely most famous quote declares all spheres of life falling under the dominion of Christ and thereby bearing some sort of implications for Christian behavior. However, setting aside the specifically Reformed subcultures where Kuyper's Neo-Calvinism held influence, American Evangelicalism's larger "whole-life ethic" is likely a more direct descendent of nineteenth-century pietism born from the "Christian perfectionism" visions associated with Oberlin College, Charles Finney, Phoebe Palmer, and others.
67. Work and careerism can easily fall guilty of this: one of the most heavily cited faith and work books warns of work loyalties "slowly crushing" the individual by way of becoming a "neurotic fabrication of our self-worth." See Timothy Keller and Katherine Leary Alsdorf, *Every Good Endeavor: Connecting Your Work to God's Work* (New York: Penguin Books, 2014).
68. This may represent a both creative but ultimately reactive adaptation to the conditions of creative-class work: there is little evidence that evangelical identities—or for that matter, any other religious identities—are mounting measurable resistance to the pulls of workism. Studies breaking down work hours broken by religious affiliation reveal religious identity has little independent effect on average number of hours worked. See Lisa Keister, *Faith and Money: How Religion Contributes to Wealth and Poverty* (New York: Cambridge University Press, 2011). Observed variations are more directly attributable to occupational and socioeconomic factors exogenous to

religious affiliation. Interviews with evangelicals in the most elite positions of government, education, and media echo this finding: elite evangelicals expressed a great deal of emotional duress and regret generated by the challenge of balancing a high-demand career with church and family, but there was no discernable pattern of career sacrifices made in the interests of religious commitments. See Lindsay, *Faith in the Halls of Power*. The noted exception to this absence of pushback is white conservative Protestant women, who as a group demonstrate the weakest attachments to the paid labor market. See Jennifer Glass and Jerry Jacobs, "Childhood Religious Conservatism and Adult Attainment among Black and White Women," *Social Forces* 83 (2005): 555–579. How women interface with the faith and work space is explored in detail in the next chapter. But among conservative Protestant women, their rates of work are highly correlated with lower education attainment and earlier investments in marriage and childbearing. On the larger question of religious pushback against the economic sphere, I evaluate the complexities of labeling this phenomenon a case of religious accommodationism in Chapter 7.

69. Martin Luther, *Works of Martin Luther: With Introduction and Notes*, transl. Adolph Spaeth (Philadelphia, PA: A. J. Holman y, 1915), 241.
70. Douglas W. Franks, *Less than Conquerors: How Evangelicals Entered the Twentieth Century* (Grand Rapids, MI: Eerdmans, 1986), 136. Religious scholar Betty A. Deberg provides a valuable corrective to Franks's account that speaks to the diverging experience of Protestant women in this same era. See DeBorg, *Ungodly Women: Gender and the First Wave of American Fundamentalism* (Minneapolis, MN: Fortress Press, 1990), 145–146.
71. Daniel Rodgers, *The Work Ethic in Industrial America, 1865–1917* (New Haven,CT: Yale University Press, 1973), 111.
72. Similar observations are made by Robert Maples Anderson regarding Pentecostal groups that gradually splintered away from Holiness, Keswick, Methodist, and Baptist currents in the 1890s and 1900s. See Anderson, *Visions of the Disinherited: The Making of American Pentecostalism* (Eugene, OR: Wipf & Stock, 1992), 223–240.
73. R. H. Tawney, *Religion and the Rise of Capitalism* (New York: Harcourt, Brace, 1926), 200.
74. Echoing Berger's pronouncement, sociologist Brian Wilson posited the modern industrial order was antagonistic to religious interferences, attributing this tension to traditionalism's alleged incompatibility with the conveyor belt's dependence on indifferent technical imperatives. See Wilson, *Contemporary Transformations of Religion* (New York: Oxford University Press, 1976), 20.
75. Jose Casanova, *Public Religions in the Modern World* (Chicago: University of Chicago Press, 1994).
76. Elinor Scarbrough, "Materialist-Postmaterialist Value Orientations," in *Beliefs in Government*, Vol. 4: *The Impact of Values*, ed. Jan W. van Deth and Elinor Scarbrough (New York: Oxford University Press, 1995), 123–159.
77. Hansfried Kellner and Frank W. Heuberger, "Modernizing Work: New Frontiers in Business Consulting," in *Hidden Technocrats: The New Class and New Capitalism.*,

ed. Hansfried Kellner and Frank W. Heuberger (New Brunswick, NJ: Transaction, 1992), 57.

78. Paul Heelas and Linda Woodhead, "Homeless Minds Today?," in *Peter Berger and the Study of Religion*, ed. Linda Woodhead, Paul Heelas, and David Martin (New York: Routledge, 2001), 43–72. See also Gordon E. Dehler and M. Ann Welsch, "The Experience of Work: Spirituality and the New Workplace," in *Handbook of Workplace Spirituality and Organizational Performance*, ed. Robert A. Giacalone and Carole L. Jurkiewicz (New York: M. E. Sharpe, 2003),108–122
79. Boltanski and Chiapello, *The New Spirit*, 459.
80. Ibid., 97.
81. Robert Jackall, *Moral Mazes: The World of Corporate Managers* (New York: Oxford University Press, 2010), 115.
82. For discussion of this potential conflict with other spiritual identities and practices in the workplace, see Robert A. Giacalone and Carole L. Jurkiewicz (eds.), *Handbook of Workplace Spirituality and Organizational Performance* (New York: M. E. Sharpe, 2003).
83. G. K. Chesterton, *Utopia of Usurers and Other Essays* (New York: Boni & Liveright, 1917), 37.
84. Tawney, *Religion and the Rise of Capitalism*, 203–204.

## Chapter 5

1. Details taken from Kathryn Teresa Long, *The Revival of 1857–58: Interpreting an American Religious Awakening* (New York: Oxford University Press, 1998).
2. Quoted in David B. Freeland, *A History and Evaluation of Workplace Ministry in America* (Knoxville, TN: unpublished thesis project, 2012), 36.
3. Joe M. Carroll, *Experience God in Your Workplace: Insights and Stories to Help You Connect More Meaningfully with God in Your Work* (Indianapolis, IN: Dog Ear, 2015).
4. Robert Tribken, "The Fulton Street Prayer Meetings and the Revival of 1857/58: The Workplace Connection," *Center for Faith and Enterprise Blog*, March 29, 2019. Accessed online: http://faithandenterprise.org/the-fulton-street-prayer-meetings
5. An example of a typology of work types and labor practices can be found in Colin C. Williams, "Non-Commodified Labour," in *The Routledge Companion to Alternative Organization*, ed. Martin Parker, George Cheney, Valerie Fournier, and Chris Land (New York: Routledge, 2014), 105–119. Williams presents a two-axis grid of labor: a left-right spectrum of commodified versus non-commodified and an up-down spectrum of monetized versus non-monetized. The faith and work conversation mainly addresses "formal, paid labor in the private sector," which occupies only one corner of this grid.
6. Dorothy Sayers's writing on work is the exception here, but her position in the United Kingdom and her religious affiliation (Anglicanism) outside any American revivalist

or fundamentalist tradition likely means that her ideas were retroactively canonized into the movement later in the twentieth century.

7. These statements about recurring vocational inferiority reflect anecdotal observations from events and interviews. For Billy Graham's ongoing ranking at the top of the "most admired" list, see Frank Newport, "In the News: Billy Graham 'Most Admired' List 61 Times," *Gallup*, February 21, 2018. Accessed online: https://news.gallup.com/poll/228089/news-billy-graham-admired-list-times.aspx.
8. This observation was ultimately part of a message on humility and resisting self-righteousness, as well as resisting cultural ideas of heroic individualism and narcissism. But this message of humility did not challenge the view that entrepreneurs *did* in fact occupy the highest status position among Christians: the lesson on humility here seemed more intended to express the familiar idea that "with great power comes great responsibility."
9. Studies of workers have long shown a "pragmatic acceptance" of work and unexpectedly high levels of workers reporting that their work gives them a sense of meaning. See Michael Mann, "The Social Cohesion of Liberal Democracy," *American Sociological Review* 35, no. 3 (1970): 423–439 and Robert Wuthnow, *Poor Richard's Principle: Recovering the American Dream Through the Moral Dimension of Work, Business, and Money* (Princeton, NJ: Princeton University Press, 1996).
10. For discussion of work replacing forms of disappearing community, see Jay A. Conger, *Spirit at Work: Discovering the Spirituality in Leadership* (San Francisco, CA: Jossey-Bass, 1994).
11. See Alex Rosenblat, *Uberland: How Algorithms Are Rewriting the Rules of Work* (Oakland: University of California Press, 2018) and Colin Lecher, "How Amazon Automatically Tracks and Fires Warehouse Workers for 'Productivity,'" *The Verge*, April 25, 2019. Accessed online: https://www.theverge.com/2019/4/25/18516004/amazon-warehouse-fulfillment-centers-productivity-firing-terminations.
12. Elinor Scarbrough, "Materialist-Postmaterialist Value Orientations," in *Beliefs in Government*, Vol. 4: *The Impact of Values*, ed. Jan W. van Deth and Elinor Scarbrough (New York: Oxford University Press, 1995), 123–159. A 2017 study of changes in seventy-eight different countries since the 1970s suggested that a society's movement toward white-collar employment over blue-collar or agricultural jobs correlated with increasing levels of individualistic practices like living alone, valuing friends and family less, and valuing self-expression, even controlling for socioeconomic development. This supports the conclusions of other post-materialist scholars that not only economic development but also occupational shifts can drive cultural movement toward post-materialist values. See Henri C. Santos, Michael E. W. Varnum, and Igor Grossmann, "Global Increases in Individualism," *Psychological Science* 28, no. 9 (2017): 1228–1239.
13. Some of these topics were taken from Stephen Edgell, Heidi Gottfried, and Edward Granter (eds.), *The SAGE Handbook of the Sociology of Work and Employment* (Thousand Oaks, CA: SAGE Publications, 2015). The point made here is *not* simply that the faith and work movement fails to exhibit the same comprehensive, meticulous, and often politically left-of-center orientation that characterizes contemporary

sociology of work, at least in terms of avoiding discussions of power, stratification, intersectional identities, and criticisms of income distribution within capitalism. Such a difference would not be particularly surprising. What the sociology of work discipline provides, however, is a point of comparison that brings into focus what faith and work generally omits and how those omissions are patterned by a seemingly parochial conception of work and work issues.

14. Quotation taken from event program provided to all event attendees.
15. The only types of careers that prove exceptional to this exclusion are various occupations related to the arts, which are often incorporated into the movement despite not being traditional breadwinner jobs.
16. Jennifer L. Berdahl, Marianne Cooper, Peter Glick, Robert W. Livingston, and Joan C. Williams, "Work as a Masculinity Context," *Journal of Social Issues* 74, no. 3 (2018): 422–448; and Erin M. Reid, Olivia Amanda O'Neill, and Mary Blair-Loy, "Masculinity in Male-Dominated Occupations: How Teams, Time, and Tasks Shape Masculinity Contests," *Journal of Social Issues* 74, no. 3 (2018): 579–606.
17. For discussion, see Laura Nash and Scotty McLennan, *Church on Sunday, Work on Monday: The Challenge of Fusing Christian Values in Business Life* (San Francisco: Jossey-Bass, 2001), 155-183
18. Max Weber, *The Protestant Ethic and the Spirit of Capitalism*, trans. Talcott Parsons (New York: Routledge Classics, 2004), 32.
19. Long, *The Revival of 1857–58*.
20. Gail Bederman, "'The Women Have Had Charge of the Church Work Long Enough': The Men and Religion Forward Movement of 1911–1912 and the Masculinization of Middle-Class Protestantism," *American Quarterly* 41 no. 3 (1989): 432–465.
21. Hammond, *God's Businessmen*, 79.
22. Margaret Lamberts Bendroth, *Fundamentalism and Gender, 1875 to the Present* (New Haven, CT: Yale University Press, 1993), 81.
23. David T. Morgan, "The Revivalist as Patriot: Billy Sunday and World War I," *Journal of Presbyterian History* 51, no. 2 (1973): 188–215.
24. Bendroth, *Fundamentalism and Gender*, 81.
25. Grem, *The Blessings of Business*, 38.
26. Hammond, *God's Businessmen*, 82. Hammond reprints a poem that appears in two lay-targeted publications of the time (p. 78): Leave it to the ministers, And soon the church will die, Leave it to the women-folks, And the young will pass you by, For the church is all that lifts us from the coarse and selfish mob, And the church that is to prosper needs the layman on the job.
27. Ibid., 42–43.
28. There is little ambiguity regarding these figures' status in the contemporary movement: LeTourneau and Garrison were formally inducted into a list of "pioneer" thinkers for the movement at the 2014 and 2018 Faith and Work Summits, respectively. The 2016 summit that fell between these events was organized by the Center for Faith and Work that operates out of R. G. LeTourneau's namesake university.

29. Amy Kenna, Amanda Knoke, and Bob Paulson, "God at Work: Is the Church on the Job?," *Decision Magazine*, July 1, 2004. Accessed online: http://www.geocities.ws/dcen2003/BGEA3.html.
30. Colleen W. Colaner and Steven M. Giles, "The Baby Blanket or the Briefcase: The Impact of Evangelical Role Ideologies on Career and Mothering Aspirations of Female Evangelical College Students," *Sex Roles* 58, no. 7 (2008): 526–534. For evidence that many evangelicals are in practice "pragmatic egalitarians," see Sally K. Gallagher, "The Marginalization of Evangelical Feminism," *Sociology of Religion* 65, no 3 (2004): 215–237.
31. Katelyn Beaty, *A Woman's Place: A Christian Vision for Your Calling in the Office, the Home, and the World* (New York: Howard Books, 2007).
32. The 2010s were an era of a very significant shifts, well-publicized disputes, and surging attention granted to nationally known evangelical female leaders and authors. For a fuller account, see Kate Bowler, *The Preacher's Wife: The Precarious Power of Evangelical Women Celebrities* (Princeton, NJ: Princeton University Press, 2020). *Christianity Today* has covered several different phenomena related to this arena, from increasing political polarization of well-known figures to the overall surge in popularity of female writers, scholars, and conference speakers. Two specifically relevant points: Kate Shellnutt, in a 2016 article, claimed the rise of figures like popular minister Beth Moore and author Jen Hatmaker represented a "delocalization" of women's ministry leadership, as evangelical laity now felt personally connected with these bestselling authors and online personalities. "Christian women increasingly look to nationally known figures for spiritual formation and inspiration—especially when they don't see leaders who look like them stepping up in their own churches," writes Shellnutt. See Shellnutt, "The Bigger Story Behind Jen Hatmaker," *Christianity Today*, November 15, 2016. Accessed online: https://www.christianitytoday.com/ct/2016/november-web-only/bigger-story-behind-jen-hatmaker.html. Anglican priest and author Tish Harris Warren points to these bestselling authors as harnessing creative channels for women to exercise influence from within traditions that deny them official positions of authority, instead drawing an audience around relatable writing, storytelling, and sharing life experiences. See Warren, "Who's in Charge of the Christian Blogosphere?," *Christianity Today*, April 27, 2017. Accessed online: https://www.christianitytoday.com/women/2017/april/whos-in-charge-of-christian-blogosphere.html. What both of these insights reveal is that female, career-minded writers and teachers may—by necessity—employ creative means to use their talents and gifts in the evangelical space, with any sort of resulting "status standoff" with clergy playing out far differently than that of the career-minded male worker.
33. Diane Paddison, *Practical Wisdom for Young Professional Women* (Grand Rapids, MI: Zondervan, 2011), 10.
34. Advertisement available at: http://65058.inspyred.com/images/LydiaNewsletter1.pdf.
35. Website accessed online: https://www.propelwomen.org.
36. Kate Harris, *Wonder Women: Navigating the Challenges of Motherhood, Career, and Identity* (Grand Rapids, MI: Zondervan, 2013). See also Chelsea Smith's sermon "Let's

Talk about Work," which was delivered at a women's conference organized by the high-profile non-denominational megachurch Churchome. https://www.youtube.com/watch?v=QcGFH7cNnRw.

37. See Joan C. Williams, *Unbending Gender* (New York: Oxford University Press, 2000).
38. Marilynne Cooper, "Being the 'Go-To-Guy': Fatherhood, Masculinity, and the Organization of Work in Silicon Valley," *Qualitative Sociology* 23, no. 4 (2000): 379–405, Mary Blair-Loy, *Competing Devotions: Career and Family among Women Executives* (Cambridge, MA: Harvard University Press, 2003), Erin Kelly, Samantha K. Ammons, Kelly Chermack, and Phyllis Moen, "Gendered Challenge, Gendered Response: Confronting the Ideal Worker Norm in a White-Collar Organization," *Gender & Society* 24, no. 3 (2010): 281–303.
39. Marilynne Cooper defines the "Superdad" category of masculinity as one in which men attempt to "meet all work and family obligations without sacrificing anything in either sphere." See Cooper, "Being the 'Go-To-Guy,'" 391.

## Chapter 6

1. James A. Sloan, *The Great Question Answered; or, Is Slavery a Sin (Per se?) Answered According to the Teaching of the Scriptures* (Memphis, TN: Hutton, Gallaway, 1857), 248.
2. True W. Hoit, *The Right of American Slavery* (St. Louis, MO: L. Bushnell, 1860), 22.
3. Brooks's talk can be accessed online at: http://asburyproject.org/media/orlando-2016/.
4. Bruce Caldwell, writing an intellectual biography of Hayek, recounts: "Although a small group of libertarians and conservatives always read him with enthusiasm, for much of the century Hayek was a subject of ridicule, contempt, or, even worse for a man of ideas, indifference." Caldwell also observes that Hayek's own school of thought, the Austrian school, largely sat on the sidelines of the many economic "revolutions" (Keynesian, econometrics, etc.) that formal economics underwent across the twentieth century, effectively marginalizing its star thinkers from the discipline's central debates. See Bruce Caldwell, *Hayek's Challenge: An Intellectual Biography of F. A. Hayek* (Chicago: University of Chicago Press, 2005), 2–3. One of the places Hayek's thought has been taken up with enthusiasm is in the Reconstructionist movement within Protestant theology, a theocratic-leaning branch of Protestantism I discuss in detail in Chapter 8. See Michael J. McVicar, "Christian Reconstructionism and the Austrian School of Economics," in *Hayek: A Collaborative Biography, Part IX: The Divine Right of the Free Market*, ed. Robert Leeson (New York: Palgrave Macmillan, 2013), 191–247.
5. One person I consulted on the high proportion of non-white attendees at this event said the enrollment of the seminary itself was disproportionately non-white, which may have shaped the networks of people who heard of the event. Another suggested some attendees had come into town to attend a much larger event featuring T. D.

Jakes—a popular Black pastor—and may have seen the Asbury conference as a convenient (and free) event to tack onto their schedule.

6. Mariya Strauss, "'Faith-Washing' Right-Wing Economics: How the Right Is Marketing Medicare's Demise," *The Public Eye*, Fall 2015, https://web.archive.org/web/20160115230445/https://www.politicalresearch.org/2015/11/14/faith-washing-right-wing-economics-how-the-right-is-marketing-medicares-demise/.
7. P. D. Anthony's work *The Ideology of Work* (London: Tavistock, 1977) examines cultural frameworks related to work exclusively through this ideological function: "Ideologies of work . . . are primarily directed at subordinates; their function is to explain the relative position of the subordinate and to influence his beliefs and his behavior concerning the activities he is required to perform. An ideology of work is a defense of subordination . . ." (p. 3).
8. Michel Mollat and Philippe Wolff, *The Popular Revolutions of the Late Middle Ages* (London: Allen & Unwin, 1973), 306. Quoted in Nicholas Abercrombie, Stephen Hill, and Bryan S. Turner, *The Dominant Ideology Thesis* (Boston: Allen & Unwin, 1980), 75.
9. E. P. Thompson, "The Transforming Power of the Cross," in Thompson, *The Making of the English Working Class* (New York: Vintage Books, 1963), 350–400; Reinhard Bendix, *Managerial Ideologies in the Course of Industrialization* (New York: John Wiley & Sons, 1956); Daniel Rodgers, *The Work Ethic in Industrial America, 1865–1917* (New Haven, CT: Yale University Press, 1973); Herbert G. Gutman, *Work, Culture, & Society: An Industrializing America* (New York: Vintage Books, 1976), For examples of how individualist and social Christianity blended together in serving these disciplinary impulses, see discussions in Ken Fones-Wolf, *Trade Union Gospel: Christianity and Labor in Industrial Philadelphia, 1865–1915* (Philadelphia: Temple University Press, 1989); Lundén, *Business and Religion in the American 1920s*; Robert Wauzzinsk, *Between God and Gold: Protestant Evangelicalism and the Industrial Revolution, 1820–1914* (Cranberry, NJ: Associated University Presses, 1993); and Thekla Ellen Joiner, *Sin in the City: Chicago and Revivalism 1880–1920* (Columbia: University of Missouri Press, 2007). Fones-Wolf makes the important point that, by the end of the nineteenth century, much of the American working class did not descend from a white Protestant tradition and was thereby not as likely to subscribe to any sort of "Protestant ethic" that might be disseminated by elites.
10. A somewhat significant exception to this would be the very common discussions of "leadership" in business which, while almost always focusing on personal ethics and behaviors, is at times hard to distinguish from managerial styles or techniques. My point here, however, is that there's a subtle but important difference between learning to "manage/lead like Jesus" and "constructing employee performance outcomes like Jesus," the latter of which would almost certainly not be a topic of discussion.
11. David Miller and Dennis LoRusso both explore the gap between the faith and work movement and the workplace spirituality world. Miller speaks from experience in narrating the poor initial reception his faith and work message received at a work and spirituality conference. See Miller, *God at Work*; and James Dennis LoRusso, *Spirituality, Corporate Culture, and American Business: The Neoliberal Ethic and the*

*Spirit of Global Capitalism* (New York: Bloomsbury Academic, 2017). Some of the disconnect is the product of the awkward incongruence between the tradition-bound religious "faith" of evangelical Protestantism and the far less defined "spirituality" that animates the workplace spirituality movement. Miller himself has come to serve as the most prominent crossover point between workplace spirituality and the faith and work movement, contributing to a 2013 handbook for researchers and practitioners in workplace spirituality. See David Miller and Timothy Ewest, "Faith at Work (Religious Perspectives): Protestant Accents in Faith and Work," in *Handbook of Faith and Spirituality in the Workplace: Emerging Research and Practice*, ed. Judi Neal (New York: Springer, 2013), 69–84.

12. Some of the mid-century leaders were notorious for proclaiming the promise that Christian principles promised higher profits and success, a strand of the movement explored in Chapter 8.
13. The most complete diagnoses of this perception of atomistic actors uninfluenced by structures and historical factors can be found in Christian Smith, *American Evangelicalism: Embattled and Thriving* (Chicago: University of Chicago Press, 1998), 187–217; Michael Emerson and Christian Smith, *Divided by Faith: Evangelical Religion and the Problem of Race in America* (New York: Oxford University Press, 2000), 76–83; James Davison Hunter, *To Change the World: The Irony, The Tragedy, and Possibility of Christianity in the Late Modern World* (New York: Oxford University Press, 2010), 26–27.
14. Awareness of such structures shaped how conservative Protestants from earlier eras directed the focus of their ministries. For example, in 1886, Chicago revivalist Dwight L. Moody capitalized on business leaders' anxieties and fears concerning unrest after the Haymarket affair to raise $250,000 to support Bible classes for working-class laborers and the poor. Moody pledged to train what he called "gapmen" who could bridge the emerging chasm between clergy and the working class, instructing these men to "lay their lives alongside of the laboring classes and the poor and bring the gospel to bear on their lives" (quoted in Joiner, *Sin in the City*, 58). The underlying intention, of course, was placating workers and preventing further labor unrest. It is difficult to imagine leaders in the contemporary faith and work movement perceiving this sort of class-based gap existing, much less taking upon themselves the challenge of positioning themselves within such a gap.
15. A review of evangelical job training curricula makes the compelling case that such materials do in fact aim paternalistic messaging at lower-status and unemployed workers. See Gretchen Purser and Brian Hennigan, "Cleaning Toilets for Jesus," *Jacobin*, June 30, 2017, https://www.jacobinmag.com/2017/06/work-to-welfare-unemployment-christian-right-jobs-for-life. But these curricula would, for a variety of reasons explored in the earlier parts of this book, be unlikely to find their way to a faith and work conference or other resources associated with the movement.
16. It should be noted that this event, the Gospel at Work event, did not receive any financial backing from the three major funding sources examined in this chapter. This is further evidence of how ubiquitous this messaging is.

17. Max Weber, *The Protestant Ethic and the Spirit of Capitalism*, trans. Talcott Parsons (New York: Routledge Classics, 2004), 124.
18. Lester DeKoster, *Work: The Meaning of Your Life, A Christian Perspective* (Grand Rapids, MI: Christian's Library Press, 2010), 27.
19. Kelvin Knight and Ronald Beadle, "Virtue and Meaningful Work" *Business Ethics Quarterly* 22, no. 2 (2012): 433–450.
20. A comprehensive historical source examining pro-slavery arguments among evangelicals is John Patrick Daley, *When Slavery Was Called Freedom: Evangelicalism, Proslavery, and the Cause of the Civil War* (Lexington: University of Kentucky, 2002). Daley outlines formulations of arguments by ministers that slavery and "free labor" were not all that different due to neither ultimately escaping a universal God-ordained "servitude" for all individuals. Quoting Presbyterian James Sloan, "Wherever there is capital there will be servitude. You may call this relation free or slave labor—whatever you choose—but it is a matter of very small importance in a practical view whether the service rendered be voluntary or involuntary. . . . Christians do not belong to themselves . . . the real difference [between free and slave labor] is only in the mode of punishment" (p. 124). Another Presbyterian leader, James Henley Thornwell, made a similar claim of equivalence: "What is it that makes a man a slave? We answer the obligation that to labor for another, determined by the Providence of God, independently of the provisions of a contract. . . . God's command is often as stringent upon the free laborer, and determines, with as stern a mandate, what contracts he shall make. Neither can be said to select his employments" (p. 124). In many ways, this mode of defining free labor as so grueling that it is on par with slavery is hardly a framework for "dignifying" work, but the end result is the same: providing Providential assurance that all workers, free or slave, find themselves in the setting and position to which they should submit without protest.
21. True W. Hoit, *The Right of American Slavery* (St. Louis, MO: L. Bushnell, 1860), 22.
22. Sloan, *The Great Question Answered*, 69.
23. Charles Colcock Jones, *Catechism, of Scripture Doctrine and Practice: For Families and Sabbath Schools Designed Also for the Oral Instruction of Colored Persons* (New York: Leavitt, Trow, 1845), 130–131.
24. Yale theologian Miroslav Volf wrote an early faith and work book that specifically criticized approaches to faith and work that "ennoble dehumanizing work" at the expense of calls for altering the structures producing such work. See Volf, *Work in the Spirit: Toward a Theology of Work* (New York: Oxford University Press, 1991). A handful of other faith and work texts have picked up this critique as well. Among resources produced by the libertarian organizations mentioned above, however, such a worry is largely absent.
25. Michael Luo and Laurie Goodstein. "Emphasis Shifts for New Breed of Evangelicals," *New York Times*, May 21, 2007, https://www.nytimes.com/2007/05/21/us/21evangelical.html; Laura Session Stepp, "Why Young Evangelicals Are Leaving the Church," *CNN*, December 16, 2011, https://www.cnn.com/2011/12/16/opinion/stepp-millennials-church/index.html; Deborah Jian Lee, "Millennials: Why the Young Religious Right Is Leaning Left," *Time*, October 20, 2015, http://time.com/4078909/evangeli

cal-millennials/. A 2017 analysis of religious left efforts that might span religious groups in the United States found a number of factors working against the emergence of a coherent coalition. A leading obstacle is the steadily growing level of religious disaffiliation, paired with increasingly unfavorable views of religion among those identifying as liberals. See Daniel Cox, "Don't Bet on the Emergence of a 'Religious Left,' *FiveThirtyEight*, April 20, 2017. https://fivethirtyeight.com/features/dont-bet-on-the-emergence-of-a-religious-left/

26. Confirming this tight partnership, a thirty-minute documentary funded by Kern on faith and work at one point appeared on AEI's Values and Capitalism website, focused largely on a roundtable conversation among Katherine Leary Alsdorf, Christopher Brooks, David Blanchard, and Gregory Thornbury. This video can now be accessed on the Institute for Faith, Work, and Economic's website: https://tifwe.org/film-to-whom-is-given-business-for-the-common-good/
27. Evan Sparks, "Intellectual Capital" *Philanthropy Roundtable*, Spring 2011. Accessed online: https://web.archive.org/web/20130118213257/https://www.philanthropyroundtable.org/topic/excellence_in_philanthropy/intellectual_capital
28. Anne R. Bradley, "Voting with Your Feet to Serve the Common Good," *Washington Times*, May 12, 2016, p. 7.
29. Gerardo Marti, *American Blindspot: Race, Class, Religion, and the Trump Presidency* (New York: Rowman & Littlefield, 2020), 113, 133. Chapter 3 discusses earlier forms of politicized Protestant theologies in American history.
30. While the other primers delve into a strange grab bag of libertarian and politically conservative ideas, the Wesleyan primer—*How God Makes the World a Better Place*—never strays far from John Wesley's own social concerns and theology. The authors seem to have been afforded more editorial freedom: the cited contemporary thinkers and theorists are largely centrist-to-left sociologists. Sowell, Novak, Friedman, and the Austrian economists are completely absent.
31. To draw just a few quotations from the Baptist, Lutheran, Reformed, and Pentecostal primers: "We need to pursue policies that encourage the poor to become active image bearers of God." "At the very least, this ought to give us pause; is it possible that our zeal for social justice encourages deadly sin?" "When the church is fulfilling its true mission—calling sinners to repentance and to new life in Christ and then nurturing them in the faith—it indirectly addresses the issue of poverty by helping to change human hearts and habits." "Americans in the past crossed rugged mountain ranges, barged down the Ohio, crossed the seemingly interminable western plains, and eked out a living in hard and intractable lands . . . these people did not want to depend on government." "Unfortunately, many people, including Christians, have been lured to buy into the notion that stewardship of the planet means that we have to support the call by 'experts' and by the federal government to support the kind of coercive . . . programs and policies being called for." This latter quote goes on to compare the efforts promoting environmental regulation to "the takeover of the Soviet Union in 1917" before comparing the "colluding" of global warming scientists and environmental policy advocates with the Pharisees and wealthy people who serve as the targets of Jesus's most pointed criticisms.

32. Accessed online: https://www.youtube.com/user/KernPastorsNetwork/playlists.
33. Hugh Whelchel, "Do Free Markets Inherently Lead to Exploitation?" *Institute for Faith, Work, and Economics*, September 8, 2014. https://tifwe.org/free-markets-and-exploitation/.
34. There seem to be inconsistencies in the Koch organization's views on social issues. The investigative journalism cited above frequently challenges the Koch brothers' publicly professed neutrality and indifference on social issues, citing the large amounts of money passed to conservative social groups advocating against feminism, LGBTQ rights, abortion rights, and other policies deemed harmful to "family values." But the Koch brothers have voiced public support to same-sex marriage rights and other more progressive social-value issues, which is likely what prevents Whelchel from fully identifying his efforts as congruent with Koch efforts. These inconsistencies appear to directly intersect with Whelchel's organization: the Institute for Faith, Work, and Economics passes several million dollars' worth of support from Koch-funded organizations to socially conservative lobbying groups.
35. Document accessed online: https://prezi.com/p28vyakm5mbn/the-oikonomia-network/.
36. There is a significant tension here that goes unexplored within the faith and work space: many adherents of libertarianism rejected and clashed with Christianity. Von Mises was deeply skeptical of the compatibility of Christianity and capitalism. He saw Christianity irreconcilable with "a free social order based on private ownership in the means of production. A living Christianity cannot, it seems, exist side by side with Capitalism. . . . Christianity must either overcome Capitalism or go under." See Ludwig Von Mises, *On Socialism* (New Haven, CT: Yale University Press, 1951), 428–429. IFWE also employs as a fellow David Kotter, a theologian at Colorado Christian University, who has given talks and produced works asserting that Ayn Rand's views are "consistent with a biblical worldview" and that the most obvious model for her John Galt character in *Atlas Shrugged* is, in fact, Jesus. Here, too, there is significant revisionist work required to present Rand's libertarianism as compatible with Christianity. Rand herself famously called Christianity "dangerously other-oriented" and "the best possible kindergarten of communism." See Tyler O'Neil, "Ayn Rand's Libertarian Hero John Galt was Modeled on Jesus, Christian Panelist Argues," *The Christian Post*, February 18, 2014. Accessed online: https://www.christianpost.com/news/ayn-rands-libertarian-hero-john-galt-was-modeled-on-jesus-christian-panelist-argues-114729/.

## Chapter 7

1. Max Weber, *The Protestant Ethic and the Spirit of Capitalism*, trans. Talcott Parsons (New York: Routledge Classics, 2004), 101.
2. Weber, *The Protestant Ethic*, 124.

3. Though less active in the field now, Lindsay was earlier in his career a sociologist of religion. Lindsay's sociological work *Faith in the Halls of Power*, which surveys evangelicals in positions of power, made up the first wave of his now larger project of interviewing leaders of all religious backgrounds across industries. See Michael Lindsay, *Faith in the Halls of Power: How Evangelicals Joined the American Elite* (New York: Oxford University Press, 2007).
4. Jeff Haanen, "Michael Lindsay: Go Where Decisions Are Made," *Christianity Today*, August 6, 2014. Accessed online: https://www.christianitytoday.com/ct/2014/august-web-only/michael-lindsay-you-have-to-be-in-room.html.
5. Details on Redeemer Presbyterian Church and Keller drawn from William M. McMillan, "Contextualization, Big Apple Style: Making Conservative Christianity More Palatable in Modern Day Manhattan," *Symposia* 5 (2013): 1–16; and Lindsay, *Faith in the Halls of Power*.
6. Not only do New Yorkers on average work more hours than their professional counterparts in other cities, but many of the occupational fields identified as common at Redeemer are some of the most time-demanding fields among careers today.
7. Richard Florida, "Cities and the Creative Class," *Cities & Community* 2, no. 1 (2003): 4.
8. Scott M. Stringer, "The Hardest Working Cities," *NYC Economic Brief, Office of the New York City Controller*, March 2015. https://comptroller.nyc.gov/wp-content/uploads/documents/Longest_Work_Weeks_March_2015.pdf.
9. Richard Florida and Charlotta Mellander, "Segregated City: The Geography of Economic Segregation in America's Metros," *The Martin Prosperity Institute*, September 6, 2014. http://martinprosperity.org/content/the-divided-city-and-the-shape-of-the-new-metropolis/.
10. Ted Melinik and Carol Morello, "Washington: A World Apart," *Washington Post*, November 9, 2013. https://www.washingtonpost.com/sf/local/2013/11/09/washington-a-world-apart/.
11. Samantha Sharf, "Full List: America's Most Expensive ZIP Codes," *Forbes*, November 28, 2017. https://www.forbes.com/sites/samanthasharf/2017/11/28/full-list-americas-most-expensive-zip-codes-2017/#7858f14e5d19.
12. Attaching the term "humanism" may seem anachronistic or antagonistic to Kuyperianism: Kuyper was adamantly against the humanism of his day, asserting it fundamentally erred in trying to build a society de novo, grounded only in the free will of the individual. My usage of the term here reflects Kuyper's resurrection of a Renaissance-grounded humanism as embodied in Calvin. Kuyper himself saw a "close relation" existing between Calvin and humanism: "In as far as humanism endeavored to substitute life in this world for eternity, every Calvinist opposed the humanist. But inasmuch as the humanist counted himself with a plea for a proper acknowledgement of secular life, the Calvinist was an ally." A similar humanism is also championed in the thought of J. Gresham Machen who, as Marsden observes, saw the need to preserve the virtues of Renaissance humanism amidst the more culturally oppositional pulls of fundamentalism. When he was still at Princeton, Machen called for an enthusiastic cultivation of arts, science, and culture "with all the enthusiasm of the veriest humanist, but at the same time consecrate them to the service of

our God." Such a stance would come to inspire Carl Henry (discussed below) who also looked back to the Renaissance as a source of "deep meanings" that Christians might possibly be able to retrieve. Another Evangelical scholar who conferred equal worth to Renaissance ideas was Christian education champion Frank Gaebelein, who explicitly referred to himself as a "Christian humanist." See Albert R. Beck, *All Truth is God's Truth: The Life and Ideas of Frank E. Gaebelein* (Waco, TX: Baylor University, unpublished dissertation, 2008).

13. See David Harrington Watt, "Fundamentalists of the 1920s and 1930s," In *Fundamentalism: Perspectives on a Contested History,* Edited by Simon A. Wood and David Harrington Watt, (Columbia, SC: University of South Carolina, 2014). Geroge Marsden argues the "backwoods, rural, and uneducated" depiction of fundamentalists owes its prevalence to the descriptions produced by journalist H. L. Mencken after the Scopes Monkey Trial and failed to realistically depict the scope and fuller influence of the movement. Robert Wenger compares the biographies of forty prominent leaders from fundamentalist and modernist groups (largely prominent between 1918 and 1933) to conclude that modernist leadership on average held a greater number of advanced degrees but geographic footprints of each camp largely mirrored the U.S. population and U.S. churchgoing population at the time. Wenger also broke down congregational numbers and found fundamentalism's greater numeric strength east of the Mississippi and north of the Mason-Dixon line, with Pennsylvania seemingly serving as fundamentalism's strongest source of adherents and supporters. See Wenger, *Social Thought in American Fundamentalism.*
14. For an overview of the Church of God's opposition to industrialism, wealth, and materialism, see Mickey Crews, *The Church of God: A Social History* (Knoxville: University of Tennessee Press, 1990), 12–13.
15. Kuyper's thought remains largely irrelevant to many arms of evangelicalism, particularly those who have preserved a more culture-denying pre-millennialism or separatist orientations of fundamentalism or restorationist churches. Kuyperianism also has little foothold among Pentecostals, Anabaptist groups, Latino Evangelicals, progressive evangelicals, or multicultural evangelical settings with greater access to non-white theological currents. .
16. Molly Worthen, *Apostles of Reason: The Crisis of Authority in American Evangelicalism* (New York: Oxford University Press, 2014), 221.
17. Joel Carpenter, "The Perils of Prosperity: Neo-Calvinism and the Future of Religious Colleges," in *The Future of Religious Colleges*, ed. Paul J. Dovre (Grand Rapids, MI: Eerdmans, 2002), 185-207.James C. Turner, "Something to Be Reckoned With: The Evangelical Mind Awakens," *Commonweal* 126 (1999): 11–23.
18. Abraham Kuyper, *Lectures on Calvinism* (Grand Rapids, MI: Eerdmans, 1961), iii.
19. David Naugle, *Worldview: The History of a Concept* (Grand Rapids, MI: William B. Eerdmans, 2002), 17.
20. Abraham Kuyper, *Lectures on* Calvinism (Peabody, MA: Hendrickson Publishers, 2008),11–12.
21. For a sample of writing from this journal, see James D. Bratt and Ronald A. Wells (eds.), *The Best of The Reformed Journal* (Grand Rapids, MI: Eerdmans, 2011).

22. George Marsden, "The State of Evangelical Christian Scholarship," *Reformed Journal* 37 (1987): 14.
23. Carl F. H. Henry, "The Vigor of the New Evangelicalism," *Christian Life*, January (1948): 30.
24. Worthen, *Apostles of Reason*.
25. See Sara Diamond, *Roads to Dominion: Right-Wing Movements and Political Power in the United States* (New York: Guilford Press, 1995).
26. Dutch Reformed Church, *Human Relations and the South African Scene in the Light of* Scripture (Cape Town: National book Printers, 1976). For commentary by sympathetic Kuyperians, see Richard Mouw, "Calvin's Legacy for Public Theology," *Political Theology* 10, no. 3 (2009): 431–446; and Mark Rathbone, "Sphere Sovereignty and Irreducibility: The Ambiguous Use of Abraham Kuyper's Ideas during the Time of Apartheid in South Africa," *Koers* 80, no. 1 (2015): 1–18.
27. Chuck Colson's book *How Now Shall We Live* is perhaps the most popular work that promotes the cultural mandate to wider evangelicalism. Colson was guided to Kuyper by Michael Cromartie, who later became an influential evangelical in the think tank world who served as vice president of the Ethics and Public Policy Center. According to an interview with Richard Mouw, soon after Colson became a well-known, newly converted evangelical in the 1970s, Cromartie set up a meeting between Colson and a large number of Calvin College faculty members to essentially pose a theological intervention on Colson's public theology, which Colson himself recognized was underdeveloped. Colson would go on to put Kuyper at the foundation of his work: "I've done my best to popularize Kuyper, because that's what's so desperately needed in the Western civilization today: looking at all life through God's way." Quotation from Colson taken from Owen Strachan, *The Colson Way: Loving Your Neighbor and Living with Faith in a Hostile World* (Nashville, TN: Thomas Nelson, 2015).
28. Nicholas Wolterstorff, *Until Justice and Peace Embrace* (Grand Rapids, MI: William B. Eerdmans, 1983)
29. George M. Marsden, *The Twilight of the American Enlightenment: The 1950s and the Crisis of Liberal Belief* (New York: Basic Books, 2014).
30. Franklin Graham, "Christ Our Sovereign King," published December 1, 2020. Accessed online: https://decisionmagazine.com/franklin-graham-christ-our-sovereign-king/.
31. Katherine Stewart, "The Roots of Josh Hawley's Rage," *New York Times*, January 11, 2021. Accessed online: https://www.nytimes.com/2021/01/11/opinion/josh-hawley-religion-democracy.html.
32. Quoted in Marsden, *Fundamentalism and American Culture*, 210–211.
33. Theologies of creation rooted in earlier forms of Calvinism identified far greater antithesis between Christian callings and nature itself, the latter of which could very well contain countervailing forces that must be militantly overcome by Christian action. For a fuller account of how these battles with forces instilled a reformist impulse within Calvinism, see Michael Walzer, *The Revolution of the Saints* (Cambridge, MA: Harvard University Press, 1965).

34. Georg Wünsch, *Evangelische Wirtschaftsethik* (translated as *Protestant Economic Ethics*) (Tübingen: J. C. B. Mohr, 1927). Quoted in H. Richard Niebuhr, *The Social Sources of Denominationalism* (New York: Henry Holt, 1929), 97.
35. Abraham Kuyper, "Sphere Sovereignty," In *Abraham Kuyper: A Centennial Reader* ed. by James D. Bratt (Grand Rapids, M: Eerdmans, 1998), 488.
36. Abraham Kuyper, *The Problems of Poverty* (Grand Rapids, MI: Baker Book House, 1991), 30.
37. Abraham Kuyper, *Lectures on Calvinism* (Peabody, MA: Hendrickson, 2008), 104–106.
38. Chuck Colson and Nancy Pearce, *How Now Shall We Live?* (Carol Stream, IL: Tyndale House, 1999), xii.
39. Kuyper's views are categorized by Christian theologians as adhering to amillennialism. This perspective sees the millennial reign of Christ as not a coming earthly reality—what pre-millennialists promised would be ushered in by Christ's return—but instead a spiritual reality in which the church now resides. Christ's return will still establish his reign on earth, but amillennialism does not adhere to a dramatic burning up or passing away of the world itself. Some adaptations of this view contend that our own material labor and fruits have bearing on the next age, which allows them to take on eternal significance. Clearly not all the Kuyper-influenced evangelical writers and thinkers fully abandon pre-millennialism, but my observations in the faith and work space suggest the pre-millennialism of the nineteenth century and even that of Billy Graham or Tim LaHaye bear no influence on the conversation.
40. The most systematic discussion of faith and work peeling away from pre-millennialism appears in Volf, *Work in the Spirit*. Volf's work is occasionally cited in contemporary faith and work books, but by and large the rejection of pre-millennialism goes unaddressed by faith and work leaders.
41. Faith and work lectures and books frequently cite amillennial or post-millennial theologians like George Eldon Ladd, Oscar Cullmann, N. T. Wright, Al Wolters, and Christopher J. H. Wright.
42. C. I. Scofield's religious instruction specifically related to work provides the best example of a "man your station" pre-millennial theology of work. See Scofield, *The New Life in Christ* (Chicago: The Bible Institute Colportage Association, 1915).
43. Though only tangentially related to eschatology, faith and work leaders at times promote understandings of heaven that feature work and labor, a belief which serves to imbue present work with eternal significance by emphasizing workers' continual participation in work for all eternity. As Keller and Alsdorf argue in *Every Good Endeavor*, the "heavenly city will be cultivated and maintained by workers whose callings find their ultimate fulfillment in eternity." These claims are generally arrived at by way of criticizing the disembodied, immaterial, and overly spiritualized vision of heaven which is believed to be fueling a spiritual–material dualism in our this-worldly lives, one judged antithetical to visions of redeeming work and recognizing its eternal significance. As a point of contrast, an 1855 sermon by Baptist pastor Charles Spurgeon stakes out a remarkably different view of heaven: "To my mind, one of the best views of heaven is, that it is a land of rest—especially to the working man. Those who have

not had to work hard, think they will love heaven as a place of service. That is very true. But to the working man, to the man who toils with his brain or with his hands, it must ever be a sweet thought that there is a land where we shall rest. Soon, this voice will never be strained again; soon, these lungs will never have to exert themselves beyond their power; soon, this brain shall not be racked for thought; but I shall sit at the banquet-table of God; yea, I shall recline on the bosom of Abraham, and be at ease for ever." The writings of Scofield also contrast a this-worldly toil with the rest offered by the next. Such a contrast violates the more Romanticist elements of the faith and work movement, which insists that present toil represents participation in activity closely connected to the eventual restoration and renewal of all things, as discussed in Chapter 4. Volf's *Work in the Spirit* provides greater exploration of the theological differences between these views.

44. Some events that occurred amidst the time of my data collecting: in *Burwell v. Hobby Lobby Stores, Inc.*, the Supreme Court ruled that for-profit corporations could refuse to provide contraception for female employees on grounds of religious conviction. A Christian-owned cake business in Oregon was found guilty of violating a state non-discrimination ordination in their refusal to make a cake for a lesbian couple. The Religious Freedom Restoration Act—defending business owners' rights to deny services in cases where religious convictions were violated—was also passed in Indiana, with its main endorser, Indiana governor Mike Pence, then joining a national political campaign for vice president. White evangelicals were also navigating the supercharged rhetoric of the 2016 Republican primary and then the general presidential election, which saw many white evangelical leaders place their support behind Donald Trump. Setting aside the cases where I specifically brought up such occurrences in interviews, no interviewee or speaker at an event addressed any of these developments.
45. Perceptions of one's social stability or precarity are just as much cultural and phenomenological as they are products of economic or social positioning, so objective measures of socioeconomic stability are generally poor predictors of how populations perceive threats to their own status. Political scientists studying the rise of populism and authoritarian groups have attested that support for these groups typically revolves around cultural anxieties surrounding immigration and threats to the preservation of white cultural homogeneity. The argument advanced here is not that creative-class evangelicals have necessarily defected from supporting populist causes or candidates now popular on the right, but merely that they have unique *cultural, social, and economic* resources that may be driving a wedge between their own perceptions of American institutions at large and the perceptions of other conservative voters.
46. The survey of the most frequent speakers at faith and work events revealed that 43.5 percent of leaders identified as "conservative" or "very conservative." Though I requested to survey the political views of several hundred attendees at a major faith and work event, my request was politely denied by the event's lead coordinator. According to a staffer I spoke with at the event, the leader coordinator was apparently quite puzzled as to why anyone would want to survey this event's attendees for

their political views, which in this leader's mind seemed quite disconnected from the event's topic.

47. Equating Christian purposes with those goods and ends already present within cultural spheres has a longer history in the Christian tradition. H. Richard Niebuhr, in his survey of Christian orientations to culture, labels such approaches the "Christ within culture" approach. See Niebuhr, *Christ and Culture* (New York: HarperCollins, 2001).
48. H. Russell Botman, "Is Blood Thicker than Justice? The Legacy of Abraham Kuyper for Southern Africa," in *Religion, Pluralism, and Public Life: Abraham Kuyper's Legacy for the Twenty-First Century*, ed. L. E. Lugo (Grand Rapids, MI: William B. Eerdmans, 2000).
49. For examples, see S. A. Cortright and Michael J. Naughton, *Rethinking the Purpose of Business: Interdisciplinary Essays from the Catholic Social Tradition* (Notre Dame, IN: University of Notre Dame Press, 2002). Andrew V. Abela and Joseph E. Capizzi (eds.), *A Catechism for Business: Tough Ethical Questions and Insights from Catholic Social Teaching* (Washington, DC: Catholic University of American Press, 2014).
50. Charles Tripp, *Islam and the Moral Economy: The Challenge of Capitalism* (New York: Cambridge University Press, 2006).
51. This is not to say there are not a steady flow of economic and business books written by authors who possess evangelical credentials. However, no author or particular tradition of evangelical ethics seems to exercise any observable influence within the faith and work space.
52. Charles Taylor, *Sources of the Self: The Making of Modern Identity* (Cambridge, MA: Harvard University Press, 1989), 224. See Chapter 4 for discussion of this parallel.
53. The wider theoretical questions of accommodationism are discussed in James Davison Hunter's research on evangelicals navigating the "quandary" of modernity. See Hunter, *American Evangelicalism: Conservative Religion and the Quandary of Modernity* (New Brunswick, NJ: Rutgers University Press, 1983). The present use of this concept, however, is more narrowly focused on accommodation with the conditions, practices, and logics of creative-class capitalism rather than the much broader question of accommodating modernity.
54. Schmalzbauer himself considers evangelicals' entry into two particular knowledge-economy professions: higher education and the media. Here I am applying his insights to a slightly wider case of professions engaged by the faith and work movement, which gathers many knowledge-economy and creative-class professions.
55. These organizations are at times omitted from lists of faith and work organizations due to their very specialized function. It also becomes difficult at times to distinguish a professional group from other "special purpose" groups. But included here would be groups like the Fellowship of Christian Magicians, the Christian Legal Society, the Christian Chiropractors Association, etc. See Wuthnow, *The Restructuring of American Religion*, 100–131.
56. Pew Forum on Religion and Public Life, *U.S. Religious Landscape Survey* (Washington, DC: Pew Research Center, 2015). https://www.pewforum.org/religious-landscape-study/.

57. James D. Davidson, Rachel Kraus, and Scott Morrissey, "Presidential Appointments and Religious Stratification in the United States, 1789–2003," *Journal for the Scientific Study of Religion* 44, no. 4 (2005): 485–495.
58. Pew Forum, *U.S. Religious Landscape*.
59. H. Richard Niebuhr, *The Social Sources of Denominationalism* (New York: Henry Holt, 1929), 71.
60. Quotations taken from a summary of the talk printed in a contemporary newspaper, "Vital Problems Were Discussed," *Rochester Democrat and Chronicle*, Wednesday, February 21, 1906, and also from Miller, *God at Work*.
61. See Mark Thomas Edwards, *The Right of the Protestant Left: God's Totalitarianism* (New York: Palgrave Macmillan, 2012), 133. According to Edwards's account, WCC leaders Henry Van Dusen and J. H. Oldham both advocated for redeveloping conceptions of vocation at the 1954 meeting. Edwards also notes that socialist theologian Paul Tillich, having become impressed by the "men of conscience" he lectured at Harvard's business school, had also begun developing a "theology of business" around the same time.
62. Two other sets of developments exhibited a thirty-year gap between Mainline Protestantism and white Evangelicalism. The 1950s was the era of generative production of laity-targeted books on the topic of theology of the laity, written by Mainline thinkers. Evangelicalism's own book market appears to have hit new heights in the 1980s. In 1974, Andover Newton Theological School, a Mainline seminary, initiated the Andover Newton Laity Project, made up of working groups of laity and seminary professors meeting to explore the challenges of vocation in specific fields and occupations. Edited volumes and reports summarized these group's experiences. Out of this project emerged Andover's Center for the Ministry of the Laity in the 1980s. Evangelical colleges and seminaries were trailing behind by about thirty years: faith and work and vocational discernment centers came to populate nearly every evangelical college and seminary in the 2010s, largely due to the financial backing of the Kern Family Foundation and the Lilly Endowment.
63. Perhaps somewhat counterintuitively, Mainline leaders' most persisting influence in the world of vocation and work is likely its strong presence in ecumenical efforts that end up serving a wider range of Christian spaces. Mainline theologians occupy several places of leadership in Lilly Endowment–backed initiatives such as the Forum for Theological Exploration and the Council for Independent College's Network for Vocation in Undergraduate Education (NetVUE). For these organizations, the concept of vocation and calling spans both secular and clerical roles, as the organization seeks to inspire laity to become more involved in Christian communities. Individuals affiliated with these projects have produced several books on vocation and purpose, including Timothy Clydedale's *The Purposeful Graduate: Why Colleges Must Talk to Students about Vocation*, David Cunningham's trilogy of edited volumes on vocation in higher education, and two anthologies of Christian thinkers exploring vocation: *Callings: Twenty Centuries of Christian Wisdom on Vocation*, edited by William C. Placher, and *Leading Lives That Matter: What We Should Do and Who We Should Be*, edited by Mark R. Schwen and Dorothy C. Bass.

64. For an overview of Mainline efforts' evolution after 1970, see, *Shape-Shifting Capital.*
65. This center pivoted its surviving energies toward developing Robert Greenleaf's "spiritualized leadership" principles and other managerial efforts within the workplace spirituality movement. See George González, *Shape-Shifting Capital: Spiritual Management, Critical Theory, and the Ethnographic Project* (Lexington, KY: Lexington Books, 2015).
66. Ray's *Working* is a more sociologically informed and theologically rich text than most Evangelical texts exploring the final topics. The final chapter lands on a "sacramental theology of work" that endorses not only an invitation to co-creation and participating in God's "economy of grace"—echoing what have become standard Evangelical themes—but also champions worker co-ops, living wage, and solidarity with the poor.
67. Statistics from Robert Wuthnow, "Beyond Quiet influence? Possibilities for the Protestant Mainline," in *The Quiet Hand of God: Faith-Based Activism and the Public Role of Mainline Protestantism*, ed. Robert Wuthnow and John H. Evans (Berkeley: University of California Press, 2002), 381–403.

## Chapter 8

1. Quoted in Weber, *The Protestant Ethic and the Spirit of Capitalism*, 118.
2. Here I have omitted from analysis some modes of Black Protestantism that have historically occupied a distinct position in relation to wider American society. While some specific traditions and movements are explicitly addressed in the following analysis, the complex heterogeneity among Black Protestant churches—ranging from more sectarian and more pietistic to more activist-oriented forms of faith—prevents any singular categorization of how Black Protestantism relates to the economic sector. Black Protestant churches have also historically played a unique in relation to the congregants they serve, a role which reflects the structural obstacles and economic marginalization many Black congregants have faced over the history of the United States. This non-agentic mode of relating to the economic sector lessens the useful points of comparison between these traditions and the faith and work movement, which occupies an equally distinct (but very distant) socioeconomic profile. For a typology of Black churches that expands beyond Protestantism, see Hans A. Baer and Merrill Singer, *African-American Religion in the Twentieth Century: Varieties of Protest and Accommodation* (Knoxville: University of Tennessee Press, 1992).
3. Tawney, *Religion and the Rise of Capitalism*, 227.
4. The notion of sect, first developed by theologian Ernst Troeltsch, is defined and developed in Rodney Stark and William Bainbridge, *The Future of Religion* (Berkeley: University of California Press, 1985), 49–50.
5. James Halteman, "A Mennonite Approach to Business Ethics," in *Spiritual Goods: Faith Traditions and the Practice of Business*, ed. Stewart W. Herman and Arthur Gross-Schaefer (Bowling Green, OH: Philosophy Documentation Center, 2001), 277.

6. Quoted in Calvin Redekop, Sephen C. Ainlay, and Robert Siemens, *Mennonite Entrepreneurs* (Baltimore, MD: Johns Hopkins University Press, 1995), 46.
7. Halteman, "A Mennonite Approach."
8. Quoted in Redekop, Ainlay, and Siemens, *Mennonite Entrepreneurs*, 46.
9. Richard Cawardine, "Charles Seller's 'Antinomians' and 'Arminians': Methodists and the Market Revolution," in *God and Mammon: Protestants, Money, and the Market, 1790–1860*, ed. Mark Noll (New York: Oxford University Press, 2002), 75–98; and Douglas Strong, *Perfectionist Politics: Abolitionism and the Religious Tensions of American Democracy* (Syracuse, NY: Syracuse University Press, 1999).
10. Lewis V. Baldwin, *Invisible Strands in African Methodism: A History of the African Union Methodist Protestant and Union American Methodist Episcopal Churches, 1805–1980* (Metuchen, NJ: The American Theological Library Association, 1983).
11. Nancy Jean Davis and Robert V. Robinson, *Claiming Society for God: Religious Movements and Social Welfare: Egypt, Israel, Italy, and the United States* (Bloomington: Indiana University Press, 2012), 113–142.
12. Liston Pope, *Millhands and Preachers: A Study of Gastonia* (New Haven, CT: Yale University Press, 1942).
13. For an overview of the Church of God's opposition to industrialism, wealth, and materialism, see Mickey Crews, *The Church of God: A Social History* (Knoxville: University of Tennessee Press, 1990), 12–13.
14. Quoted in Mike King, *Quakernomics: An Ethical Capitalism* (New York: Anthem Press, 2014), 111.
15. For an account of evolving views of wealth among Quakers, see T. A. B. Corley, "Changing Quaker Attitudes to Wealth, 1690–1950," in *Business and Wealth in Modern Britain*, ed. David Jeremy (New York: Routledge, 1998), 137–152.
16. Historian Mickey Crews recounts that Church of God leaders were largely critical of middle-class churches around the turn of the century but subsequently moved closer to that socioeconomic position themselves by the time they joined the National Association of Evangelicals in 1942. See Crews, *The Church of God*, 146–148.
17. For the longer history of conservative Protestant parachurch organizations navigating loyalties to the interests of their donors, see Ken Fones-Wolf, *Trade Union Gospel: Christianity and Labor in Industrial Philadelphia, 1865–1915* (Philadelphia: Temple University Press, 1989), Joiner, *Sin in the City*; Ronald C. White, "Youth Ministry at the Center: A Case Study of Young Life," in *Re-Forming the Center: American Protestantism, 1900 to Present*, ed. Douglas Jacobsen and William Vance Trollinger, Jr. (Grand Rapids, MI: Eerdmans, 1998), 361–380; Kim Phillips-Fein, *Invisible Hands: The Businessmen's Crusade against the New Deal* (New York: W. W. Norton, 2009); and Grem, *The Blessings of Business*.
18. Diamond, *Roads to Dominion*, 246. See also Ammerman, "North American Protestant Fundamentalism," 49–54.
19. William Martin, *With God on Our Side: The Rise of the Religious Right* (New York: Broadway Books, 1996), 356.
20. Fuller Seminary faculty member Peter Wagner served as theologian, lead spokesperson, and self-appointed historian of the movement Most of this history is taken

from Wagner, *Dominion! How Kingdom Action Can Change the World* (Grand Rapids, MI: Chosen Books, 2008); and Brad Christerson and Richard Flory, *The Rise of Network Christianity: How Independent Leaders Are Changing the Religious Landscape* (New York: Oxford University Press, 2017).

21. A newspaper article describing these movements' connection with then-presidential candidate Rick Perry describes New Apostolic Reformation adherents as having a "growing fascination with infiltrating politics and government" as well as "climb[ing] the commanding heights" of seven cultural institutions in order to "lord over society." See Forrest Wilder, "Rick Perry's Army of God," *The Texas Observer* August 3, 2011. Accessed online: https://www.texasobserver.org/rick-perrys-army-of-god/. Other articles from the same era tie 2016 presidential candidates Ted Cruz and Michelle Bachman to the movement. See John Fea, "Ted Cruz's Campaign Is Fueled by Dominionist Vision for America," *Washington Post*, February 4, 2016. Republished online: https://religionnews.com/2016/02/04/ted-cruzs-campaign-fueled-dominionist-vision-america-commentary/
22. See R. Douglas Geivett and Holly Pivec, *A New Apostolic Reformation? A Biblical Response to a Worldwide Movement* (Bellingham, WA: Lexham Press, 2014).
23. Wagner discusses the theories of culture change in Randall Collins and James Davison Hunter. Hillman also cites these theorists in an April 5, 2018 webinar, which can be accessed online: https://www.slideshare.net/oshillman/7m-cultureshaping-webinar.
24. In over a hundred hours of fieldwork—including attendance at major national conferences—there were no references to Seven Mountains theology and very little detectable influence of any Pentecostal theology. One interviewee, on being asked about exposure to Seven Mountains Theology, recalled a speaker promoting the framework at a 2014 national conference. However, both the interviewee's recount of this event and the event's program (provided by the interviewee on request) indicated Seven Mountains theology was addressed by only one of the twenty-four different speakers at the event.
25. Phone interview, 10/31/2016. The leaders Hillman identified as currently active in the faith and work space are involved in CEO-focused groups, which were largely outside the pool of leaders studied. I discuss the existence of this parallel executive-centered space in the Appendix.
26. This explanation of other efforts proving to draw wider audiences might be complemented by the entrance of outside funding sources, which did not fund any of the charismatic or Dominionist "first wave actors," while boosting resources of the second-wave actors.
27. Geographic disparity is based on the locations of Dominionist-inspired faith and work conferences, which favored the South (San Antonio, Atlanta, North Carolina) over the Pacific Northwest or the Northeast, where creative-class populations have been more prevalent. On education levels, the 2014 Religious Landscapes Survey places two major Pentecostal denominations at the lowest end of the education attainment spectrum: 11 percent of Church of God (Cleveland, Tennessee) adherents have college degrees, while for the Assemblies of God this percentage goes up to 15 percent. This compares to the national average of 27 percent. One-third of adherents

within the Presbyterian Church in America have college degrees, representing the highest-educated Evangelical denomination (but notably trailing behind six Mainline Protestant denominations). Many leaders in the faith and work movement are affiliated with the Presbyterian Church of America, which also served as a major conduit for the spread of Neo-Calvinist Kuyperianism discussed in Chapter 7.

28. Previous histories of the faith and work movement have neglected the influence of Dominionist theology. However, one history notes the movement divided into three major approaches around the year 2000: a "Neo-Calvinist 'Genesis 1 & 2' Focus," an "Evangelical 'Business as Mission' Focus," and a "Pentecostal 'Cultural Transformation' Focus," the latter of which should be identified with the Dominionism discussed here. See Darren Shearer, "The Marketplace Christianity Movement: A Brief History (1930–Present)," *Theology of Business Institute*. http://www.theologyofbusiness.com/the-marketplace-christianity-movement-a-brief-history-1930-present/.
29. Kate Bowler, *Blessed: A History of the American Prosperity Gospel*, New York: Oxford University Press, 2013). The intellectual genealogy of Prosperity Gospel originates far outside the fundamentalist world indexed earlier. E. W. Kenyon, originally a Methodist pastor from New York, drifted through several careers before landing at Emerson College of Oratory in Boston. It was here that he encountered the "New Thought" movement, a spiritual-philosophical system of thought that drew together transcendentalism and Christian conceptions of healing to assign primacy to the mind as the root cause of disease. After having a born-again experience in response to a sermon by Moody-associate A. J. Gordon, Kenyon adapted "New Thought" into an otherwise orthodox nineteenth-century revivalist Christianity, positioning faith as the mental element capable of unlocking spiritual power to overcome conditions. He went on to found a Bible institute and to write several books which would later influence (and be largely plagiarized by) influential mid-century Pentecostal Kenneth Hagin, who founded the "Word of Faith" movement, a branch of the contemporary Prosperity Gospel. Hagin and other influential pastors like Oral Roberts took promises of health and wealth to the masses by way of televangelism.
30. Faith and work demographics are generalized from the statistics on faith and work leaders, faith and work event attendees, and interview responses by leaders on who made up their audiences in most settings. These demographics are outlined more in Chapter 3.
31. Cited in Scott Schieman and Jong Jung, "'Practical Divine Influence': Socioeconomic Status and Belief in the Prosperity Gospel," *Journal for the Scientific Study of Religion* 51, no. 4 (2012): 746.
32. LifeWay Research, "Churchgoers Views—Prosperity." Accessed online: http://lifewayresearch.com/wp-content/uploads/2018/07/American-Churchgoers-Prosperity-2017.pdf.
33. Eric L. McDaniel, "What Kind of Christian Are You? Religious Ideologies and Political Attitudes," *Journal for the Scientific Study of Religion* 55, no. 2 (2016): 288–307. See also Hanna Rosin, "Did Christianity Cause the Crash?" *The Atlantic* (December 2009) Accessed online: https://www.theatlantic.com/magazine/archive/2009/12/did-christianity-cause-the-crash/307764/; and Ryan P. Burge, "Do Americans Believe in

the Prosperity Gospel? Here's What the Data Says," *Religion in Public* (November 21, 2017). Accessed online: https://religioninpublic.blog/2017/11/21/do-americans-believe-in-the-prosperity-gospel-heres-what-the-data-says/.

34. Matthew Tallman, *Demos Shakarian: The Life, Legacy, and Vision of a Full Gospel Business Man* (Lexington, KY: Emeth Press, 2010).
35. Quoted in Grem, *The Blessings of Business*, 58.
36. Gerardo Marti, "Ego-Affirming Evangelicalism: How a Hollywood Church Appropriates Religion for Workers in the Creative Class," *Sociology of Religion* 71, no. 1 (2010): 52–75.
37. The faith and work movement also maintains Weber's more sober and rational understanding of this-worldly asceticism rather than much of the Prosperity Gospel's affirmation of "affect as a sign of the power of the truth of faith." See Richard Flory and Kimon H. Sargeant, "Conclusion: Pentecostalism in Global Perspective," in *Spirit and Power: The Growth and Global Impact of Pentecostalism*, ed. Donald E. Miller, Kimon H. Sargeant, and Richard Flory (New York: Oxford University Press, 2013), 314.
38. These three books are: *Your Work Matters to God* (1990) by Doug Sherman and William Hendricks; *The Fabric of This World: Inquiries into Calling, Career Choice, and the Design of Human Work* (1990) by Lee Hardy; and the previously discussed *Every Good Endeavor: Connecting Your Work to God's Work* (2012) by Tim Keller and Katherine Leary Alsdorf. All three root their calls for meaningful work in Bellah and his coauthors' observation that modern society had lost a sense of shared vocation. They then include the same quote from Bellah et al. in their first few pages: "To make a real difference . . . [there would have to be] a reappropriation of the idea of vocation or calling, a return in a new way to the idea of work as contribution to the good of all and not merely as a means to one's own advancement."
39. Amy Sherman, *Kingdom Calling: Vocational Stewardship for the Common Good* (Downers Grove, IL: InterVarsity Press, 2011), 45.
40. Sherman's wider writings and organizational affiliation grant her impeccable conservative credentials: during the 1990s she wrote several pieces promoting conservative ideas on welfare reform that were published and promoted by conservative policy think tanks. She maintains affiliation with the Acton Institute and the Sagamore Institute, a nonpartisan think tank in Indianapolis that promotes private philanthropic efforts and "enterprise solutions to poverty" as superior to governmental programs for assisting those in need. But within the faith and work space, she seems to occupy a status as the leader who "does the social justice thing," as mentioned above. This status reflects the truncated range of political and economic perspectives present in the faith and work movement: without any progressive or radical voices in the space, Sherman's push toward vocational "activism"—primarily channeled toward private, voluntary actions—is perceived as relatively progressive.
41. David W. Sapp, "Southern Baptist Response to the American Economy, 1900–1980," *Baptist History and Heritage* 16 (1981): 7.
42. Doug Sherman and William Hendricks, *Your Work Matters to God* (Colorado Springs, CO: NavPress, 1990), 178.

43. See Mark Noll, "Protestant Reasoning about Money and the Economy, 1790–1860: A Preliminary Probe," in *God and Mammon: Protestants, Money, and the Market, 1790–1860*, ed. Mark Noll (New York: Oxford University Press, 2002), 75–98
44. See Weber, *The Protestant Ethic and the Spirit of Capitalism*, 53–80, 102–125; Ernst Troeltsch, *The Social Teaching of the Christian Churches* (Chicago: University of Chicago Press, 1981), 812–815; Tawney, *Religion and the Rise of Capitalism*, 189–210; and Niebuhr, *The Social Sources of Denominationalism*, 77–105. Tawney and Niebuhr's assessments spared little judgment on Calvinism's affinity for accommodating bourgeois and capitalist ethics, Niebuhr asserts the Reformation "in its final outcome . . . established churches which offered religious sanctuary to bourgeoisie and nobility but sent the poor away empty to find some other home for their faith." He sees Calvin's preference for the Old Testament over the New Testament as a shrewd move to preclude the "inconvenient counsel of Jesus on wealth" to instead teach the bourgeois "what [they] were very ready to believe—that prosperity is the reward of virtue and poverty the affliction of sin" (pp. 92, 96).
45. Lance Wallnau, *God's Chaos Candidate: Donald J. Trump and the American Unraveling* (Keller, TX: Killer Sheep Media, 2016).
46. Damon Berry, "Voting in the Kingdom: Prophecy Voters, the New Apostolic Reformation, and Christian Support for Trump," *Nova Religio* 23, no. 4 (2020): 69–93. The Trump campaign's choice to launch the "Evangelicals for Trump" initiative at a Latino congregation in Florida—headed by a Pentecostal minister known for his luxurious wealth and Prosperity Gospel teaching—captures this widening and reconfiguring of who makes up the constituency of political evangelicalism.
47. Ryan Burge, "Think Evangelicals Are Dying? Depends on How You Define Evangelical," *Religion Unplugged* (February 10, 2021). Accessed online: https://religionunplugged.com/news/2021/2/10/think-us-evangelicals-are-dying-out-that-depends-how-you-define-evangelicalism.
48. John Cotton, "Christ the Foundation of Life," in *The Puritans in America*, ed. Alan Heimert and Andrew Delbanco (Cambridge, MA: Harvard University Press, 1985), 31.
49. See Robert Wuthnow's discussion of ethnoreligious communities in Wuthnow, "New Directions in the Study of Religion and Economic Life," in *The Handbook of Economic Sociology*, ed. Neil J. Smelser and Richard Swedberg (New York: Russell Sage Foundation, 2005), 608–612.
50. Robert Nisbet, *The Quest for Community* (New York: Galaxy Books, 1953), 94.
51. Max Weber, *The Protestant Ethic and the Spirit of Capitalism*, trans. Talcott Parsons (New York: Routledge Classics, 2004), 124.

## Appendix

1. Paul DiMaggio, "Cultural Entrepreneurship in Nineteenth-Century Boston: The Creation of an Organizational Base for High Culture in America," *Media, Culture, and Society* 4 (1982): 33–50
2. For a fuller account of invasive and infiltrating accounts of institutional change, see Julie Battilana, Bernard Leca, and Eva Boxenbaum, "How Actors Change Institutions: Toward a Theory of Institutional Entrepreneurship," *The Academy of Management Annals* 3, no. 1 (2009): 65–107.
3. Peter Berger and Thomas Luckmann, *The Social Construction of Reality: A Treatise in the Sociology of Knowledge* (Garden City, NY: Anchor Books, 1966).
4. For a more comprehensive explanation of criterion purposive sampling, see Michael Quinn Patton, *Qualitative Evaluation and Research Methods*, 2nd edition (Newbury Park, CA: SAGE Publications, 1990)
5. Pierre Bourdieu and Loïc J. D. Wacquant, *An Invitation to Reflexive Sociology* (Chicago: University of Chicago Press, 1992).
6. There were two exceptions: *New York Times* columnist David Brooks spoke at a 2014 Center for Faith and Work conference. Paypal founder Peter Thiel was briefly listed as a speaker for at 2016 Center for Faith and Work conference before disappearing from event advertising prior to the event. Thiel's name in the months leading up to the event, a period that also saw him enter the political fray in agreeing to speak at the 2016 Republican National Convention. Event coordinators did not respond to my question on why Thiel was removed from the lineup, but certainly the very public political endorsement of a presidential candidate may have played a role, as such an endorsement would be unusual for a faith and work speaker.
7. The most comprehensive summary of the movement is Mats Tunehag, Wayne McGee, and Josie Plummer, "Business as Mission: Lausanne Occasional Paper No. 59," in *A New Vision, a New Heart, a Renewed Call*, Vol. 3, ed. David Claydon (Pasadena, CA: William Carey Library, 2005), 281–376 and C. Neal Johnson, *Business as Mission: A Comprehensive Guide to Theory and Practice* (Downers Grove, IL: IVP, 2010).
8. The America's Best Hope website describes its lineups as "inspiring industry CEOs, relevant entertainment figures, and thought leaders around the country," which suggests that event coordinators draw upon speakers' bureaus to construct such lineups of well-known speakers.
9. Jeffrey M. Berry, "Validity and Reliability Issues in Elite Interviewing," *Political Science and Politics* 35, no. 4 (2002): 679–682.
10. One difficult methodological question revolved around confidentiality in these event spaces. Conferences largely operate in a liminal space between public and private: they are publicly advertised, place speakers in front of mass audiences for public viewing, and are very frequently live-streamed online or recorded and broadcast later in their entirety. They certainly do not take place in private workspace or private residences, a conceptualization of "private space" appearing in the research ethics guidelines. Yet there is also a private intimacy to conferences: attendees must register ahead of time

to gain admittance, the subcultural feel can at times incite a "backstage" collegiality among committed movement enthusiasts, and interactions between attendees can often take the form of informal, personal interactions. I incorporated my university ethics board's standard that an interaction is public when participants "do not have an expectation of privacy." As a result, for conferences that were open to the public—and particularly for any event that was live-streamed or later posted videos of conference sessions—I have disclosed the names and content of these talks in my accounts of the events. In cases where sessions were not broadcast and access was more restricted, I have not revealed the names of speakers or any attributes of the event that would make the speaker immediately identifiable. Modifications to this rule of thumb were required for one case: I drew on an event observation solely to assess the sponsoring organization's objectives and how it presented its motivations for being active in the particular movement. This case was the campus ministry leaders conference coordinated by the Lilly Endowment, which was outlined in Chapter 7. No recordings of this event were posted online afterward and, unlike other events, this was an invitation-only event, limited to ministry leaders and their guests. In this case, while revealing the name of the conference was necessary to tie it to the argument being presented, in the interest of affording privacy to participants, I did not identify the name of the speaker of the event and only provided quotations that very closely mirror what is also available online through that organization's own website.

11. I do not identify these events by name out of respect for the privacy of individuals who almost certainly participated with a general expectation that their participation and comments were not "on the record."
12. John D. McCarthy and Mayer N. Zald, "Resource Mobilization and Social Movements: A Partial Theory," *American Journal of Sociology* 82, no. 6 (1977): 1212–1241.
13. For a more expansive presentation and interpretation of the 1992 data, see Robert Wuthnow, *God and Mammon in America* (New York: Free Press, 1994). For Baylor Religion Survey Wave III, see Baylor University, *The Baylor Religion Survey, Wave III* (Waco, TX: Baylor Institute for Studies of Religion, 2010). For the 2011 Public Religion Research Institute, see Robert P. Jones and Daniel Cox, "The 2011 American Values Survey: The Mormon Question, Economic Inequality, and the 2012 Presidential Campaign," *PRRI* November 8, 2011. http://www.prri.org/research/2011-american-values-survey/.
14. The historical narrative in Chapter 6 regarding the historical development of "cultural engagement orientations" of evangelicalism was directly aided by reading these books, particularly those from the 1960s and 1970s. It appeared the authors of these non-work-oriented "faith and work books" were articulating such uncommon ideas, relative to the evangelical subculture of the time period, that the Seattle working group committee saw them as laying important groundwork for the cultural frameworks that would open up the space for faith and work. My conversations with figures active in the Christian book publishing world in the 1970s suggest that these books were not big sellers, so their perspectives may have been marginalized and largely ignored, only retroactively canonized into the faith and work world.

15. Timothy Gloege, *Guaranteed Pure: The Moody Bible Institute, Business, and the Making of Modern Evangelicalism* (Chapel Hill: University of North Carolina Press, 2015).
16. One press—Revell—regularly advertised a full catalog of both fundamentalist and modernist writers, despite the periodicals themselves leaving no ambiguity regarding their evaluation of those modernist writers. But to honor the proud separatism of the larger subculture, all authors' biographies were ascertained from secondary sources: those affiliated with modernist or progressive groups like the Federal Council of Churches in America were dropped from the sample.

# Index

*For the benefit of digital users, indexed terms that span two pages (e.g., 52–53) may, on occasion, appear on only one of those pages.*